ANATOMY
of a *MELODY*
The interactive guide to jazz improvisation

Javier Arau

Other books by the author

ANATOMY
of a *MELODY*
The interactive guide to jazz improvisation

Javier Arau

NEW YORK JAZZ ACADEMY PRESS
Jackson Heights, New York

Published by
NEW YORK JAZZ ACADEMY PRESS
a division of New York Jazz Academy®.
Jackson Heights, New York
www.nyjazzacademy.com

Cover artwork:
Martirosyan, Marietta. *The Sound of Colors.*
2025, oil on canvas. Private collection, New York.

Illustrations by Maya Arau.
Music typesetting by Javier Arau.

306 pp.

For more information about this book, including ordering and permissions,
visit www.javierarau.com.

Library of Congress Cataloging-in-Publication Data

Arau, Javier, 1975–
  Anatomy of a melody: the interactive guide to jazz improvisation / Javier Arau.
    p.   cm.

  Includes bibliographical references (p.   ) and index.
  ISBN 9798992534610 (spiral bound) — ISBN 9798992534603 (epub) —
  ISBN 9798992534627 (hardcover) — ISBN 9798992534658 (paperback)
  1. Jazz—Instruction and study.   2. Improvisation (Music)—Instruction and study.
  3. Melody—Analysis, appreciation.   4. Jazz—Theory.   I. Title.

MT68.A73 2025
781.65/076—dc23
LCCN 2025936089

Printed in the United States of America.
10 9 8 7 6 5 4 3 2 1

For all the thinkers, filled with a passionate curiosity, ever-searching for solutions to the greatest musical puzzles.

"If there's something you don't understand,
you have to go humbly to it.
You don't go to school and sit down and say
I know what you're getting ready to teach me,
you know?
You sit there and you learn.
You open your mind.
You absorb.
You've got to be still to do this."[1]

— **John Coltrane, tenor saxophonist and composer**

Contents

2 Playing With Purpose Chord Tone Target Notes, Transposition, and Key Centers 35

PART 1

PART 2

3 Night and Day Minor Key Melodic Targets and the Dorian Mode 63

PART 1

8 Night Shift Minor ii-V-i, Modal Mixture, and the Altered Dominant **207**

PART 1

PART 2

Preface

Challenges

The art of improvisation is shrouded in a certain gorgeous and inspired mystery. To the uninitiated, jazz music can sound as if it is being played by magicians who are conjuring up intricate sounds out of thin air. I am going to venture a guess that each of us has heard someone playing some engaging improvised solo and immediately thought, "How did they just play that?! How on Earth did that melody just appear?" I've asked this sort of question over and over for decades, ever since I first started learning jazz. It's a question that begs to be answered through extensive research, diligent practice, and plenty of active listening. Yet, even after years of concerted effort, there is still a likelihood that a wide chasm persists between the question and any truly meaningful answer. That gulf presents the biggest puzzle and challenge of all.

This disconnect is an ugly beauty. A real problem. We are drawn to jazz music as fans of the great improvisers., the master melodists. The creativity and artistry of these giants qualifies them in my mind as "immortals." But when we first begin to form and create melody, we are but mortal infants. Jazz study can lead to great joy and fulfillment; it can also lead to frustration, failure, and actual despair, in part because we cannot escape the fact that our end goal — making melodies along the immortal lines of Chet Baker or Dexter Gordon — often remains years and years away. Too many players end up swimming and then drowning fast, skipping many of the steps they should take before jumping into improvising on standard jazz repertoire.

There's hope, though, so please don't despair. After all, many musicians have delved into jazz as beginning improvisers and have become entirely successful as improvising artists. What we need foremost are tools that allow us to take small steps, digesting bits of music, one at a time, all while empowering us to fully realize our own artistry every step of the way.

My Story

I wrote this book wishing that I had benefitted from a book like this while I was first learning how to improvise. I first heard saxophonist Charlie Parker when I was 11 years old and, from that moment onward, I approached every solo I heard as a code waiting to be cracked. While local pros were helping me develop my craft on the instrument, I was turning to recordings of classic masters — Parker, John Coltrane, Julian "Cannonball" Adderley, Sonny Rollins — yearning to gain insight into how they could play with such creativity. My route to developing as a jazz musician was composed nearly entirely of transcribing solos. Whenever I faced a chord progression and couldn't understand how to play over it, I sought out a recorded solo and transcribed it. I likened this process, every single time, to getting a private lesson from a master.

There is a common approach to learning called *end-gaining*, a term used in the Alexander Technique. To end-gain means to reach for your goal by focusing on the end result. In music, I end-gained constantly. If I wanted to learn how to improvise on "Giant Steps," I would transcribe "Giant Steps" from as many performances as I could and learn to play them all. The problem with end-gaining is that it tends to ignore process and process is what leads to productive and meaningful results. I may have wanted to learn "Giant Steps," and the transcribing was certainly valuable, but I needed tools to help me with smaller steps along the way. "Giant Steps" itself was composed in the key of E-flat yet I had never even learned how to improvise on an E-flat major scale at a slow tempo. By ignoring process, I can't help but think I slowed down my own development as a budding improviser.

What I continued to affirm as a music student over many decades was that transcribing was one step of many, all which contributed to a process that helped demystify jazz improvisation as an art form. Each small step — including scale and line manipulation, ear training, theory study, composition, deep listening — not only laid a broader musical foundation but also served as essential tools for advancing my artistic development.

I was mentored as a young student by many of the greatest improvisers in jazz history and, fortunately, most of them were both motivating and quite direct in their teaching. At age 15, I was trading fours with Dizzy Gillespie and, at age 18, my transcription of Joe Henderson's solo on "Lush Life" was accepted for publication in *Jazz Educators Journal*, with Henderson himself taking an active interest in my development. Dave Brubeck personally contributed to financing my college education and, as a graduate student at New England Conservatory (NEC), my mentors — George Russell, Bob Brookmeyer, George Garzone, and Jerry Bergonzi — nurtured my musical welfare.

Solutions

In my first few years living in New York City, I divided my teaching hours between private students and university classrooms and I began to further hone my craft and approach. Eventually, I started wanting to develop a wider platform for teaching and research, in part to try out many of my own pedagogical ideas.

I founded New York Jazz Academy® in 2009. The school quickly became a vibrant incubator for jazz teaching and learning throughout New York City, eventually reaching thousands of students in more than 70 countries worldwide. This book is the culmination of those decades of field research, presenting a method that is holistic and balanced, introducing hundreds of small steps for the musician while focusing on the ultimate goal of helping each learner realize their full artistic potential. Just as the teachings and topics here have been tried and tested by thousands of students since NYJA®'s inception, it is my goal that this book will resonate with every type of reader, regardless of their level of musicianship and prior musical experience.

Ultimately, this book is entirely about you and your own process, which is about to become quite creative (and mostly pain-free). Here's hoping that you may unlock the great mysteries of jazz improvisation finding immense joy along your way.

Acknowledgements

My lifelong love of music was nurtured from the very beginning. I'm still amazed to think that folk legend Pete Seeger serenaded me as an infant during his workshops at McCabe's Guitar Shop in Santa Monica—moments made possible by my parents, Suzanne and José. Those early experiences, and countless others they shared with me as I grew up, helped shape the musician I would become. I am deeply grateful for the world they opened to me.

Thanks to my teachers, especially Mark Tulga, who taught me from very early on the significance of the details in jazz style; Bob Brookmeyer, who held nothing back, always aiming for the truth in improvisation and composition; George Russell, who made it clear that passionate performance matters and that music theory is living, breathing, and ever-changing; Jerry Bergonzi, for helping me tune in to the smallest facets of chord connection and motivic development; Ken Schaphorst, for helping me bridge an early divide between my classical and jazz concepts; Steve Jordheim, for shaping my understanding of the saxophone and chamber music; Allen Gimbel, for guiding my passion as a composer; George Garzone, for teaching me that intent matters; Dizzy Gillespie, who in a fleeting moment, by teaching me exactly how to tap my foot, changed my approach to music entirely; Joe Henderson, who demonstrated deep and generous care for my work as a saxophonist and young scholar; Maria Schneider, Jim McNeely, Michael Abene, and Mike Holober, all of whom supported me as a composer; trumpeter Bill Berry, who did me a great favor by shouting to me in the middle of a solo on Duke Ellington's "Caravan," "No! Stop playing the C blues scale! 'Caravan' is in F minor!" (a simple, humbling moment that again changed my world).

To many other teachers, each of whom contributed so much to my understanding of music, including Woody Mankowski, Tom Washatka, John Harmon, Allan Chase, Lee Hyla, John Heiss, Robert Cogan, Joe Maneri, Peter Row, Matthew Michelic, John Lutterman, John Benson, Paul Contos, Craig Faniani, Wayne Reimers, Shelley Denny, Rick Baker, and Ron Foggia; my Alexander Technique teacher, Mark Josefsberg, and my high school sophomore year English teacher, June Gatewood, who instilled in me an appreciation for detail in grammar and sentence diagramming (now a lost art!). Others who inspired me as a young musician, including Russell Ferrante, who cared enough to encourage and welcome a very young fan, even going so far as to send me a postcard from Blue Note Jazz Club in NYC (seriously, who does this?!); Jimmy Lyons, Chick Corea, and Clark Terry, each of whom supported my efforts as a young musician; Greg Perkins, Tom Peron, and Bud Spangler, each of whom believed deeply in me and helped me spread my own wings.

To many in the field who supported me and inspired me in various ways, including Tony Bennett, who personally helped young musicians study with me at NYJA®; Les Silver and Fred Weiner, who supported me as an artist and entrepreneur; Antonio J. Garcia, John Ephland, Fred Sturm, Ken Dorn, and Thomas Erdmann, who cheered me on as I delved into scholarship at a young age; Evan Eisenberg, Matthew

Budman, Brian Pertl, José Encarnación, Steve Treseler, Darcy James Argue, and George Engelhard, who continue to provide inspiration as writers and scholars.

To many friends and colleagues, from whom I have learned so much, including Tom Dempsey, Michael Webster, David Engelhard, Peck Allmond, Lindsey Horner, Pete Zimmer, Jay Leonhart, Ron McClure, Alex Nguyen, Tippan Phasuk, Tammy Scheffer, Aubrey Johnson, Wayne Escoffery, Carolyn Leonhart, Jon Mele, Lorne Watson, Andrew Lim, Dave Allen, Chris Rogers, Mike Fahie, J.C. Sanford, Ayn Inserto, John Ray, Adam Birnbaum, Dave Ambrosio, Ron Horton, Danilo Perez, Patricia Zarate Perez, Dan Blankinship, Daniel Bennett, Alan Ferber, Jeff Fairbanks, Sunny Knable, Michael Nelson, and Alex Arcone. To the many who had direct involvement with this book, including Brad Carman, Gaston Kaisin, Giacomo Tagliavia, Alan Benner, Tom Pamperin, Shannon Bates, and the many readers who offered their insights into various drafts.

Special thanks to Marietta Martirosyan, who created her mesmerizing oil painting, *The Sound of Colors*, specifically for this book, my sister and valuable editor María del Carmen Arau Ribeiro, my brothers Matthew and José, my in-laws Peggy and David Stare, and my entire extended family. Extra special thanks to my wife Kelley, my daughter Juliet, and my daughter Maya, who created the dozens of illustrations inside this book, including the inspiring and often whimsical "Zen Jazz Master."

I ntroduction

Your Story

Why are you here?

When was the very first time that jazz music had a lasting impact on you? Where were you at the time? What helped you transition from being a listener to becoming an active performer? At some point, you caught the "jazz bug," leaving you with a requisite and perennial hunger, an insatiable appetite for more. Close your eyes and try to remember the very first time you ever tried to improvise. Rather than first trying to recall your own efforts, what do you remember about your surroundings? What do you remember about your emotions? Were you excited? Happy? Anxious? Afraid? If you are fearful of improvising, know that you are not alone. Let's confront this head on. Why the fear? It is in part because we have a fear of failure. In musical improvisation, we fear the "wrong" notes. We want to sound exactly like what we are hearing from others. That is usually unrealistic. We must manage expectations and come to a fuller understanding of process and progress. Familiarity and confidence helps quell fear. To gain confidence, you must experience success.

This book will guide you along a path where every step encourages exploration. While some failure is to be expected, the goal is for you to experience ample success along the way. Consider *Anatomy of a Melody: The interactive guide to jazz improvisation* to be a roadmap assisting you on a very personal journey. The book has been crafted to offer an approach to jazz improvisation that helps solidify the musical foundations upon which all great artistry can develop, keeping a steady focus on musical detail and process. At the same time, your interaction with the book is meant to inspire and awaken your passion and interests as a musician.

What do you want to learn?

Take a look at the following gorgeous melodic line improvised by the great saxophonist, Sonny Stitt, on the jazz classic "Avalon." It's pretty safe to assume that you would love to be able to improvise a melodic line as elegant as Stitt's. How do you get to the point where you can play a line like this though?

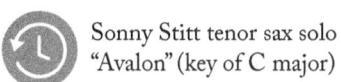

Sonny Stitt tenor sax solo
"Avalon" (key of C major)

If you want to play like Sonny Stitt, first try backing up a bit. Long before learning how to improvise at this advanced level, you must absorb many small steps along the way, handling each with detailed care. Regardless of how disparate some melodies may be, they are often composed of the same basic elements.

Roll up your sleeves and really dig in!

This book is meant not only to be read but also to be applied on a musical instrument so that the musician can work through the ideas presented. Some of the biggest obstacles the musician faces are in application, where sometimes even seemingly basic concepts can be quite a challenge. Perhaps you can play some major scales but are not able to play certain minor scale fragments from memory. Maybe you can play "Twinkle, twinkle, little star" in the key of C but you struggle with the same simple melody in the key of A-flat. You might be entrenched with playing a traditional 12-bar blues at a medium tempo in the key of F but you struggle with playing at a slow tempo with added chromatic chord changes.

Think small and think big. On the road to fluency, map it all out, articulating your own artistic goals:

1. Know what you like and what you dream of achieving.

2. Consider what fundamentals are and how to internalize and apply them.

3. Stay curious and observe what components great music comprises. What are the essential building blocks you need to learn to develop as an improvising artist?

Book Format

Scaffolding

This book delves into musical concepts as they relate to melody, rhythm, harmony, and form. Scaffolding is abundant, giving each student an opportunity to develop well in one area before proceeding to the next area. The topics covered here are presented in a historical context and in the form of a how-to guide for creating your own improvisations through careful practice of exercises and other concrete elements. Learning the *Anatomy of a Melody* will focus your attention on three parts in a progressive and iterative approach.

- UNIT ONE addresses fundamental concepts in melodic and rhythmic construction, examining a single chord at a time.

- UNIT TWO introduces harmony and simple chord progressions, limited to two chords at a time, all relating to a single tonic key.

- UNIT THREE explores fundamentals in a broader context, introducing 3- and 4-chord groupings, including the "Holy Trinity" — the ii-V-I progression — and chromatic applications in bebop jazz and beyond.

By design, the material for each unit seldom moves beyond the key of C, which leaves the transposition to the musician, with this movement to new keys posed as a central challenge throughout the book.

Nearly every topic is presented as a mini-lesson of only 1-2 pages for maximum ease of cross-referencing hundreds of topics, most of which are also easily accessible in the Index. Material may be used in private lessons or in a classroom setting. The book serves as a comprehensive text for teaching improvisation and jazz styles, a text for teaching theory and harmony, and as an all-purpose reference guide to jazz music. Chapters allow for plenty of teacher/student interaction and each topic is introduced to enhance immediate success and understanding. Assignments and goals for each chapter are also clarified, enabling you to review and reinforce ideas.

Symbols and sections

Each page of this book is crafted to engage the musician, both visually and musically. Below are symbols and sections that will help keep you focused while giving you structure and guidance throughout.

	Zen Jazz Master Says	Zen Jazz Master is quite a guide. When he speaks, everyone listens.
	Historical Example	Masterful examples from throughout history are prevalent in each chapter.
	Tip	Want to better apply the material? Tip shares quick and effective advice.
	Challenge	Rise to the challenges, which include healthy doses of transposition!
	Improvise	Now's your chance to go for it! From 1-chord vamps to full repertoire.
	Compose	Cross-train and develop your voice with composition assignments.
	Ear Training	It all starts with developing your ear via many creative exercises.
	Inquiry Box	Added insight into specific topics, presented in a bite-sized format.
	Listening Guide	Not sure what to listen to? Let these suggestions serve as your guide.
Solo	**Spotlight**	Explore the melody of a specific improvised solo.
	Topic	Topics are meant to cover only 1-3 pages at a time so you can focus without distractions.
	Masterclass	Break up your flow with an added masterclass on a special topic.
	Smackdown!	Compare two approaches in a head-to-head matchup.
	Investigate	Delve deeply into one particular area of study and come out refreshed.
	Song Study	Learn from a masterwork, including lead sheets, chord charts, and more.
	Improvise	Finally, a chance to improvise on a tune. Time to spread your wings!

Beginning Conclusions

What's the expectation?

It's a winding and adventurous road ahead. Manage your expectations carefully and take extra care to ensure that you celebrate the small steps in the present moment. Assuming you put in the practice and the work, you are exactly where you should be. If you need some cheering on, make sure to come on back and read this introduction again. Learning a jazz composition is a bit different than learning an entry-level classical piece on an instrument. While the chord progression for "Autumn Leaves" may be more forgiving than, say, the progression for Wayne Shorter's "Fee-Fi-Fo-Fum," what you choose to play over "Autumn Leaves" will change throughout your life. Each piece in the repertoire is a lifelong pursuit and, for this reason, no jazz composition is only for "beginner level" musicians.

Artistry need not wait for mastery

While this book addresses the craft involved in becoming a fluent improviser, great jazz musicians are not simply plugging in scales that change with each chord. There are exceptions to the rules of jazz theory in great solos, which makes improvisation and artistic success all the more fascinating. The bottom line? You have to know the rules to break the rules.

Artistry really knows no boundaries and demands no clear set of prerequisites. You already possess a singular musical voice whether you are fully aware of this or not. You can always play something meaningful and intentional, right now. Artistry need not wait for mastery. The decisions a soloist makes can always be artistic ones. When given the right tools, you can start making artistic choices even after learning only a handful of notes.

How to supplement the book?

So many elements of jazz style need to be studied beyond a book. If you really want to develop, you must also supplement your studies. Here are a few strong suggestions:

1. Get a teacher.
2. Learn with others.
3. Reread and re-apply. The book is meant to be tackled with different layers in mind. Your first pass through the book will feel much different than your second pass.

Final words

Will you be a fluent improviser after finishing this book? Possibly! Will you be able to improvise at all? Definitely! How quickly and well you progress depends in part on you and how hard you work for it. Improvisation takes practice, discipline, thought, and, most importantly, imagination. My hope is that, by the time you finish this book, you will understand, deeply, how to approach music and craft a solo with wings. I'll be with you every step of the way and I'm definitely looking forward to taking this journey with you.

UNIT ONE

Melody and Rhythm

- Fundamental building blocks
- Major and minor melody
- Navigating 1-chord progressions

Chapter 1
- Major Scale Fragments
- Rhythmic Placement
- Motivic Development

Chapter 2
- Chord Tone Target Notes
- Transposition
- Key Centers

Chapter 3
- Minor Scales
- Minor Key Melodic Targets
- Dorian Mode

"The word 'Jazz,' as far as I can see or can remember, was when I was a little boy, five years old. The year of 1905. In those days it was called <u>Rag Time Music</u>. And when ever there was a <u>dance</u> or a <u>Lawn Party</u> the Band (consisted) of six men, would stand in front of the place on the Side Walk and play a half hour of good rag time music. And <u>us</u> kids would stand or dance on the other side of the street until they went inside. That was the only way that we young kids could get the..." [2]

— Louis Armstrong, trumpeter, composer, and founding father of jazz
(excerpted in his own handwriting)

1 A Perfect Tonic

Major Scale Fragments, Rhythm, and Motivic Development

Why does some music draw us in? What really causes a listener to stop and listen closely? Is it the emotion felt when hearing it? Is it something as abstract and undefined as the simple sound or feel of the work? A great piece of music is built with artistry, regardless of how rudimentary or complex. What lies beneath, under the surface, contains details and answers. To begin to understand how to craft a great melody, one that affects us, we must delve into the fundamental components that structure the anatomy of the melody. Of the two parts of this chapter, first part introduces the building blocks of rhythm and the major scale. The second part offers an exploration of motivic development and other core elements in great musical melodies throughout history. The tools introduced here will be used for a lifetime, helping give breath to every engaging and artistic musical phrase.

Contents

TOPICS
- The Simplest Melody
- Counting Rhythm
- Strong vs. Weak Beats
- Scale Degrees
- Syncopation
- "The Charleston"
- *Clave*
- Major Scale Workout
- Rhythmic Meter
- Compound and Irregular Meter
- "Twinkle, twinkle" Workout
- Motivic Development
- Motivic Development among Masterworks
- Scale Pattern as Motif
- Diatonic Intervals
- Common Diatonic Intervals
- Interval as Thematic Motif
- 1-Measure Rhythms
- Cut Time
- Rhythmic Matrix
- Double-time and Half-time Feel
- Articulation and Style
- Oppositions
- Melodic Examples
- Melodic Architecture
- Composition 101
- Music Notation Basics

EAR TRAINING
- "Mary had a little lamb"
- "Twinkle, twinkle, little star"
- Envisioning the Rhythm Section

MASTERCLASS
- How to play swing eighths

INVESTIGATE
- Two Views: Major Scale Construction

SONG STUDY
- Major Scale Fragments ("Lean on me")

COMPOSE
- C Major Melody
- Write your own rhythms

IMPROVISE
- Free Improv (over C Major)
- Using Scale Fragments (C Major vamp)
- Play-Rest
- Interval as Thematic Motif
- Major Scale Workout

LISTENING GUIDE
- Swing Scale Artists
- Audiation Using Classic Melodies
- Songs Featuring *Clave* Rhythm

ZEN JAZZ MASTER SAYS
- Rhythm is king!

HISTORICAL EXAMPLES
- "Hot Cross Buns" (Traditional)
- "Frère Jacques" (Traditional)
- "Itsy Bitsy Spider" (Traditional)
- "I want to be happy" (Youmans/Caesar)
- "Jingle Bells" (Traditional)
- "Love me or leave me" (Donaldson/Kahn)
- "The Charleston" (Johnson/Mack)
- "I'm a little teapot" (Traditional)
- "My Bonnie lies over the ocean" (Traditional)
- "Hickory Dickory Dock" (Traditional)
- *Symphony No. 5* (Ludwig van Beethoven)
- "Old MacDonald had a farm" (Traditional)
- Louis Armstrong trumpet solo "St. Louis Blues"
- "Avalon" (Jolson/DeSylva/Rose)
- "When the Saints Go Marching In" (Traditional)
- "C Jam Blues" (Duke Ellington)
- "Deed I do" (Hirsch/Rose)
- "Over the Rainbow" (Harold Arlen)
- "St. Louis Blues" (W. C. Handy)
- "Amazing Grace" (Traditional)
- Hank Mobley tenor sax solo "Home Cookin'"

The Simplest Melody

At first glance, the musical example below seems to be the simplest melody, an entirely inconsequential three-note bit — C-D-E. Perhaps surprisingly, it also contains a world of musical structure and detail, offering a concise example of four primary elements of music — pitch, harmony, rhythm, and form. *Pitch* and *rhythm* are the most obvious since each melodic pitch also receives a rhythmic value. *Harmony* is implied by the final resolution, establishing a clear harmonic relationship between the first and last pitch. The term *form* refers to any musical element's implicit structure, whether a simple phrase or entire song, and can be described in terms of its length — so this simple melody's form is only one measure long and among the smallest of melodic statements.

EX. 1.1
Even the simplest melody includes four primary elements of music.

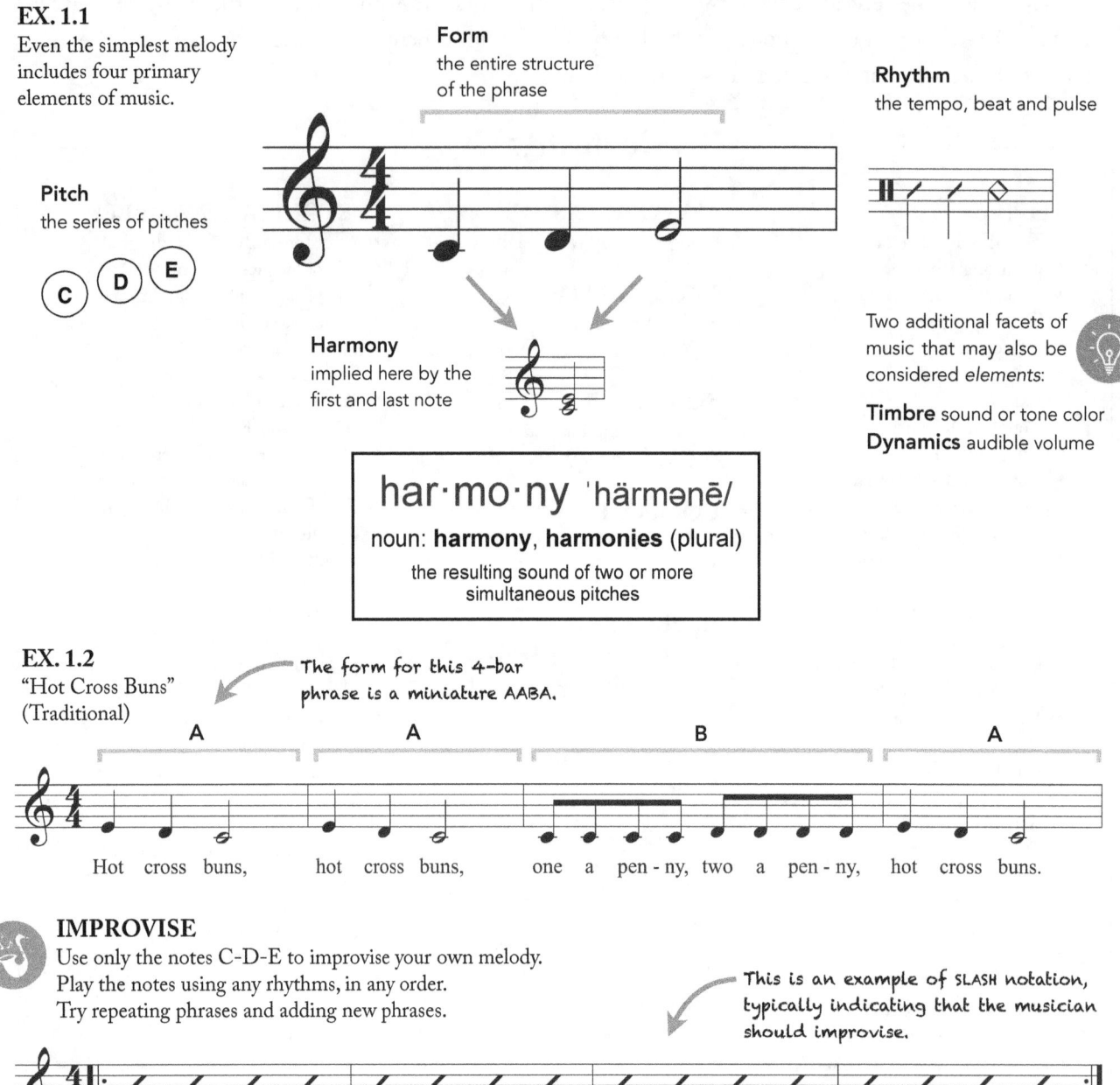

Form
the entire structure of the phrase

Rhythm
the tempo, beat and pulse

Pitch
the series of pitches

C D E

Harmony
implied here by the first and last note

Two additional facets of music that may also be considered *elements*:

Timbre sound or tone color
Dynamics audible volume

har·mo·ny ˈhärmənē/
noun: **harmony**, **harmonies** (plural)
the resulting sound of two or more simultaneous pitches

EX. 1.2
"Hot Cross Buns"
(Traditional)

The form for this 4-bar phrase is a miniature AABA.

A   A   B   A

Hot cross buns,   hot cross buns,   one a pen-ny, two a pen-ny,   hot cross buns.

IMPROVISE
Use only the notes C-D-E to improvise your own melody.
Play the notes using any rhythms, in any order.
Try repeating phrases and adding new phrases.

This is an example of SLASH notation, typically indicating that the musician should improvise.

Counting Rhythm

Rhythm is easy to hear but, to develop a high level of rhythmic precision, you will benefit from moving beyond your ear's intuition to deciphering the details of printed rhythms. Examine exactly how many beats it takes to move from one note to another in any given measure. When counting the rhythm below, notice the variety of note types, including *eighth notes*, *quarter notes*, *half notes*, and *whole notes*, with some notes counted for multiple beats and others counted for less than a beat. This is not at all an exhaustive list of rhythmic choices, as there are many other types of rhythmic options available in music. The 4/4 at the beginning of the line is a *time signature* indicating a *meter* of 4 quarter-note beats per measure.

EX. 1.3
Use numbers "1 2 3 4" for the downbeats and the "+" ("and") symbol for upbeats.

Use parentheses when the beat is not articulated. This happens when a note is held out for more than 1 beat and when a note is tied to a previous note. Parentheses are also placed around any beat that is a rest.

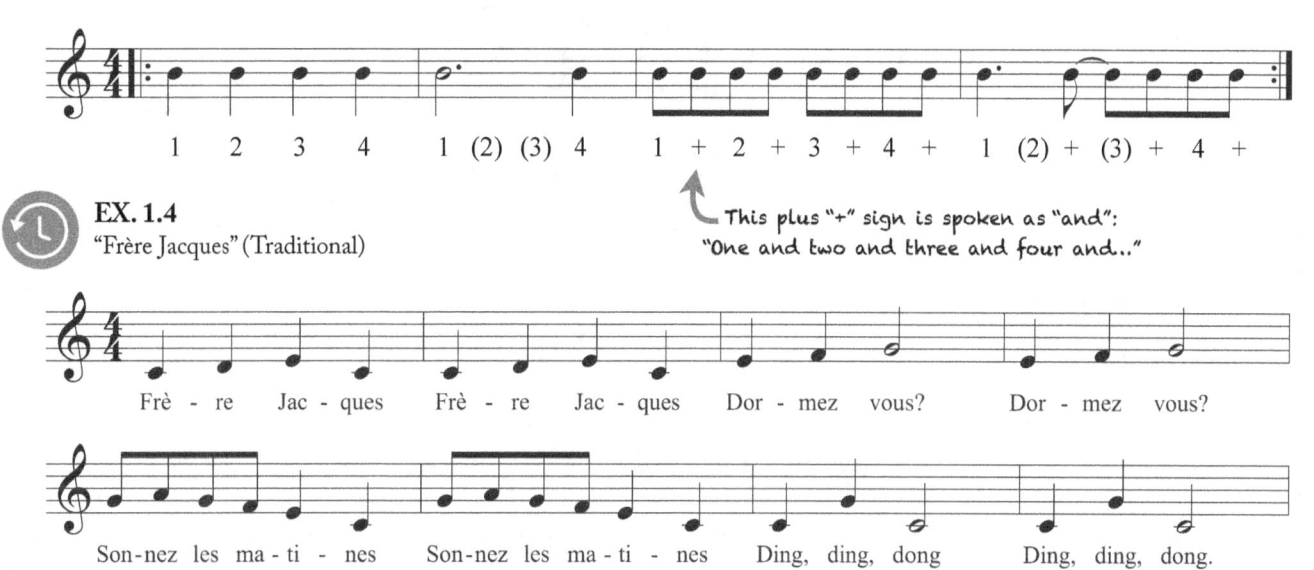

EX. 1.4
"Frère Jacques" (Traditional)

This plus "+" sign is spoken as "and": "One and two and three and four and.."

Strong vs. weak beats

All spoken language includes strong and weak beats
Recite or sing "Frère Jacques" or "Twinkle, twinkle, little star" and you will immediately hear both strong and weak beats.

In 4/4 meter, strong beats are typically beats 1 and 3.

In 4/4 meter, weak beats are typically beats 2 and 4, as well as any upbeats.

What about accents?
Accents may or may not coincide only with strong beats since they can be placed on any beat, whether up or down. When weak beats are accented, the rhythm can feel surprising and inspired.

Write the rhythmic counts under each note below.

EX. 1.5
Strong beats 1 and 3

Hear the melodic resolutions on beat 3.

Investigate   Two Views: Major Scale Construction

At the top of a skilled artist's list of tools is the *major scale*, which may be used to create countless melodies. Of the 12 major scales, the most accessible is the C major scale, composed only of the white keys on the piano. What follows are two approaches to constructing the C major scale. Every major scale is constructed in the same manner so an understanding of one scale will help develop fluency with all 12 major scales.

View #1 **Whole step, half step**

This traditional method uses intervals of whole steps and half steps to construct a major scale. Start with an initial pitch then add notes following the sequence "Whole, whole, half, whole, whole, whole, half."

EX. 1.6
Piano map and "white key" letter names

> **W** Whole step
> **h** half step

EX. 1.7
C major scale construction, "whole step, half step" method

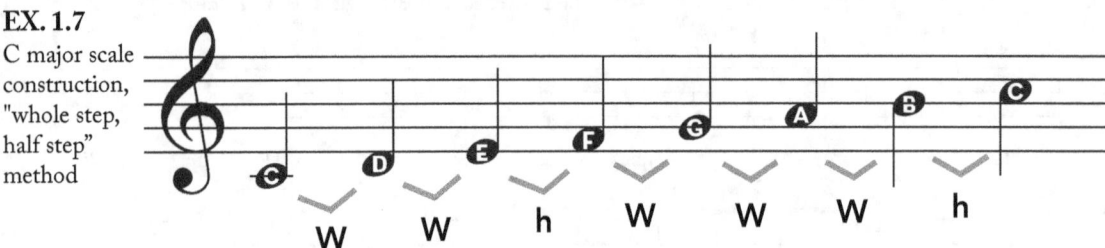

A **half step** is the shortest distance between two notes on the piano. A **whole step** is a distance totaling two half steps. The interval from B to C is a half step but the interval from A to B is a whole step. A half step up from A would land on the black key between A and B.

View #2 **Scale fragments**

The major scale is composed of two 4-note scale fragments called *tetrachords*. Both the lower and upper tetrachords in the major scale sound identical because they share the same intervallic formula. Think of this as "1 2 3 plus a half step" — consisting of a first pitch ("1"), then a second pitch up a whole step ("2"), a third pitch up another whole step ("3"), and lastly a fourth pitch up a half step.

EX. 1.8
C major scale construction using scale fragments: "1 2 3, plus a half step" method

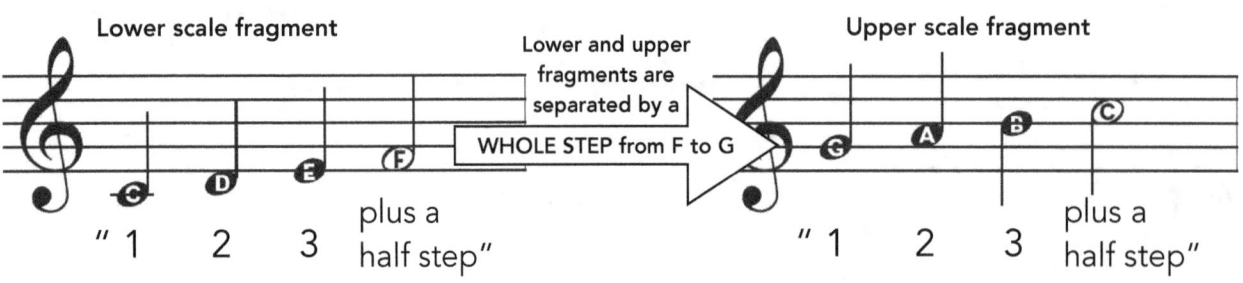

Scale Degrees

When reading music, the ultimate goal is to be able to feel, hear, understand, internalize, and perform absolutely any piece of written music in any context. While reaching this level of mastery may seem a lofty goal, you can speed up your development by using three approaches to identify any pitch: *letter name*, *scale degree*, and *solfège syllable*. Each approach will strengthen your understanding of the pitch material while also helping to train your ear. Internalize these strengths by taking the extra step of writing out the numbers and syllables. Also practice singing them (even if singing is not a strong suit!).

Guess each song below
before you play it.

> **Letter names** C, D, E...
> **Scale degrees** $\hat{1}$, $\hat{2}$, $\hat{3}$...
> **Solfège syllables** Do, Re, Mi...

$\hat{1}$ vs. $\hat{1}$: The scale degree carat "∧" formally sits atop the scale degree number, which may also be presented informally, without a carat.

EX. 1.9
Scale degree/*solfège* examples

In many places around the world, the 7th is called SI, not TI.

①

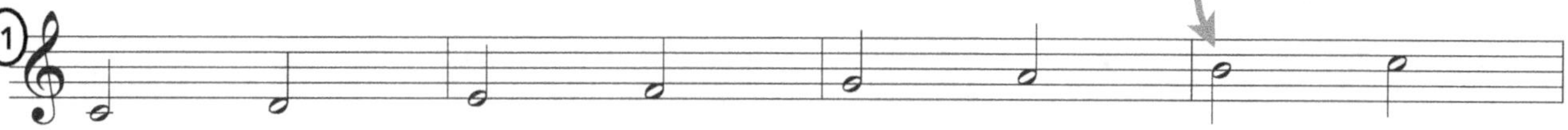

$\hat{1}$	$\hat{2}$	$\hat{3}$	$\hat{4}$	$\hat{5}$	$\hat{6}$	$\hat{7}$	$\hat{1}$ (or 8)
Do	Re	Mi	Fa	Sol	La	Ti	Do

②

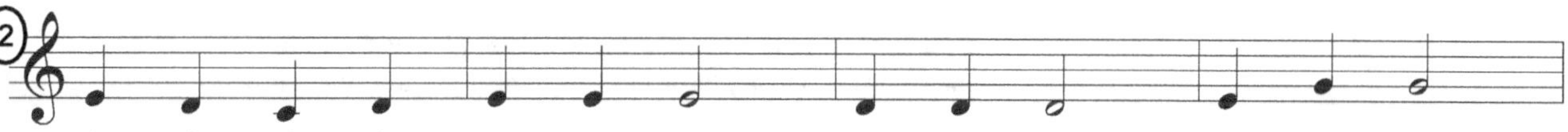

$\hat{3}$	$\hat{2}$	$\hat{1}$	$\hat{2}$	$\hat{3}$	$\hat{3}$	$\hat{3}$	$\hat{2}$	$\hat{2}$	$\hat{2}$	$\hat{3}$	$\hat{5}$	$\hat{5}$
Mi	Re	Do	Re	Mi	Mi	Mi	Re	Re	Re	Mi	Sol	Sol

③

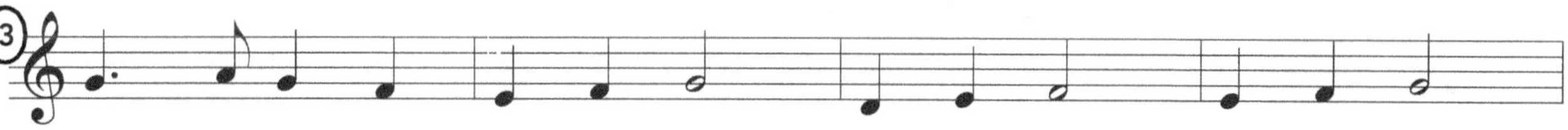

$\hat{5}$	$\hat{6}$	$\hat{5}$	$\hat{4}$	$\hat{3}$	$\hat{4}$	$\hat{5}$	$\hat{2}$	$\hat{3}$	$\hat{4}$	$\hat{3}$	$\hat{4}$	$\hat{5}$
Sol	La	Sol	Fa	Mi	Fa	Sol	Re	Mi	Fa	Mi	Fa	Sol

④

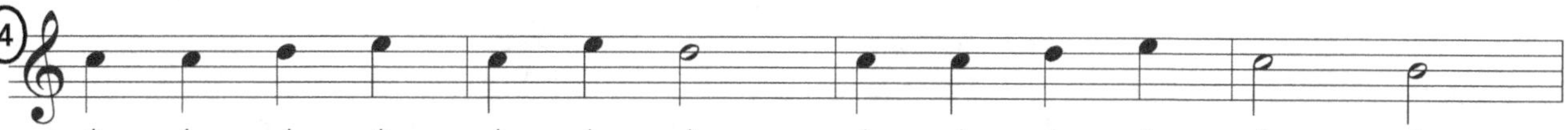

$\hat{1}$	$\hat{1}$	$\hat{2}$	$\hat{3}$	$\hat{1}$	$\hat{3}$	$\hat{2}$	$\hat{1}$	$\hat{1}$	$\hat{2}$	$\hat{3}$	$\hat{1}$	$\hat{7}$
Do	Do	Re	Mi	Do	Mi	Re	Do	Do	Re	Mi	Do	Ti

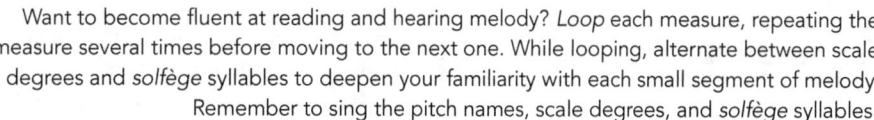

Want to become fluent at reading and hearing melody? *Loop* each measure, repeating the measure several times before moving to the next one. While looping, alternate between scale degrees and *solfège* syllables to deepen your familiarity with each small segment of melody. Remember to sing the pitch names, scale degrees, and *solfège* syllables.

Syncopation

Consider the many simple songs that use downbeat rhythms. *Syncopation* is the antithesis of straight rhythm, as it places accents on weak beats that may pull the ear away from the downbeat pulse. The first set of examples below contrast straight quarter notes with an accented and syncopated beat 2 (and the displacement of a typically strong beat 3). Other examples address straight and syncopated eighth notes, where upbeat accents add an element of interest.

EX. 1.10
Straight quarter note rhythm, strong beats 1 and 3 emphasized

EX. 1.11
Syncopated quarter note rhythm, emphasis on beat 2 instead of beat 3

Label the syncopated rhythms on "I want to be happy" below.

EX. 1.12
"I want to be happy"
(Youmans/Caesar)

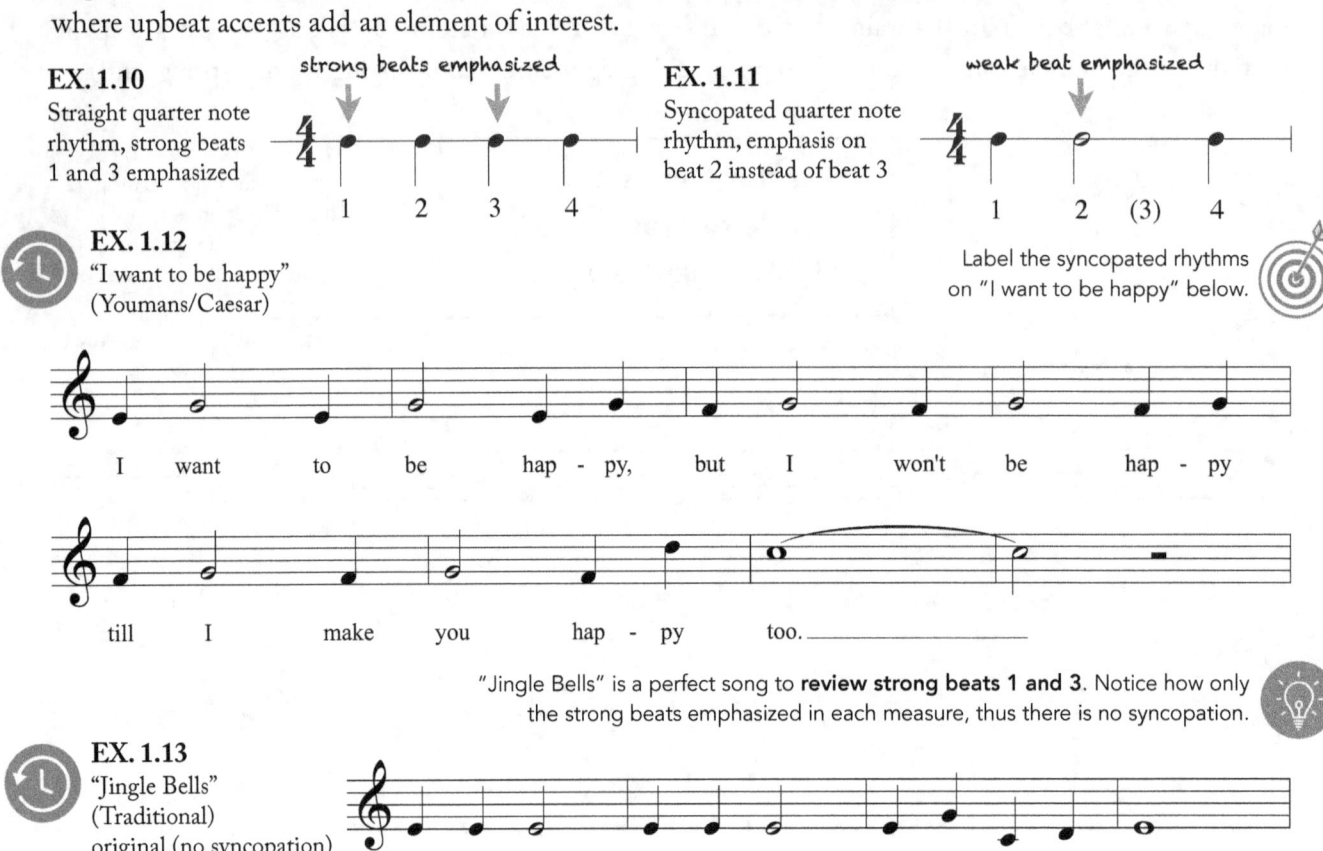

"Jingle Bells" is a perfect song to **review strong beats 1 and 3**. Notice how only the strong beats emphasized in each measure, thus there is no syncopation.

EX. 1.13
"Jingle Bells"
(Traditional)
original (no syncopation)

EX. 1.14
"Jingle Bells"
with added
8th note syncopations

EX 1.15
"Love me or leave me"
(Donaldson/Kahn)

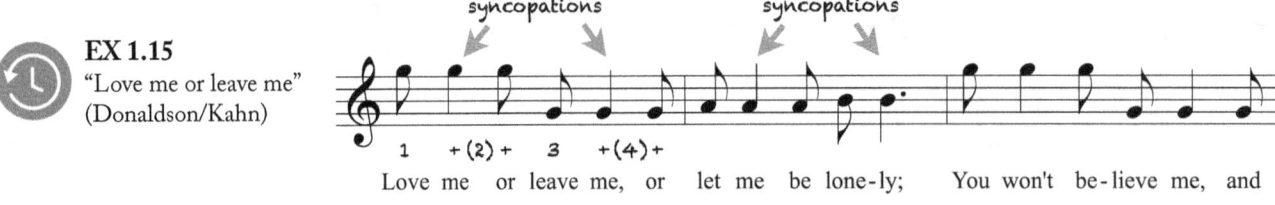

Write in the counting for every rhythm on this page. Every measure will use some or all of the following numbers and their upbeats, each notated with a plus (+): 1 + 2 + 3 + 4 + . Use parentheses for rests and any tied notes.

"The Charleston"

Consider a military march as the quintessential straight rhythm, comprising a steady downbeat pulse, each beat like a foot placed in front of the other ("Left, right, left!"). "The Charleston" rhythm is pervasive in jazz music and is a quintessential syncopation that deliberately adds rhythmic surprise to the more predictable march rhythm. Originally a dance rhythm, "The Charleston" breaks the monotony of downbeats with an occasional quick-footed move on an upbeat. An anticipation of beat 3, the accent on the "and" of beat 2 is "The Charleston's" defining characteristic, adding significant rhythmic energy.

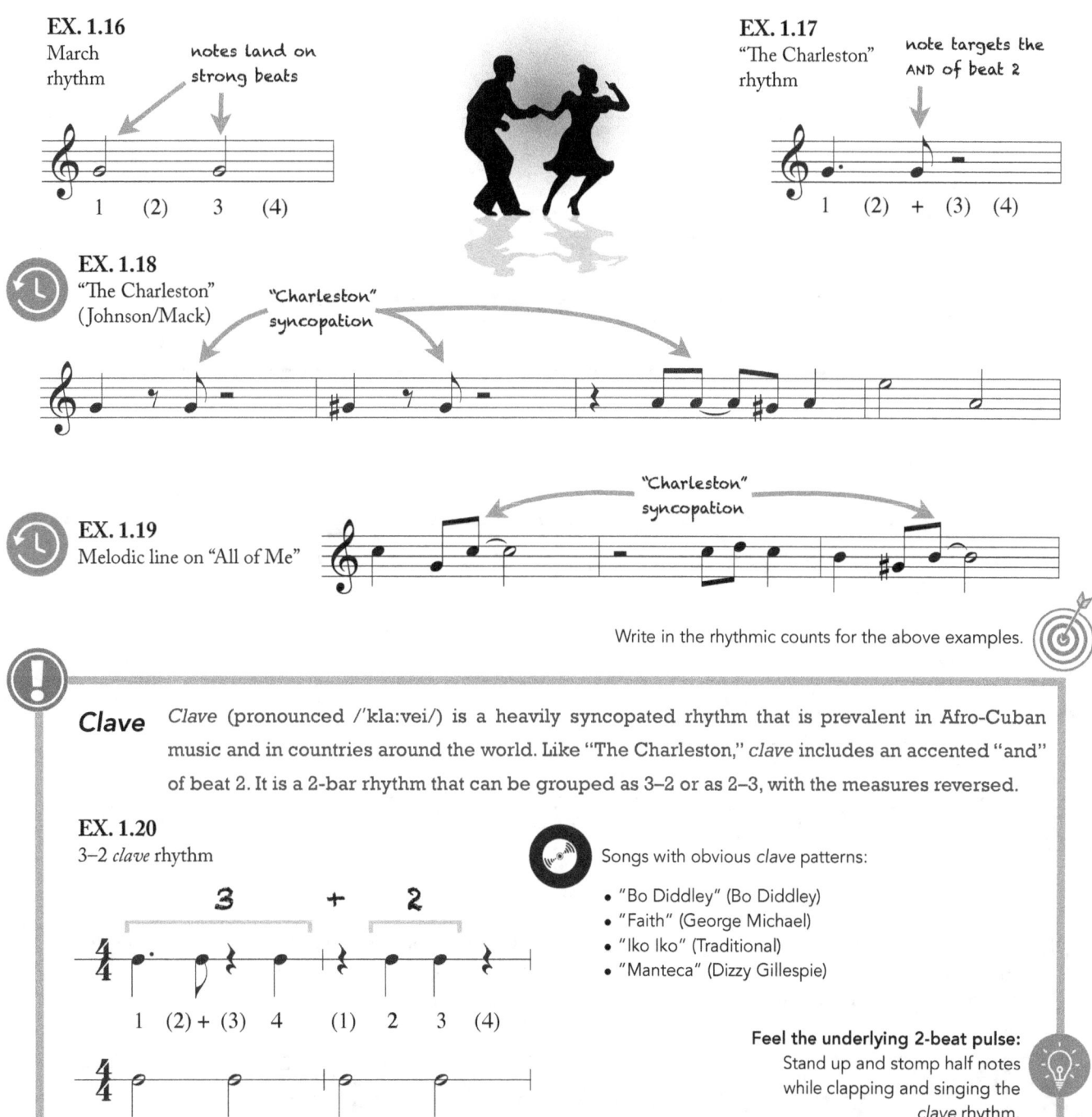

EX. 1.16
March rhythm

notes land on strong beats

1 (2) 3 (4)

EX. 1.17
"The Charleston" rhythm

note targets the AND of beat 2

1 (2) + (3) (4)

EX. 1.18
"The Charleston" (Johnson/Mack)

"Charleston" syncopation

EX. 1.19
Melodic line on "All of Me"

"Charleston" syncopation

Write in the rhythmic counts for the above examples.

Clave   *Clave* (pronounced /ˈklaːveɪ/) is a heavily syncopated rhythm that is prevalent in Afro-Cuban music and in countries around the world. Like "The Charleston," *clave* includes an accented "and" of beat 2. It is a 2-bar rhythm that can be grouped as 3–2 or as 2–3, with the measures reversed.

EX. 1.20
3–2 clave rhythm

3 + **2**

1 (2) + (3) 4 (1) 2 3 (4)

Songs with obvious *clave* patterns:

- "Bo Diddley" (Bo Diddley)
- "Faith" (George Michael)
- "Iko Iko" (Traditional)
- "Manteca" (Dizzy Gillespie)

Feel the underlying 2-beat pulse:
Stand up and stomp half notes while clapping and singing the *clave* rhythm.

Song Study | Major Scale Fragments ("Lean on me")

The first four notes of the major scale can contribute to making myriad memorable melodies. The following exercise uses the lower fragment of the C major scale. It also illustrates how something that sounds technical, like the term "fragment," is also highly artistic and musical. Practicing the same phrase over both the lower and upper fragments helps with mastering the major scale.

EX. 1.21
C major scale, lower fragment

Need to take a breath?
This is a natural break
in the music.

Pitch collection challenge!

Can you hear how the major scale fragment exercise above sound like "Lean on me"?
Add a combination of the following pitches in **measures 3-4** and complete the phrase:

C D E

EX. 1.22
C major scale, lower fragment,
looped for greater fluency

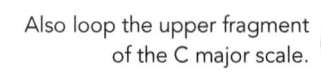

Also loop the upper fragment
of the C major scale.

IMPROVISE
Use only C-D-E-F or G-A-B-C and improvise your own melody.
Play the notes using any rhythms, in any order.
Try repeating phrases and adding new phrases.

Does using all those scale notes above feel like a bit too much?
Limit yourself to just a handful of notes. For example,
use only the lower fragment of your major scale.

EX. 1.23
Melodic example, limited to only the
lower fragment of the C major scale

Major Scale Workout

Scales are not meant to be played merely ascending and descending in full. A much more thorough major scale workout will help add variety to scale practice. The first C major scale exercise below uses the 5th scale degree, G, as a *pivot* point and includes all the pitches of the major scale. The exercise helps illustrate the difference between *steps*, *skips*, and *leaps*. For the second exercise below, maintain an awareness of both the lower and upper fragments of the major scale.

> **Step** up or down to the next note (G up to A, G down to F)
> **Skip** up or down but first skip over a note (G up to B, G down to E)
> **Leap** up or down but first skip over more than one note (G up to C, G down to D)

EX. 1.24
Step-skip-leap exercise
(C major scale, pivoting from G)

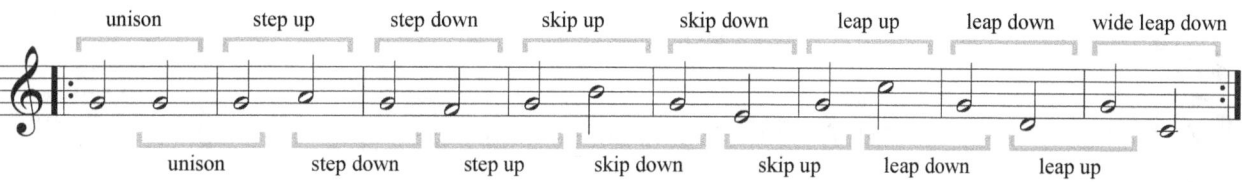

EX. 1.25
Melodic exercise
(C major scale)

The 7th scale degree (B), also called the LEADING TONE, can appear in a lower octave UNDER the root (C) since scales can encompass multiple octaves.

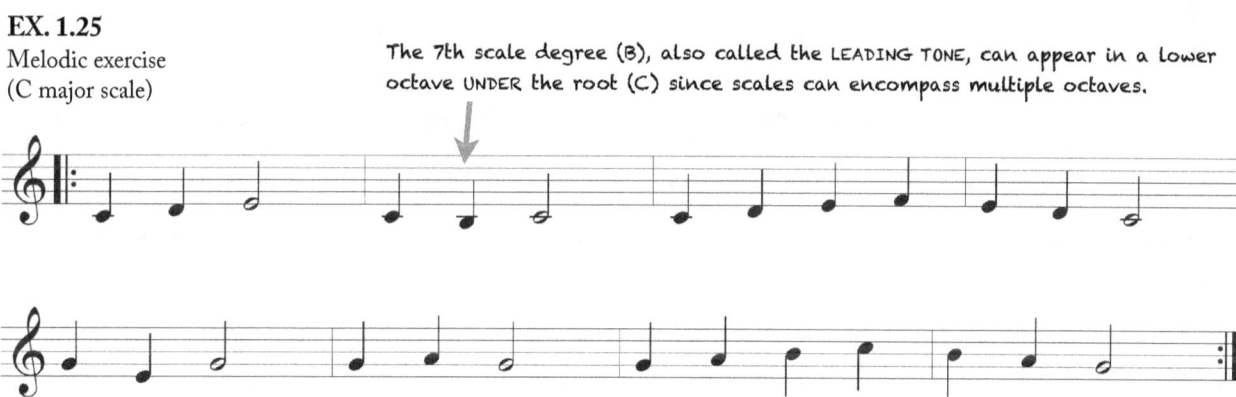

 As a variation, practice the above exercise by shortening all the notes (using **staccato**).

 Play "Mary had a little lamb" using the C major scale without looking (entirely by ear).

 Notate "Mary had a little lamb" using the C major scale.

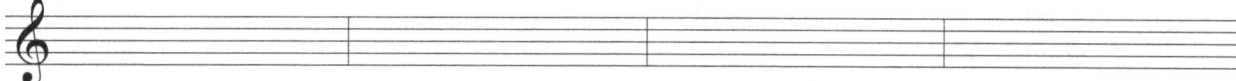

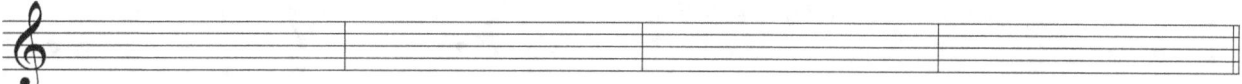

Rhythmic Meter

Rhythmic meter presents a precise organization of rhythm, grouping beats into patterns. The most common meter is 4/4 time (also called *common time*), which organizes rhythm into 4 quarter-note beats per measure. 4/4 is classified as *simple meter* because each beat is divided into two equal parts — 2 eighth notes. Each of the 3 beats in 3/4 time is also divisible by 2, as are the 2 beats in 2/4 time. Each of these simple meters organizes rhythm into distinct patterns.

Top: Number of <u>beats</u> per measure ("four")

Bottom: <u>Value</u> of each beat ("quarter notes")

EX. 1.26
"I'm a little teapot"
(Traditional)

I'm a lit-tle tea pot short and stout.
1 + 2 + 3   4   1   2   3 (4)

Top: Number of <u>beats</u> per measure ("three")

Bottom: <u>Value</u> of each beat ("quarter notes")

EX. 1.27
"My Bonnie lies over the ocean"
(Traditional)

My Bon - nie lies   ov - er the   o - cean,
3   1 (2) + 3   1   2   3   1   2 (3)

For every example below, count the beats and subdivisions out loud with a slow and steady beat.

 4/4 is also called *common time*.

2/4 is also called *simple duple* with 2 beats per measure.

Duple vs. Triple: 4/4 is considered a *simple duple* meter since the 4 beats per measure are evenly divided by 2. 3/4 is *simple triple* since its 3 beats can be divided evenly only by 3.

Compound and irregular meter

Compound meter differs from simple meter in that it divides each beat into three equal parts so the beat is a dotted quarter note comprising 3 eighth notes. 6/8 time tends to be grouped into 2 beats of 3 eighth notes each.

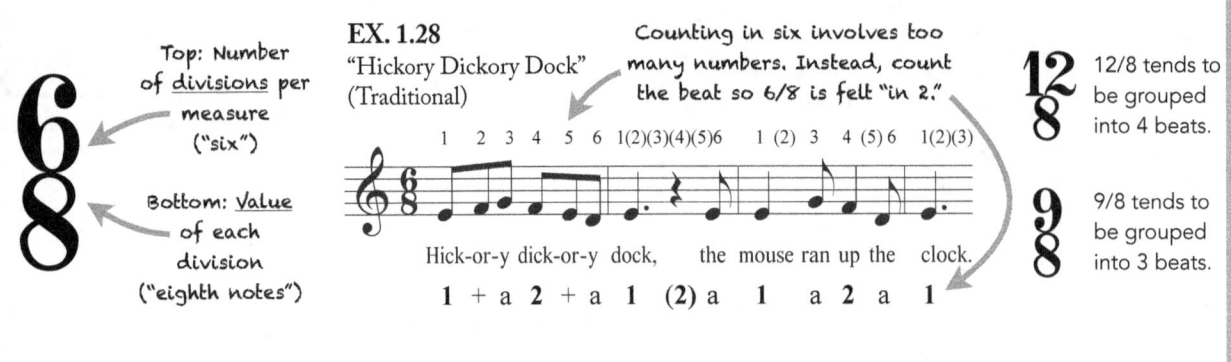

Top: Number of <u>divisions</u> per measure ("six")

Bottom: <u>Value</u> of each division ("eighth notes")

EX. 1.28
"Hickory Dickory Dock"
(Traditional)

Counting in six involves too many numbers. Instead, count the beat so 6/8 is felt "in 2."

1 2 3 4 5 6 1(2)(3)(4)(5)6 1 (2) 3 4 (5) 6 1(2)(3)

Hick-or-y dick-or-y dock,   the mouse ran up the   clock.
1 + a 2 + a 1 (2) a 1   a 2 a 1

12/8 tends to be grouped into 4 beats.

9/8 tends to be grouped into 3 beats.

Irregular meter, also called *odd* or *mixed,* includes rhythmic groupings that mix up duple and triple. For example, 5/4 might be grouped as 3 beats plus 2 beats; 7/8 might be grouped as 2 beats of 2 eighths plus 1 beat of 3 eighths.

EX. 1.29
5/4 time signature

EX. 1.30
7/8 time signature

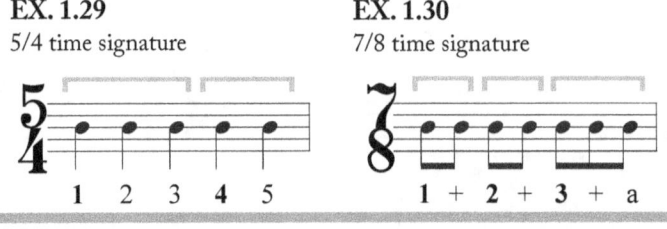

1 2 3 4 5   1 + 2 + 3 + a

Masterclass   How to Play Swing Eighths

The basics

Most people learn that swing eighth notes look like straight eighth notes but they should be played so they *sound like eighth note triplets*. This is a good starting place.

EX. 1.31
How swing eighth notes LOOK

EX. 1.32
How swing eighth notes SOUND

What you need to know

Swing eighths are not always played like triplets. There are different rates of swing. Think of a graph — *The Swing Scale* — where, to the very left are completely straight eighth notes (0% swing) and, on the right, is a radically swung eighth note (100% swing), closer to a dotted eighth followed by a sixteenth note. Right in the middle (50% swing) is the triplet-laced swing pattern that you first learn. Pre-dating jazz, turn of the century ragtime falls to the far left of the scale. Jazz of the '20s and '30s, popularized by swing dances including the Charleston and Lindy Hop, moves far right. Bebop of the '40s keeps closer to the middle, while trends since the 1950s have moved eighth notes farther left again, approaching perhaps 30-40% swing.

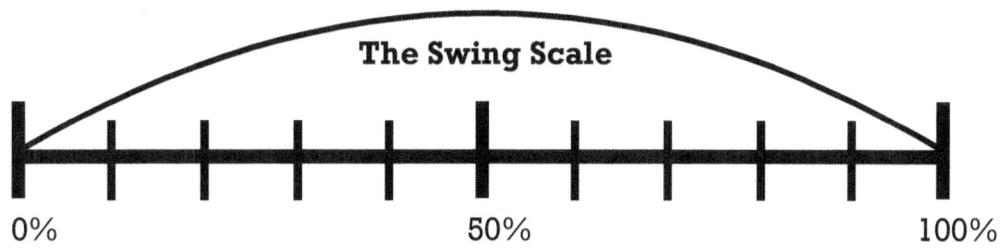

The swing illusion

It may come as a surprise that swing eighths are not always played by changing the rhythm. By playing straight eighth notes and accenting the upbeats, you can create an illusion of swing. Try playing the exercises below. Can you hear *the swing illusion*? Keeping the swing illusion in mind can help you play closer to 30-40% swing.

EX. 1.33
Straight eighths

EX. 1.34
Straight eighths with accented upbeats

Try playing this triplet-laced phrase and compare it to the previous accented example. How large a difference is there between the two examples?

Begin listening to the varying degrees of swing played by these great jazz players.

- **30%** John Coltrane "Moment's Notice"
- **50%** Charlie Parker "Bloomdido"
- **70%** Louis Armstrong "St. Louis Blues"
- **10-90%** Jelly Roll Morton "The Crave"

Continue to experiment with playing different rates of swing. Through practice and experience, you will begin to develop **your own concept of swing**, which will help give you a personal and mature sense of jazz style.

"Twinkle, twinkle" Workout

 Include a combination of singing, *audiation*, and playing your instrument on every piece you learn:

1. Sing "Twinkle, twinkle, little star" with lyrics:

   Twinkle, twinkle, little star
   How I wonder what you are
   Up above the world so high
   Like a diamond in the sky
   Twinkle, twinkle, little star
   How I wonder what you are

2. Sing "Twinkle, twinkle, little star" again, singing "*doo*" for every syllable.

3. Sing a drone C while *audiating* (imagining, using only your mind's ear) "Twinkle, Twinkle, Little Star."

4. Repeat steps 1-3 then skip to step 5.

5. Play "Twinkle, twinkle, little star" on your instrument, entirely by ear.

Write out "Twinkle, twinkle, little star" in C major.

C C G G — — — — — — — — — — — — . — —

— — — — — — — — — — — — — — — —

— — — — — — — — — — — — — — — —

 Do you want to try this workout with another tune?
Here is a short list of alternatives:

- "Bye Bye Blackbird"
- "Joy to the World"
- "They can't take that away from me"
- "Someone to Watch over Me"
- "Avalon"
- "It's only a paper moon"
- "Limbo Jazz"
- "Tiger Rag"

Improvise   Play-Rest

The complement to rhythm is rest — complete silence. After you play a phrase, try pausing for a few beats. The silence at the end adds meaning to your phrasing. Practicing the examples below will also help you become fluent with the sound of various phrase lengths. Aim for clarity here. When a phrase ends, make sure it ends. Do not let your notes spill over into any rests (easier said than done!).

IMPROVISE
Play 1 Measure + 1 Beat

The slashes here represent SLASH NOTATION, which commonly indicates your opportunity to improvise.

The RHYTHMIC NOTATION here indicates that any pitch may be played on this single beat.

IMPROVISE
Play 2, Rest 2

IMPROVISE
Play 3, Rest 1

IMPROVISE
Rest 1, Play 1

Close your eyes. Envision the rhythm section and count the beats per measure above. For each example, simply imagine which measures to play and which measures to rest. This practice strategy will help you keep your place in each 4-bar phrase.

As you improvise each set of Play-Rest phrases, imagine that every time you are playing, someone is **touching your shoulder** gently. During the rests, your shoulder is no longer touched. Hand on means PLAY; hand off means REST!

Motivic Development

Entire compositions and improvisations may be based on small sets of notes — termed *motifs* (or *motives*, *themes*, *cells*, etc.). A motif may involve any musical entity. While quite commonly introduced as a limited pitch set, a motif may instead involve only a rhythm, a dynamic or shift in dynamics, a gesture, or another element. The essence is that the motif introduces a thematic idea that may be developed across a musical work, giving the work an inherent integrity.

EX. 1.35
"C Jam Blues" rhythm only
(Duke Ellington)

Duke Ellington's "C Jam Blues" is already ripe for motivic development. Notice how the motifs in subsequent examples **derive from its theme**.

EX. 1.36
Short and simple upbeat motif

Pitch collection challenge!
Create the melody of "C Jam Blues" above by adding a combination of only the following pitches:

C G

EX. 1.37
Short 2-note motif, developed both ascending and descending

Eighth note rest, in place of a note, adds a welcome moment of surprise.

EX. 1.38
Various motifs

steps   skips   repeated pitch   neighbor notes

angular, wide intervals   whisper/stillness   gestural flourish   rest

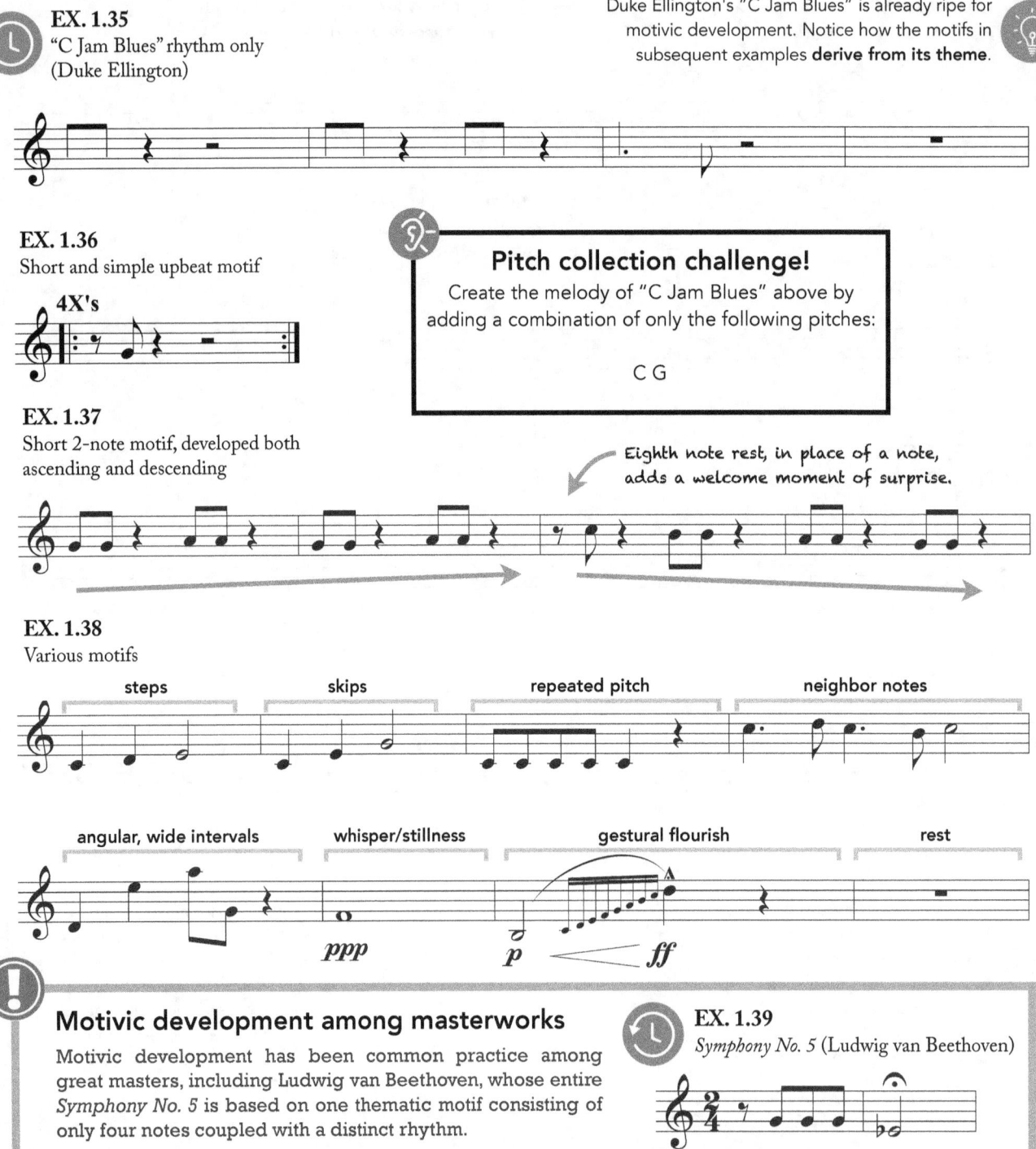

Motivic development among masterworks

Motivic development has been common practice among great masters, including Ludwig van Beethoven, whose entire *Symphony No. 5* is based on one thematic motif consisting of only four notes coupled with a distinct rhythm.

EX. 1.39
Symphony No. 5 (Ludwig van Beethoven)

Scale Pattern as Motif

Even the smallest handful of notes from a major scale pattern may be used as a motif ripe for further development. The C major scale patterns below illustrate how, when using a scale pattern as motif, the melody will remain strong and logical. One reason for this is that each scale pattern establishes a clear shape that helps give the melody an inherent structure. Presented below are six distinct scale pattern shapes, followed by examples of these shapes unfolding across multiple measures.

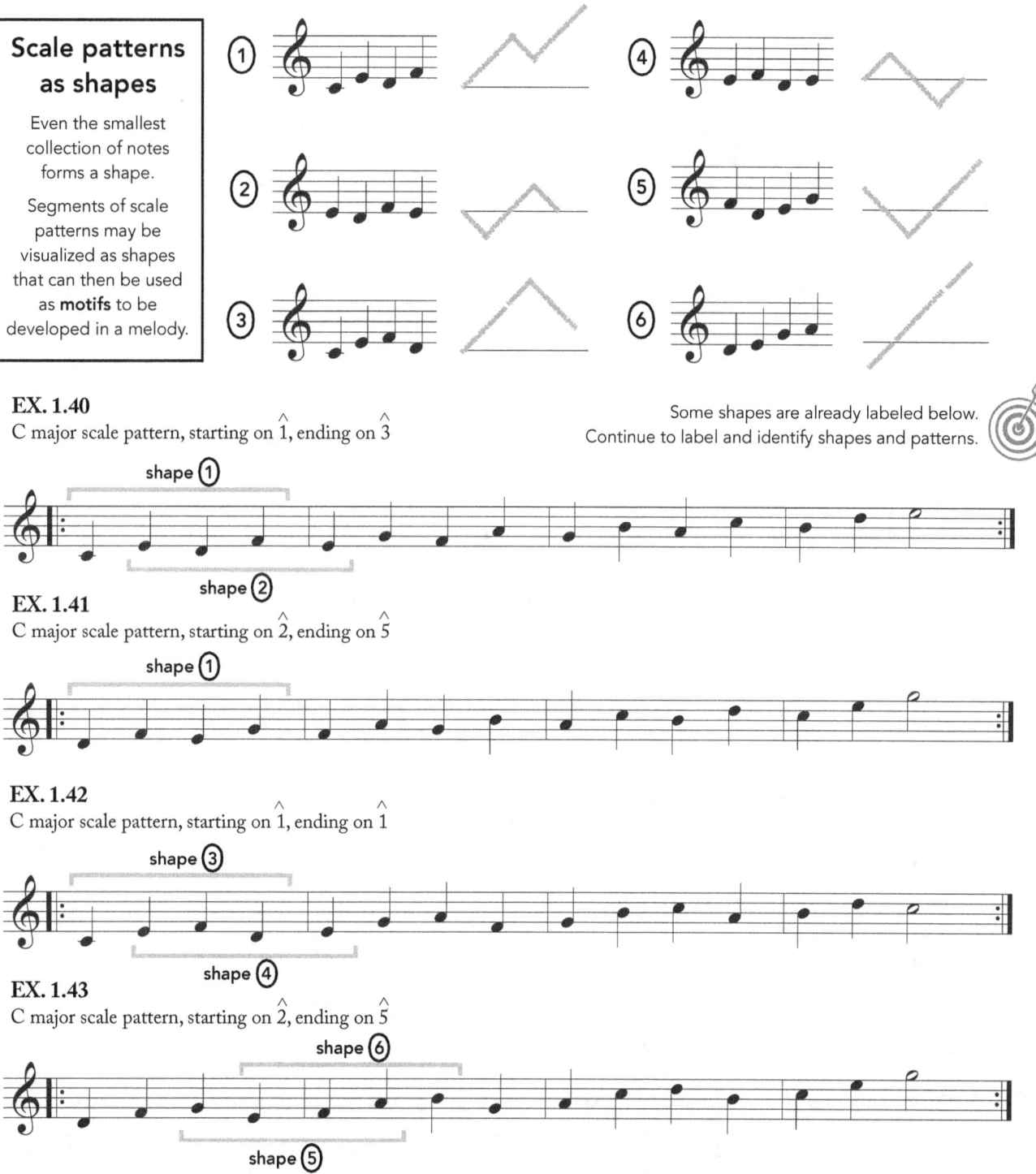

Scale patterns as shapes

Even the smallest collection of notes forms a shape.

Segments of scale patterns may be visualized as shapes that can then be used as **motifs** to be developed in a melody.

EX. 1.40
C major scale pattern, starting on $\hat{1}$, ending on $\hat{3}$

Some shapes are already labeled below. Continue to label and identify shapes and patterns.

EX. 1.41
C major scale pattern, starting on $\hat{2}$, ending on $\hat{5}$

EX. 1.42
C major scale pattern, starting on $\hat{1}$, ending on $\hat{1}$

EX. 1.43
C major scale pattern, starting on $\hat{2}$, ending on $\hat{5}$

Diatonic Intervals

Consider a clock face, its hands measuring various intervals of time, illustrating the passing seconds, minutes, and hours. A *musical interval* is also a measurement — the distance between two notes. Any series of notes, even the major scale itself, is comprised of intervals. Determine the interval between any two notes in a major scale by counting the number of scale steps it takes to move from one to the other. Get to know both the sounds and names of *diatonic intervals* as they relate to the C major scale.

di·a·ton·ic ˈdīəˈtänik/
adjective involving only notes from the scale and key, without any chromatic alteration

in·ter·val ˈin(t)ərvəl/ noun: **interval**
plural noun: **intervals**; adjective: **intervallic** (-vălˈĭk)
1. Distance in time. 2. Distance between two notes.

EX. 1.44
Diatonic interval exercise
(C major scale)

VERY IMPORTANT!
Get to know the SOUND
of each interval.

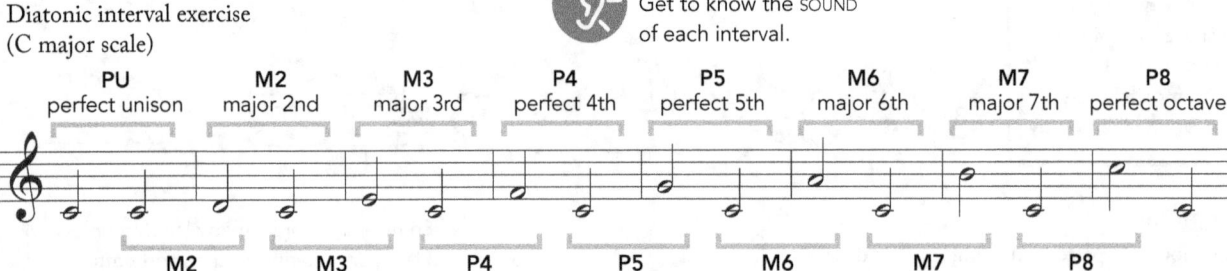

EX. 1.45
Old MacDonald (Traditional)
diatonic interval study

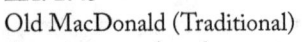
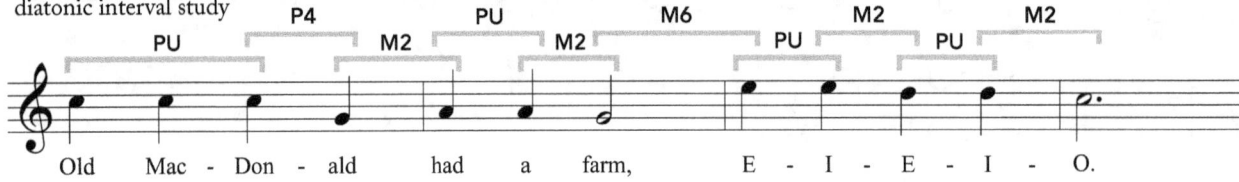

Old Mac - Don - ald had a farm, E - I - E - I - O.

When counting the number of scale steps, **always include the starting note.**
For example: G up to E = G-A-B-C-D-E = 1-2-3-4-5-6 = MAJOR 6th (M6) interval

Common diatonic intervals

Below are common interval names and examples (within the C major scale). Determine the interval by counting all the scale steps between the two notes. Always count the starting note.

NAME:	PU perfect unison	m2 minor 2nd	M2 major 2nd	m3 minor 3rd	M3 major 3rd	P4 perfect 4th
EXAMPLE:	E stays on E E-E 1-1	E up to F E-F 1-2	F up to G F-G 1-2	G down to E G-F-E 1-2-3	A down to F A-G-F 1-2-3	G up to C G-A-B-C 1-2-3-4
NAME:	P5 perfect 5th	m6 minor 6th	M6 major 6th	m7 minor 7th	M7 major 7th	P8 perfect octave
EXAMPLE:	E up to B E-F-G-A-B 1-2-3-4-5	E up to C E-F-G-A-B-C 1-2-3-4-5-6	G up to E G-A-B-C-D-E 1-2-3-4-5-6	D up to C D-E-F-G-A-B-C 1-2-3-4-5-6-7	C up to B C-D-E-F-G-A-B 1-2-3-4-5-6-7	E up to E E-F-G-A-B-C-D-E 1-2-3-4-5-6-7-8

Interval as Thematic Motif

The use of an interval as thematic motif can add immediate clarity to a melody. The interval chosen, such as a perfect 5th (P5) or a minor 3rd (m3), may be repeated or it may develop to involve other intervals. This intervallic development gives the melody an inevitability and internal logic.

EX. 1.46
Perfect 5th
as motif

Imagine each interval below as if it is **a character in an unfolding story**.
Do you hear the distinguishing characteristics in each melody below?

EX. 1.47
Major/minor 3rd
as motif

EX. 1.48
Louis Armstrong trumpet solo
"St. Louis Blues"

IMPROVISE

First choose an interval as motif then improvise.

1-Measure Rhythms

Small rhythmic cells, even when only one measure long, are memorable, purposeful, and highly engaging. Get to know 1-measure rhythms by ear, by sight, and by feel. Practice them in multiple tempos and feels, from swing to straight eighths. Notice the details, particularly how some of these rhythms are syncopated and others are not. These rhythms may be used with any combination of pitches.

EX. 1.49
1-measure rhythms

Loop each 1-measure rhythm below, playing through each one repeatedly, in tempo. Also write in the counts for each.

EX. 1.50
Major scale *étude* using rhythm ⑤

EX. 1.51
Rhythm ③ with added pitches

Repeat the *étude* above, using a different 1-measure rhythm each time.

Cut Time

At a slow or medium tempo, the quarter-note beat defines the rhythmic pulse but, when the tempo gets particularly fast, the pulse naturally changes to the half note. Just like 4/4 measures, *cut time* measures include four quarter notes but each cut time measure is counted in 2, instead of in 4, with each half note receiving a count. Also known as *double time*, cut time can help keep a fast tempo relaxed and easy. Both "Avalon" and "When the Saints" may be played from medium tempo to a very fast double-time tempo.

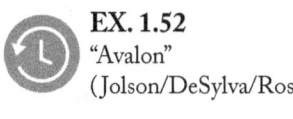

EX. 1.52
"Avalon"
(Jolson/DeSylva/Rose)

EX. 1.53
"When the Saints Go Marching In"
(Traditional)

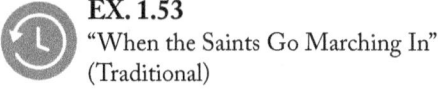

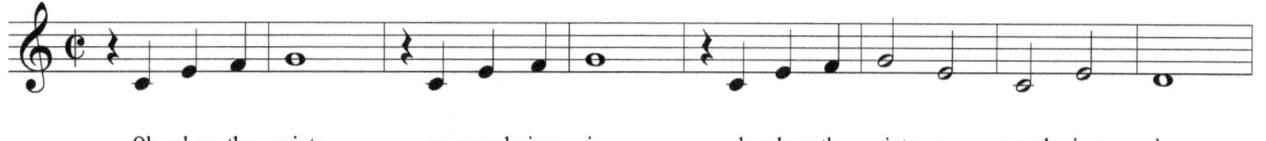

Oh when the saints   go march-ing   in,   oh when the saints go   march - ing   in,

---

**Common time
vs.
cut time**

Common time, or *4/4 time*, and cut time both use the "C" symbol but cut time adds a vertical line dividing the "C" in half lengthwise. Cut time is felt "in 2," as if it is written in 2/2 meter, with two half-note beats.

EX. 1.54
Quarter-note pulse,
common time (4/4), felt "in 4"

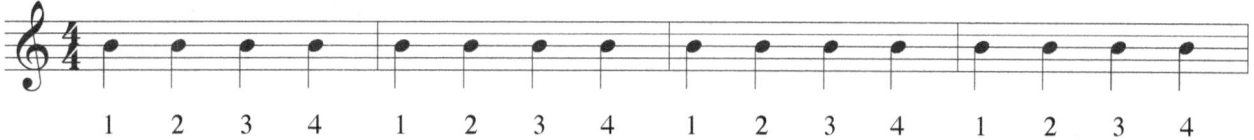

1   2   3   4   1   2   3   4   1   2   3   4   1   2   3   4

EX. 1.55
Half-note pulse,
cut time, felt "in 2"

1   2   1   2   1   2   1   2

Cut time can help **keep a fast tempo relaxed and easy.** For the above up-tempo examples, try tapping or counting quarter notes per measure. Then try again but tap or count half notes. Do the quarter notes get stressful? Do the half notes give the tempo a lighter and easier feel?

Rhythmic Matrix

Whether you are playing entirely solo or with other musicians, your music is being played over a *rhythmic matrix* that acts as an underlying rhythmic engine, informing your performance. Understanding this matrix is essential to unlocking your potential to swing, communicate, and play creatively. Under your melodic line, the matrix may be comprised of any beat pattern — a steady stream of eighth notes, eighth-note triplets, sixteenth notes, half notes, a combination of half notes and quarter notes, and more. The most common matrix is counted in 4/4 time, a simple meter with four quarter notes forming a pulse under the melody. Consider this akin to a tapping foot, a metronome click, or even a simple march down the street. At any moment, you can "march to the beat of a different drum" by imagining any other rhythmic value or pulse for your matrix, offering each measure a simultaneous subdivision of beats.

EX. 1.56
The rhythmic matrix in common time (4/4), including common rhythmic values

Most melodies employ a **combination of rhythmic values**, which can help sustain musical interest and momentum.

A rhythmic variation commonly used in jazz is *double-time feel*. Double time, also known as cut time, involves speeding up the underlying tempo but double-time feel keeps the underlying tempo the same while speeding up the rhythms played over the pulse, only implying the cut-time rhythm.

In the 4/4 examples below, the **underlying tempo and pulse remain constant**. In the cut time example, the tempo is twice as fast.

EX. 1.57
Original-time feel in 4/4

The original 8th-note rhythm is played over a quarter note pulse.

EX. 1.58
Double time (cut time)

EX. 1.59
Double-time feel in 4/4

The double-time rhythms here move twice as fast, implying a double-time feel but not actual double time since the underlying tempo remains constant and does not double.

Articulation and Style

In any genre of music, how the music is played really makes all the difference. The performer's sound and style shape every phrase. Notice below how dynamics and articulation shape the character of each phrase. Of particular importance is how upbeat accents help the music swing.

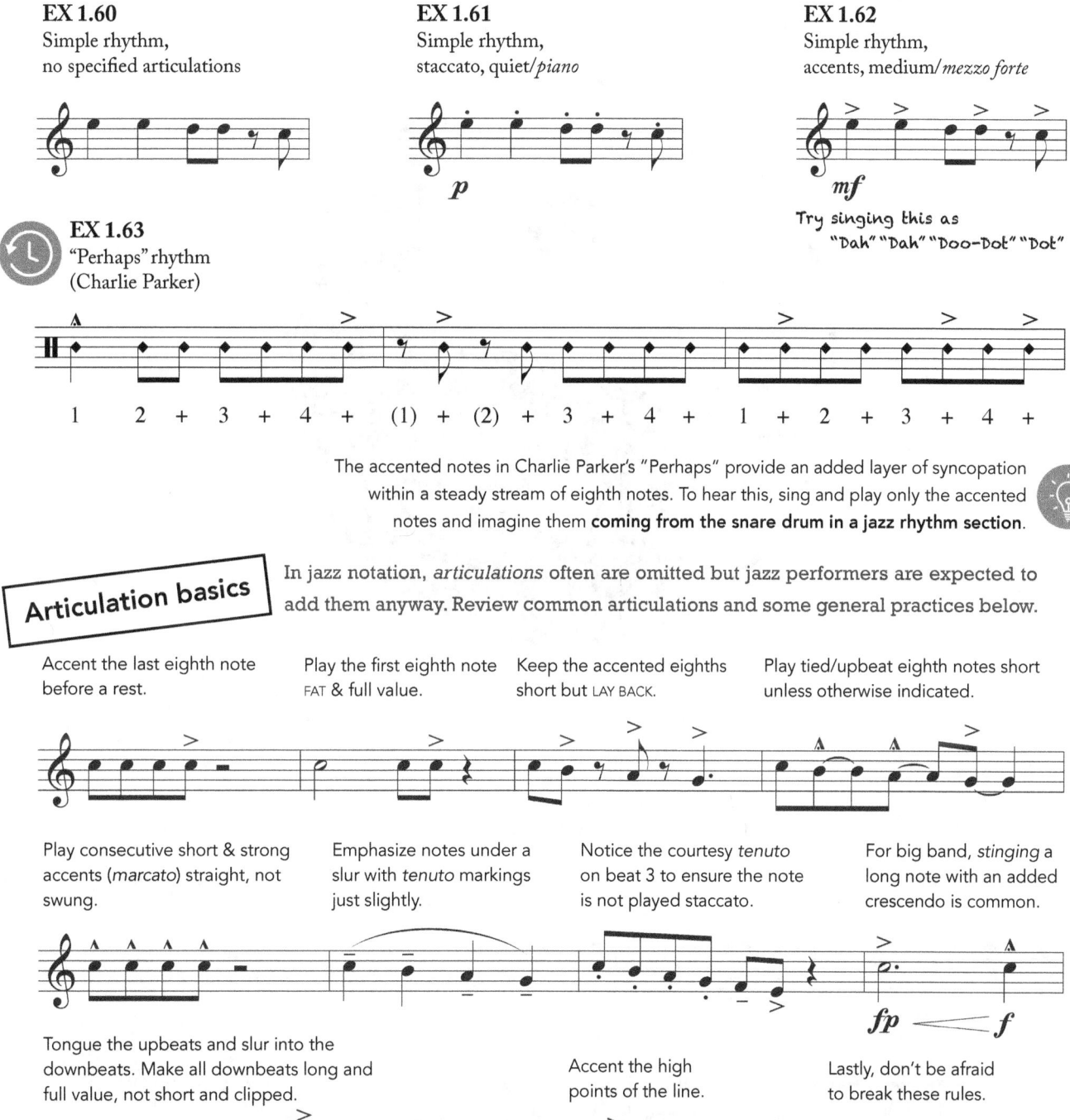

EX 1.60
Simple rhythm,
no specified articulations

EX 1.61
Simple rhythm,
staccato, quiet/*piano*

EX 1.62
Simple rhythm,
accents, medium/*mezzo forte*

Try singing this as
"Dah" "Dah" "Doo-Dot" "Dot"

EX 1.63
"Perhaps" rhythm
(Charlie Parker)

1   2   +   3   +   4   +   (1)   +   (2)   +   3   +   4   +   1   +   2   +   3   +   4   +

The accented notes in Charlie Parker's "Perhaps" provide an added layer of syncopation within a steady stream of eighth notes. To hear this, sing and play only the accented notes and imagine them **coming from the snare drum in a jazz rhythm section**.

Articulation basics

In jazz notation, *articulations* often are omitted but jazz performers are expected to add them anyway. Review common articulations and some general practices below.

Accent the last eighth note before a rest.

Play the first eighth note FAT & full value.

Keep the accented eighths short but LAY BACK.

Play tied/upbeat eighth notes short unless otherwise indicated.

Play consecutive short & strong accents (*marcato*) straight, not swung.

Emphasize notes under a slur with *tenuto* markings just slightly.

Notice the courtesy *tenuto* on beat 3 to ensure the note is not played staccato.

For big band, *stinging* a long note with an added crescendo is common.

Tongue the upbeats and slur into the downbeats. Make all downbeats long and full value, not short and clipped.

Accent the high points of the line.

Lastly, don't be afraid to break these rules.

1   +   2   +   3   +   4   +   1   2   +   a   3   +   (4)

Oppositions

Oppositions are all around us. We wake each morning and sleep each night. We breathe in then breathe out. The sun sets; the moon rises. Music also achieves balance through oppositions. Rhythm can be fast then slow. Melody can move up then down. Themes and phrases can be varied or repetitious. Significantly, a key to crafting a successful melody lies in understanding and applying musical oppositions. Consider the oppositions below then continue to think of other likely oppositions.

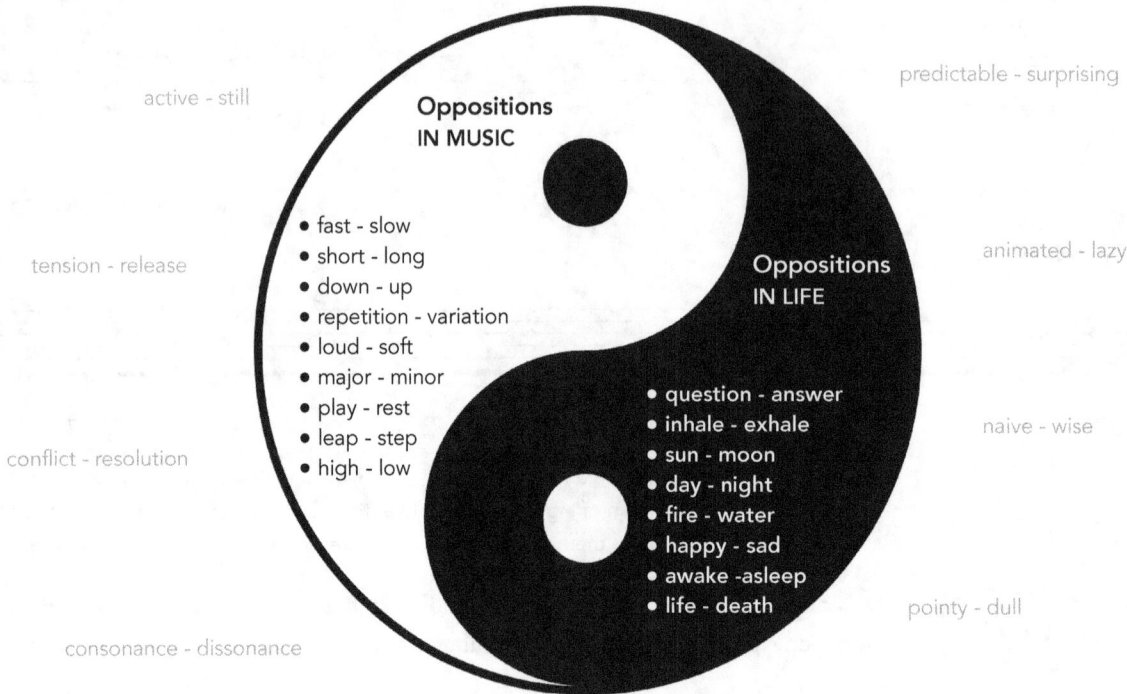

active - still

predictable - surprising

tension - release

animated - lazy

Oppositions
IN MUSIC

- fast - slow
- short - long
- down - up
- repetition - variation
- loud - soft
- major - minor
- play - rest
- leap - step
- high - low

Oppositions
IN LIFE

- question - answer
- inhale - exhale
- sun - moon
- day - night
- fire - water
- happy - sad
- awake - asleep
- life - death

conflict - resolution

naive - wise

consonance - dissonance

pointy - dull

Which musical oppositions can you identify
in the Duke Ellington classic below?

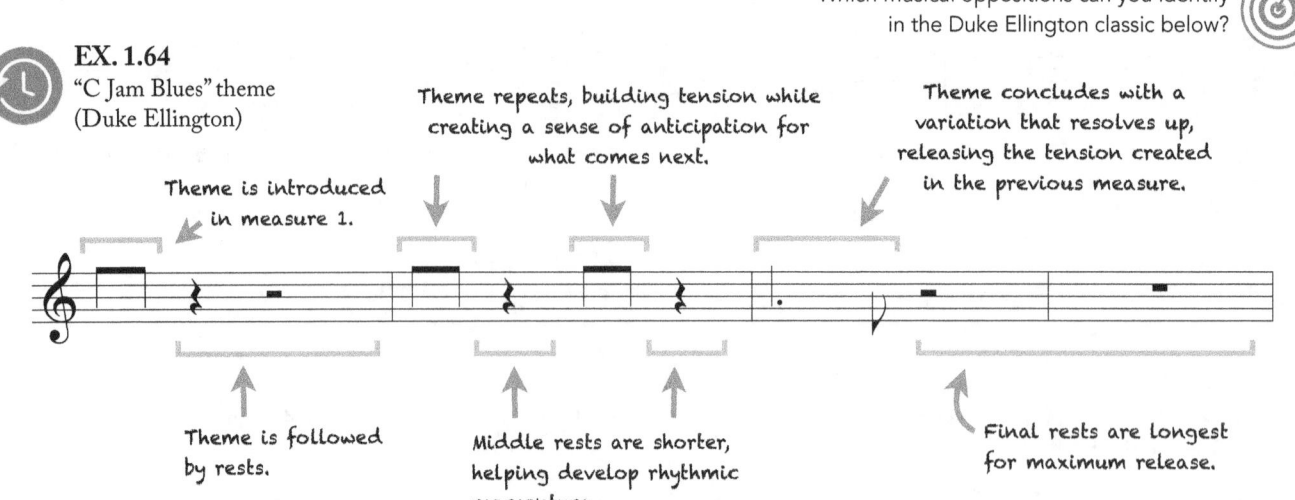

EX. 1.64
"C Jam Blues" theme
(Duke Ellington)

Theme is introduced
in measure 1.

Theme repeats, building tension while
creating a sense of anticipation for
what comes next.

Theme concludes with a
variation that resolves up,
releasing the tension created
in the previous measure.

Theme is followed
by rests.

Middle rests are shorter,
helping develop rhythmic
momentum.

Final rests are longest
for maximum release.

Do not jump straight into analysis. **Get to know the sound of the music first.**
This will help facilitate a stronger understanding of oppositions and other details.

Melodic Examples

Jazz improvisation covers much of the same artistic ground as musical composition. Any melody contains distinct characteristics. Take some time to examine the following compositions. What sort of characteristics stand out? Can you identify similarities and oppositions in each melodic example?

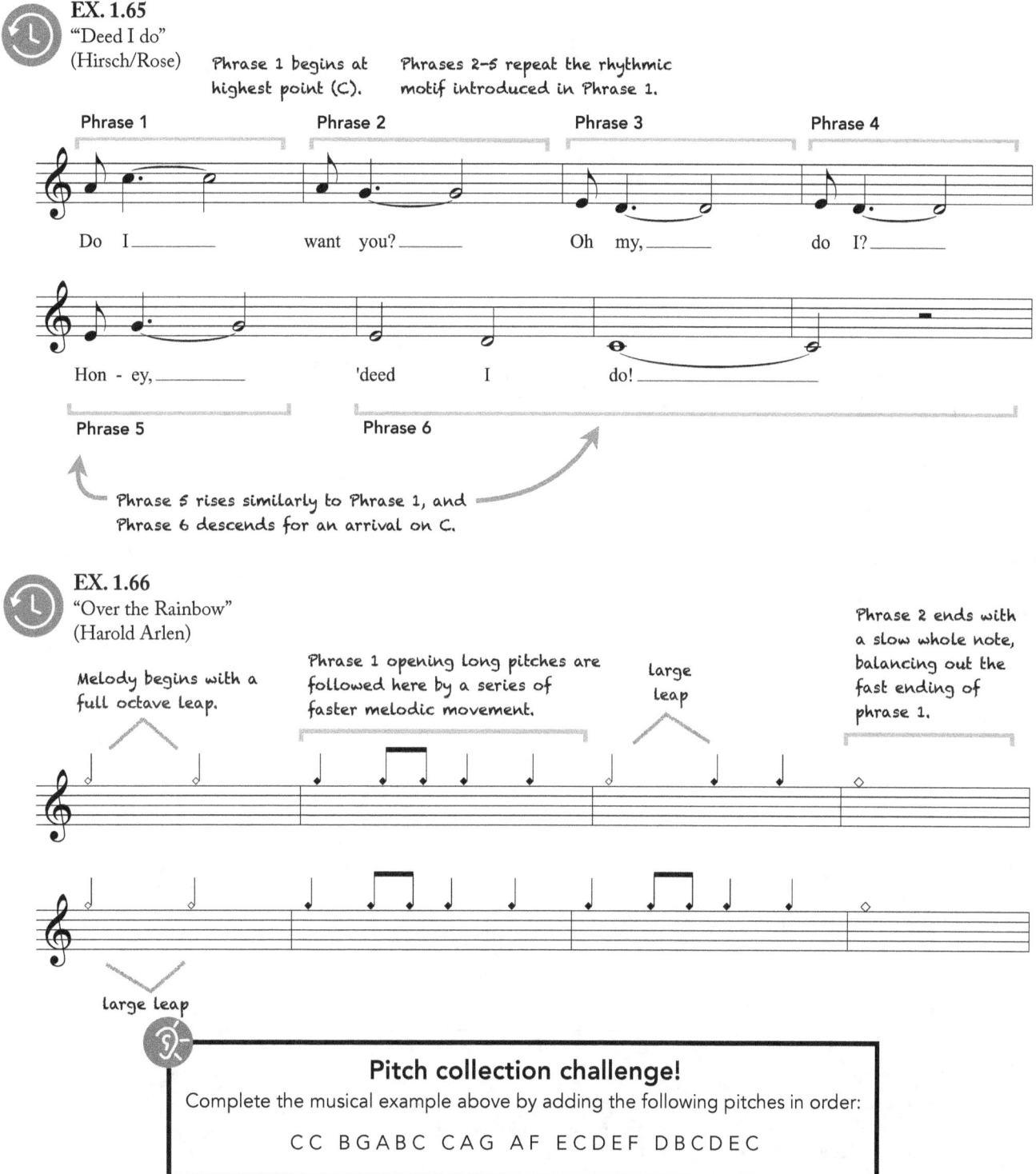

EX. 1.65
"Deed I do"
(Hirsch/Rose)

Phrase 1 begins at highest point (C).

Phrases 2-5 repeat the rhythmic motif introduced in Phrase 1.

Phrase 5 rises similarly to Phrase 1, and Phrase 6 descends for an arrival on C.

EX. 1.66
"Over the Rainbow"
(Harold Arlen)

Melody begins with a full octave leap.

Phrase 1 opening long pitches are followed here by a series of faster melodic movement.

large leap

Phrase 2 ends with a slow whole note, balancing out the fast ending of phrase 1.

large leap

Pitch collection challenge!
Complete the musical example above by adding the following pitches in order:

C C B G A B C C A G A F E C D E F D B C D E C

Melodic Architecture

Melodic phrases take on distinct shapes. These shapes are sometimes referred to as *melodic architecture*, conjuring up images of structures and buildings. Visualizing melody can help with artistic interpretation of each phrase and offers another method of understanding. The examples below are rooted in C major, the thin horizontal line indicating the note C. The melody forms above and below that central pitch.

EX. 1.67
"St. Louis Blues"
(W. C. Handy)

Carefully examine the melodic shapes below, including their high and low points, imagining **the composer as an architect**.

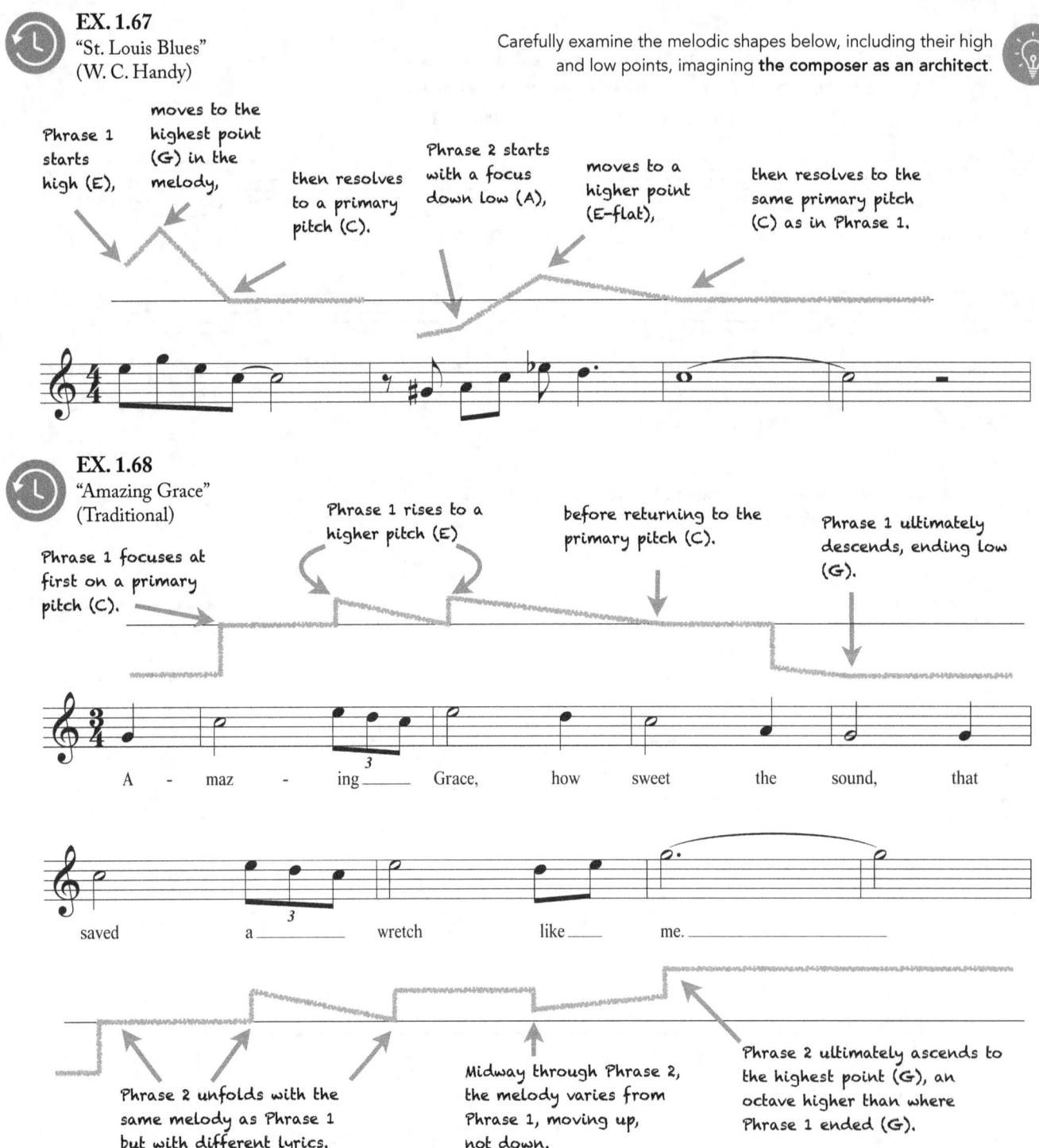

Phrase 1 starts high (E), moves to the highest point (G) in the melody, then resolves to a primary pitch (C). **Phrase 2 starts with a focus down low (A),** moves to a higher point (E-flat), then resolves to the same primary pitch (C) as in Phrase 1.

EX. 1.68
"Amazing Grace"
(Traditional)

Phrase 1 focuses at first on a primary pitch (C). Phrase 1 rises to a higher pitch (E) before returning to the primary pitch (C). Phrase 1 ultimately descends, ending low (G).

A - maz - ing —— Grace, how sweet the sound, that

saved a —— wretch like —— me. ——

Phrase 2 unfolds with the same melody as Phrase 1 but with different lyrics. Midway through Phrase 2, the melody varies from Phrase 1, moving up, not down. Phrase 2 ultimately ascends to the highest point (G), an octave higher than where Phrase 1 ended (G).

Composition 101

How do you compose a melody? It's simple, and it involves an easy-to-remember formula:

1. Write down a note.
2. Write down a second note.
3. Write down a third note that follows the second note.
4. Keep going!

 Don't judge your work at this stage. Your goal should be only to generate more content. Once you have composed a significant amount of music then you could begin editing. But, at first, there won't be enough to edit. **Keep composing with no worries**. It's the best approach you can take when you first begin and you will grow naturally, whether or not you judge your own work so early in the creative process.

 Compose your own melody using the C major scale.

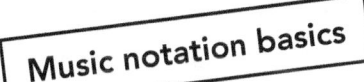 Whether for review or to gain more fluency, taking ample time to understand music notation is essential for all musicians. Here are some fundamentals:

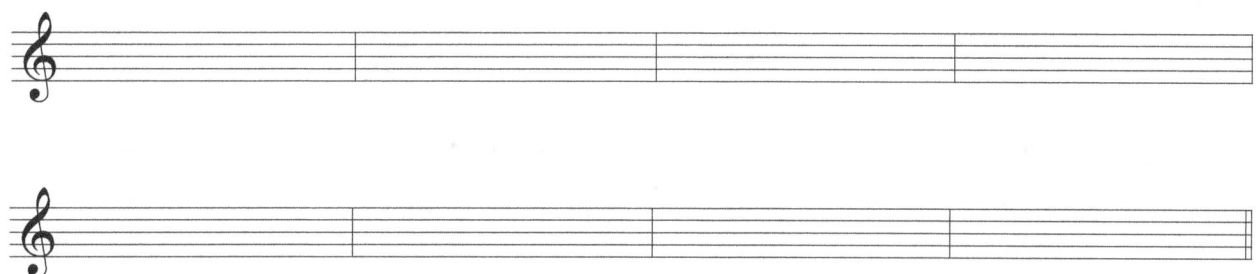

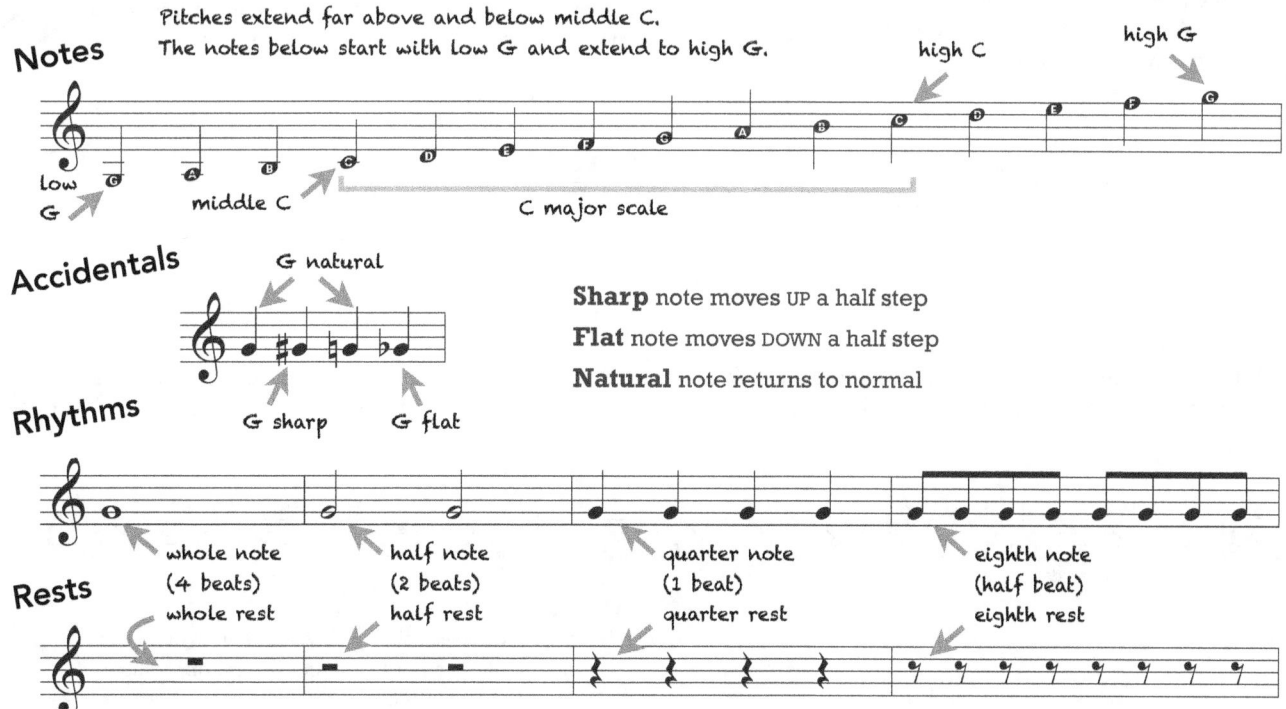

Sharp note moves UP a half step

Flat note moves DOWN a half step

Natural note returns to normal

Improvise   Major Scale Workout

Before improvising, examine the following examples, both in 4/4 meter. Notice how tenor saxophonist Hank Mobley uses only notes from the major scale while piquing interest and including variety by adding in a triplet and a scale pattern. While the entire major scale might end up being used by the time an improvised line has ended, melodies commonly unfold through the use of small scale fragments. The second example features a syncopated 1-measure rhythm that starts with a rest and emphasizes the "and" of beat 2.

EX. 1.69
Hank Mobley tenor sax solo
"Home Cookin'"

EX. 1.70
1-measure rhythm examples
(eighth note rest alteration)

Circle the one stretch of all eight consecutive C major scale notes in Hank Mobley's solo above.

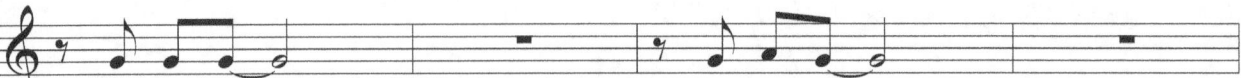

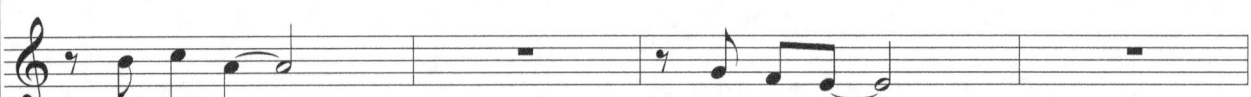

Write your own 1-measure rhythms in 4/4. Consider whether the rhythm you write is one that would want to use as a motif while improvising a melody.

What should you do during the rests above? You are not playing during the rests but the music keeps on! **Continue counting the beats** while also feeling the underlying pulse of the phrase.

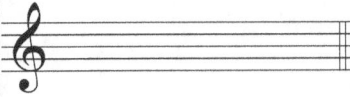

IMPROVISE
Improvise using major scale fragments in your key of C. Can you think of scale degrees while soloing?

Keep your improvisation **slow, simple, and repetitive** and be sure to use rests to balance your solo.

C

After you improvise slowly, vary your tempo and style. Remember to continue to use oppositions. slow-fast, up-down, soft-loud, long-short, etc.

Zen Jazz Master says:

Rhythm is king!

If you don't believe this, then you have never heard tenor saxophonist Illinois Jacquet play an incredible solo almost entirely on one pitch! A great jazz solo doesn't need a ton of notes but it always needs a great sense of rhythm. When you solo, make your notes burst with rhythm, whether slow half note or fast sixteenth. If you are only playing quarter notes, play them in a "pocket" with the rhythm section. If you are playing swing, then swing hard!

Great players who don't tend to play a ton of notes:

Eddie "Lockjaw" Davis

Paul Desmond

Illinois Jacquet

Miles Davis

Ahmad Jamal

Count Basie

"Rhythm" is also a great word to use when playing HANGMAN!

R-H-Y-T-H-M.

Only one vowel and it's a "Y."

No one starts with "Y" when playing Hangman.

Try it. Your opponents won't know what hit them.

Chapter 1 Achievements

Congratulations!

You are one step closer to jazz nirvana.

Here is a partial list of what you've achieved:

- Recognizing the major scale and its many melodic facets
- Using scale degrees and simple rhythms while improvising
- Identifying motifs and oppositions in melody
- Improvising on a major scale
- Developing fundamental skills in ear training and music notation

Are you ready for the next chapter?

Answer these questions to determine whether you are prepared to continue to the next chapter:

- **Do you understand** basic major scale construction and scale degrees?

  If "Yes," move to the next chapter.
  If "No," review this chapter.

- **Can you hear** simple melodies in your head before you play them?

  If "Yes," move to the next chapter.
  If "No," don't fret. Move to the next chapter anyway. The ear will take some more time and material to develop.

- **Can you read** basic music notation with ease?

  If "Yes," move to the next chapter.
  If "No," review this chapter AND move to the next chapter. Your reading ability should improve with more practice and more material.

- **Do you want** to learn about chord tones, target notes, and key centers?

  If "Yes," move to the next chapter.
  If "No," you have two choices: (1) move to the next chapter anyway and see what piques your interest or (2) close this book and come back when you're hungry to learn more!

Playing with Purpose

Chord Tone Target Notes, Transposition, and Key Centers

Crafting a melody is really not much different than forming phrases and sentences when writing a short story or when engaging in a conversation. Each melodic phrase has three parts — a beginning, middle, and end — most often intersecting with harmony and rhythm via target notes. Targets help give a melody structure and direction and, without them, a melody risks being formless and lacking in meaning. Chord tone target notes serve as an introduction to harmony, leading to an exploration of the concepts of transposition within all twelve major key centers.

Contents

TOPICS
- Chord Tones
- Passing Tones
- Major Scale Tendencies
- Chord Tone Target Notes
- Ready, Set, Aim!
  (for rhythmic accuracy)
- What is your intent?
- Target Note Exercises
- Diatonic Enclosures
  and Approach Notes
- Diatonic Enclosures
  and Scale Patterns
- C vs. CMaj7 vs. C6
- Which major chord to use?
- Maintaining Complete
  Rhythmic Control
- Putting It All Together
- Historical Target Examples
- The Chromatic Scale
- Enharmonic Spelling
- Using Imagery to
  Remember Accidentals
- Chromatic Intervals
- Chromatic Neighbors
- Transposition Down a Whole Step
- Transposition Using Scale Fragments
- Transposition Workout
- 12 Major Scales
- Circle of Fifths
- Key Signatures
- Key Center Workout

EAR TRAINING
- Chord Triad Audiation
- Creative Counting
- Rhythmic Ear Training
- Sing Lester Young's
  "Lester leaps in" solo

MASTERCLASS
- Four Parts of Practice:
  Mind, Body, Ear, Soul

INVESTIGATE
- Note Grouping

SOLO SPOTLIGHT
- Lester Young tenor sax solo
  "Lester leaps in"

COMPOSE
- Scale Pattern Incorporating
  Enclosures
- 8 Measures Using
  C Major Scale Target Notes

IMPROVISE
- Chord Tone Target Notes
- C Major Vamp Using
  Varying Tempos
- Improvise in Various
  Major Keys

LISTENING GUIDE
- Songs Featuring
  Neighbor Notes and Enclosures
- Style and Nuance in Lester
  Young's "Lester Leap In" Solo

ZEN JAZZ MASTER SAYS
- Train your ear!

HISTORICAL EXAMPLES
- "The Star-Spangled Banner"
  (Key/Smith)
- "Taps" (Traditional)
- "Joy to the World/Antioch"
  (George Frideric Handel)
- "Blue Moon"
  (Rodgers/Hart)
- "Sunday"
  (Cohn/Miller/Styne/Krueger)
- "Stardust" (Hoagy Carmichael)
- Charlie Parker alto sax solo
  "Lay your habits down"
- "Sweet Georgia Brown"
  (Bernie/Pinkard/Casey)
- "Lester leaps in" (Lester Young)
- "Freddie Freeloader (Davis/Kelly)
- "Always" (Irving Berlin)
- "Für Elise" (Ludwig van Beethoven)
- "Down by the Riverside" (Traditional)
- "Yankee Doodle" (Traditional)
- "When the Saints Go Marching in"
  (Traditional)
- "Twinkle, twinkle, little star"
  (Wolfgang Amadeus Mozart)
- "Three Blind Mice" (Traditional)
- "Skip to my Lou" (Traditional)

Chord Tones

When two or more pitches are heard simultaneously, a harmony is created. Chords, commonly comprising three or more simultaneous pitches, are central to harmony. The notes within a chord — *chord tones* — may be played together simultaneously or played one at a time. The chord below, a C major triad, uses the first, third, and fifth (1-3-5) scale degrees of the C major scale. The following musical examples illustrate its use in famous melodies.

EX. 2.1
C major chord triad composed of C major scale degrees (1-3-5).

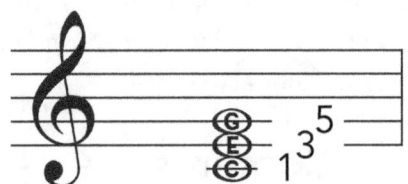

Chords in any octave

Chord tones may be placed in any octave. A C major triad is always labeled with scale degrees 1-3-5, whether played high or low.

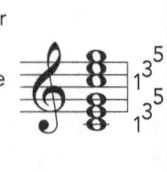

1. Sit at a piano and **play** the C major chord triad above.
2. Stop playing the chord and **audiate**, hearing the chord tones in your mind.
3. **Play** the chord again, and **sing** each chord tone. If you don't have access to a piano, only audiate and sing.

ter·ti·ar·y /ˈtərSHēˌerē/
adjective: **tertiary**
tertiary harmony uses chords based on thirds (intervals)

A chord **arpeggio** is created when all chord tones are played consecutively, as in "The Star-Spangled Banner."

EX. 2.2
"The Star-Spangled Banner" (Key/Smith)

5   3   1   3   5   1
Oh__ say, can you   see?

EX. 2.3
"Taps" (Traditional)

Finish writing in the scale degrees for "Taps" below.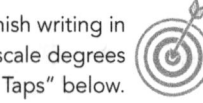

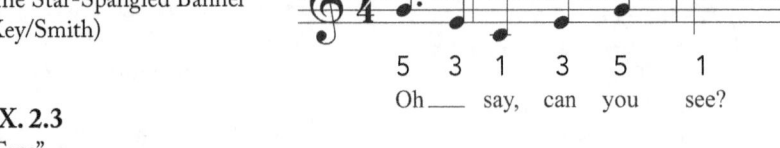

5 5 1   5 1 3

Passing tones

Passing tones are notes in a scale that sit between chord tones. Within any major scale, scale degrees 2-4-6-7 are passing tones that lead to the major triad chord tones 1-3-5. Melodies may be composed of any combination of chord tones and passing tones.

EX. 2.4
C major scale, including chord tones (CT) and passing tones (PT)

EX. 2.5
"Joy to the World/Antioch" (George Frideric Handel)

Circle the chord tones in "Joy to the World" below.

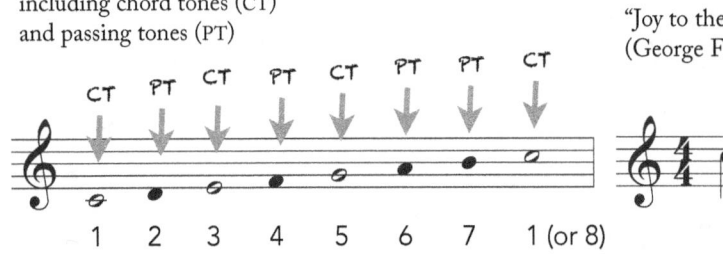
CT PT CT PT CT PT PT CT
1   2   3   4   5   6   7   1 (or 8)

Major Scale Tendencies and Chord Tone Target Notes

Within the major scale, chord tones 1-3-5 offer moments of resolution and release. The tendency of the remaining notes, passing tones 2-4-6-7, is to resolve up or down to the nearest chord tone by step. Passing tones may also be considered lower or upper neighbor notes and offer moments of tension until they resolve to chord tones. *Target notes*, also called *goal tones*, function as melodic arrival points, both mid-phrase and at phrase ends that are often but not always chord tones. In these early stages of targeting, most chord tone target notes will be placed on strong beats (beats 1 and 3 in 4/4 time).

EX. 2.6
C major scale tendencies

UN Upper Neighbor **CT** Chord Tone
LN Lower Neighbor **PT** Passing Tone

Visualize a neighbor note as truly being the note's neighbor. The note gets out of bed, walks outside to pick up the newspaper, looks next door and says, *"Hello, neighbor!"*

EX. 2.7
C major triad and upper neighbors

EX. 2.8
C major triad and lower neighbors

EX. 2.9
C major passing tone exercise

EX. 2.10
"Blue Moon" (Rodgers/Hart), rhythm only

Pitch collection challenge!
Complete the musical example above by adding the following pitches in order:

G E G F G A G G F G E D E F E E D D D E C C A C

Also write in all scale degrees then circle the chord tone target notes in "Blue Moon" (key of C major).

Ready, Set, Aim! (for rhythmic accuracy)

How well do you know your major chord tone targets and passing tones? Become familiar with exactly how many notes fit target notes and how to align these target notes with specific beats in a measure. By preparing for rhythmic accuracy, you are preparing for a purposeful and informed improvisation.

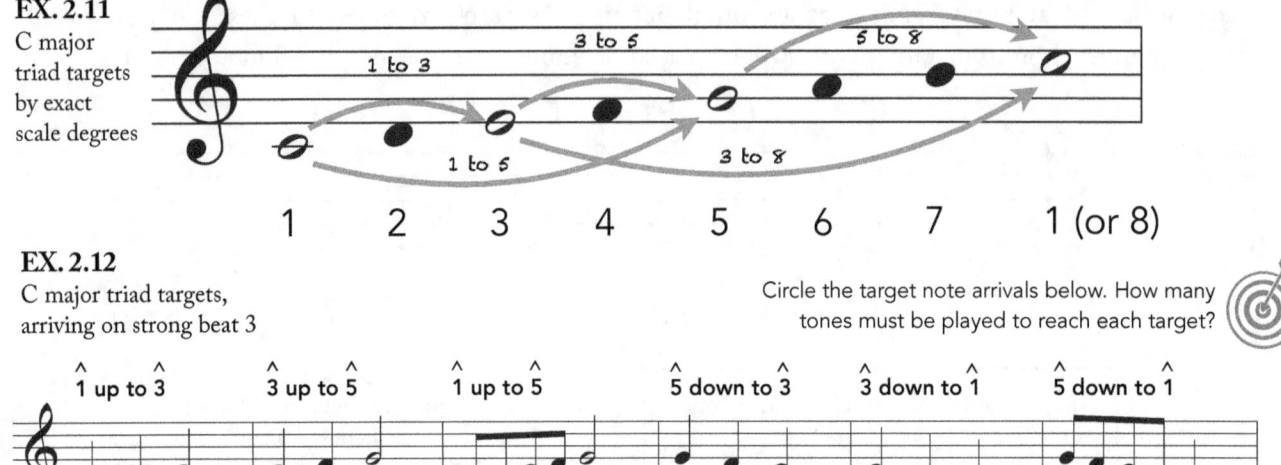

EX. 2.11
C major
triad targets
by exact
scale degrees

EX. 2.12
C major triad targets,
arriving on strong beat 3

Circle the target note arrivals below. How many
tones must be played to reach each target?

What is your intent?

What is the *intended* goal? Beat 1 of measure 2 (also called "bar 2")? If so, the first row of examples below miss their intended targets. This not to say the first row is entirely wrong but the examples are definitely inaccurate. To reach the intended beat 1, bar 2 target, the rhythm of select notes is changed in the second row. The third row adds rests, displacing the notes so that they arrive on time.

EX. 2.13.1
INACCURATE! Target misses beat 1, bar 2, landing instead on beat 4, bar 1

EX. 2.14.1
INACCURATE! Target misses beat 1, bar 2, landing instead on beat 4, bar 1

EX. 2.15.1
INACCURATE! Target misses beat 1, bar 2, landing instead on beat 4, bar 1

EX. 2.13.2
ACCURATE! Target lands on beat 1, bar 2

EX. 2.14.2
ACCURATE! Target lands on beat 1, bar 2

EX. 2.15.2
ACCURATE! Target lands on beat 1, bar 2

EX. 2.13.3
ACCURATE! Target lands on beat 1, bar 2

EX. 2.14.3
ACCURATE! Target lands on beat 1, bar 2

EX. 2.15.3
ACCURATE! Target lands on beat 1, bar 2

Target Note Exercises

The following exercises focus on landing C major chord tone targets on beat 1 (and sometimes beat 3). In the short *étude* below, pay close attention to the details, including times when the scale turns around and moves back down.

EX. 2.16
Target note *étude*

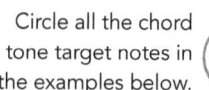

Circle all the chord tone target notes in the examples below.

Swing the above *étude* and change to a syncopated rhythm in the 2nd measure of each 2-bar phrase.

Rest-play target note exercise

When you first rest then play, you allow yourself to hear and feel the beat, giving time for planning a bit how you are going to arrive at the new target. If playing with a rhythm section or accompanist, you also give the music a chance to set the stage before you make your entrance. Because we tend to play first then rest, the reversal here will come as a welcome breath of fresh air.

EX. 2.17
Rest then play

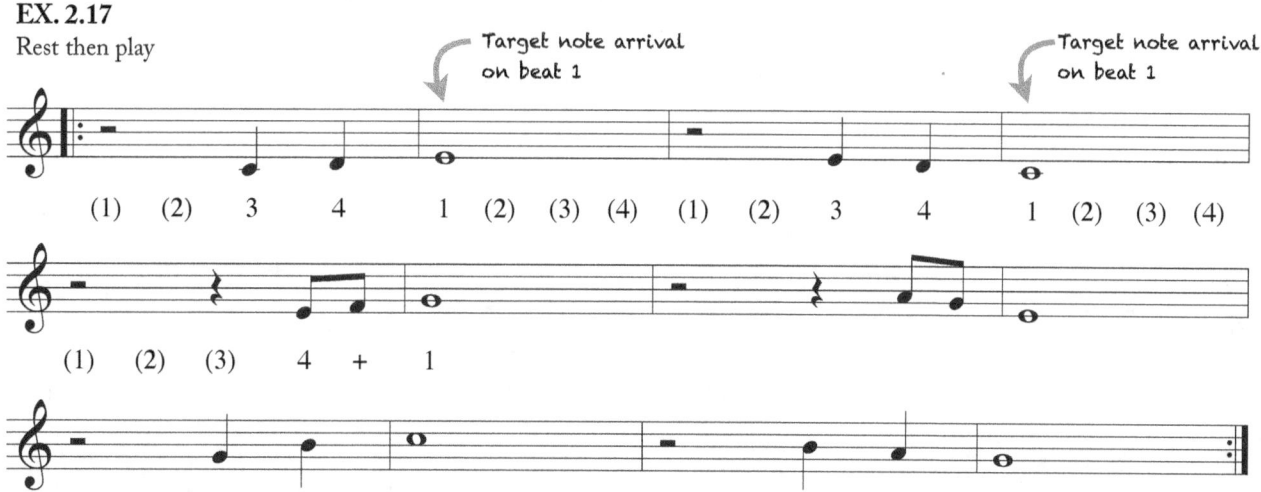

Target note arrival on beat 1

Target note arrival on beat 1

(1)   (2)   3   4   1   (2)   (3)   (4)   (1)   (2)   3   4   1   (2)   (3)   (4)

(1)   (2)   (3)   4   +   1

 Get creative with counting! In 4/4 meter, count at least 8 measures of quarter notes but count some of the beats out loud while keeping other beats silent.

Write in the remaining rhythmic values above. Pay close attention to which numbers need to be in parentheses and why.

Diatonic Enclosures and Approach Notes

A chord tone is approached either by leap, skip, or step. *Neighbor notes* (also called *neighbor tones* or *approach notes*) approach the chord tone by step, either from above (upper neighbor) or below (lower neighbor). *Diatonic enclosures* are comprised of at least two neighbor notes (upper and lower) and these neighbors enclose the target note from above and below.

Consider enclosures as adding variety to scale shapes while also helping to align a melodic target with **a particular rhythmic goal**.

EX. 2.18
Diatonic enclosures (C major)

EX 2.19
"Sunday"
(Cohn/Miller/Styne/Krueger)

I'm   blue   ev-'ry Mon-day,   Think-ing   o-ver Sun-day,

EX 2.20
"Stardust"
(Hoagy Carmichael)
First and last phrases of melody

And now the pur-ple dusk of twi-light time.   A me-mo-ry of love's ref-rain.

Enclosures and intent

How and when to use an *enclosure* may depend on *intent*. Both of the examples below use the C major scale and target high C. The first example arrives on the *and* of beat 4, bar 1. The second example uses an enclosure to help the phrase arrive on beat 1, bar 2. Both versions sound good! Which one is correct really depends on the player's intention. If the intent is to land on the strong beat 1, then the enclosure is useful. If the intent is to anticipate beat 1, bar 2, then the enclosure need not be used at all.

EX. 2.21
Major scale targeting the *and* of beat 4, bar 1

early arrival (anticipation) on the AND of beat 4

1 + 2 + 3 + 4 + (1)(2)(3)(4)

EX. 2.22
Major scale targeting beat 1, bar 2, using an enclosure

enclosure

beat 1 arrival at target note

1 + 2 + 3 + 4 + 1 (2)(3)(4)

Look for neighbor notes and enclosures in the following songs:

- "Twinkle, twinkle, little star"
- "When the Saints Go Marching in"
- "Bye Bye Blackbird"
- "Tea for Two"

- "Triste"
- "Bernie's Tune"
- "Solar"
- "Time to Say Goodbye"

What about the following example? Is this an enclosure? Why or why not?

Diatonic Enclosures and Scale Patterns

When moving up or down a scale, you have a 50/50 chance of landing your final target note on a strong beat. If you use an enclosure, you skip over a scale step before landing your target, increasing your odds to 100%. The examples below explore upward and downward enclosures throughout the entire C major scale.

You may also use enclosures with smaller **scale fragments** instead of complete scales. The scale fragments below target beat 3.

EX. 2.23
Scale fragments
and enclosures

In the examples below, finish writing in the scale degrees for every note. Also finish circling all enclosed targets.

EX. 2.24
Enclosure exercise,
descending major scale targets

EX. 2.25
Enclosure exercise,
descending major scale targets

Write your own scale pattern incorporating enclosures.

C vs. CMaj7 vs. C6

A chord often is notated only as a chord symbol placed above a staff system. The symbol "C" signifies a C major triad, which includes only the scale degrees 1-3-5. If any other notes are added to the chord, these are *chord extensions* and the chord symbol helps signify what notes have been added (or subtracted). The three chord symbols below — C, CMaj7, and C6 — are all variants of the same chord — C major. All three chords may function as the root chord in the key of C major since their core triad (scale degrees 1-3-5) is identical, yet each sounds slightly different from the next. Many musicians replace C with C6 or CMaj7 and vice versa.

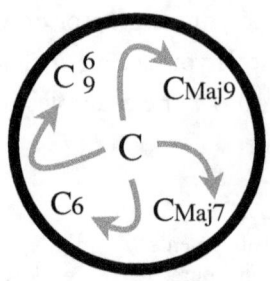

C major triad includes many variations, all meaning "C major"

EX. 2.26
C, CMaj7, C6 chords

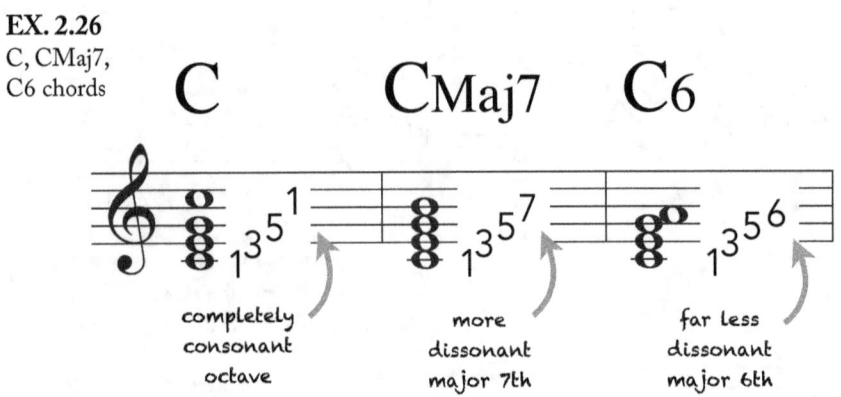

Listen for the **details and distinctions** of each chord. Can you hear, in CMaj7 for instance, how the major 7th (the note B) actively interacts in dissonance with the chord's root (the note C)? Compare this to the C6 chord, where the major 6th (the note A) interacts with the chord's 5th (the note G).

EX. 2.27
C, CMaj7, C6 arpeggios

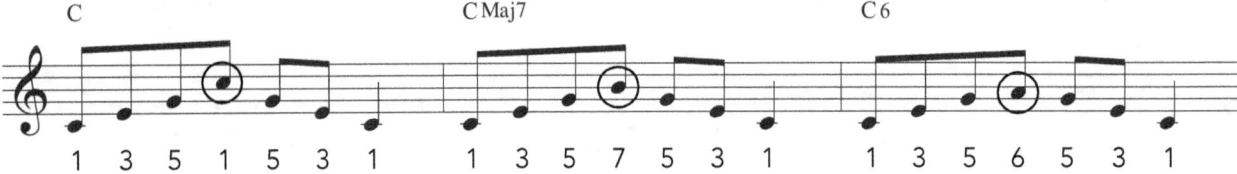

EX. 2.28
"When You're Smiling" (Shay/Fisher/Goodwin)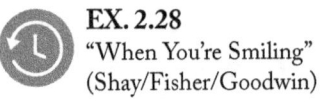

"When You're Smiling" introduces **three types of C major** — C, CMaj7, and C6 — before moving to a D minor harmony. Circled notes highlight the chords' differentiating notes.

Which major chord to use?

Which *chord type* is used while performing might depend entirely on personal taste. The player must decide which sound works best for the moment. This could involve playing only simple triads, or it might mean adding some 6ths and 7ths or even higher extensions, including 9ths, 11ths, and 13ths!

Major chord symbols
The following symbols may all also be used to indicate a major chord with at least a major 7th extension added. If the major chord is only a triad, no symbol is needed.

Δ   Δ7 MA7 Major7

Maintaining Complete Rhythmic Control

Maintaining complete rhythmic control entails knowing all your options and melding these with your imagination so that any immediate idea can be played out. This is similar to how a chess grandmaster might approach a match, being able to envision all the moves before the game has been won. The examples below illustrate how rhythms can be manipulated to achieve precise melodic goals. Techniques include combining small phrases, rhythmic and octave displacement, and targeted melodic direction through careful use of pivots.

EX. 2.29
Rhythm is a stream of constant eighth notes but rhythmic variety comes from changes in direction

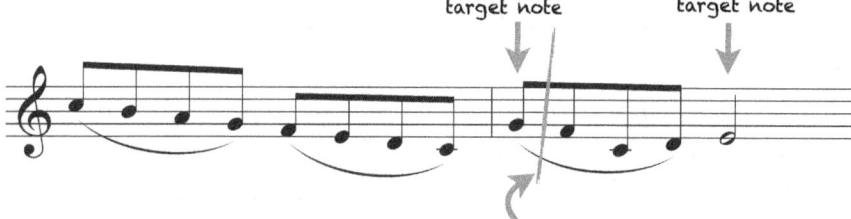

Since there are clearly two target notes in the melody above, **consider the whole line as two phrases combined**, with the second phrase starting on the "and" of beat 1, bar 2. This is a natural starting point since it immediately follows the first target note arrival on beat 1, bar 2.

EX. 2.30
C major scale with octave displacement and pivot (with beat 1 rhythmic displacement)

EX. 2.31
C major scale without octave displacement or pivot (with beat 1 rhythmic displacement)

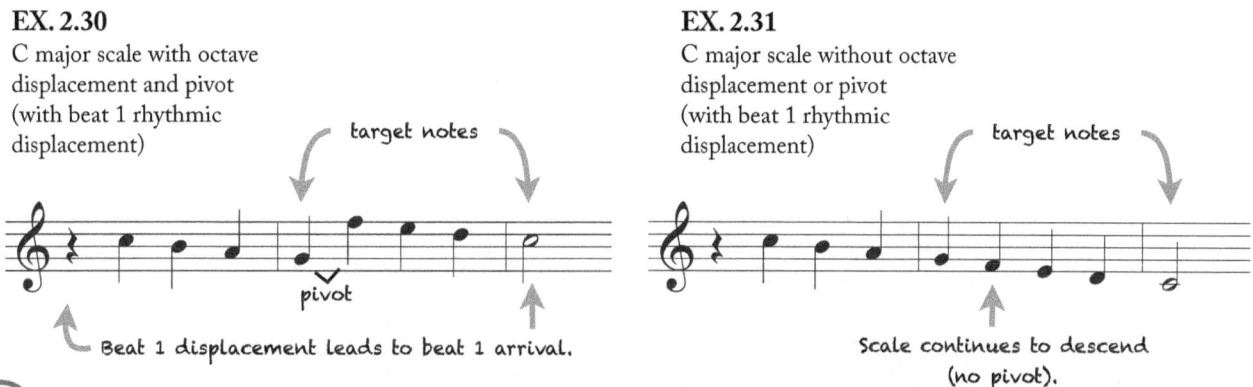

Putting it all together

A melodic line is built from many parts, with note groupings that include scale fragments, octave displacements and pivots, neighbor notes, enclosures, and carefully placed target notes. Put it all together and you have the makings of a long line, filled with musical interest.

Create and practice similar perpetual motion exercises in other keys.

EX. 2.32
Perpetual motion exercise (constant eighths)

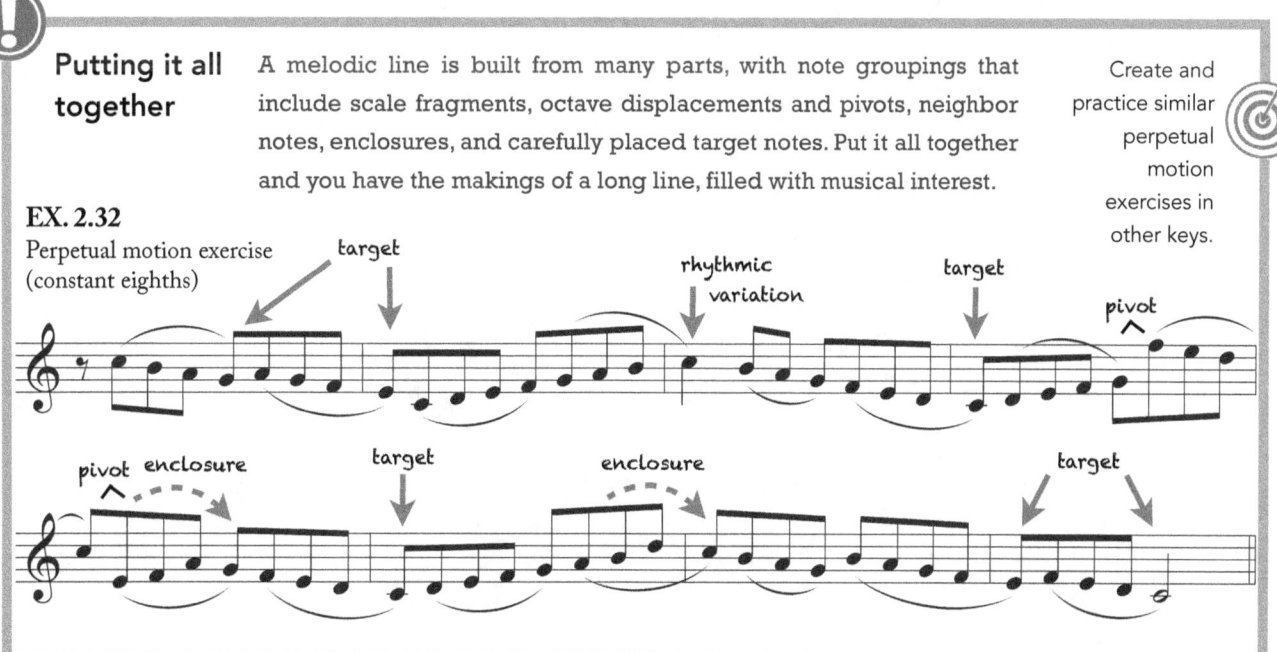

Masterclass

Four Parts of Practice:
— page 1 of 2 —
Mind, Body, Ear, Soul

If you want to be a great musician, you are going to find very quickly that simply practicing your instrument as much as possible is not going to be enough to get you to where you want to be. Until you actually break down your practice into certain elements, you won't be maximizing your potential.

Individualized practice gives you an opportunity to nurture yourself and your artistry. Practice does not simply involve your body and your instrument. Through practice, you have a rare opportunity to work on all aspects of your being. You will see the best long-term results if you continue to nurture four elements — *mind*, *body*, *ear*, and *soul*. When you practice, try setting aside time and energy to ensure you are addressing each one. This is particularly important because you may naturally gravitate toward only a couple of these elements. So, if you tend to be a musician who does well focusing on body and mind (e.g. practicing *études* and scales), you may need to set aside extra time to work on your ear and soul.

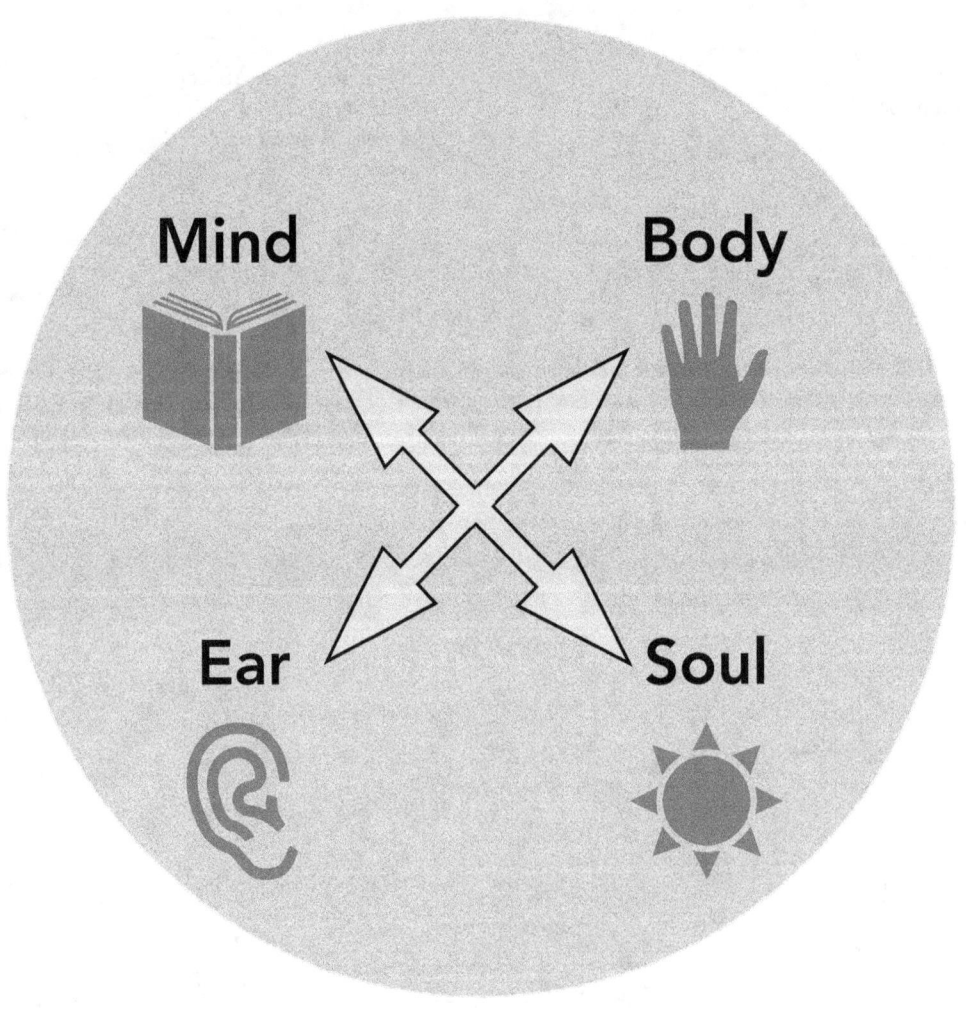

Masterclass

Four Parts of Practice:
— page 2 of 2 —
Mind, Body, Ear, Soul

Mind

You are most likely using your *mind* more than any other element but don't back off! There's more work to be done with the mind to refine what you know. A focus on scale steps, harmonic and rhythmic relationships, intervallic structures, and other elements will help strengthen your artistry. In addition, you need your mind to be active, helping to create imaginative musical shapes and phrases.

Body

Muscle memory matters and, just as an athlete requires training with multiple repetitions, so do you. You must begin to absorb your material at different tempos, keys, styles, and more, which takes significant physical work on your instrument. Your *body* must also become entirely connected from head to toe, with your breath, your limbs, and your core all acting in physical harmony.

Ear

The *ear* can be trained. Having a good ear is not common. We live in a visual society, where ears are seldom trained. The goal of ear development is not only to be able to identify notes, intervals, and harmonies. We need our ears to unlock our creativity, helping us make artistically valuable choices as improvisers. One of the simplest and most enjoyable ways to develop your ear is to engage in active listening. This is an easy task because it requires you only to take a break and listen to music intently, giving the music your full attention rather than relegating it to the background. This form of active listening can occur both on and off the instrument.

Soul

Your *soul* matters most. Without it, you will not resonate as a performer. In your soul lies your deepest and most profound passions and the reasons for your artistry. Nurture your soul by practicing earnestly and with purpose. Do not take your practice time for granted — ever! Also nurture your soul beyond your practice regimen through other means, perhaps including mindfulness, meditation, extracurricular activities, journaling, reading, studying other works of art, listening to music, and giving to others.

Historical Target Examples

Improvisers and composers intentionally target specific notes to give clarity to their melodic lines. The following historical examples of target notes include references to classic improvisations and compositions. The rhythmic momentum here tends to lead to targets on beats 1 and 3, the strong beats of each 4/4 measure. Use your ear for the pitch collection challenge below and reveal select melodies.

EX. 2.33
Charlie Parker alto sax solo
"Lay your habits down"

EX. 2.34
"Sweet Georgia Brown"
(Bernie/Pinkard/Casey)

No   gal made has   got   a   shade   on   Sweet   Geor - gia   Brown. __

Pitch collection challenge!
Complete select musical examples below by
adding the following pitches in order:

EX. 2.35 G A C C C C C E G C A G A C C C C C E G C
EX. 2.36 A G A G D C A G

EX. 2.35
"Lester leaps in"
(Lester Young)

EX. 2.36
"Freddie Freeloader"
(Davis/Kelly)

The following two examples feature some **targeted notes that are not C major chord tones.** The variety helps add interest to the melodic line.

EX. 2.37
"Always" (Irving Berlin)

I'll __ be lov-ing you,   al - ways, ___   With   a love that's true,   al - ways. ___

Every example below uses only diatonic notes in C major. Circle the pitches that are definitely target notes.
Do you see any other pitches that you think might be target notes but you are not sure? Why or why not?

Improvise   Chord Tone Target Notes

TOOLS TO USE:

1. Scale fragments
2. Rhythmic displacement and variety
3. Syncopation
4. Neighbor notes
5. Enclosures

Before you begin improvising, **decide** what you would like to accomplish. What is your focus? Are you going to limit yourself to one scale fragment at a time? One rhythm? Are you going to rest then play? Use primarily eighth notes? Quarter notes? Half notes? Loud vs. soft? If this seems like too many questions, then pick one for starters.

IMPROVISE
Play 1 measure then end on beat 1 target note

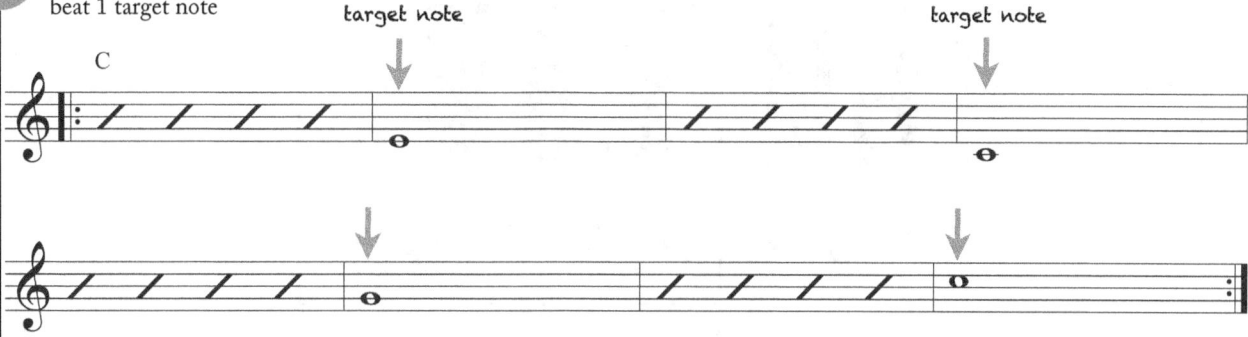

Rhythmic ear training: Tap your foot on a chosen beat (e.g. beat 3 only) while playing each line below.

Hold out whole notes while tapping your foot

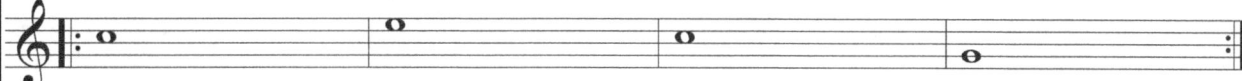

Play or sing while tapping your foot

IMPROVISE
Improvise over a 4-measure vamp using varying tempos in the key of C major.

A **vamp** is a small repeated section that typically includes only 1 to 4 chords, usually no longer than 4 to 8 measures, as a foundation for an improvising soloist. Always strive to become familiar with a vamp's exact length.

Give yourself some tools for the improvisation exercise above! Write down your major scale and make sure you know your pitch options. Then, consciously assign a 1-measure rhythm as theme throughout.

Major scale

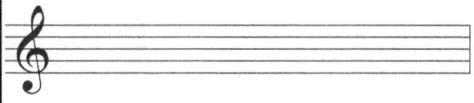

1-measure rhythm

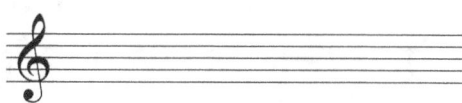

The Chromatic Scale

The *chromatic scale* is composed solely of notes separated by half-step intervals. While the C major scale uses only the white keys on the piano, the C chromatic scale uses all the piano keys, both black and white. The chromatic scale has a distinct engaging sound that is used extensively in most musical genres. Understanding the chromatic scale will help unlock other scales and multiple key centers, including all 12 major scales and keys.

EX. 2.38
Piano map, including all "white and black note" letter names

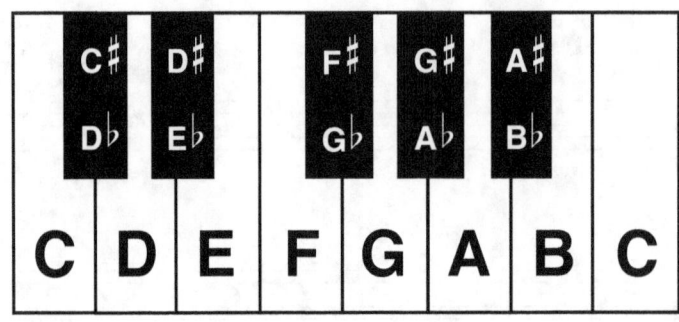

EX. 2.39
C chromatic scale

Common practice:
Use sharps (♯)
on the way UP.
Use flats (♭)
on the way DOWN.

Enharmonic spelling

Every flatted or sharped note has an enharmonic equivalent. For example, A♯ is also B♭, G♯ is also A♭. Here is the complete list of enharmonic spellings:

C♯ = D♭	E♯ = F	A♯ = B♭
D♯ = E♭	F♯ = G♭	C♭ = B
E = F♭	G♯ = A♭	B♯ = C

Using imagery to remember accidentals

To remember the functions of accidentals (sharp, flat, natural signs), use the following creative imagery.

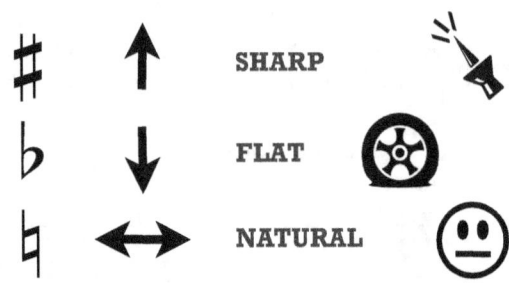

SHARP — moves the note UP a half step…so… when you sit on a **SHARP TACK**, you jump UP!

FLAT — moves the note DOWN a half step…so… when you get a **FLAT TIRE**, your car goes DOWN.

NATURAL — returns the note to NORMAL…so… when you want to be **NORMAL**, be NATURAL!

Chromatic Intervals

The chromatic scale uses all 12 notes on the piano keyboard and can start on any note. If it starts on C, it is called the C chromatic scale. If it starts on D, it is called the D chromatic scale, and so on. Every interval can be found embedded within the chromatic scale, including not just half steps (minor 2nd intervals) but also M2, m3, M3, P4, d5, P5, m6, M6, m7, M7, and P8 intervals.

EX. 2.40
Intervals within the
C chromatic scale

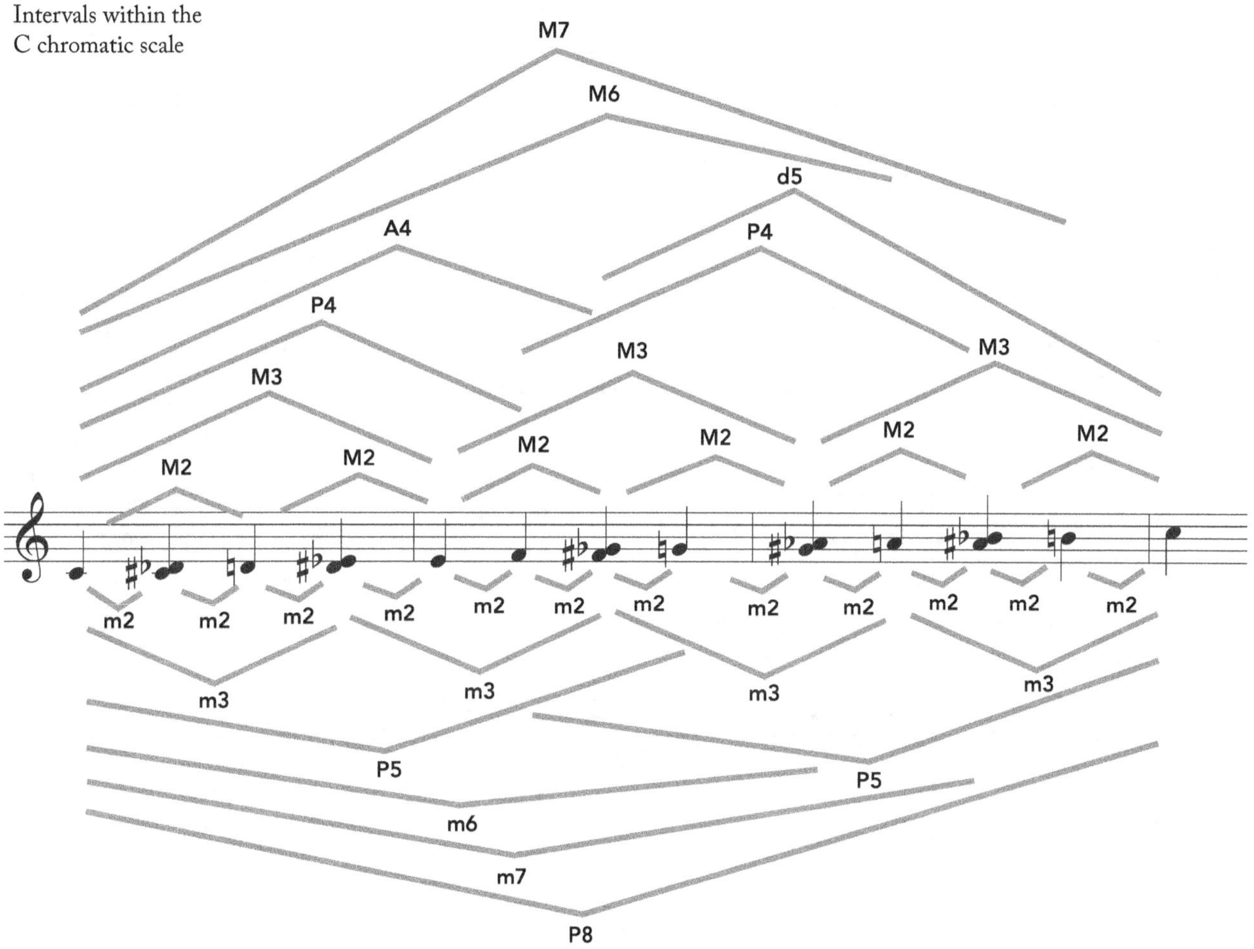

PU perfect unison	d5 diminished 5th
AU augmented unison	P5 perfect 5th
m2 minor 2nd	A5 augmented 5th
M2 major 2nd	m6 minor 6h
A2 augmented 2nd	M6 major 6th
m3 minor 3rd	A6 augmented 6th
M3 major 3rd	m7 minor 7th
P4 perfect 4th	M7 major 7th
A4 augmented 4th	P8 perfect octave

- Where are the whole steps (major 2nd, or M2, intervals)?
- Where are the half steps (minor 2nd, or m2, intervals)?
- Major thirds?
- Minor thirds?
- Fourths?
- Fifths?
- Sixths?
- Sevenths?
- BONUS: How do intervals change when using different enharmonic equivalents? For instance, the interval between C and E-flat is a minor 3rd. But what is the interval between C and D-sharp?

Chromatic Neighbors

In most of the following examples, *chromatic neighbors*, also called *chromatic approach notes*, are always a half step above or below any note and tend to be placed before a target note's strong beat arrival. Chromatic approach notes may also be placed on downbeats, adding dissonance and melodic color.

EX. 2.41
Lower chromatic neighbors,
C major scale

1   2   3   4   5   6   7

EX. 2.42
Lower chromatic neighbors,
C major chord triad

1   3   5

EX. 2.43
Upper chromatic neighbors,
C major scale

7   6   5   4   3   2   1

EX. 2.44
Upper chromatic neighbors,
C major chord triad

5   3   1

chromatic neighbors,
all on downbeats

EX. 2.45
Chromatic neighbor
pattern (C triad)

These patterns and historical examples all prominently feature **lower chromatic neighbors**, which can ornament both chord tones and non-chord tones.

chromatic lower
neighbor

EX. 2.46
"Für Elise"
(Ludwig van Beethoven)

Circle the chromatic neighbors in "Down by the Riverside." Also play it removing the chromatic accidentals, using only notes from the major scale. Do you prefer the chromatic or diatonic version?

EX. 2.47
"Down by the Riverside"
(Traditional)

I'm gon-na   lay down   my   sword and shield   Down   by   the   riv-er - side

1.

Down   by   the   riv-er - side   Down   by   the   riv-er - side   Gon-na

2.

riv-er - side___   And   stu-dy,_____   war   no   more._____

Transposition Down a Whole Step

There are 12 major keys, each corresponding to the 12 physical keys within the octave on a piano keyboard. By practicing in different keys, you will begin to understand how all 12 major scales are constructed. Pay close attention, in particular, to the scale fragments that are bracketed below. Whether transposed down a whole step from C major to B-flat major or to any another key, these fragments are always composed of two whole steps and one half step (WWh) and separated from each other by a whole step (W).

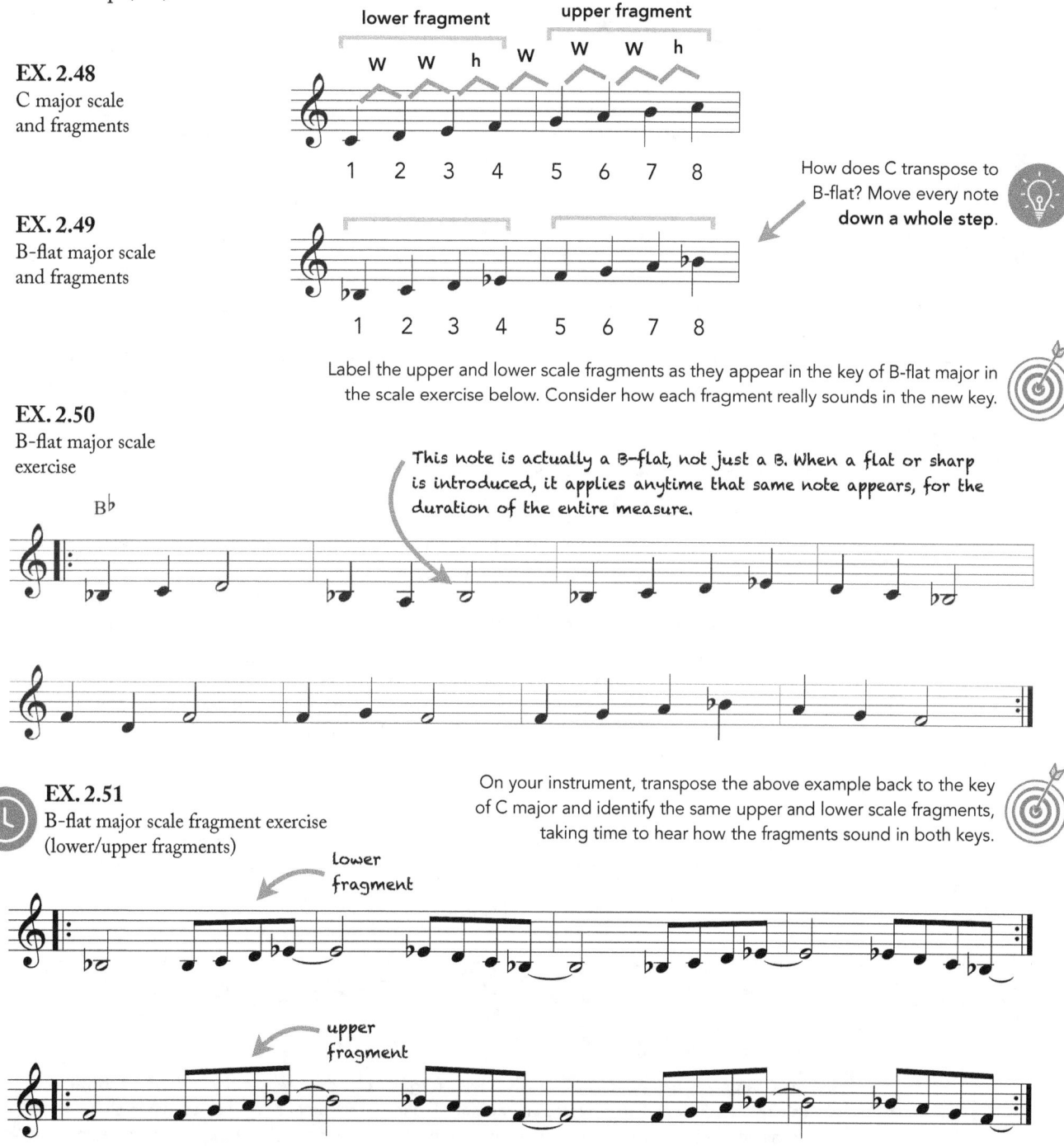

EX. 2.48
C major scale
and fragments

How does C transpose to B-flat? Move every note **down a whole step**.

EX. 2.49
B-flat major scale
and fragments

Label the upper and lower scale fragments as they appear in the key of B-flat major in the scale exercise below. Consider how each fragment really sounds in the new key.

EX. 2.50
B-flat major scale
exercise

This note is actually a B-flat, not just a B. When a flat or sharp is introduced, it applies anytime that same note appears, for the duration of the entire measure.

EX. 2.51
B-flat major scale fragment exercise
(lower/upper fragments)

On your instrument, transpose the above example back to the key of C major and identify the same upper and lower scale fragments, taking time to hear how the fragments sound in both keys.

lower fragment

upper fragment

Transposition Using Scale Fragments

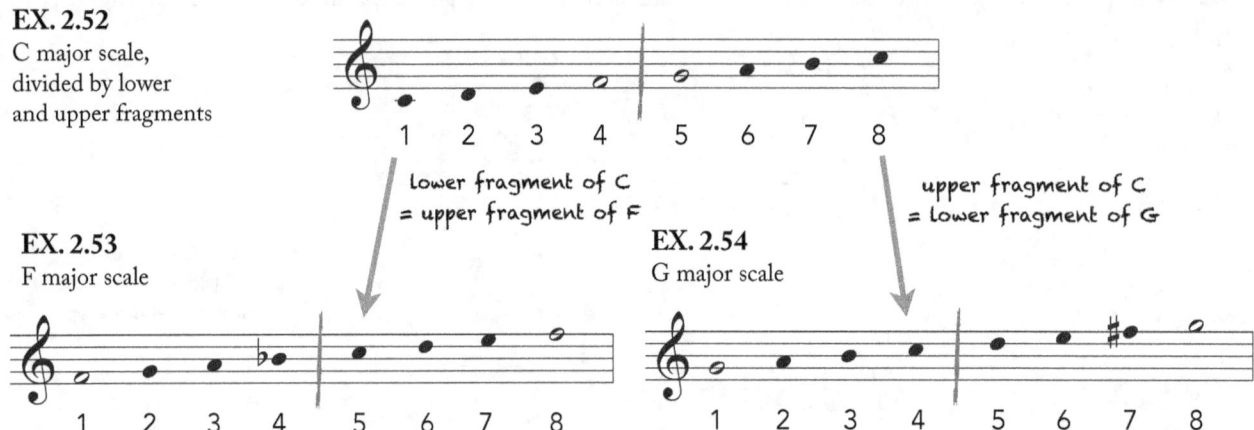

3 keys in 1 scale (C major)

Did you know that embedded within every major scale are the fragments from two other major scales? This means that three keys can be derived from one scale, always stemming from scale degrees 1-4-5. Embedded within C major are also four-note fragments (or *tetrachords*) used in F major and G major.

EX. 2.52
C major scale, divided by lower and upper fragments

1   2   3   4   5   6   7   8

lower fragment of C = upper fragment of F

upper fragment of C = lower fragment of G

EX. 2.53
F major scale

1   2   3   4   5   6   7   8

EX. 2.54
G major scale

1   2   3   4   5   6   7   8

3 keys in 1 scale (G major)

Below is another example of three major scales being derived from one major scale, this time using the G major scale. Use the following tools to master every major scale, easily coming up with "3 keys in 1" anywhere.

- Using scale numbers in C major, recall that the embedded "3 keys in 1," (C major, F major, G major) stemmed from scale degrees 1-4-5.

- In the G major scale below, "1-4-5" is "G-C-D." Thus, the three keys derived from G major are G major, C major, and D major.

  - The bottom fragment of G major (G-A-B-C) is also the top fragment of C major.
  - The top fragment of G major (D-E-F#-G) is also the bottom fragment of D major.

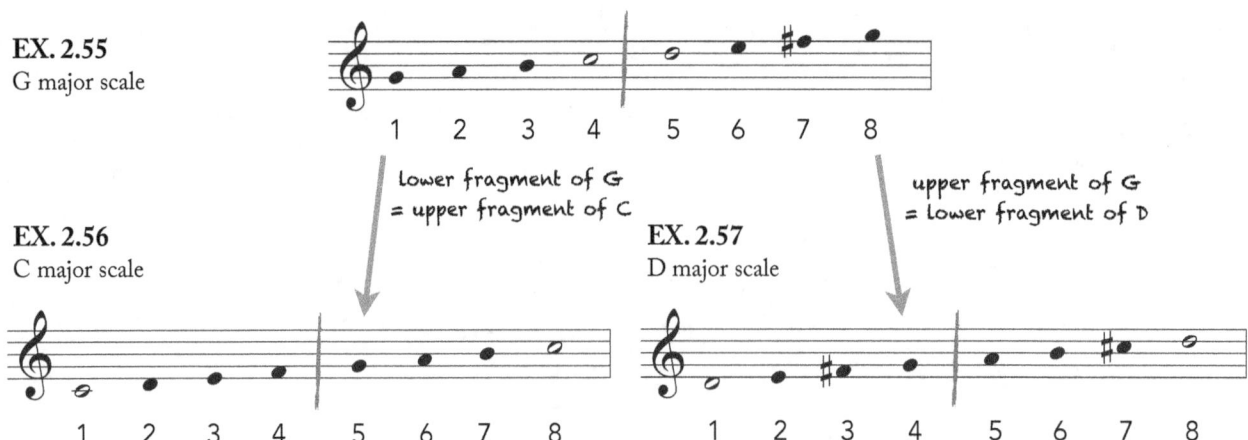

EX. 2.55
G major scale

1   2   3   4   5   6   7   8

lower fragment of G = upper fragment of C

upper fragment of G = lower fragment of D

EX. 2.56
C major scale

1   2   3   4   5   6   7   8

EX. 2.57
D major scale

1   2   3   4   5   6   7   8

When starting with the original scale, the **lower fragment** belongs to another scale that **subtracts one sharp** (or adds one flat). The **upper fragment** belongs to another scale that **adds one sharp** (or subtracts one flat). In the example above, the original scale is G major (1 sharp). The lower fragment becomes part of C major (no sharps/flats). The upper fragment becomes D major (2 sharps).

Transposition Workout

Learn all 12 keys quickly by becoming familiar with *12 major scale tetrachords*. While the ultimate goal is to gain fluency with all 12 major scales, instead of starting with the entire scale, start with only the first four notes. By starting with only one tetrachord in each key, the goal becomes far more attainable.

Do not skimp over these tetrachords.
Really make an effort to get to know each one, practicing them in isolation and in groups.

EX. 2.58
Major scale tetrachords, ascending by half step

W   W   h

W   W   h

"Open" indicates that the repeated section may be played an indefinite number of times.

Open

EX. 2.59
Fragment fluency loop
(try with all tetrachords)

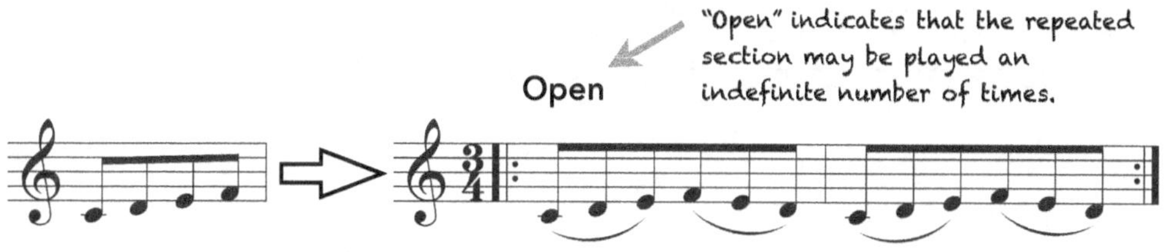

EX. 2.60
"Yankee Doodle"
(key of G major)

One of the best methods for becoming familiar with new major keys is to practice familiar songs based on the major scale. Practice "Yankee Doodle" below in the key of G major. Then, try transposing the melody to D major or any other key.

Also try practicing "Lean on me" in new keys, including G major and D major.

12 Major Scales

All *12 major scales* MUST be memorized and internalized. Each scale is strongly associated with a *key center* that often forms the tonal basis for a musical composition. Some immediate goals are below.

Goals

1. Get to know the *specific sound* of each major scale while learning every note and pitch name.

2. Hear and understand the *intervallic relationships* between each note in each scale, where each half step is, compared to where each whole step is, in addition to the wider embedded intervals.

3. Understand how each upper and lower fragment *relates* to another major scale (annotated below).

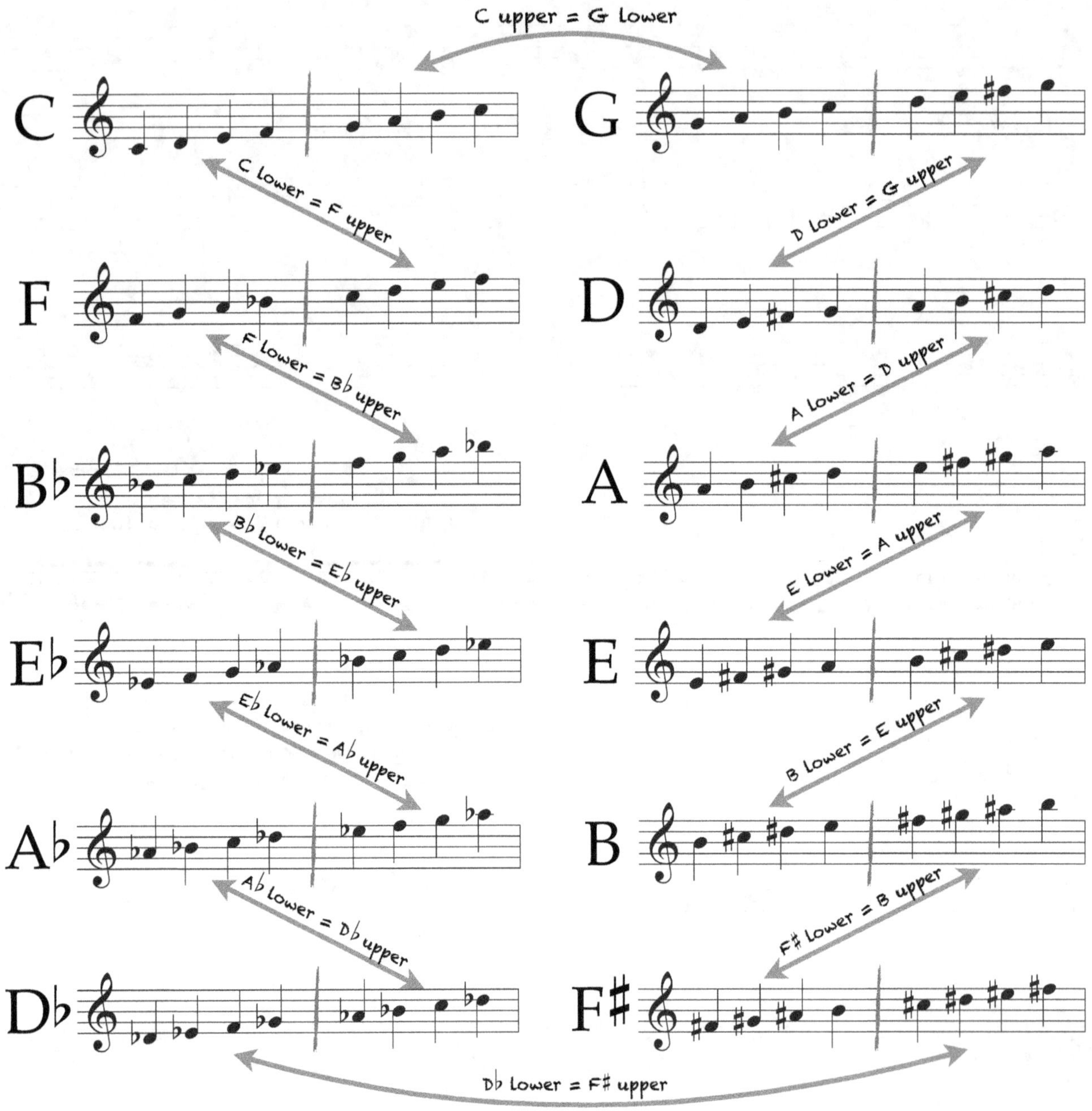

C upper = G lower

C

G

C Lower = F upper

D Lower = G upper

F

D

F Lower = Bb upper

A Lower = D upper

Bb

A

Bb Lower = Eb upper

E Lower = A upper

Eb

E

Eb Lower = Ab upper

B Lower = E upper

Ab

B

Ab Lower = Db upper

F# Lower = B upper

Db

F#

Db Lower = F# upper

Learn scales one fragment at a time. Take time to learn how upper and lower 4-note fragments of each major scale **relate to the other major scales**. Every lower fragment becomes an upper fragment in another scale and vice versa.

Circle of Fifths

The *circle of fifths* illustrates how each of the 12 keys are interrelated. The key of C major is presented in the top center, with no flats and no sharps.

Moving counterclockwise
(to the left)
adds a flat (♭)
to each new key.

Moving clockwise
(to the right)
adds a sharp (♯)
to each new key.

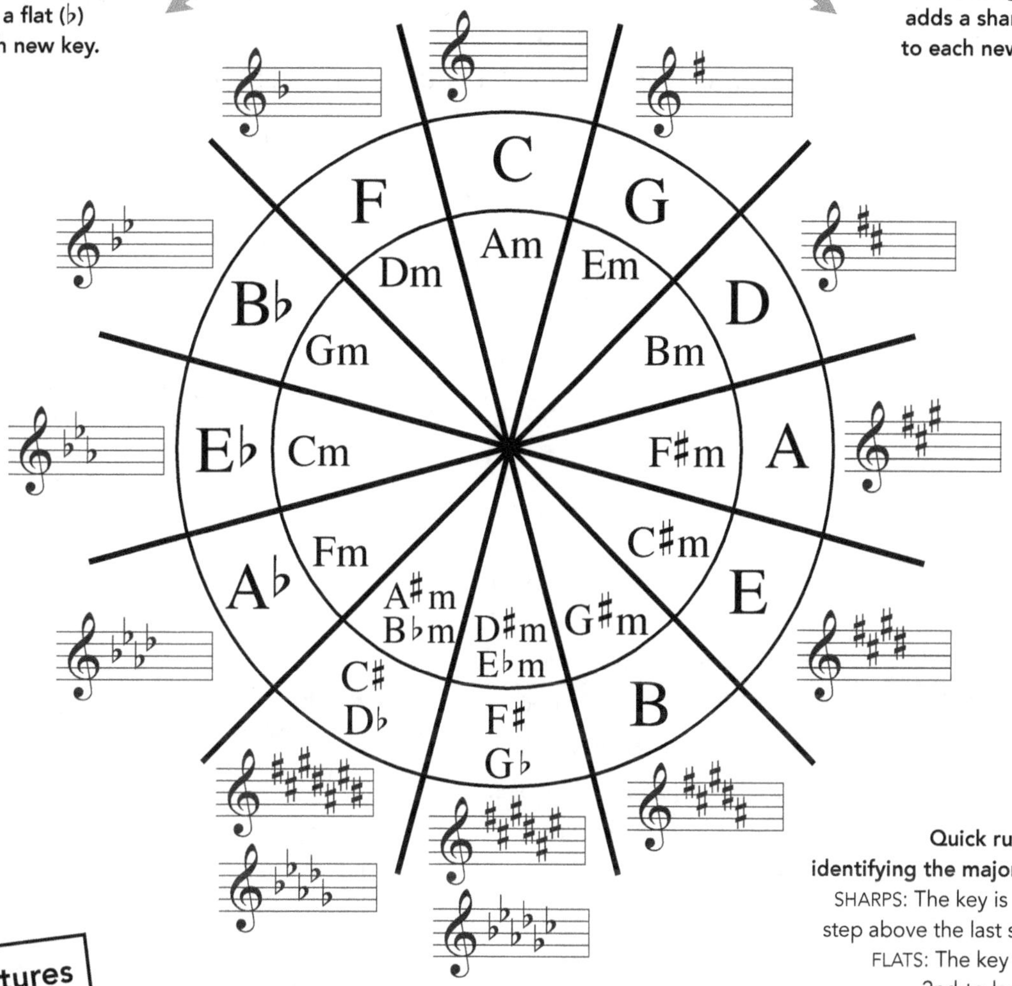

**Quick rule for
identifying the major key:**
SHARPS: The key is 1 half
step above the last sharp.
FLATS: The key is the
2nd-to-last flat.

Key signatures

Each key in the circle of fifths has its own *key signature* containing a specific number of flats or sharps. While these flats or sharps could be written next to each note, using a key signature at the beginning of the staff keeps the notation simpler while also helping identify the key at a glance.

Order of FLATS: BEADGCF
(**BEAD G**ot **C**aught **F**irst)

Order of SHARPS: FCGDAEB
(**F**at **C**ats **G**o **D**own **A**lleys
Eating **B**aloney)

Key signatures help clean up
written notation. Which of the two
versions to the left looks clearer
(and what key are they in)?

Investigate

Note Grouping
page 1 of 3

"In music it's not about the notes, it's what happens in between the notes."[3]
— Isaac Stern, violinist

To become the best performer you can be, you will want to delve into a concept called *note grouping*. How the musician interprets groups of notes will greatly alter the artistry of any performance. To begin to understand how note grouping works, first take a closer look at positive and negative space in music. *Positive space* can be considered whatever is the most visually and audibly obvious while *negative space* tends to be more subtle.

Positive or negative space
which do you see —
a vase of flowers
or a pair of faces?

Major scale in thirds

In the case of the major scale played in thirds, ascending thirds (each a *skip* up) constitute positive space. Between the ascending thirds is a connecting interval, a descending second (a *step* down). This step down constitutes negative space and is less obvious because it exists between the repetitions of the scale pattern, acting as a musical complement.

EX. 2.61
C major scale in thirds

Emphasizing positive space

The thirds here are marked with dashed slurs. Focusing on the thirds reinforces the downbeat start for each grouping of thirds.

EX. 2.62
C major scale in thirds,
emphasizing positive space

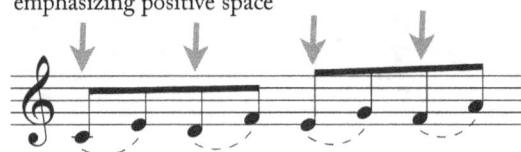

Emphasizing negative space

The steps between the thirds are emphasized, allowing the negative space to come to the foreground.

EX. 2.63
C major scale in thirds,
emphasizing negative space

EX. 2.64
C major scale in thirds,
emphasizing negative space

 Insert an eighth note rest on beat 1 to help hear the negative space within the note grouping.

Investigate

Note Grouping
page 2 of 3

Consider two ways to hear music — the way it LOOKS and the way it FEELS. Take a common phrase with four quarter notes per measure: the tendency is to simply play each note while counting "1, 2, 3, 4." Learning to play music this way highlights the visually obvious positive space of the musical canvas. Instead of playing the music the way it looks, the performer can change the note groupings of the melody to bring forth the negative space and forward momentum in a more nuanced and artistic interpretation.

How music looks (positive space)

Rhythm tends to START on beat 1 of a measure. The printed page also reinforces this image, with barlines boxing in the notes of each measure. Note groupings that highlight this visual positive space inevitably start by emphasizing beat 1 at the beginning of each measure — "1234, 1234." Although these note groupings allow us to hear how the rhythm aligns, they often make the music sound unnatural and halting, creating little to no melodic forward motion.

EX. 2.65
Scale grouping, emphasizing positive space

Beat 1 is emphasized and it serves as a point of departure. Little to no forward motion is created.

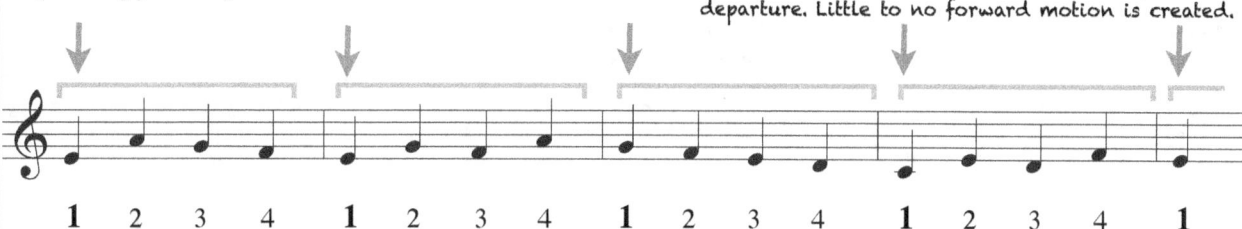

1 2 3 4   1 2 3 4   1 2 3 4   1 2 3 4   1

How music feels (negative space)

In contrast to rhythm, melody tends to LEAD to beat 1. The same beat 1 that was considered a rhythmic point of departure above now functions as a melodic point of arrival at the end of the phrase. To understand melody, we group our notes here differently, as "2341, 2341." These groupings are visually less obvious and may be considered negative space. They are essential to capturing the feel and momentum of any melody.

EX. 2.66
Scale grouping, emphasizing negative space

By changing the note groupings, forward motion is created, leading to beat 1 as a point of arrival.

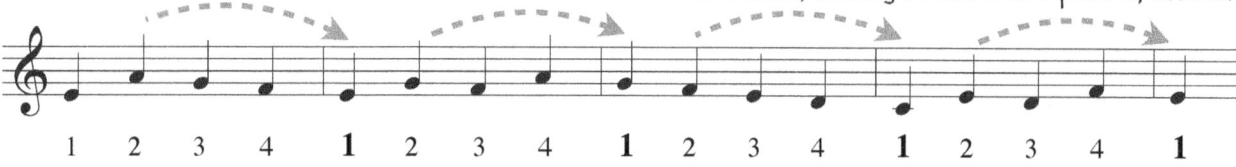

1 2 3 4   1 2 3 4   1 2 3 4   1 2 3 4   1

EX. 2.67
Scale grouping in 8ths, emphasizing negative space

We can also distinguish positive and negative space when examining **eighth note groupings**, with momentum leading to beats 1 and 3 — "+2+**3**, +4+**1**." (Spoken "and two and THREE and four and ONE.")

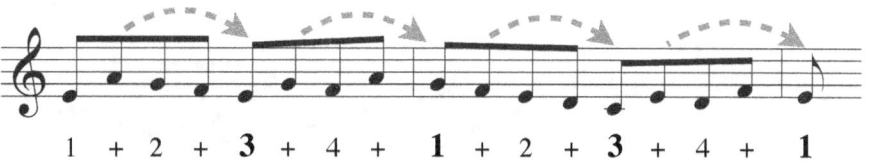

1 + 2 + **3** + 4 +   **1** + 2 + **3** + 4 +   **1**

Investigate

Note Grouping
page 3 of 3

Chord arpeggios

If the melody is played solely as written, the ear hears the notes as if they are trapped between barlines, where strong beat 1 is a point of departure — the start of a phrase. Placing *fermatas* on strong beats lengthens their rhythmic value and help the ear hear the forward momentum carrying each arpeggio to a clear target — as if each beat 1 (and 3) is a point of arrival.

EX. 2.68
Chord arpeggio exercise

Notes are grouped according to the visual beaming of eighth notes, boxed within barlines and lacking forward momentum.

EX. 2.69
Chord arpeggios with fermatas

EX. 2.70
How fermatas sound

Fermatas help the ear hear the strong beat arrival following each chord arpeggio.

Use these fermatas only as a **practice tool**. They should not be used in actual performance.

Bebop jazz line

Below is an excerpt from alto saxophonist Charlie Parker's iconic bebop jazz line on "Anthropology." Pay very close attention to the slur markings. Articulating the upbeats while slurring into the downbeats is quite common in jazz performance. Keep the downbeat eighth notes long and full-value, not inadvertently clipped and staccato.

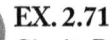

EX. 2.71
Charlie Parker alto sax solo "Anthropology"

EX. 2.72
"Anthropology" solo with fermatas

EX. 2.73
How fermatas sound

Solo 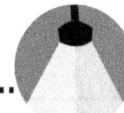 Spotlight

Lester Young, tenor sax "Lester leaps in"

Tenor saxophonist Lester Young's influence in music cannot be understated. His unparalleled ability to improvise a coherent and engaging melody is evident in the opening phrases of his iconic performance on "Lester leaps in." The opening bars of his improvisation include a focus on chord tone target notes while also using chromatic neighbors and light rhythmic syncopation.

EX. 2.74
Lester Young tenor sax solo
"Lester leaps in"
(key of C major)

Repeated C tonic on strong beats establishes a memorable opening motif.

This C is a surprise, not only because it is so high but also because it starts on beat 2, providing some syncopation.

The skip up to E provides enough variation to build interest.

Write in all the scale degrees below. Notice which scale degrees are used to form a major pentatonic

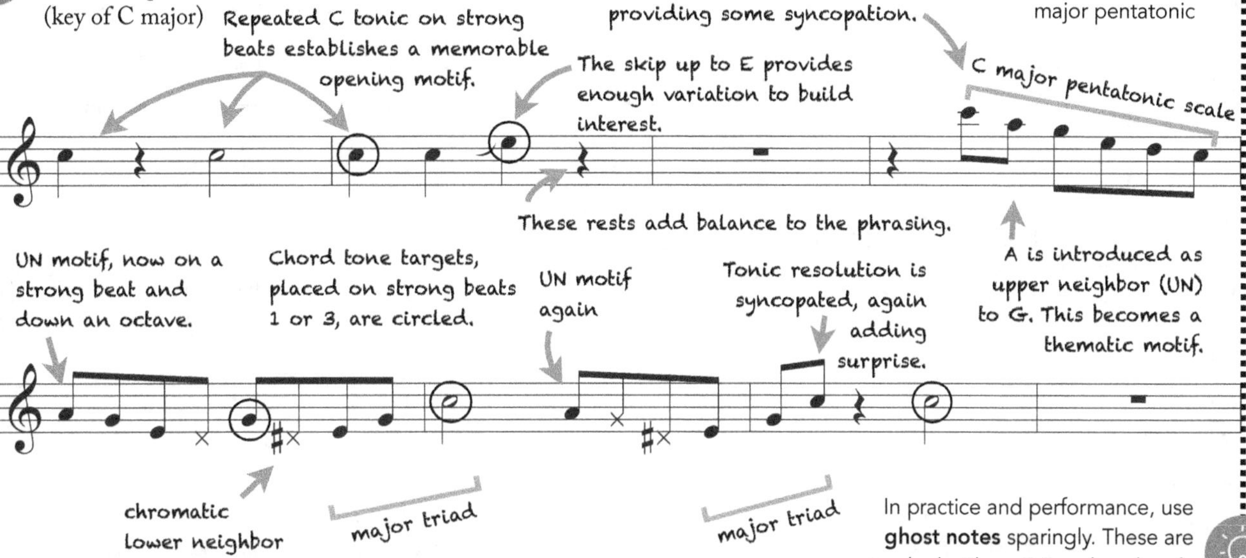

C major pentatonic scale

These rests add balance to the phrasing.

A is introduced as upper neighbor (UN) to G. This becomes a thematic motif.

UN motif, now on a strong beat and down an octave.

Chord tone targets, placed on strong beats 1 or 3, are circled.

UN motif again

Tonic resolution is syncopated, again adding surprise.

chromatic lower neighbor

major triad

major triad

In practice and performance, use **ghost notes** sparingly. These are marked with an "x" and are barely audible. Overusing ghost notes strips the improvised line of its rhythmic momentum.

The written notes above can only present a partial view. For full effect, listen to Lester Young's performance, noticing the subtle layers of style and nuance throughout.

Transposition workout

Lester Young's "Lester leaps in" solo should be played and memorized in all 12 major keys. Start by learning it in the original key of B-flat. Use the staff systems below to notate it completely. The key signature (2 flats) and first two measures are already written out for you.

EX. 2.75
Lester Young tenor sax solo
"Lester leaps in" (key of B-flat)

Learn Lester Young's opening phrases at various tempos. For an added challenge, listen to the whole solo and learn it in its entirety.

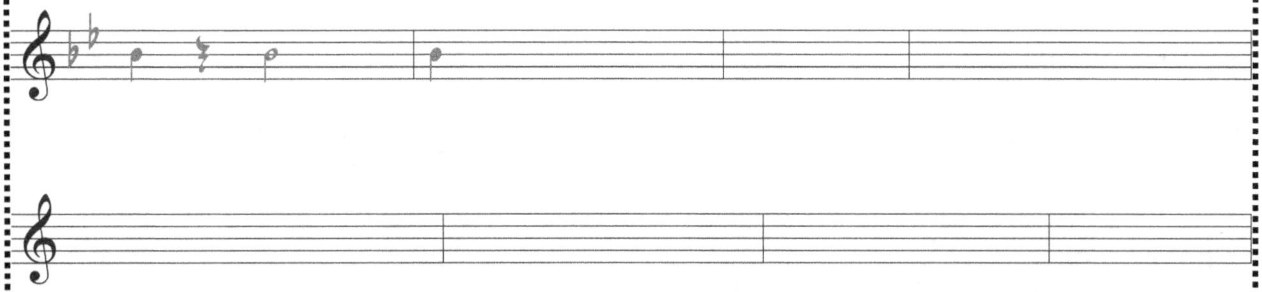

Internalize Lester Young's solo to the point where you can sing it, both with the recording and a cappella.

Improvise   Key Center Workout

To gain fluency in all 12 major keys, become familiar with key signatures while practicing with simple melodies, like familiar folk songs, nursery rhymes, and other compositions. Each key center takes significant care and study. The first example below presents the classic jazz composition "When the Saints Go Marching in" in the key of C major. First finish writing in all the scale degrees then transpose it to a new key of your choice. For the remaining examples, use the given scale degree numbers to help aid in transposing from one key to another, following the steps outlined below.

EX 2.76
"When the Saints Go Marching in"
(Traditional)

Make sure you understand a song's **scale degrees in the key of C major** before you transpose.

1 3 4 5

Oh when the saints go march-ing in,   Oh when the saints go march-ing in,

Step 1 Write in the key signature for the new key.

Step 2 Under the staff, write in the song's scale degrees.

Finish writing out the scale degrees for the C major version above, then finish transposing "When the Saints" to the key of D major below.

Step 3 Use the scale degrees (and your ear) to write out the melody in the new key.

1 3 4 5

Write in the pitches for the three songs below, each in a different major key. Scale degrees are given. Start by first writing in the key signature at the beginning of each staff system.

"Twinkle twinkle, little star" (Wolfgang Amadeus Mozart)

1 1 5 5   6 6 5   4 4 3 3   2 2 1

"Three Blind Mice" (Traditional)

3 2 1   3 2 1   5 4 4 3   5 4 4 3

"Skip to my Lou" (Traditional)

3 1   3 3 3 5   2   7   2 2 4

IMPROVISE
First improvise in the key of C major then transpose to other keys. Consider which scale degree numbers match your notes.

C

Zen Jazz Master says:

Train your ear!

What do you think it means to *have a good ear*? Some people think having a good ear means that you have perfect pitch and can identify, literally, every note anyone plays. Perfect pitch might be important to some but, if you were not born with perfect pitch, never fear. A person with a truly good ear possesses many more significant traits.

A musician with good ear traits...

listens well across the band

Notice what the drummer is playing, whether the bassist is playing a walking bass line or not, and whether the pianist is playing sparsely or not.

pays attention to dynamics

Can you tell whether you are playing too soft or loud? Can you place an effective crescendo? Can you interact playfully with the other musicians by changing your dynamics?

knows when to leave space

Keep track of your intensity level. If things have gotten too intense for too long, you might lose your purpose. It might be time to take it down a notch by leaving more space.

has strong rhythmic sense

Know how rhythms lie across a measure. Learn to hear and repeat rhythms quickly. Find a "pocket" and play in it, whether it is ahead of, on, or behind the beat.

has a good sense of relative pitch

A good sense of relative pitch is more important than perfect pitch but it can be difficult to develop. The ability to hear intervals, melodies and harmonic progressions takes practice and concentration. You need this as a musician to play so keep working on improving your relative pitch sense. Isolated ear training can be effective but developing a better understanding of music theory, improving your technique on your instrument, and gaining more playing experience can help your ear too.

Chapter 2 Achievements

Congratulations!

You are one step closer to jazz nirvana.

Here is a partial list of what you've achieved:

- Differentiating between chord tones and passing tones
- Understanding diatonic enclosures and approach notes
- Using scale fragments in transposition
- Internalizing note groupings to help with rhythmic momentum
- Improvising using chord tone target notes in various key centers

Are You Ready for the Next Chapter?

Answer these questions to determine whether you are prepared to continue to the next chapter:

- **Do you understand** the difference between diatonic and chromatic neighbor notes?

   If "Yes," move to the next chapter.
   If "No," review this chapter.

- **Do you recall** basic C major chord tones, and how to approach them as targets?

   If "Yes," move to the next chapter.
   If "No," review this chapter AND move to the next chapter. Your understanding and retention of target notes will come from review and from application and practice.

- **Can you conceive of** note groupings in both positive and negative space?

   If "Yes," move to the next chapter.
   If "No," don't fret. Move to the next chapter anyway. Understanding note groupings takes time.

- **Do you want** to learn about modes, including Dorian minor?

   If "Yes," move to the next chapter.
   If "No," you have two choices: (1) move to the next chapter anyway and see what piques your interest or (2) resign yourself to learning only nursery rhymes since the Dorian mode is heard constantly in jazz, rock, pop, and more!

3 Night and Day
Minor Key Melodic Targets and the Dorian Mode

Minor keys, often thought to possess a sad or forlorn sound quality, are perhaps even more common than major. In fact, while there is only one type of major scale, there are many minor scale types, including natural, melodic, harmonic, and Dorian. This chapter thoroughly explores the differences and similarities of minor scale types. A particularly deep dive into Dorian also serves as an entry point into a more general study of modes. Melodic architecture and direction, tension and release within scales, and the creative benefits of improvisation using minor scale fragments are also addressed in detail.

Contents

TOPICS
- Major vs. Minor
- The First Five Notes in Minor
- Four Minor Scales and Properties
- Minor Scale Tension and Release
- Melodic Architecture and Direction
- Minor Scale Patterns
- Minor Scale Pattern Workout
- Four Parts of Pattern Practice
- Turning the Pattern Around
- Modes of the Major Scale
- Dorian Minor Scale Tendencies
- Dorian Minor Scale Fragments
- Modal Jazz
- Solo Transcription 101
- Ways to Practice a Transcribed Solo

EAR TRAINING
- Audiate and sing (various)
- Differentiating Minor Scale Types
- Transpose "Scarborough Fair"
- Dorian Minor Exercises
- Transcribe Miles Davis' "So What" solo

MASTERCLASS
- Alternative Minor Scales
- The Diminished Scale (almost minor!)
- South Indian *Ragas*

INVESTIGATE
- Two Views: Natural Minor Scale
- Two Views: Dorian Minor Scale

SONG STUDY
- "Scarborough Fair" (Traditional)
- "So What" (Davis/Chambers)

HISTORICAL EXAMPLES
- "Mary had a 'sad' little lamb" (Traditional)
- "St. James Infirmary" (Irving Mills)
- Lester Young tenor sax solo "Blue Lester"

SOLO SPOTLIGHT
- Chet Baker trumpet solo "Summertime"
- Miles Davis trumpet solo "So What"
- Stanley Turrentine tenor sax solo "Impressions"

COMPOSE
- C Minor Scale Type
- Minor Scale Pattern
- Minor Melody
- Dorian Minor Melody

IMPROVISE
- Four Minor Scales
- Freely improvise using D Dorian minor + 2 new keys
- D Dorian Minor Scale Fragments and Targets
- "So What" (Davis/Chambers)

SMACKDOWN!
- Modes vs. Scales

LISTENING GUIDE
- Songs in Minor Keys

ZEN JAZZ MASTER SAYS
- Getting Lost

Major vs. Minor

Major and minor chord triads are nearly identical except for the 3rd scale degree which, in minor, is lowered a half step. The *major* triad, formed with scale degrees 1-3-5, becomes *minor* with scale degrees 1-♭3-5. When comparing chord triads below, hear how the major 3rd renders the sound of the major chord *bright as day* while the minor 3rd renders the sound of the minor chord *dark as night*.

MAJOR
BRIGHT AS DAY

MINOR
DARK AS NIGHT

EX. 3.1
C major
chord triad

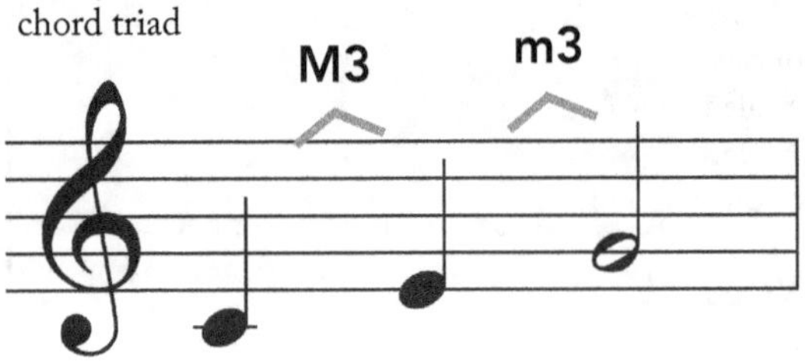

M3   m3

1   3   5

"Bright   as   day___"

EX. 3.2
C minor
chord triad

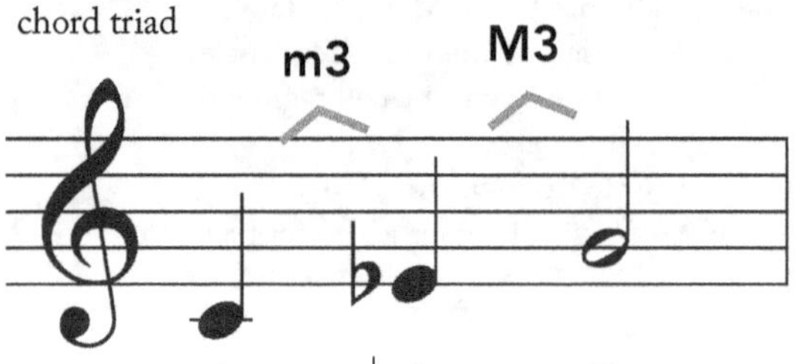

m3   M3

1   ♭3   5

"Dark   as   night___"

| **M3** | major 3rd interval |
| **m3** | minor 3rd interval |

EX. 3.3
Alternating C major and
C minor chord triads

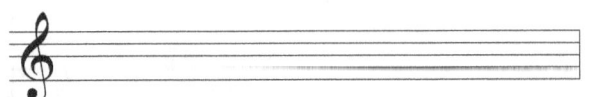

major   minor   major   minor

When forming chord triads in any key, start with the first five notes of a major scale. Then skip from scale degrees 1 to 3 and 5, flatting the 3rd to change it to minor. Try this by ear or use the staff provided to write it out.

The First Five Notes in Minor

The first five notes of the C minor scale are almost the same as the C major scale. The minor difference comes from lowering the 3rd scale degree a half step. These five notes are a constant across most different types of minor scales. Delve more deeply into this core collection of scale degrees 1 through 5.

CT | **PT** | **CT** | **PT** | **CT**

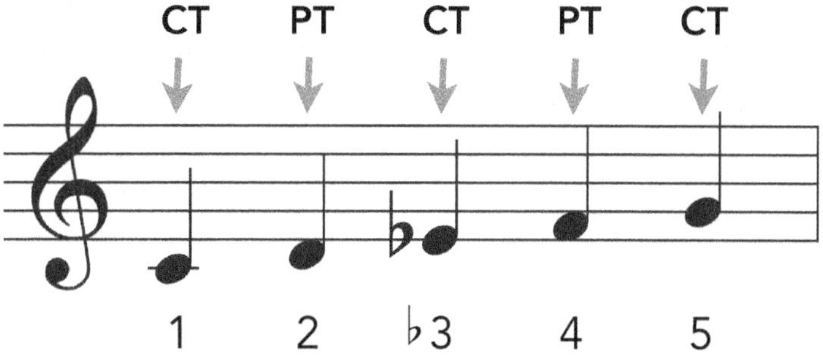

CT Chord Tone
PT Passing Tone

EX. 3.4
The first five notes of the C minor scale

1   2   ♭3   4   5

Write in the remaining scale degrees in the example below then transpose the examples on this page to another minor key of your choice.

EX. 3.5
C minor scale fragments and chord triad arpeggios

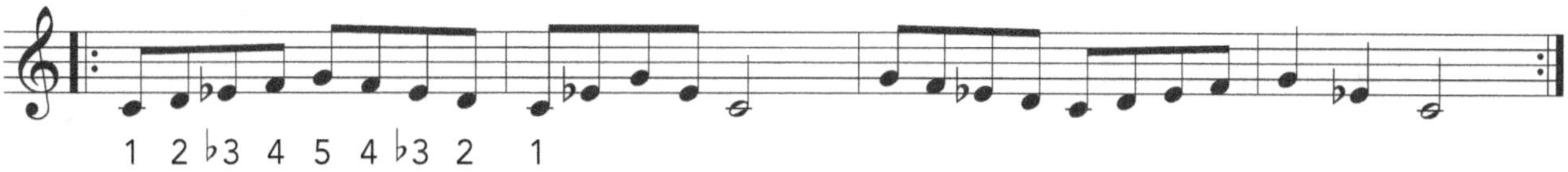

1 2 ♭3 4 5 4 ♭3 2 1

EX. 3.6
"Mary had a 'sad' little lamb"
(Traditional) (C minor version)

EX. 3.7
"St. James Infirmary"
(Irving Mills)

"St. James Infirmary" sneaks in more than the first five notes of the C minor scale. Can you spot the **rogue pitch**?

pickup notes

Adding lyrics

While lyrics give a song a deeper meaning, they also help define the rhythm since spoken language involves a clear meter and implicit accents. Speak then sing the following lyrics. Finally, insert these lyrics, with a correspondence of one syllable per note, into the staff above.

I went down to Saint James infirm'ry,
and I saw my baby there.

She was stretched on a long white table,
so sweet, so cold, so fair.

"St. James Infirmary" starts with two **pickup notes** in a pickup measure preceding measure 1. This allows for the opening phrase to target beat 1, bar 1.

Four Minor Scales and Properties

While there is only one major scale type, there are many minor scale types. The four most common minor scales — *natural*, *harmonic*, *melodic*, and *Dorian* — all share a lower scale fragment, where the first five notes remain static across all four scale types. Each upper scale fragment ends with scale degree 8, which also remains static, although scale degrees 6 and 7 change with each scale type. In the key of C minor, the lower five notes are always C-D-E♭-F-G. The upper fragment for natural minor is A♭-B♭-C but, for harmonic minor, the upper fragment is A♭-B-C.

EX. 3.8
C minor scale types, including the static lower fragment, followed by variable upper fragments.

Harmonic minor is particularly distinctive as the only minor scale that includes a **minor 3rd interval** (from ♭6 to 7).

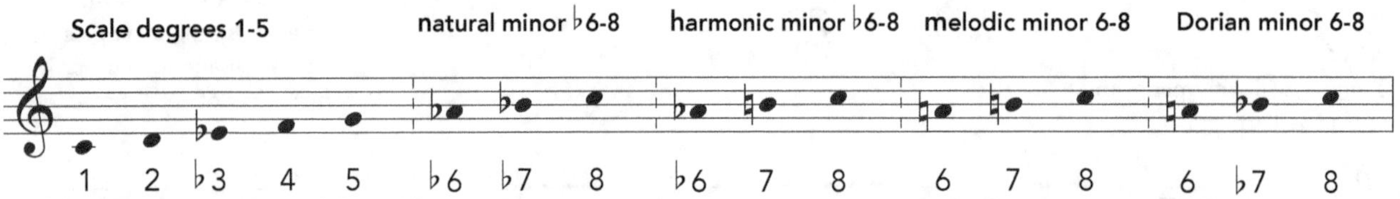
Scale degrees 1-5
natural minor ♭6-8
harmonic minor ♭6-8
melodic minor 6-8
Dorian minor 6-8
1 2 ♭3 4 5
♭6 ♭7 8
♭6 7 8
6 7 8
6 ♭7 8

EX. 3.9
C natural minor scale

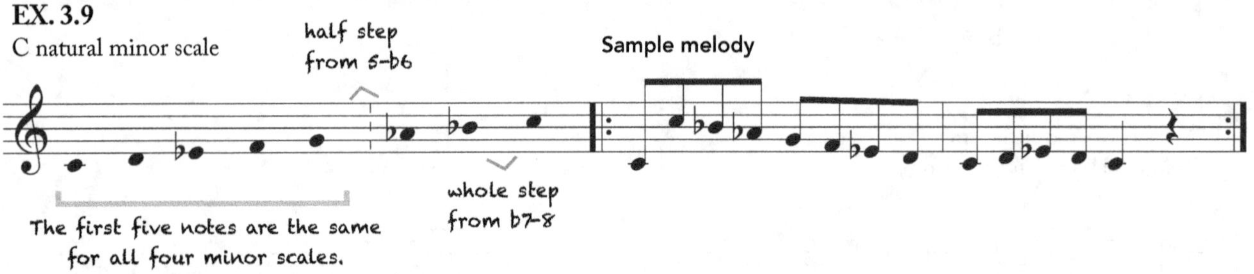
half step from 5-b6
Sample melody
whole step from b7-8
The first five notes are the same for all four minor scales.

EX. 3.10
C harmonic minor scale

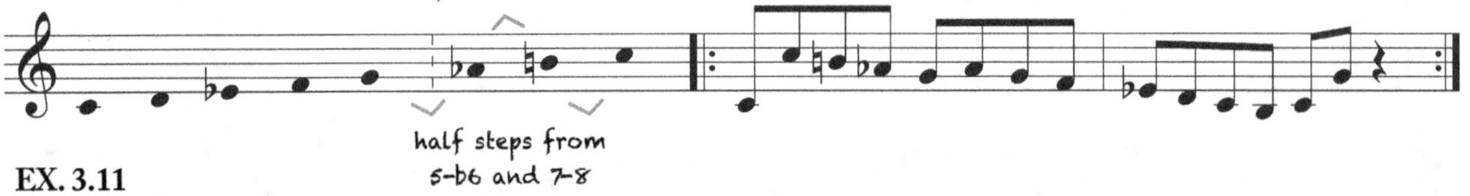
minor third from b6-7
Sample melody
half steps from 5-b6 and 7-8

EX. 3.11
C melodic minor scale
aka *jazz melodic minor*
or *ascending melodic minor*

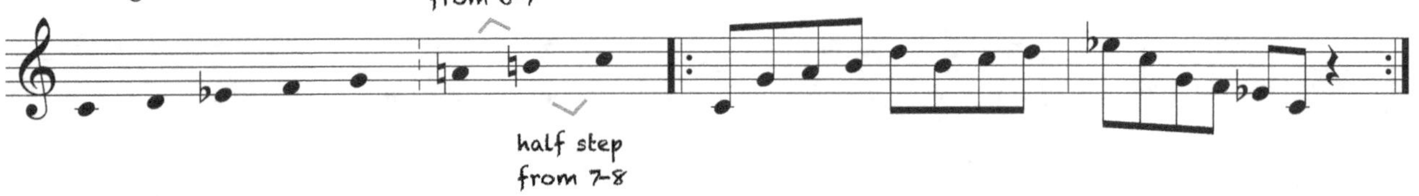
whole step from 6-7
Sample melody
half step from 7-8

EX. 3.12
C Dorian minor scale

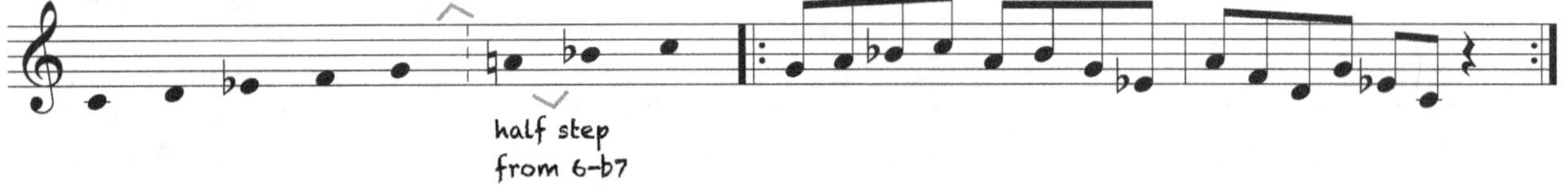
whole step from 5-6
Sample melody
half step from 6-b7

Investigate | Two Views: Natural Minor Scale

The *natural minor scale* is termed "natural" because it is derived directly from the major scale using two types of construction. The first, called *parallel minor*, keeps the same root as the major scale but lowers the 3rd, 6th, and 7th scale degrees. The second, called *relative minor*, uses the notes of the major scale but starts on the 6th scale degree of major.

View #1 | Parallel minor

To construct a parallel minor scale, start with the major scale, keeping the same root (scale degree 1), *lowering the 3rd, 6th, and 7th* scale degrees by a half step.

EX. 3.13
C major scale

EX. 3.14
C natural minor scale

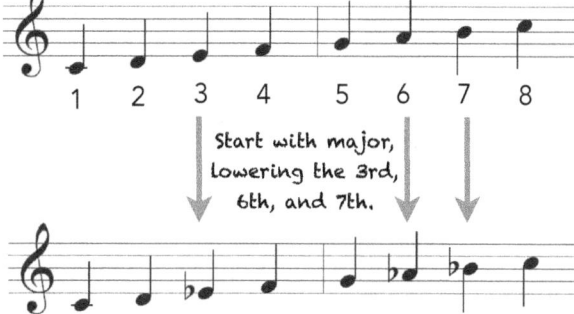

Start with major, lowering the 3rd, 6th, and 7th.

Envisioning parallel

Imagine parallel trees in nature, each sprouting from the same level ground. The ground is the key or tonic pitch of the scale (C). The tree is the type of scale (major or minor) stemming from their shared root.

View #2 | Relative minor

To construct a relative minor scale, use the same diatonic notes as the major scale (keeping the same key signature) but *start on the 6th scale degree*, which is three half steps lower than the root of the relative major.

EX. 3.15
C major scale

EX. 3.16
A natural minor scale

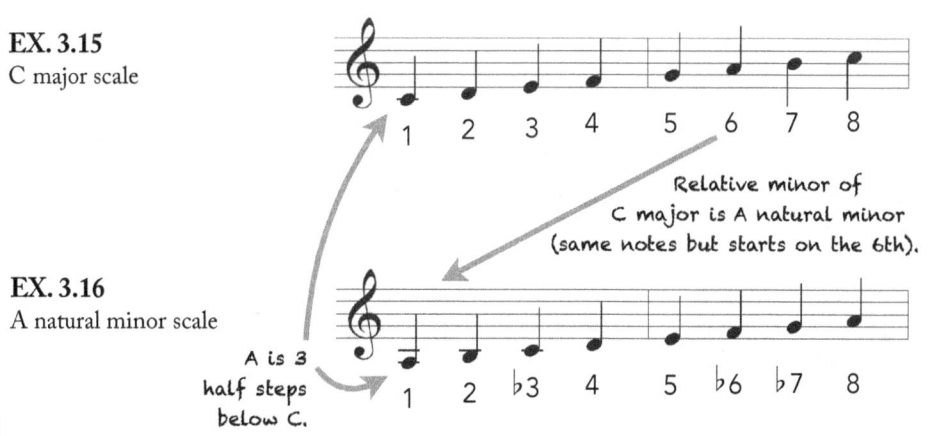

Relative minor of C major is A natural minor (same notes but starts on the 6th).

A is 3 half steps below C.

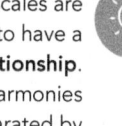

Relative major and natural minor scales are considered to have a **mediant relationship**. Mediants are harmonies or scales separated by major or minor third intervals.

di·a·ton·ic
/ˌdīəˈtänik/

adjective: **diatonic**

(of a scale, interval, etc.) involving only notes proper to the prevailing key without chromatic alteration.

Now try this process starting from the bottom! Starting with C natural minor in view #1 above, move to its relative major (E-flat major). Then start with A natural minor in view #2 above and move to its parallel major (A major).

**E-flat major scale
(relative major of C minor)**

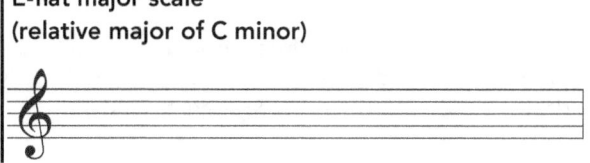

**A major scale
(parallel major of A minor)**

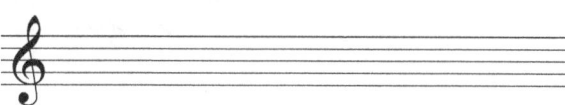

Minor Scale Tension and Release

Natural minor
Cm

5 ♭6 ♭7 8

Within every scale, some notes provide points of *tension* while others provide moments of *release*. Finding the right balance between the two is essential. Just as every inhale we take is balanced with an exhale, tension may be balanced with resolution in an effective melody. *Natural minor* scale degrees 1, ♭3, and 5 form a minor chord triad, the scale's tonic harmony, and provide moments of release or resolution. The remaining scale degrees — 2, 4, ♭6, and ♭7 — are passing tones. They are also considered non-chord tones, creating tension while tending to resolve to the nearest tonic chord tone.

EX. 3.17
C natural minor scale
(chord tones are circled)

EX. 3.18
C minor chord triad
(tonic harmony)

1   2   ♭3   4   5   ♭6   ♭7   8   5 / ♭3 / 1

EX. 3.19
Non-chord tones (tension) resolving to
circled chord tones (release)

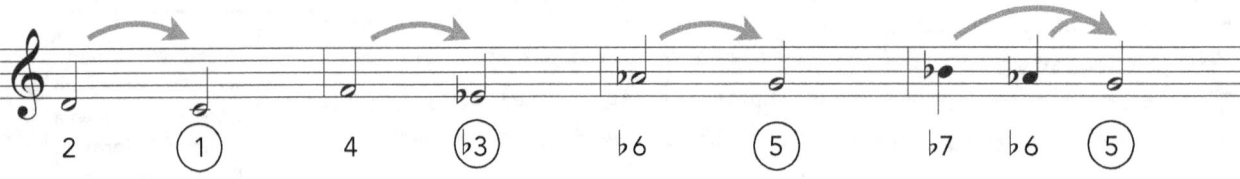

2   ①   4   ♭3   ♭6   ⑤   ♭7   ♭6   ⑤

EX. 3.20
Additive exercise
(C natural minor scale)

 Sing the additive exercise very slowly. Listen for each downward resolution to chord tones.

SPEED ROUND! How fast can you play the additive exercise above? Also play it transposed to a few new keys of your choice.

Consider every note in the natural minor scale as being a **character with a different personality**. As an example, perhaps scale degree 1 is really strong and stable and scale degree 2 is longing, more than anything, to be with 1.

Melodic Architecture and Direction

A melody can gain musical purpose and direction by centering on tonic chord tones and gradually moving from one chord tone target to another. *Melodic architecture* manifests itself in the melodic line's form and direction. In the examples below, the melodic direction involves a descent (or ascent) over time, with clear target notes emphasizing the downward (or upward) shape.

EX. 3.21
Melodic descent: Non-chord tone tension and chord-tone release (C natural minor)

Each moment of tension and release has a **distinct feel**. In the example below, get to know how flat-6 feels as it *rubs* against the 5 and feel the monumental release when a prolonged 2 finally resolves to 1.

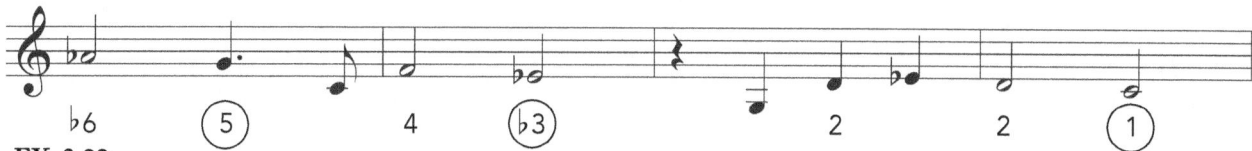

EX. 3.22
Big picture:
Moving from 1 to 5 to 1

EX. 3.23
Save the punchline:
Moving from 5 to 1

Save the punchline! Inexperienced improvisers often begin their solos on scale degree 1, providing too much resolution, too soon, but melodies very often initially withhold 1 as a central note, saving it for later in the melody.

Dissonance needs resolution

Dissonance is CLASH! Needs resolution!

Dissonance in its many forms is not necessarily a bad thing! Every note that rubs against a given harmony is aching to be resolved at some point.

Any bit of dissonance can be prolonged until the improviser decides to resolve the sound by moving to a note that matches the given harmony. Some of the most appealing improvisations actually prolong the time it takes to come to a resolution.

Minor Scale Patterns
page 1 of 2

Natural minor

Cm

5 ♭6 ♭7 8

Natural minor scale patterns help unlock various melodic targets within a key since pattern fragments tend to arrive on both chord tones and non-chord tones. Working with patterns also helps the ear grow accustomed to note groupings. In the examples below, as each 1-measure melodic fragment ascends or descends, consider which notes are considered passing tones and pickup notes.

EX. 3.24
Diatonic thirds, filled (up)

EX. 3.25
Diatonic triads (up)

Notice the **pattern shapes**, moving stepwise throughout all these measures.

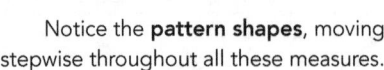

Harmonic minor

Cm

5 ♭6 7 8

The *harmonic minor scale* includes a minor 3rd interval between the scale degrees flat-6 and 7. Its other distinct interval is the minor second, a half step, which shows up three times, between scale degrees ♭3-4, 5-♭6, and 7-8. Both these distinguishing intervals continually shift to different places in the measure when running harmonic minor scale patterns. The following examples create melodic interest by combining stepwise and skipping motion throughout.

EX. 3.26
Diatonic triads (up), scale steps (down)

Write in the scale degrees for each example on this page.

EX. 3.27
Diatonic thirds 1-♭3-4-2 (up-down)

Melodic minor
Cm

Minor Scale Patterns
— page 2 of 2 —

The traditional *melodic minor scale* raises scale degrees 6 and 7 when ascending but lowers both notes when descending. In contrast, the *jazz melodic minor scale* raises scale degrees 6 and 7 when both ascending and descending. Melodic minor scale patterns seem like they would sound nearly identical to major scale patterns, given that the only difference is the flatted 3rd. The reality is that melodic minor is still entirely distinct, in part because of this minor 3rd but also because of the intervals surrounding the third, including the minor 2nd between scale degrees 2-♭3 and the major 2nd between ♭3-4.

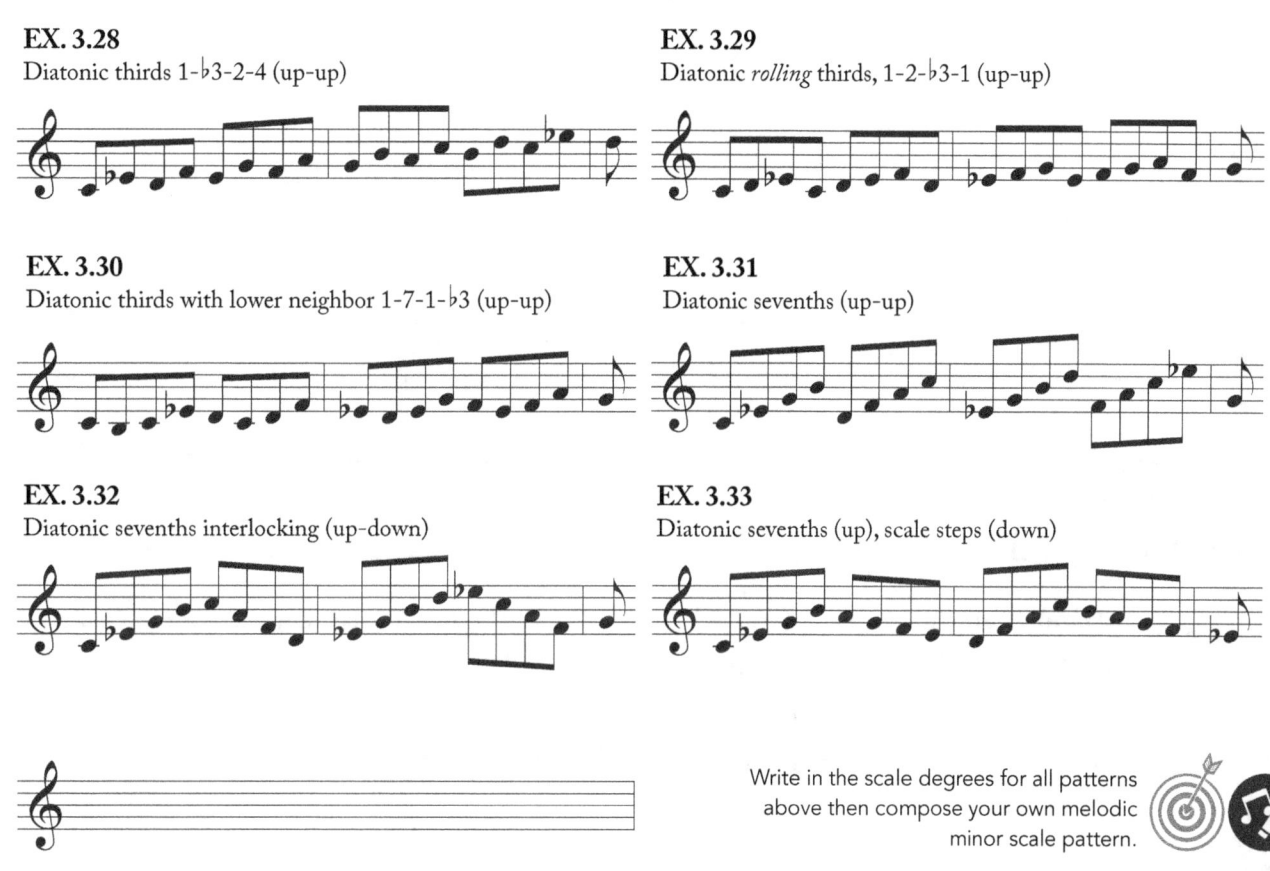

EX. 3.28
Diatonic thirds 1-♭3-2-4 (up-up)

EX. 3.29
Diatonic *rolling* thirds, 1-2-♭3-1 (up-up)

EX. 3.30
Diatonic thirds with lower neighbor 1-7-1-♭3 (up-up)

EX. 3.31
Diatonic sevenths (up-up)

EX. 3.32
Diatonic sevenths interlocking (up-down)

EX. 3.33
Diatonic sevenths (up), scale steps (down)

Write in the scale degrees for all patterns above then compose your own melodic minor scale pattern.

Turning the pattern around

The above patterns are all ascending. To turn the patterns around and make them descend, study their diatonic intervals. This will help when reversing any pattern.

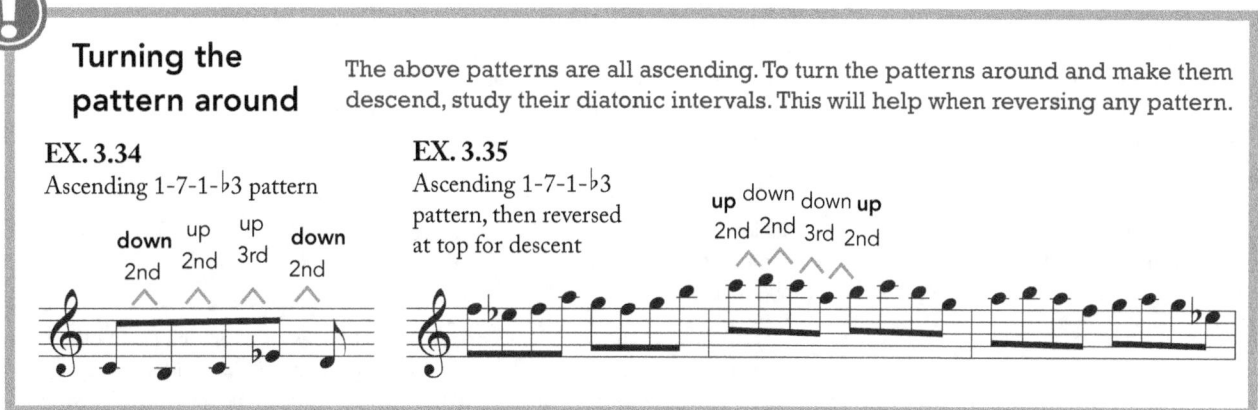

EX. 3.34
Ascending 1-7-1-♭3 pattern

EX. 3.35
Ascending 1-7-1-♭3 pattern, then reversed at top for descent

Minor Scale Pattern Workout

After choosing just one minor scale and key, write out any two patterns from the previous two pages.

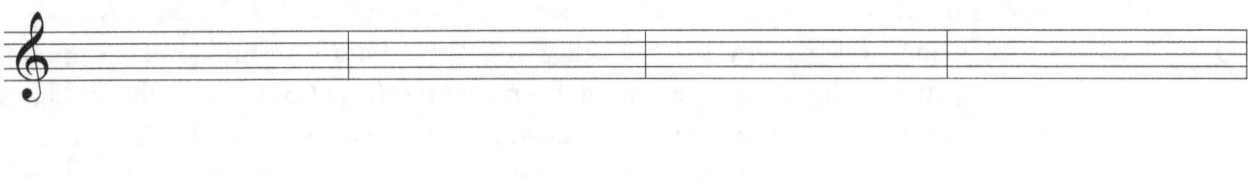

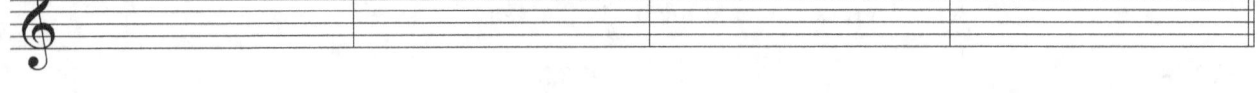

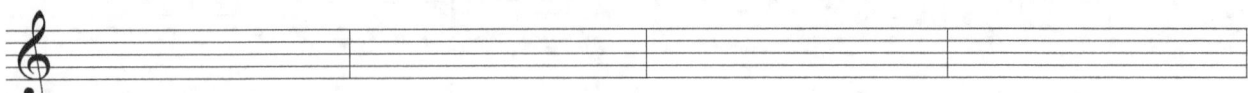

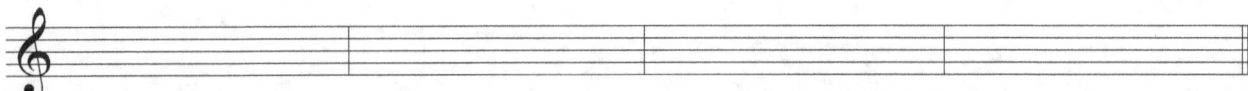

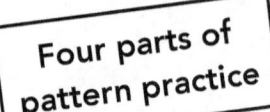

Four parts of pattern practice

Change your tempo! Tempo is a powerful variable. Practice your scale patterns at varying speeds, ranging from very slow to quick and brisk. Use a metronome to help you choose specific tempos.

Mind Study pattern pitch names, specific intervals, and pattern shapes.

Ear Differentiate between the sound of the intervals between each note.

Body Aim for accuracy with every rhythm and pitch, improving any weak spots.

Soul After deciding how you want to sound, deliver!

Minor key songs:

- "There's a Place in France"
- "When Johnny Comes Marching Home Again"
- "Stairway to Heaven"
- "Hotel California"
- "Black Magic Woman"
- "House of the Rising Sun"
- "Come Together"
- "Paint it black"
- "All Along the Watchtower"

- *Für Elise* (Beethoven)
- *Moonlight Sonata* (Beethoven)
- *Concierto de Aranjuez* (Rodrigo)
- "Great Gates of Kiev" (*Pictures at an Exhibition*) (Mussorgsky)
- *Erlkônig* (Schubert)
- *Mass in B minor* (Mozart)
- Theme from *Symphony No. 2* (Mahler)
- Theme from *Swan Lake* (Tchaikovksy)

- "We Three Kings"
- "Carol of the Bells"
- "Summertime"
- "Afro Blue"
- "Blue Bossa"
- "Black Orpheus"
- "You don't know what love is"
- "'Round Midnight"
- "Equinox"
- "St. James Infirmary"

Choose at least three works from the list above, learning each in at least two different keys. Identify the minor scale types primarily used in each.

Masterclass   Alternative Minor Scales

There is only one major scale but, even beyond the four main minor scales (natural, harmonic, melodic, and Dorian), there are many more minor scales to consider, including *double harmonic*, *Phrygian*, and *altered Dorian*. Each offers a distinct sound, united by two constants — the flatted-3rd and perfect 5th scale degrees.

EX. 3.36
C double harmonic minor
(aka *Hungarian minor*)

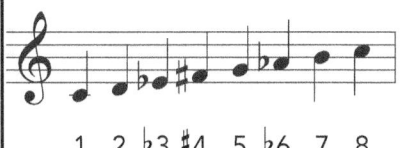

1 2 ♭3 ♯4 5 ♭6 7 8

EX. 3.37
C Phrygian minor
(aka *Spanish minor*)

1 ♭2 ♭3 4 5 ♭6 ♭7 8

EX. 3.38
C altered Dorian minor
(aka *Ukrainian minor*)

1 2 ♭3 ♯4 5 6 ♭7 8

 Compose your own C minor scale type, filling in the missing scale degrees while keeping 1, ♭3, 5, 8 intact.

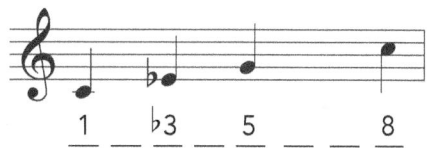

1 __ ♭3 __ 5 __ __ 8

The diminished scale (almost minor!)

The *diminished scale* is an *octatonic* scale (8 notes) that also includes a flatted 3rd. Yet instead of including a perfect 5th scale degree, the two types of diminished scales lower the 5th, both by alternating half and whole steps.

EX. 3.39
C half-whole
diminished scale

EX. 3.40
C whole-half
diminished scale

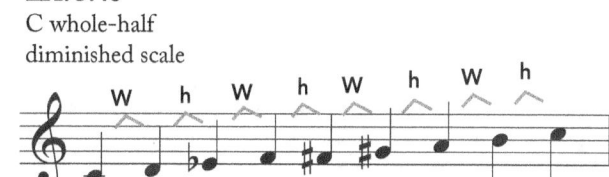

South Indian *ragas*   Cultures across every continent have long used similar musical language involving melody, harmony, and rhythm. Carnatic music of South India is based in part on *ragas* (or *raags*). At first glance, they might seem like scales but *ragas* bear some distinct attributes. Specific *ragas* are used at different times of the day and to evoke specific emotions. They often involve pitch collections that change when ascending and descending. Many *ragas* also follow schemes that elaborate beyond intervalic structure.

Raag Bageshri is an evening *raga* that includes 5 notes when ascending and 7 notes descending. During the descent, the scheme incorporates a brief re-ascent before descending entirely.

EX. 3.41
Raag Bageshri
(ascending)

Sa Ga Ma Dha Ni Sa

EX. 3.42
Raag Bageshri
(descending)

Sa Ni Dha (Ni) Pa Ma Ga Ri Sa

Instead of Western notation, Indian music uses **solfège-like syllables** and other elements.

Solo Spotlight

Chet Baker, trumpet "Summertime"

Trumpeter Chet Baker plays a masterful solo on the classic minor key composition, "Summertime." He uses elements from various minor scales, including natural, melodic, and Dorian minor. Each phrase, interspersed with plenty of rests, is also defined by clear rhythmic purpose and melodic direction.

EX. 3.43
Chet Baker trumpet solo "Summertime" (key of C minor)

This F♯, the sharp-4 of C minor, is also found in another minor scale, the **blues scale**.

C minor key signature has the same flats as E♭ major.

This E is an outlier — a chromatic passing tone between F and E♭.

Transposition workout

Prepare to transpose Chet Baker's "Summertime" solo primarily by ear to the key of your choice by writing out the new key's major scale below. Then convert the scale to minor, writing in the pitches and scale degrees for all the minor scale variations below.

EX. 3.44
Major scale

Lower the 3rd, 6th, and 7th to change the major scale to natural minor.

1 2 3 4 5 6 7 8

Scale degrees 1-5   natural minor 6-8   harmonic minor 6-8   melodic minor 6-8   Dorian minor 6-8

Improvise — Four Minor Scales

The distinct differences with each minor scale stem from their upper fragments. Improvisation via application of various minor scale types will help to distinguish these fragments. Improvising will also help you decide which minor scale fragments you prefer. Of course, the portion of the minor scale that remains constant is the bottom five notes (scale degrees 1 through 5). This lower fragment provides an anchor to the variable upper fragments. Upper vs. lower fragments also immediately suggest oppositions, which can offer melodic balance.

 Audiate then sing the following upper fragments of the C minor scale, using only scale degrees 5-8. Write on the staff the missing notes.

Minor scale degrees 5 and 8 stay the same but **6 and 7 change**.

| melodic minor | natural minor | Dorian minor | harmonic minor |

1. Choose a key.
2. Choose a minor scale.
3. Compose a melody.

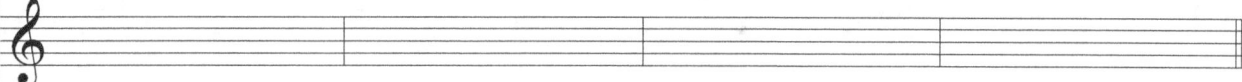

 EX. 3.45
Lester Young tenor sax solo
"Blue Lester" (C minor)

IMPROVISE
Improvise using the following scales in C minor:

1. Natural minor   4. Harmonic minor
2. Dorian minor   5. A mix of all of the above
3. Melodic minor

Lester Young uses only the **harmonic minor scale** in this solo excerpt.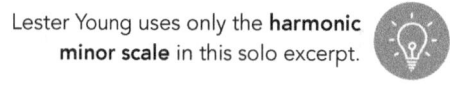

Cm

Minor chord symbols
The following symbols may all be used to indicate a C minor chord.

Cm   Cmin   C-

Improvise on the same minor chord vamp, transposed into a new key of your choice.

Modes of the Major Scale

Modes can be found within the *parent scale* of any major or minor key. For example, the parent scale in the key of C major is the C major scale. Each of the parent major scale's seven notes marks the start of one of seven modes — *Ionian, Dorian, Phrygian, Lydian, Mixolydian, Aeolian,* and *Locrian*.

Modes of the
major scale

The modes of the major scale each start on a different scale degree, from 1 to 7, and include all the diatonic notes of the major scale, simply re-ordered. Each mode has identifying characteristics, noted below with asterisks. Notice that the major scale itself is also called Ionian, the first of the seven modes, and its relative natural minor scale is Aeolian.

EX. 3.46
Modes of the C major scale

* identifying characteristic of each mode

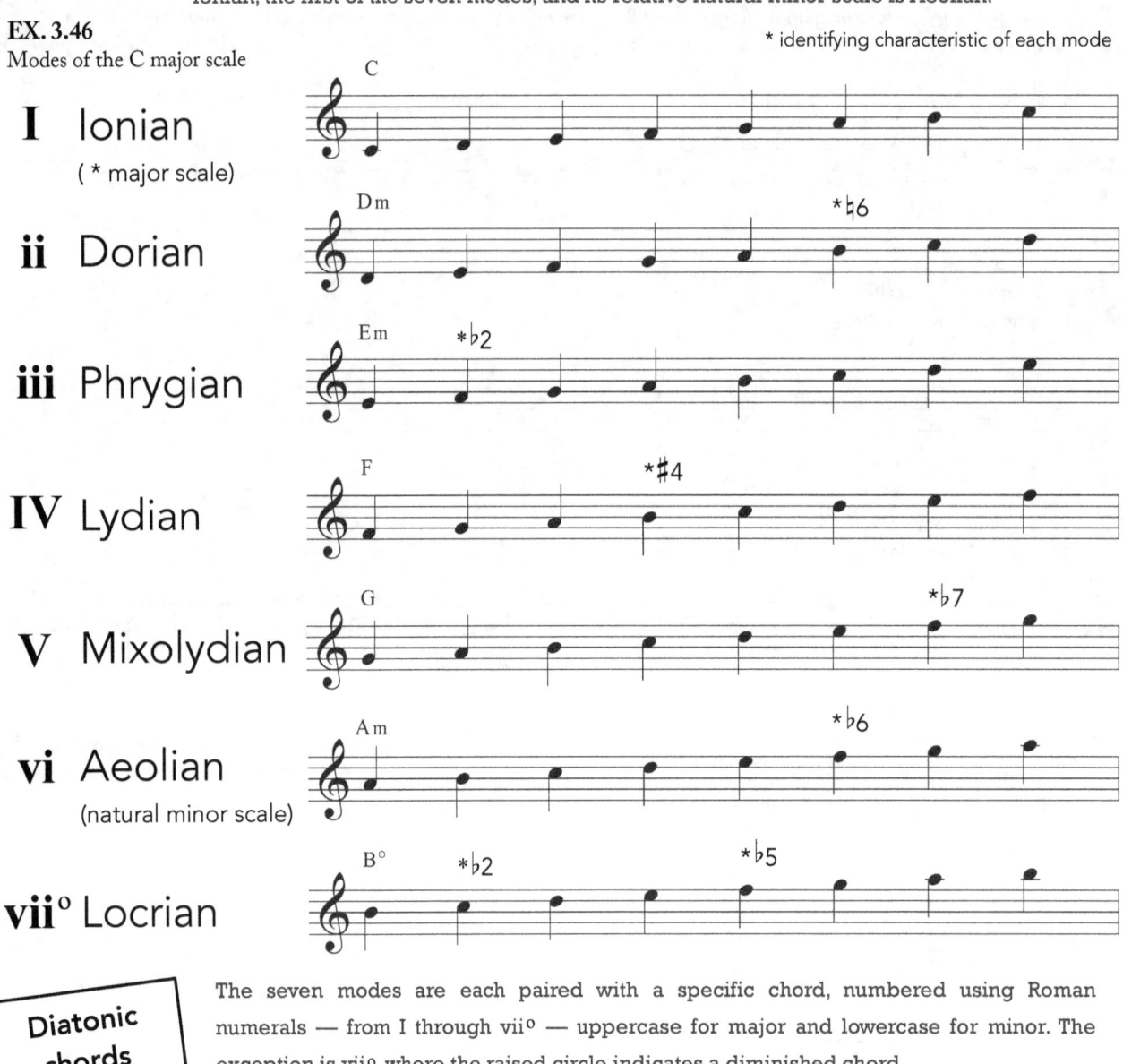

I Ionian
(* major scale)

ii Dorian

iii Phrygian

IV Lydian

V Mixolydian

vi Aeolian
(natural minor scale)

vii° Locrian

Diatonic
chords

The seven modes are each paired with a specific chord, numbered using Roman numerals — from I through vii° — uppercase for major and lowercase for minor. The exception is vii°, where the raised circle indicates a diminished chord.

EX. 3.47
Diatonic chords of the C major
scale (and their Roman numerals)

Investigate | Two Views: Dorian Minor Scale

Construct and internalize Dorian minor scales from two different vantage points: (1) starting on the 2nd scale degree of any major scale and (2) starting from the root of any major scale but lowering the 3rd and 7th degrees. This will help with hearing and mastering these scales in a variety of contexts.

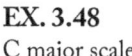

View #1 | Same notes as major scale but start on the 2nd scale degree

Movement from C major to D minor requires a shift up just one scale step. With view #1, to create the D Dorian minor scale, keep the exact same pitches as the C major scale but change the starting point from C to D. This is easier said than done since a shift like this completely changes the relationships amongst all the notes involved. A chord tone in major will now become a passing tone and target in D Dorian minor and vice versa.

EX. 3.48
C major scale

The scalar relationship in view #1 is also known as **relative**.

EX. 3.49
D Dorian minor scale, constructed from C major

View #2 | Same notes as major scale but lower the 3rd and 7th a half step

With view #2, the D Dorian minor scale is constructed by starting with the D major scale and lowering the 3rd and 7th scale degrees by a half step. The 3rd and 7th pitches are lowered, from F-sharp to F-natural and C-sharp to C-natural. Dorian minor scale numbers include a flat (♭) symbol for the 3rd and 7th, which helps clarify that both pitches have been lowered a half step.

EX. 3.50
D major scale

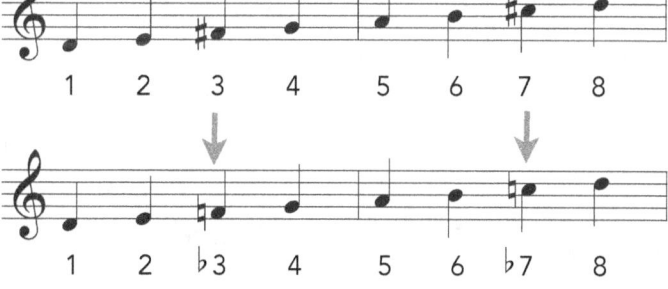

The scalar relationship in view #2 is also known as **parallel**.

EX. 3.51
D Dorian minor scale, constructed from D major

Taking this lesson in constructing Dorian minor scales, try it now in a different key below. For example, for E Dorian, view #1 would start with the D major scale while view #2 would start with the E major scale.

1. **Write out a major scale (view #1)**

2. **Write out a major scale (view #2)**

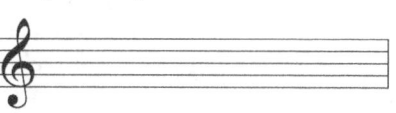

3. **Write out the Dorian scale (from both views #1 and #2)**

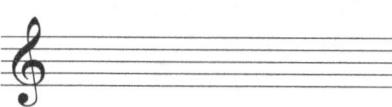

Smackdown!   Modes vs. Scales

Mode /mōd/
noun: **mode**
plural noun: **modes**

a particular diatonic set of
eight notes, spanning an
octave and found within a
major or minor scale

Scale /skāl/
noun: **scale**
plural noun: **scales**

a series of musical tones,
ascending or descending in order
of pitch, according to a specified
scheme of their intervals

All modes
are also
scales...

Modes may be considered
scale subsets, since they exist
within major and minor scales.
D Dorian minor is a scale that
is also considered a mode
since it uses the same notes as the C major scale, starting from the 2nd
scale degree. **A Aeolian minor** is also a scale and a
mode (starting on the 6th degree of C major).

...but many
scales are
not modes.

Scales are similar to modes, but
many scales are built differently
than major or minor, including
wider intervals and varied
numbers of pitches. **Diminished,
augmented, harmonic minor,**
and **chromatic** scales all meet the definition of
scales but they are definitely not modes since they
cannot be found within another major or minor scale.

EX. 3.52
D Dorian minor mode

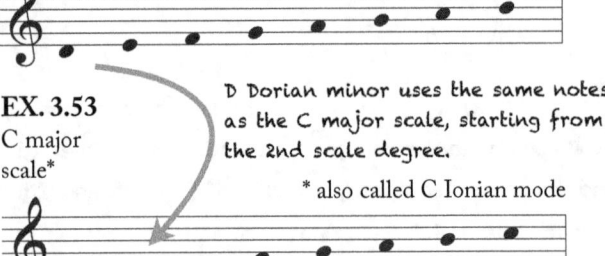

EX. 3.53
C major
scale*

D Dorian minor uses the same notes
as the C major scale, starting from
the 2nd scale degree.

* also called C Ionian mode

EX. 3.54
A Aeolian
minor mode**

Like Dorian, Aeolian
minor is also a mode of
the major scale, starting
from the 6th scale degree.

EX. 3.55
C natural
minor scale**

C natural minor scale uses the same
notes as the E-flat major scale so it is
also referred to as C Aeolian minor.

** Aeolian minor = natural minor

Other common modes (that are also scales):
Lydian, Mixolydian

Other common scales (that are *not* modes):
pentatonic, whole tone

EX. 3.56
C chromatic scale

EX. 3.57
C harmonic minor scale

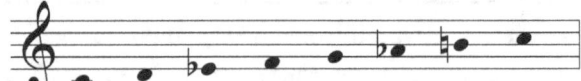

EX. 3.58
C diminished scale
(whole-half)

EX. 3.59
C augmented scale

Each scale type, by definition, is built according to a
specific set of intervals. For example, the major scale is
built on the whole and half-step intervals WWhWWWh.
For each scale above, label the specific intervals.

Dorian Minor Scale Tendencies

While D Dorian minor mode originates from C major, *Dorian minor* may establish itself as the parent scale for any composition or improvisation. If the D Dorian minor scale becomes the parent, the notes D-F-A become chord tones 1-♭3-5, providing moments of resolution as they outline a D minor chord, which, as a new tonic harmony, is designated a minor i chord and no longer considered a ii chord. The notes E-G-B become passing tones (or non-chord tones) 2-4-6 that provide tension. The parent minor triad can also commonly become a 7th chord (Dm7), which would render C, the ♭7, a chord tone.

EX. 3.60
D Dorian minor scale degree tendencies

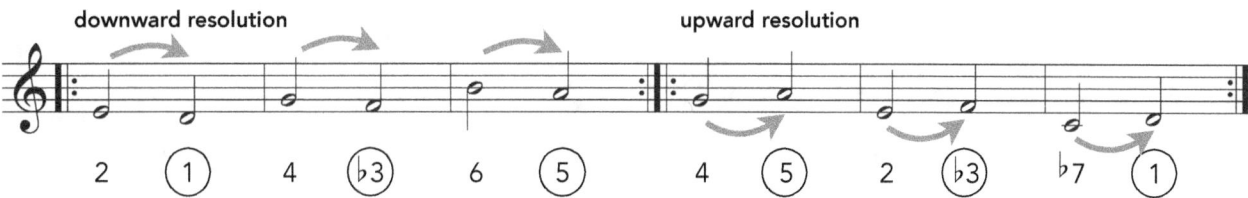

EX. 3.61
Dissonance and delayed resolutions
(D Dorian minor)

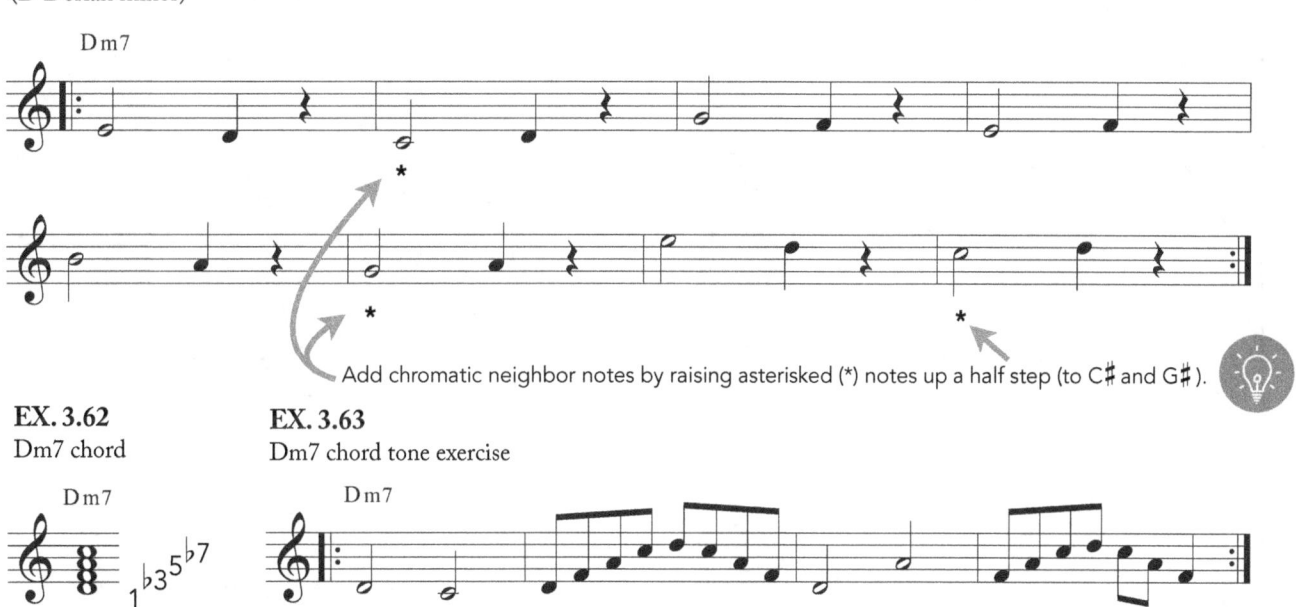

Add chromatic neighbor notes by raising asterisked (*) notes up a half step (to C♯ and G♯).

EX. 3.62
Dm7 chord

EX. 3.63
Dm7 chord tone exercise

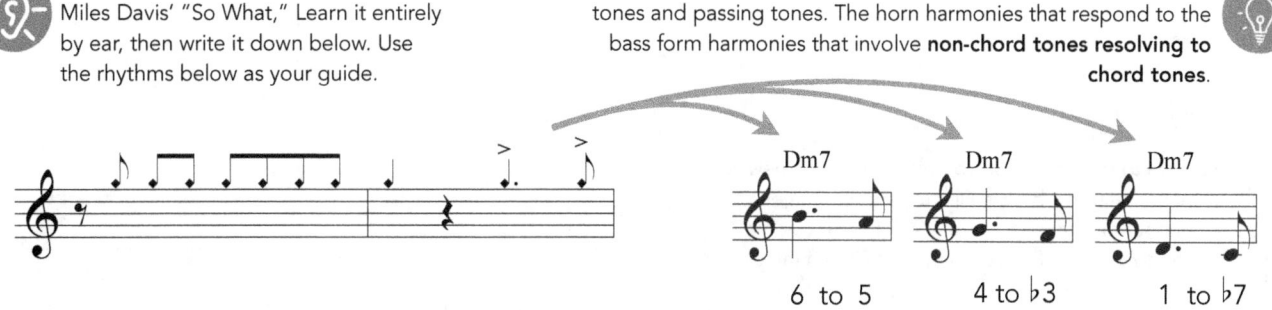

Listen to Paul Chambers' bass line on Miles Davis' "So What." Learn it entirely by ear, then write it down below. Use the rhythms below as your guide.

The bass melody of "So What" uses a combination of Dm7 chord tones and passing tones. The horn harmonies that respond to the bass form harmonies that involve **non-chord tones resolving to chord tones**.

6 to 5   4 to ♭3   1 to ♭7

Song Study — "Scarborough Fair"

The version of "Scarborough Fair" below is considered to be a D Dorian minor melody specifically because of the introduction of B-natural in measure 7. It is this 6th scale step that differentiates D Dorian minor from most other minor scale types. Notice the specific moments in each phrase when targeted D minor chord tones provide moments of release that alternate with passing tones, which often provide moments of tension.

EX 3.64
"Scarborough Fair"
(Traditional)

"Scarborough Fair" offers an opportunity to gain familiarity with the **3/4 time signature**, which allows for only 3 beats per measure, counted as "1, 2, 3."

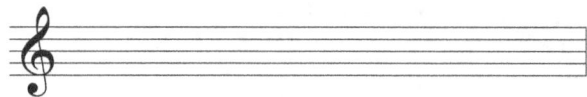

Are you go - ing to Scar - bo - rough Fair?   Pars - ley,

sage, rose - ma - ry and thyme. _____ Re -

mem - ber me to one who lives there, _____

She once was a true love of mine.

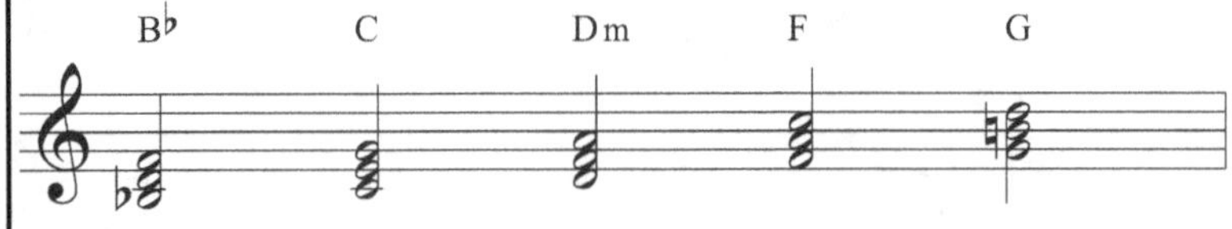

BONUS CHORD STUDY! Five chords support the melody of "Scarborough Fair." For a more advanced challenge, determine which chords accompany each measure in the song.

Bb   C   Dm   F   G

 Prepare to transpose "Scarborough Fair" to a new key of your choice, preferably by ear. First review your major scale by writing it out on the following staff. Then lower the 3rd and 7th scale degrees to make it Dorian minor.

Dorian Minor Scale Fragments
page 1 of 3

The upper and lower *scale fragments* of Dorian minor can function as their own very valuable and malleable melodic cells. Each four-note fragment (or tetrachord) can become the basis of myriad ideas for an improvising musician. Get to know how each scale fragment sounds, particularly by improvising and creating melodies with each fragment. Use the following examples to help you get started.

EX. 3.65
Upper and lower
scale fragments
(D Dorian minor)

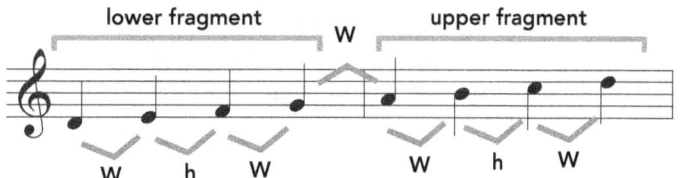

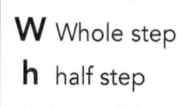

W Whole step
h half step

EX. 3.66
D Dorian minor
scale fragment exercise
(over Dm7)

Notice in the following exercise how
both the root (D) and 7th (C) are chord
tone targets since the chord is a Dm7.

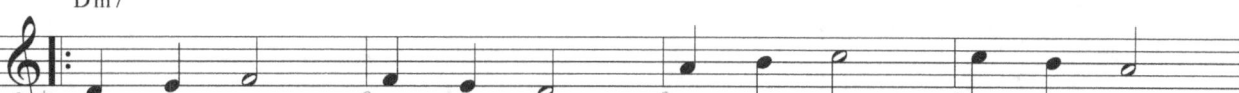

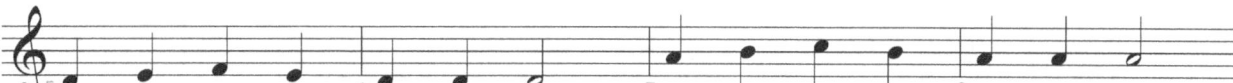

Scale fragments can stretch to multiple octaves, extending the melodic line considerably. Choose a phrase from the example above and extend it. For example, using the phrase in measures 5-6, starting with the lower fragment an octave higher, four descending phrases together form a longer line.

A fragment may include **any and all notes**
in any order. Consider upper and lower
fragments as dynamic and ever-changing.

Dorian Minor Scale Fragments
page 2 of 3

There is absolutely no need for the soloist to begin playing on beat 1 of the measure. By resting, then playing, the underlying rhythm and pulse can resound clearly. This is true whether playing solo or with accompaniment. Either way, the beats should be counted during the rests in particular. If playing with accompaniment, with a rhythm section, resting and counting gives the underlying harmonies a chance to be heard and internalized *before* the melodic line begins. The interplay between soloist and rhythm section also gains clarity.

With each phrase below, **ask if it belongs** to the lower scale fragment, upper scale fragment, or between the two.

Write in the remaining rhythmic counts for each measure below.

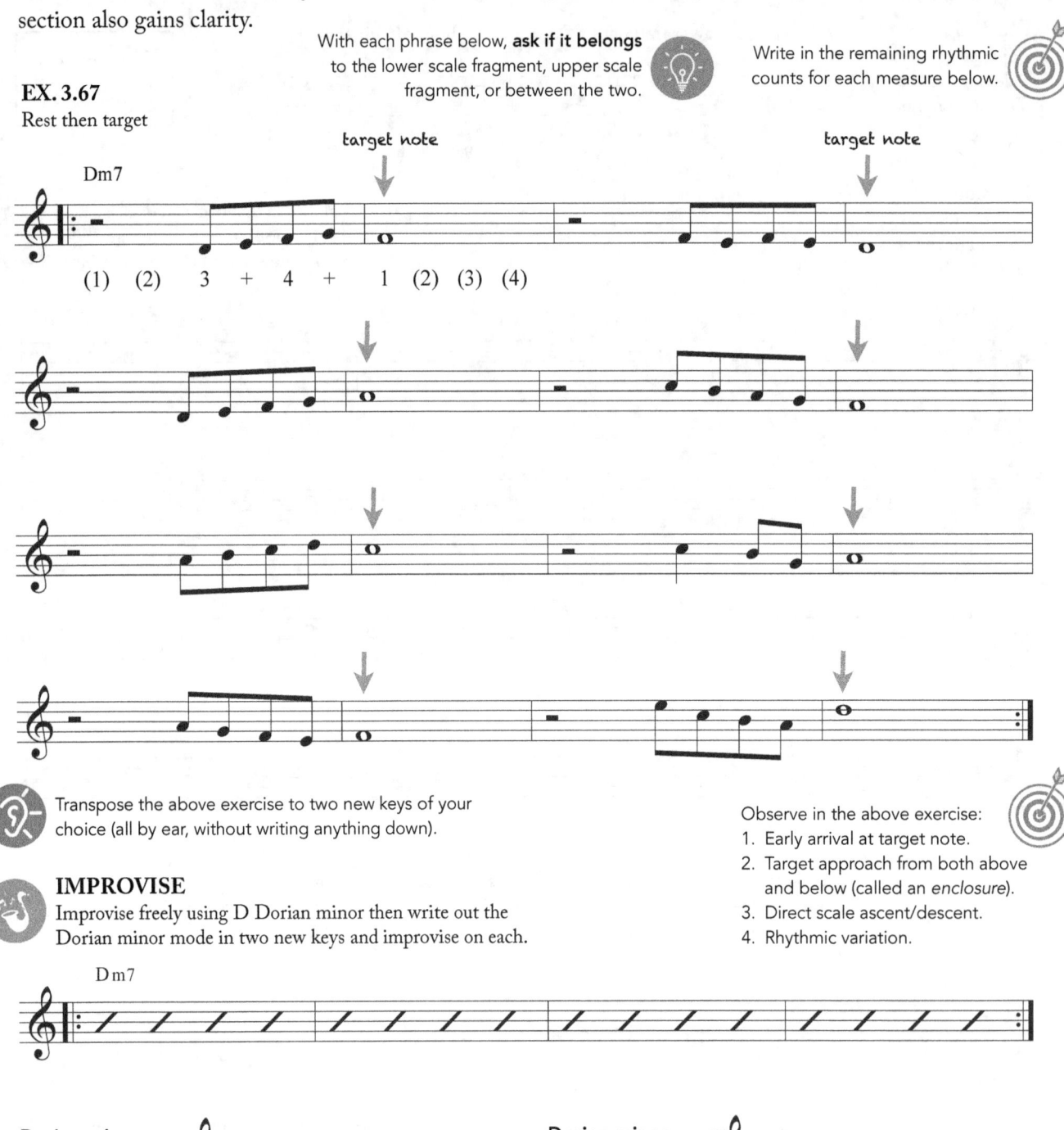

EX. 3.67
Rest then target

Transpose the above exercise to two new keys of your choice (all by ear, without writing anything down).

IMPROVISE
Improvise freely using D Dorian minor then write out the Dorian minor mode in two new keys and improvise on each.

Observe in the above exercise:
1. Early arrival at target note.
2. Target approach from both above and below (called an *enclosure*).
3. Direct scale ascent/descent.
4. Rhythmic variation.

Dorian minor
(new key 1)

Dorian minor
(new key 2)

Dorian Minor Scale Fragments
page 3 of 3

The exercise below involves improvising for one measure then holding a target note for the next measure. There is no need to play on every beat. When improvising, using a predetermined target note, start simple by resting for a couple beats then improvise using only one or two notes. The goal is to be deliberate and take time to decide on your starting fragment for each phrase.

Review the lower and upper scale fragments within Dorian minor below. Consider which intervals are used between notes. Explore altering the shape within each pattern by changing the note order. Fragments need not travel in scale order. For example, D-E-F-G can be played F-G-E-D or, using only E-F, as a partial fragment.

EX. 3.68
D Dorian minor
scale fragments

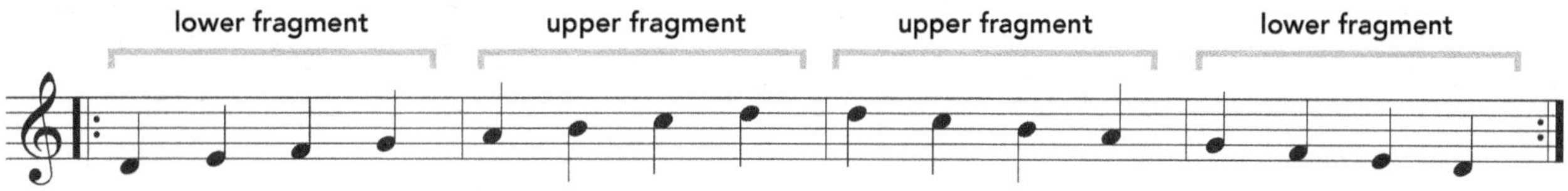

IMPROVISE
Dorian minor scale
fragments and targets

Remember: Don't always start on the first note of a fragment. **Save the punchline!**

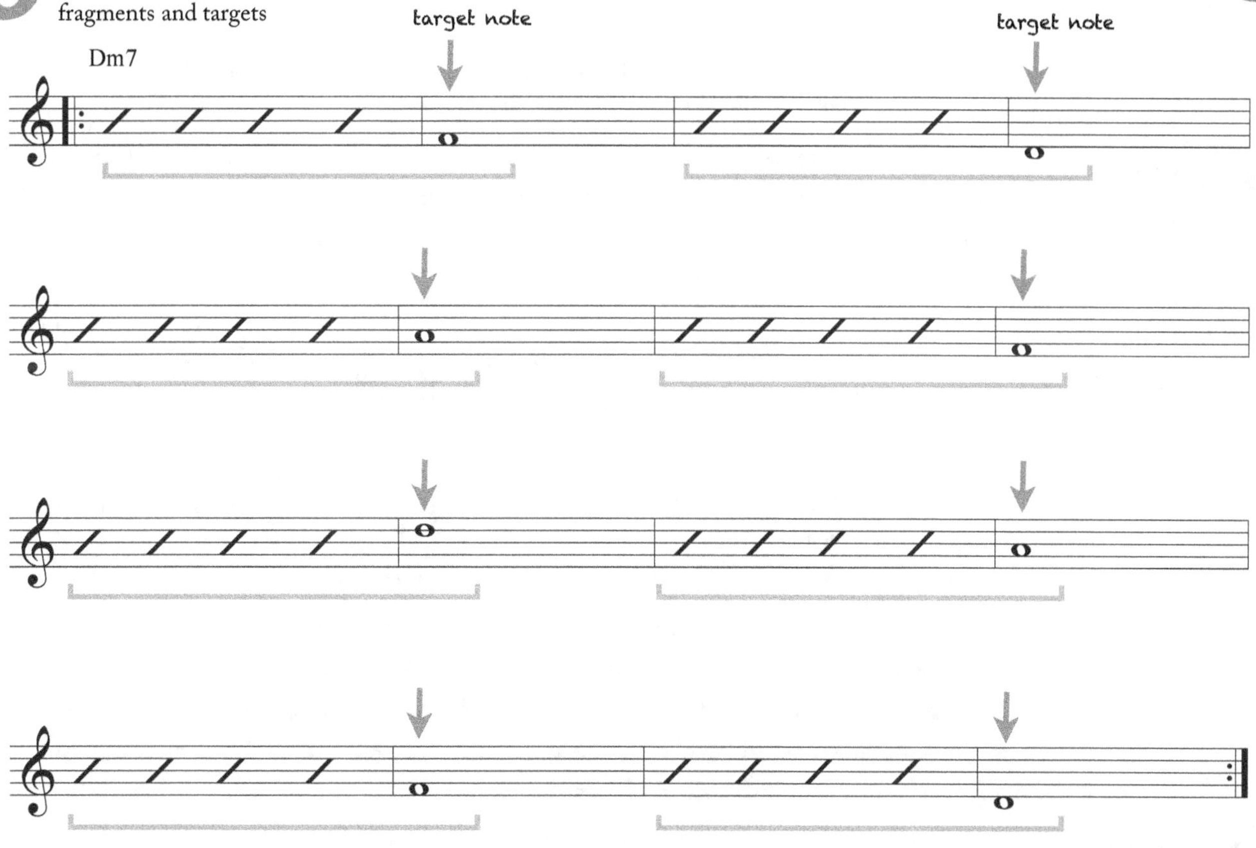

Identify whether the target note belongs to an upper or lower fragment (or both). For example, F in measure 2 belongs to the lower fragment D-E-F-G.

Song Study   "So What"
— page 1 of 2 —

"So What" is frequently played at jazz jam sessions and is based entirely on the Dorian minor mode. Featuring a bass line originated by Paul Chambers and a horn figure first performed by Miles Davis, Cannonball Adderley, and John Coltrane, "So What" helped usher in the sub-genre called *modal jazz*.

The A-section

Consider "So What" as a call and response, with the central melody played by the bassist and the response played by the horns in what is a surprising reversal of roles. The melody actually starts on a pickup measure but the phrases are still 2 bars each, with four total phrases (8 bars) in each A-section.

EX. 3.69
"So What" (Davis/Chambers), rhythm only

Write out "So What" yourself, using the rhythm below as your guide. It's easier than it seems, since most phrases are a repetition of the opening phrase.

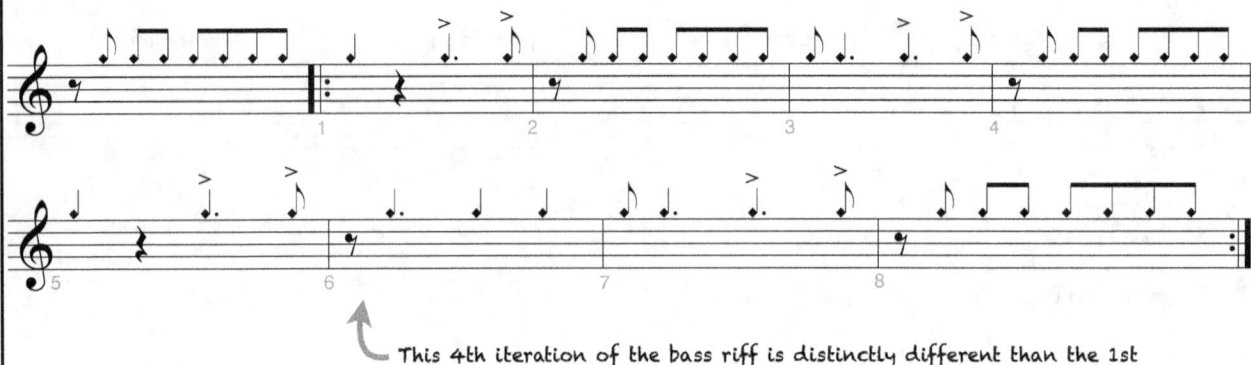

This 4th iteration of the bass riff is distinctly different than the 1st three iterations, completing the 8-measure statement.

A-section harmony

The harmony of "So What" is a blank slate. It can be entirely simple, just a Dm7 chord, or it can include many layers of harmony being played as a Dm9, Dm11, or Dm13 chord. An imaginative musician might mix in all four of these chords and possibly even more.

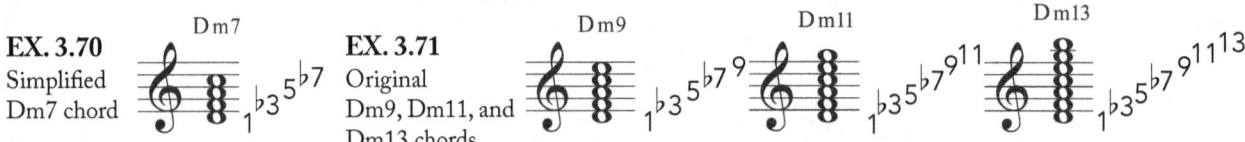

EX. 3.70
Simplified
Dm7 chord

EX. 3.71
Original
Dm9, Dm11, and
Dm13 chords

Confused about chord names? Just as scale degree 8 is also 1, the 9th, 11th, and 13th are the **same notes** as scale degrees 2, 4, and 6.

Did you know that a Dm13 chord includes **every note** of the Dorian minor scale: D, E, F, G, A, B, C?

Modal jazz

A musical sub-genre, modal jazz replaces an emphasis on form and harmonic function with an emphasis on melodic development based on modes. Modal jazz compositions tend to include fewer chords, a sparse harmonic landscape that gives improvising musicians ample space to develop ideas, governed less by a complex chord progression. A reaction to the quick pace inherent in bebop jazz, modal jazz often is played at medium or slow tempos.

Iconic modal jazz compositions:

- "So What" (Davis/Chambers)
- "Flamenco Sketches" (Miles Davis)
- "Little Sunflower" (Freddie Hubbard)
- "Freedom Jazz Dance" (Eddie Harris)
- "Canteloupe Island" (Herbie Hancock)
- "Maiden Voyage" (Herbie Hancock)

Song Study   "So What"

page 2 of 2

AABA form

"So What" is composed of four 8-measure sections, comprising what is known as a standard *32-bar AABA form*. The A-sections all sound nearly identical, each grounded in D minor. Typically, the B-section, aka the *bridge*, is the easiest to hear because it moves to a new mode (E-flat minor). A third A-section shows up after the bridge, which helps mark a final return to the original D minor harmony. To delineate the form, very often the drummer will mark the end of the final A-section with a fill that helps to usher in the next chorus. Without marking the end of a chorus, the solo section here can become confusing and unclear.

EX. 3.72
"So What" form
(32-bar AABA)

The most obvious change happens with the shift up a half step on the bridge.

Many soloists and drummers MARK the end of a chorus to help distinguish the form.

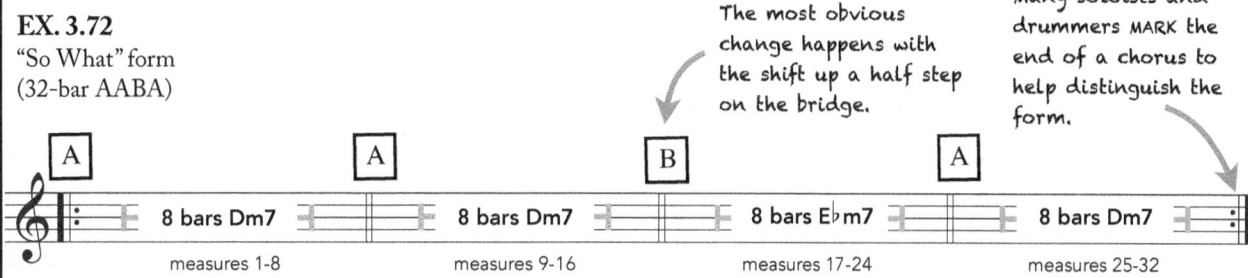

A	A	B	A
8 bars Dm7	8 bars Dm7	8 bars E♭m7	8 bars Dm7
measures 1-8	measures 9-16	measures 17-24	measures 25-32

Bridge chords

Just like the Dm13 in the A-sections, the E♭m13 in the B-section, also called *the bridge*, involves many chord extensions. At first it tends to be much easier to pare things down to an E♭m7 and E♭ Dorian minor scale.

EX. 3.73
Original chord
on the bridge

E♭m13

EX. 3.74
Simplified chord
on the bridge

E♭m7

Write out the E♭ Dorian minor scale by transposing all the notes of D Dorian minor up a half step. Then circle the chord tones for E♭m7.

D vs. E♭ Dorian

When moving between A- and B-section harmonies, look for common tones between the two scale modes. Using common tones can help bridge your idea from the A-section to the B-section (pun intended!).

EX. 3.75
D Dorian minor scale

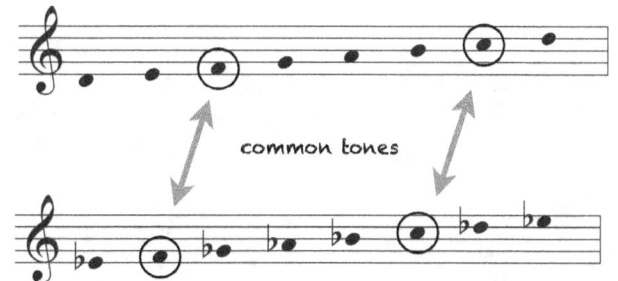

common tones

EX. 3.76
E-flat Dorian minor scale

Try holding out the note F when the Dm13 chord changes to E♭m13 on the bridge of "So What." Do you see how F is a **common tone**?

Solo  Spotlight

Miles Davis, trumpet "So What"
Stanley Turrentine, tenor sax "Impressions"

Miles Davis' trumpet solo on "So What" is perfection. Presented here is the rhythm of the first eight bars of his improvisation as well as Stanley Turrentine's tenor sax solo on "Impressions." Based on the same chord progression as "So What," "Impressions" is usually played at a faster tempo.

EX. 3.77
Miles Davis trumpet solo
"So What" (rhythm only)

Learn these solos well. They contain iconic language and timeless style pertinent to every improvising musician.

Pitch collection challenge!
Complete the rhythm excerpt above by adding the following pitches:

D C D   D A G A D D   D F A G A
D F A G A C B C B A F A G A D D   D D D D

EX. 3.78
Stanley Turrentine tenor sax solo
"Impressions"

Turrentine's solo below is played at a fairly brisk tempo. Learn the solo slowly at first, **aiming for accuracy**.

Solo Transcription 101

Jazz language is passed down from generation to generation through a time-honored tradition of *solo transcription*. Transcribing helps every musician develop a stronger ear while also providing an opportunity to practice and understand solo improvisations and especially gain valuable insight into the music of master musicians. Use the following strategies as tools to become a successful transcriber.

Be patient.

Transcription can be a long process. Enter the project with a patient mindset.

Listen.

Listen to the solo again and again, as if it's one of your favorite songs you can't stop playing. Have fun with this.

Audiate.

Imagine the solo only in your mind, away from the recording.

Sing.

Sing the solo, away from your instrument. If you are having trouble with pitch, first sing just the rhythms.

Prepare.

Prepare for success by finding the song's key. Determine whether it is major or minor. Review the key's parent scale, from which most solo notes will stem. Learning the chord progression is also a great help.

Learn.

On your instrument, learn one note at a time, eventually completing one phrase. There may be some trial and error at first but the preceding orientations will help.

Write.

While writing out the solo might be less valuable than learning a solo entirely by ear, it does allow for continued analysis and will also add to your own solo library.

Practice.

Once you've transcribed the solo, keep learning from it by practicing intently.

Using the strategies above, learn bars 1 to 16 of Miles Davis' trumpet solo on "So What" on your instrument entirely by ear.

Write out bars 8 to 16 of Miles Davis' trumpet solo on "So What." Some initial rests and rhythms have already been added.

Prepare for success by reviewing the key for "So What." Also **review and practice the parent scale** for its A-sections.

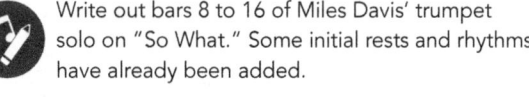

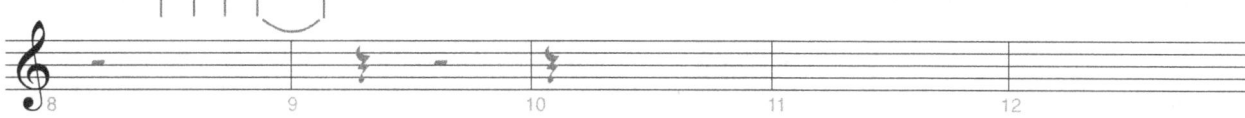

Ways to practice a transcribed solo

- Practice one phrase at a time.
- Memorize the entire solo.
- Practice repeatedly and with a metronome.
- Continue to play the solo entirely by ear.
- Learn it at multiple tempos.

- Analyze the solo.
- Write in the scale degrees.
- Write in the rhythm counts.
- Listen to the original recording and pick up all the stylistic details that are not notated.

Improvise   "So What"

One of the challenges with soloing on "So What" is that, since very little harmonic material is provided, the improviser must come up with ways to develop a full solo statement with very few parameters in place. Give it a try here!

IMPROVISE
"So What" (Davis/Chambers)

Focusing on **short rhythmic motifs** will help keep a focus on each 8-bar phrase within the 32-bar form. Offer clear phrases and ideas by using scale fragments.

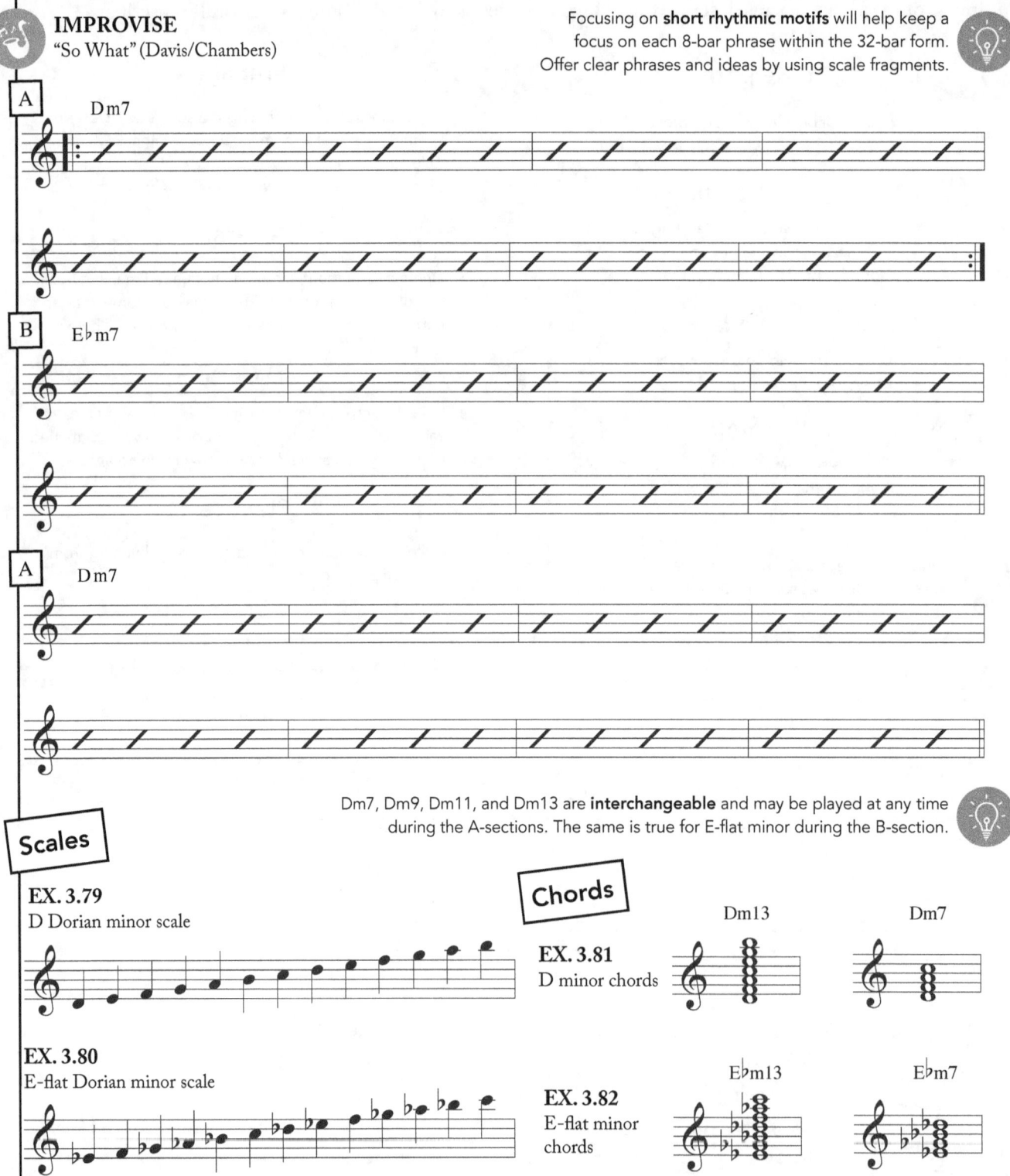

Dm7, Dm9, Dm11, and Dm13 are **interchangeable** and may be played at any time during the A-sections. The same is true for E-flat minor during the B-section.

Scales

EX. 3.79
D Dorian minor scale

EX. 3.80
E-flat Dorian minor scale

Chords

EX. 3.81
D minor chords

Dm13   Dm7

EX. 3.82
E-flat minor chords

E♭m13   E♭m7

Zen Jazz Master says:

Getting Lost

Over the years, countless jazz musicians have gotten lost while soloing on "So What." In fact, it is often a regular occurrence at amateur jam sessions. The form is easy to lose track of because the A-sections all have the same tonality and, if you improvise over more than one chorus, the last A-section can blur into the first and second A-sections. When this happens, the B-section shift can take you by surprise. Worse yet, if you get caught up in the A-section harmonies and you forget to listen and concentrate, you might miss the B-section shift altogether!

To avoid getting lost while playing multiple choruses, keep track of the top of the form and always listen to players in the rhythm section.

Chapter 3 Achievements

Congratulations!

You are one step closer to jazz nirvana.

Here is a partial list of what you've achieved:

- Exploring differences in four minor scales — natural, harmonic, melodic, and Dorian
- Using direction to establish intent in your improvisations
- Hearing upward and downward scale tendencies in Dorian minor
- Understanding differences between major and Dorian minor scales
- Improvising using target notes within the Dorian minor scale
- Creating coherent melodic structures by using scale fragments within the Dorian mode

Are you ready for the next chapter?

Answer these questions to determine whether you are prepared to continue to the next chapter:

- **Can you craft** an improvisation using each of the four main minor scale types?

     If "Yes," move to the next chapter.
     If "No," review this chapter.

- **Do you understand** the difference between a major scale and a Dorian minor scale?

     If "Yes," move to the next chapter.
     If "No," review this chapter.

- **Can you conceive** of Dorian minor in two separate scale fragments (upper and lower)?

     If "Yes," move to the next chapter.
     If "No," review this chapter.

- **Do you want** to learn more about how modes relate to each other and how to improvise over a 2-chord harmonic progression?

     If "Yes," move to the next chapter.
     If "No," then close this book and come back when you are ready to learn more! Nearly every situation in improvised music involves a chord progression and the next chapter is going to help get you started with tackling this.

UNIT TWO

Harmony and Form

- Parent keys and scales
- Navigating 2-chord progressions
- Blues form

Chapter 4
- Functional Harmony
- I-ii Chord Progressions
- Tension and Release

Chapter 5
- Dominant Harmony &
  V-I Chord Progressions
- Cadences
- Major Pentatonics

Chapter 6
- Minor Progressions
- Minor Pentatonics
- The 12-Bar Blues

"The music comes *through* you, not from you. Sometimes we lose sight of that and say, 'I'm a bad so-and-so.' There's always somebody better waiting in the wings. The other side of the coin is you can't spend your time comparing yourself to other people. Because you'll either be very vain or depressed. You have a story to tell, just like everybody else. It may be different but it's *your* story." [4]

— Kenny Barron, pianist and composer

Change is Coming
Functional Harmony & Tension and Release

Much of classic and modern jazz is based on the concept of functional harmony — how chords relate to each other. A chord progression is called a "progression" simply because each chord actually progresses to another chord. The expression "learn the changes" means to internalize how each chord functions not only in isolation but also in conjunction with other chords in the progression. The introduction of a selection of different harmonies in this chapter actually is centered on a simple progression involving only the I and ii chord. In addition to shedding light on modal and tonal harmony, the chapter also explores how targeted tensions and other devices help provide melodic nuance.

Contents

TOPICS
- Functional Harmony
- IV Chord vs. ii Chord
- Home vs. Away
- Passing Tones over I-ii
- I-ii Chord Movement
- Geometric Planes
- Harmonic Rhythm
- Lower Fragment + 5th
- I-ii Phrase Transitions
- Scale Degrees: Chords vs. Key
- I-ii Upper Fragments
- I-ii Upper Fragment Exercises
- Targeted Tension
- Historical Examples of Targeted Tension
- Non-Chord Tone Resolutions & Rhythmic Displacement
- Appoggiaturas
- Other Embellishments (Suspension, etc.)
- Parallel Motion and Contrary Motion
- Parallel Fifths
- Sequence and the Rule of Three

EAR TRAINING
- "This land is your land" Chords
- Chord Placement on Beat 1, Followed by Beats 2, 3, and 4

MASTERCLASS
- Practical Interpretation of a Lead Sheet

INVESTIGATE
- Chord Inversions
- Slash Chords vs. Polychords

SONG STUDY
- "Oh My Loving Brother" (African American Spiritual)
- "Bye Bye Blackbird" (Henderson/Dixon)

SOLO SPOTLIGHT
- Peggy Lee vocals, Miles Davis trumpet, Lee Konitz alto sax "Bye Bye Blackbird"

COMPOSE
- "Home vs. Away" Chord Progression and Melody
- Diatonic Chord Progression and Melody

IMPROVISE
- Free Improvisation on CMaj7-Dm7 Vamp
- Target Exercise on CMaj7-Dm7
- CMaj7-Dm7 Vamp (with lower fragment + fifth targets)
- Diatonic Chord Improvisation
- Rhythmic Variation and Displacements
- "Bye Bye Blackbird" (Henderson/Dixon)

SMACKDOWN!
- Modal Jazz vs. Tonal Jazz

LISTENING GUIDE
- "When You're Smiling" (Shay/Fisher/Goodwin)

HISTORICAL EXAMPLES
- "Twinkle, twinkle, little star" (W. A. Mozart)
- "My heart stood still" (Rodgers/Hart)
- "So What" (Davis/Chambers)
- "Sea Shantey" (Traditional)
- "Jeepers Creepers" (Warren/Mercer)
- "Bourbon Street Parade" (Paul Barbarin)
- "Tune Up" (Miles Davis)
- "How High the Moon" (Lewis/Hamilton)
- "But Beautiful" (Van Heusen/Burke)
- John Coltrane tenor sax solo "All the Things You Are"
- Julian "Cannonball" Adderley alto sax solo "Minority"
- "When I Fall in Love" (Young/Heyman)
- "Cheek to Cheek" (Irving Berlin)
- "Autumn Leaves" (Josef Kosma)
- "Satin Doll" (Duke Ellington)
- *Minuet in C Major, K. 6* (W.A. Mozart)
- "When the Saints Go Marching In" (Traditional)
- "Happy birthday to you" (Mildred & Patty Hill)
- Billy Tipton piano solo "Perdido"
- "Michael, row the boat ashore" (Traditional)
- "The Star-Spangled Banner" (Key/Smith)
- "Amazing Grace" (Traditional)
- "Goodnight, ladies" (Edwin Pearce Christy)
- "When You're Smiling" (Shay/Fisher/Goodwin)
- "Struttin' with Some Barbecue" (Lil Hardin Armstrong)

ZEN JAZZ MASTER SAYS
- Tell a story!

Functional Harmony
page 1 of 2

Diatonic chords are formed on every scale degree of the major scale and these harmonies all relate to their original major scale tonic. When played in conjunction with each other, they form what is called *functional harmony*, where each chord carries out a particular function. While the I chord is considered the *tonic* or *root* of the key, the V has a *dominant* function, with a strong tendency to resolve to tonic. The IV chord has a *subdominant* function, sitting below the V and tending to move to the dominant.

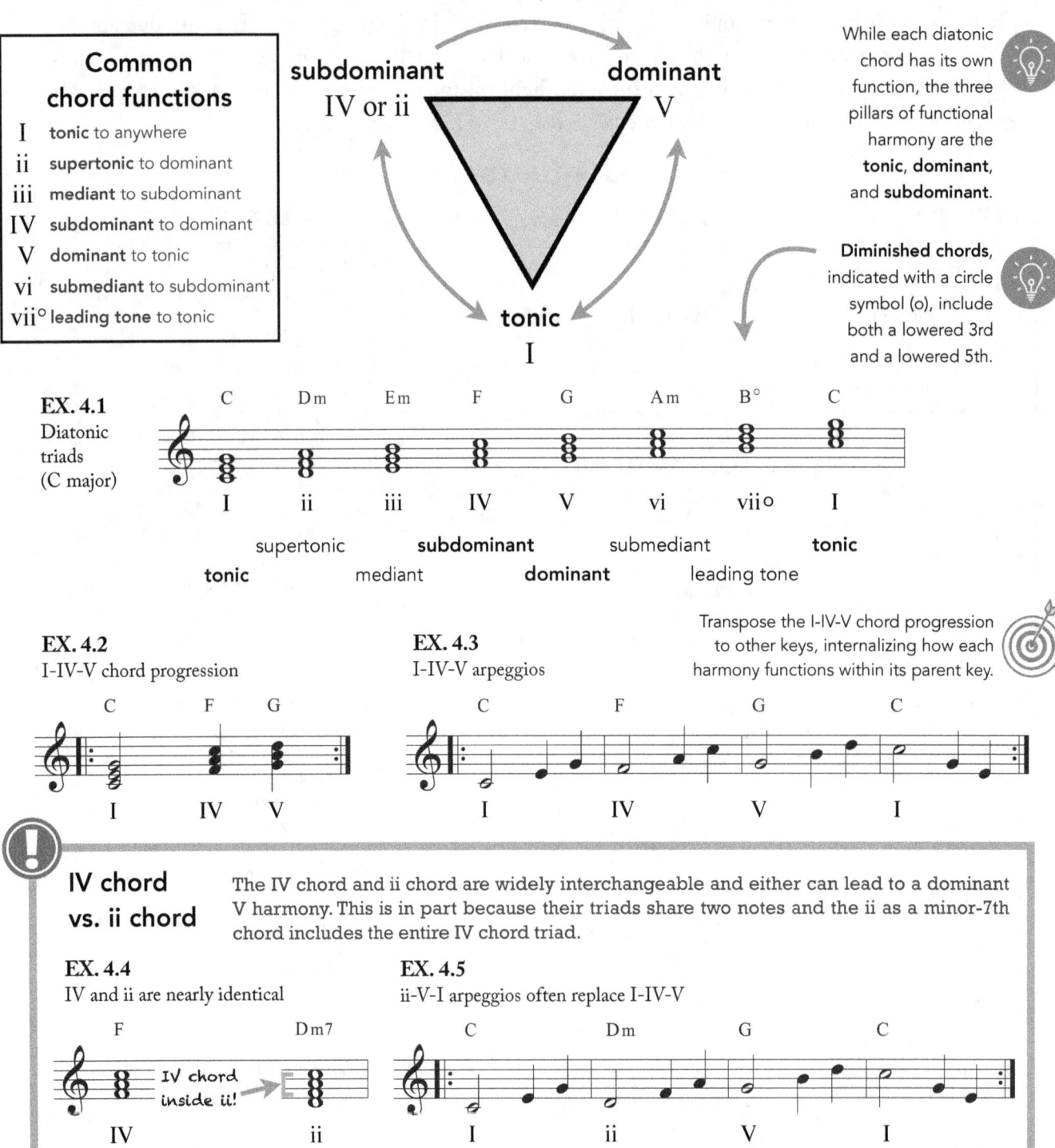

Common chord functions

I   **tonic** to anywhere
ii   **supertonic** to dominant
iii   **mediant** to subdominant
IV   **subdominant** to dominant
V   **dominant** to tonic
vi   **submediant** to subdominant
vii°   **leading tone** to tonic

subdominant — IV or ii
dominant — V
tonic — I

While each diatonic chord has its own function, the three pillars of functional harmony are the **tonic, dominant,** and **subdominant.**

Diminished chords, indicated with a circle symbol (o), include both a lowered 3rd and a lowered 5th.

EX. 4.1
Diatonic triads (C major)

C   Dm   Em   F   G   Am   B°   C
I   ii   iii   IV   V   vi   vii°   I

tonic   supertonic   mediant   **subdominant**   **dominant**   submediant   leading tone   **tonic**

EX. 4.2
I-IV-V chord progression

C   F   G
I   IV   V

EX. 4.3
I-IV-V arpeggios

C   F   G   C
I   IV   V   I

Transpose the I-IV-V chord progression to other keys, internalizing how each harmony functions within its parent key.

IV chord vs. ii chord

The IV chord and ii chord are widely interchangeable and either can lead to a dominant V harmony. This is in part because their triads share two notes and the ii as a minor-7th chord includes the entire IV chord triad.

EX. 4.4
IV and ii are nearly identical

F   Dm7
IV chord inside ii!
IV   ii

EX. 4.5
ii-V-I arpeggios often replace I-IV-V

C   Dm   G   C
I   ii   V   I

Functional Harmony

— page 2 of 2 —

Each diatonic harmony functions in one of two ways, either as (1) a *consonant* harmony that is already at a point of *resolution* (and is thus considered to be at "home") or as (2) a *dissonant* harmony that is at a point of *tension* ("away" and awaiting a return to "home"). While this is a simplification of harmonic function, it is paramount to understanding which diatonic chords fall into these two categories.

home		away	
I	C	**ii**	Dm
iii	Em	**IV**	F
vi	Am	**V**	G
		vii°	B°

Explore this two-column **home/away chart** (key of C major) at a piano or by arpeggiating on an instrument. Choose to move between each column, experiencing the tension and resolution points throughout the ensuing progression.

Change to a new key center. Get to know the home/away option in multiple keys.

How to determine "home" vs. "away"

1. Examine the basic *chord triad* of each mode from I to vii°. Do not use 7th chords for this.
2. If two chord tones match the parent I chord, that chord can be placed in the *home* column.
3. If only one chord tone matches the parent I chord, that chord is placed in the *away* column.

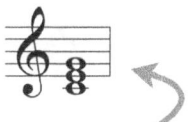

EX. 4.6
C (parent I)

I is definitively HOME.

EX. 4.7
Dm (ii)

ii chord tones do not match I at all so ii is AWAY.

EX. 4.8
Em (iii)

iii matches 2 chord tones with I so iii is HOME.

Compose a chord progression that alternates between home and away chords in the key of C major. Chords may be repeated. Write your chord symbols in the blanks provided then write them above each measure in the staff systems below. Lastly, compose a melody that complements your chord progression.

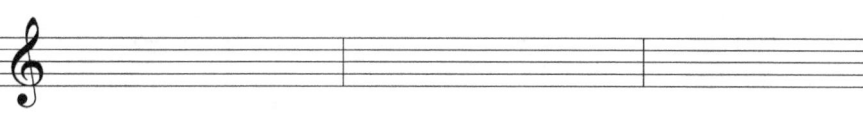

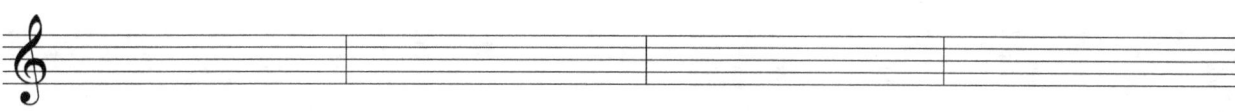

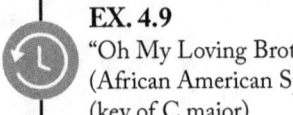
Song Study   "Oh My Loving Brother"

Nearly every phrase in "Oh My Loving Brother" begins with a set of pickup notes in the melody that then resolves to a target note on beat 1 of the next measure. Each one of these targets firmly establishes a different harmony. The song uses only the notes of the tonic major scale and provides a training ground for developing a clear understanding of diatonic harmonic function.

EX. 4.9
"Oh My Loving Brother"
(African American Spiritual)
(key of C major)

Write in matching chords for "Oh My Loving Brother."
Check your work by playing the chords you added.
If things don't sound right, change the chords until
you come up with a version you like. Notice where
and why subdominant, dominant, and tonic
harmonies are used.

Which harmonies do you prefer?
Bar 1 ("brother"): **Dm, F,** or **G7**
Bar 3 ("fire"): **C, Em, FMaj7,** or **Am**

Transpose "Oh My Loving Brother" to a new key,
Write out the first half of the melody and chords below.

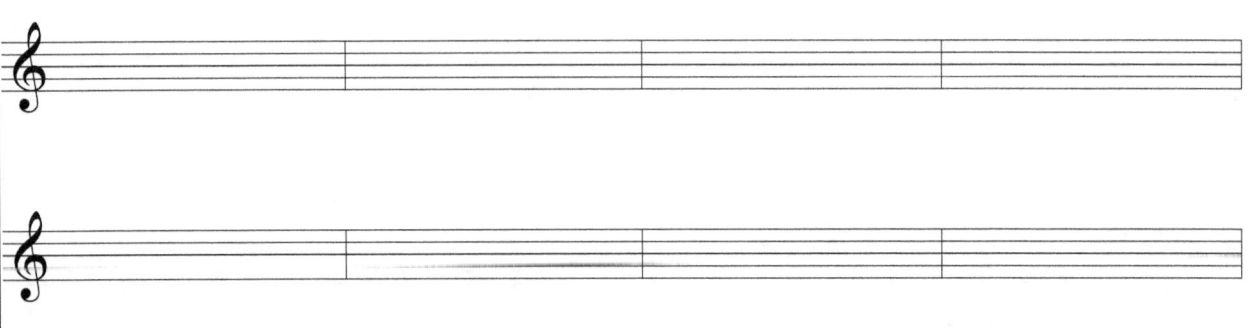

Passing Tones over I-ii

Get to know exactly how many *passing tones* get you from one chord tone to another. When you begin targeting, even with the most basic melodic lines, you'll want to have this skill firmly in place. Below are the basic building blocks that help define the I and ii chords. Practice the scales below in multiple octaves. Practice moving up and down, counting how many passing tones it takes to land on any chord tone. For example, if you want to move within the C major scale from E up to B, you have to move through three passing tones (F-G-A). Use the examples below to continue practicing.

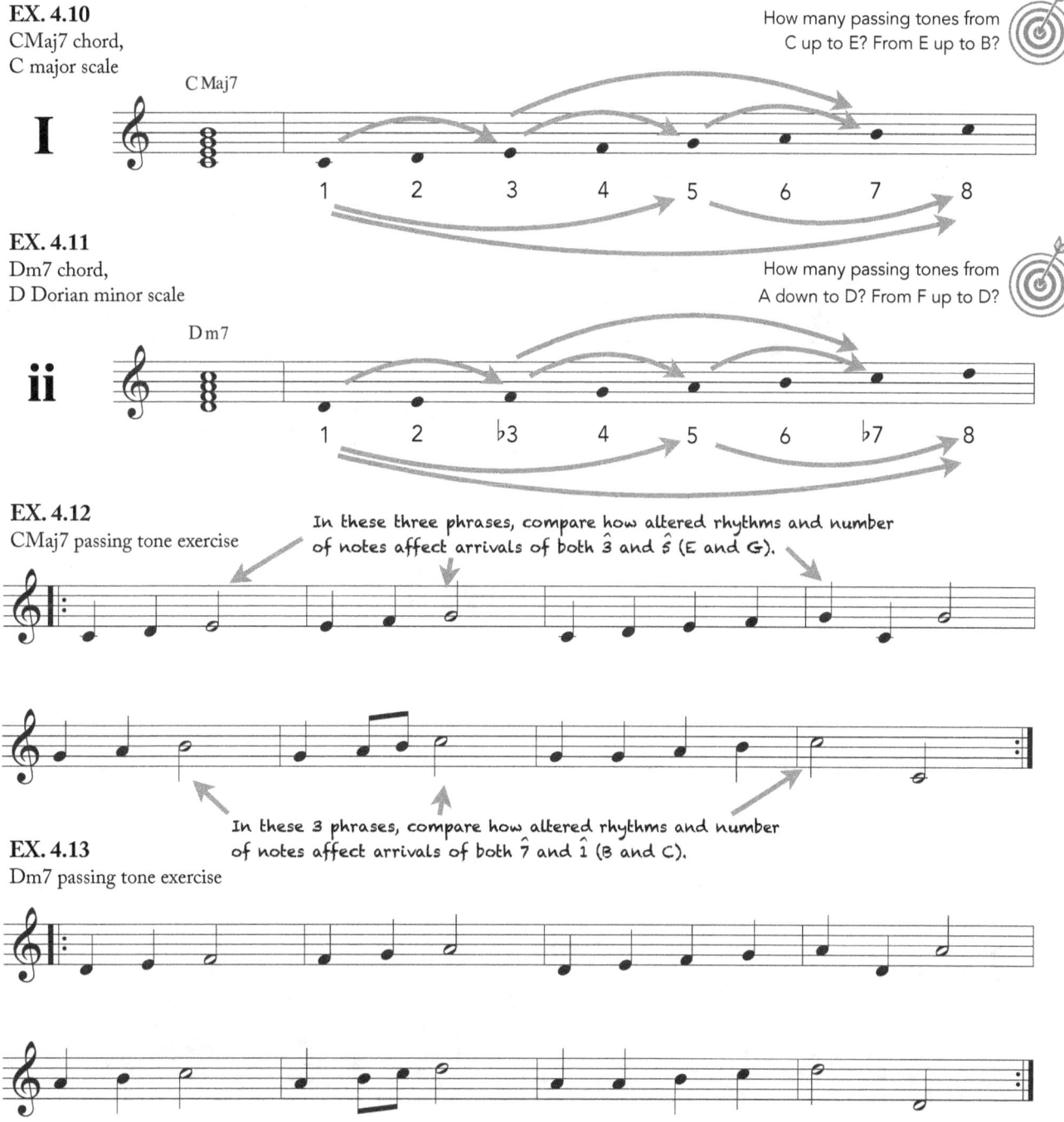

EX. 4.10
CMaj7 chord,
C major scale

How many passing tones from
C up to E? From E up to B?

I   C Maj7
1   2   3   4   5   6   7   8

EX. 4.11
Dm7 chord,
D Dorian minor scale

How many passing tones from
A down to D? From F up to D?

ii   D m7
1   2   ♭3   4   5   6   ♭7   8

EX. 4.12
CMaj7 passing tone exercise

In these three phrases, compare how altered rhythms and number
of notes affect arrivals of both 3̂ and 5̂ (E and G).

In these 3 phrases, compare how altered rhythms and number
of notes affect arrivals of both 7̂ and 1̂ (B and C).

EX. 4.13
Dm7 passing tone exercise

I-ii Chord Movement

How each chord functions within any given key is always impactful. In the key of C, a simple progression might start on a C major chord, the tonic I chord, and move up one step to a D minor chord, the ii chord. This is often called simply a *I to ii chord progression*. Lower scale fragments of both the I chord and the ii chord are created by filling in the passing tones between chord tones. An entire lower fragment of D minor (D-E-F) can easily move to C major by shifting one step up, to the C major fragment (E-F-G) centering on chord tones E and G, or one step down (C-D-E), centering on C major chord tones C and E.

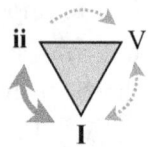

EX. 4.14
D minor lower scale fragment, resolving to C major fragments

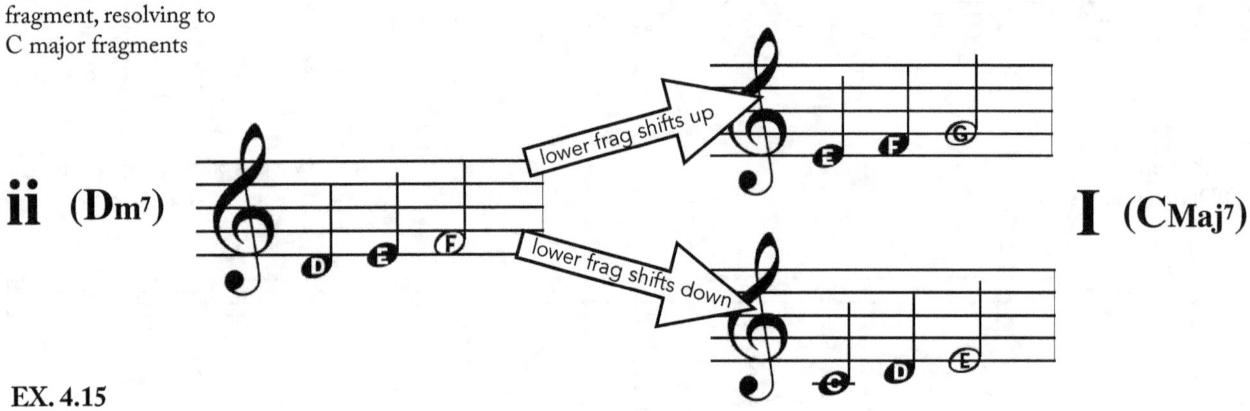

The **functional harmony graphic** above illustrates I-ii chord movement on its own and also as part of a classic ii-V-I progression.

ii (Dm⁷)   *lower frag shifts up*   E F G

lower frag shifts down   C D E

I (CMaj⁷)

EX. 4.15
Lower fragment exercise (ii-I)

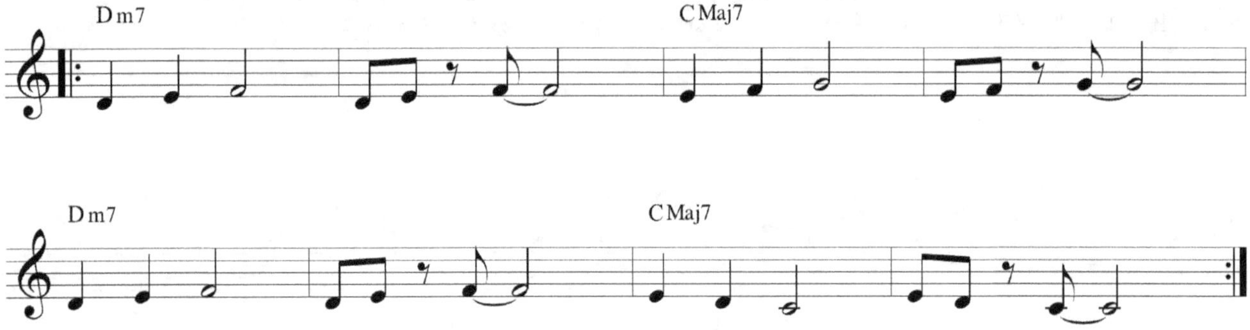

Dm7   CMaj7

Dm7   CMaj7

Geometric planes

EX. 4.16
C major (I) to D minor (ii)

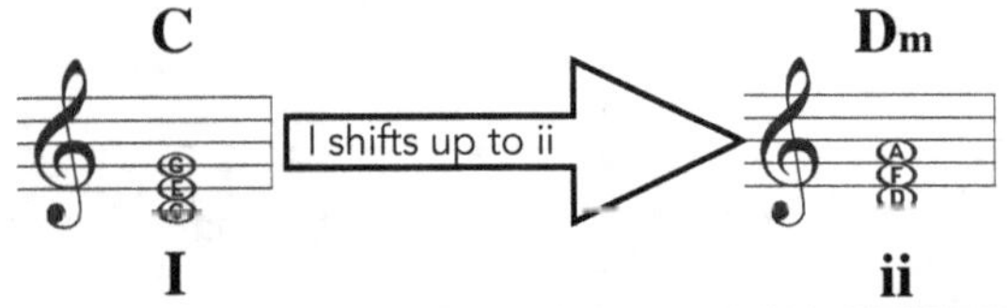

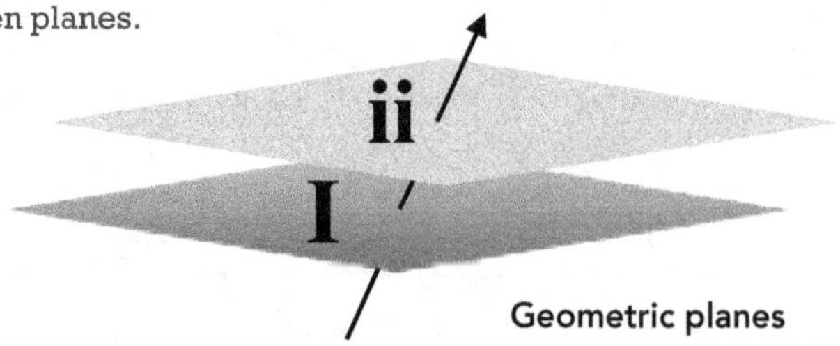

Imagine the harmonic movement between C major and D minor as a *geometric shift* with each chord on a different geometric plane and the chord progression shifting up or down between planes.

C   *I shifts up to ii*   Dm

I   ii

ii
I

Geometric planes

Harmonic Rhythm

Harmonic rhythm is defined by the placement and frequency of each new chord in a progression. Some compositions involve multiple chords per measure while other compositions stay on one chord for multiple measures. The musical examples below demonstrate various possible harmonic rhythms.

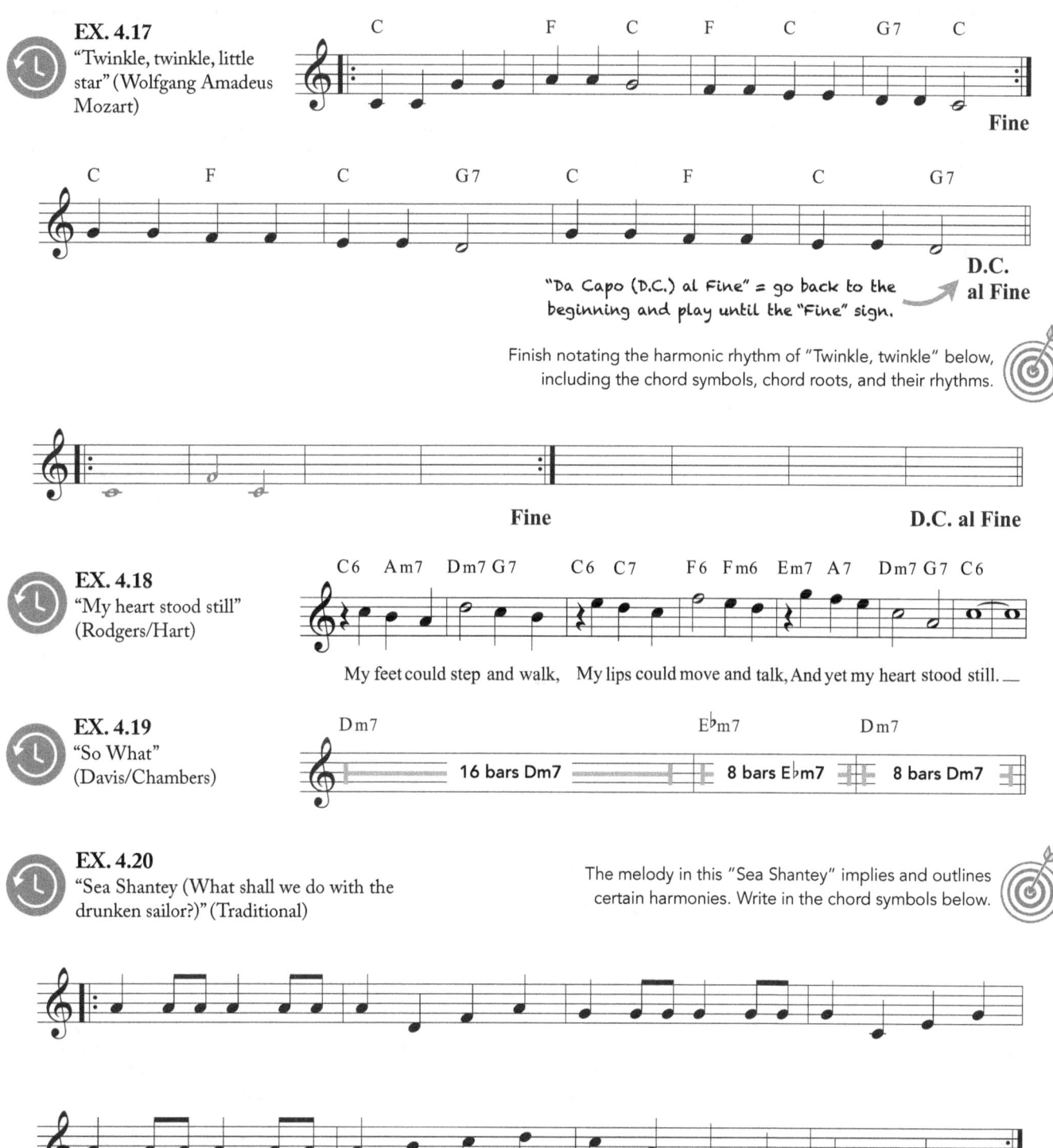

EX. 4.17
"Twinkle, twinkle, little star" (Wolfgang Amadeus Mozart)

"Da Capo (D.C.) al Fine" = go back to the beginning and play until the "Fine" sign.

Finish notating the harmonic rhythm of "Twinkle, twinkle" below, including the chord symbols, chord roots, and their rhythms.

EX. 4.18
"My heart stood still" (Rodgers/Hart)

My feet could step and walk,   My lips could move and talk, And yet my heart stood still. ___

EX. 4.19
"So What" (Davis/Chambers)

16 bars Dm7   8 bars E♭m7   8 bars Dm7

EX. 4.20
"Sea Shantey (What shall we do with the drunken sailor?)" (Traditional)

The melody in this "Sea Shantey" implies and outlines certain harmonies. Write in the chord symbols below.

Lower Fragment + 5th

Lower scale fragments function well in isolation as tetrachords but, when paired with one extra note, the 5th of the scale, even more melodic opportunities are presented. This is largely because scale degree 5 provides a particularly meaningful melodic arrival point. Rhythmically, the addition of one extra note turns the lower fragment plus the 5th into a 5-note phrase, allowing the lower fragment to start and end on a strong beat within 4/4 time.

EX. 4.21
Lower fragment + 5th for the I and ii chords in the key of C Major

EX. 4.22
Lower fragment + 5th exercise (I-ii)

All five notes need not be played. **Notes may be played out of order or removed entirely.** If the 2nd and 4th scale degree are omitted, only chord tones are left (1-3-5).

EX. 4.23
Chord tone exercise (I-ii)

IMPROVISE
Target exercise (I - ii): Improvise using (1) chord tones and passing tones then (2) only chord tones.

Learn how to transpose, considering the lower fragment + 5th for the I and ii chords in the key of D major.

On staff 1, write out the D major scale, circle the scale degrees that are the roots of I & ii chords, and write out the notes of the I & ii chords by stacking the chord tones above scale degrees 1 and 2.

On staff 2, write out 1-2-3-4-5 for both the I & ii chords in D major.

I   ii

I-ii Phrase Transitions

Do you occasionally hear gaps or spaces at the end of phrases? Such gaps are completely natural, typically resulting from either a rest or a long note being placed at the end of a measure. These gaps can be filled with notes that help transition (or connect) to other measures or phrases.

EX. 4.24
Gaps between lower scale fragments

EX. 4.25
Adding transitions (lower scale fragment + 5th)

EX. 4.26
Gaps between lower scale fragments

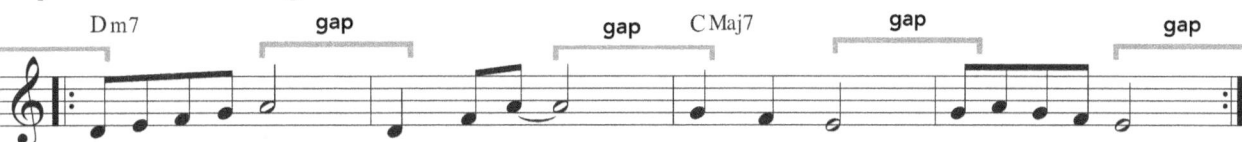

EX. 4.27
Adding transitions (lower scale fragment + 5th)

Scale degrees: chords vs. key

There are two common ways to consider scale degrees: (1) scale degrees may be labeled according to each new chord, which is considered a vertical approach, or (2) scale degrees may also be labeled in terms of the underlying key and parent scale, which is a more linear approach.

What are the **benefits of each approach** to labeling scale degrees?

EX. 4.28
Scale degrees, changing per chord (more vertical)

EX. 4.29
Scale degrees, relating to the C major parent scale/key (more linear)

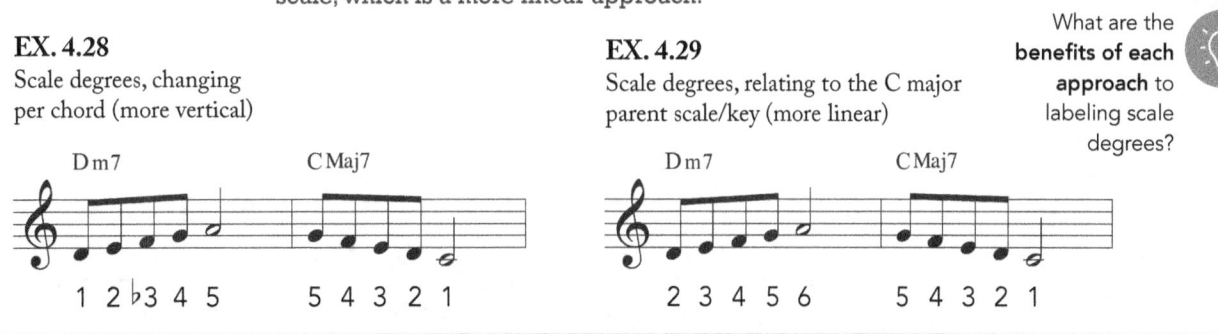

I-ii Upper Fragments

Upper scale fragments within I-ii chords are complex, in part because they offer so many target note options when resolving to the tonic I chord. In the examples below, Dm7 (the ii chord) resolves to CMaj7 (the I chord). The CMaj7 target notes include G, B, and C (scale degrees 5, 7, 1). One common pathway (G-A-B) involves the 7th of Dm7 (the note C) moving to the 7th of CMaj7 (the note B). Another pathway involves the root of Dm7 (the note D) resolving to the root of CMaj7 (the note C). Trace these pathways in all the examples below.

EX. 4.30
D minor upper fragment,
resolving to C major fragments

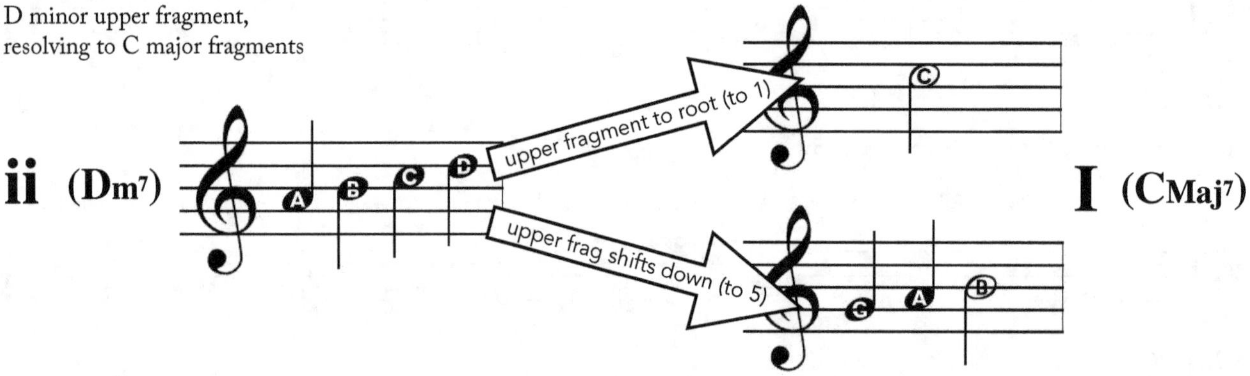

ii (Dm⁷)   **I (CMaj⁷)**

upper fragment to root (to 1)

upper frag shifts down (to 5)

EX. 4.31
Gaps between upper scale fragments

First play the following exercises as written then vary them by adding or changing rhythms.

Dm7   C Maj7

Dm7   C Maj7

EX. 4.32
Chord tone exercise (I - ii)

C Maj7

Dm7

Ultimately, the improviser **need not use all notes** in every fragment. As an example, the notes A and C could be used exclusively across both Dm7 and CMaj7 chords.

I-ii Upper Fragment Exercises

Try improvising with upper scale fragments while also reaching specific pre-determined target notes. Also notice that the one common chord tone between CMaj7 and Dm7 is the note C. How might this common tone affect your approach to improvising between the I and ii chords?

EX. 4.33
Target example (I-ii), upper fragments

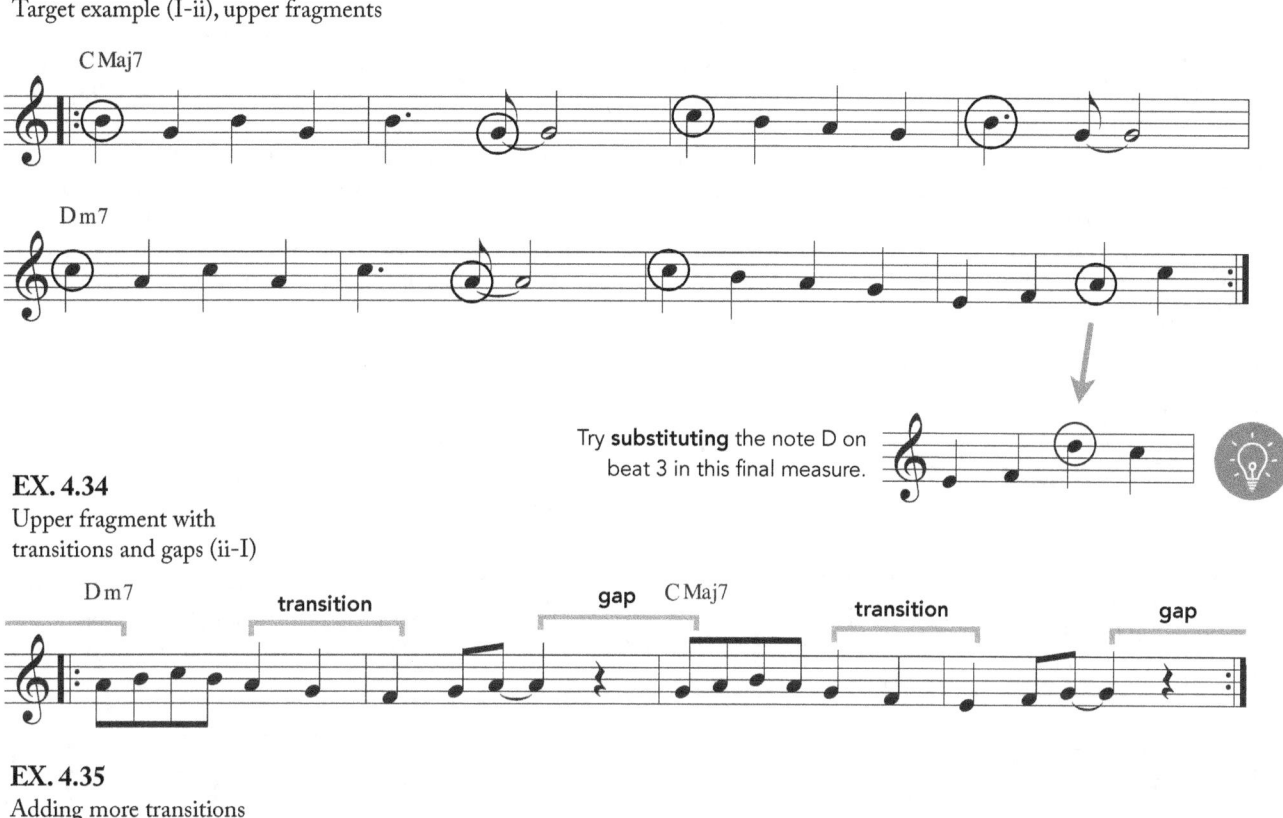

Try **substituting** the note D on beat 3 in this final measure.

EX. 4.34
Upper fragment with transitions and gaps (ii-I)

EX. 4.35
Adding more transitions (upper scale fragments)

Within each measure below, hear and feel the chord on the first beat (beat 1), followed by 3 beats that fill out the rest of the measure (beats 2, 3, 4). Make sure you can feel and hear this at varying tempos.

IMPROVISE
Improvise freely on the I-ii progression below (4 bars each chord). Your goal is to keep your place at all times.

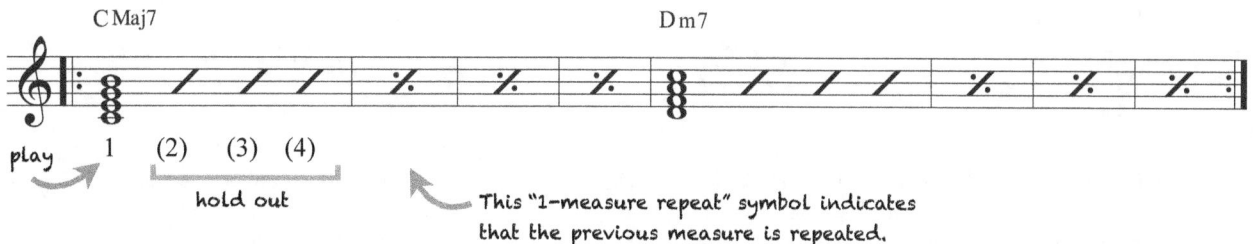

play   1   (2)   (3)   (4)

hold out

This "1-measure repeat" symbol indicates that the previous measure is repeated.

Smackdown! Modal Jazz vs. Tonal Jazz

Mod·al /ˈmōdl/
adjective: **modal**

relating to music that uses diatonic modes but is not governed by functional harmony

Ton·al /ˈtōnl/
adjective: **tonal**

relating to music using conventional keys and functional harmony

Modal jazz

Modal music can be defined based on two elements: (1) a prevalence of harmonies that encourage the **use of modes**, the scales common to the given mode (for example, D Dorian minor scale used over Dm7) and (2) the **absence of a dominant V chord**. Without a clear and present V, modal chord progressions can be enigmatic, not pointing clearly to a particular tonality.

Tonal jazz

Tonal music is governed by a **tonic-dominant** harmonic relationship. The major or minor parent key is established by the dominant V chord, which moves to the tonic I chord. Within the tonality, other harmonies are secondary and supportive of the tonic-dominant. Most classic jazz compositions are tonal although the use of modes is common to both.

EX. 4.36
Modal: minor i vamp (key of D minor)

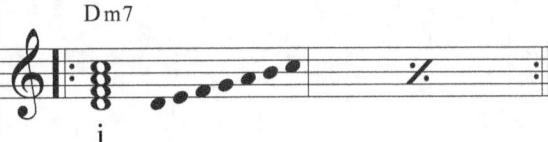

Dm7

i

Dm7 to CMaj7 is an enigmatic modal progression. Is CMaj7 the tonic, or is Dm7 the tonic?

EX. 4.37
Tonal: tonic I to dominant V (key of C major)

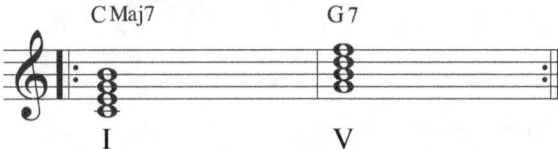

CMaj7   G7

I   V

EX. 4.38
Modal: minor ii to I, key of C major (or minor i to ♭VII, key of D minor)

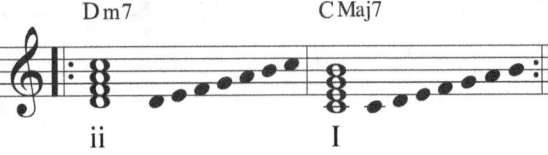

Dm7   CMaj7

ii   I

EX. 4.39
Tonal: ii to V to I (key of C major)

G7, inserted between Dm7 and CMaj7, establishes the C major tonality.

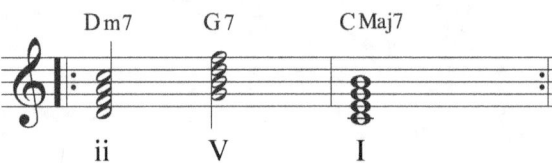

Dm7   G7   CMaj7

ii   V   I

EX. 4.40
Modal: minor i to minor v (key of D minor) (or minor iv to minor i, key of A minor)

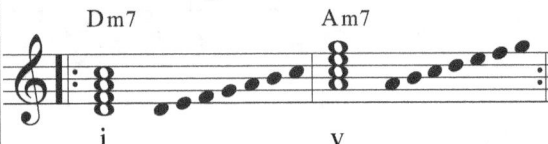

Dm7   Am7

i   v

EX. 4.41
Tonal: minor i to dominant V (key of D minor)

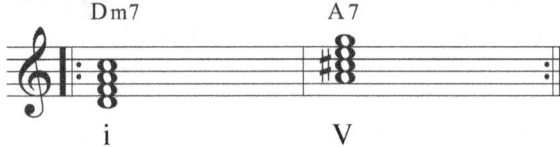

Dm7   A7

i   V

EX. 4.42
Modal: minor i to minor v (key of C minor) (or minor iv to minor i, key of G minor)

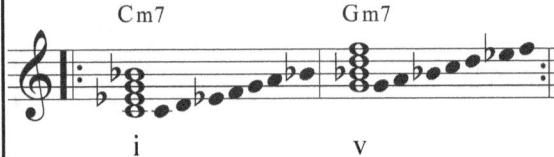

Cm7   Gm7

i   v

EX. 4.43
Tonal: minor i to dominant V (key of C minor)

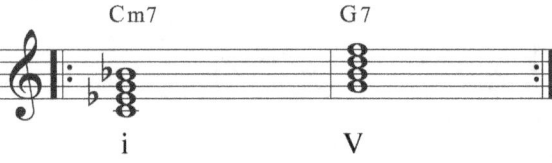

Cm7   G7

i   V

A modal composition still can be considered to be in a *key*. For example, Miles Davis' "So What" is in the **key of D minor** since it is clear that D minor is the tonic.

Study the modal progressions above and notice how each is altered and transformed into a tonal progression.

Diatonic Chord Composition Assignment

When composing your own composition using only diatonic chords, prepare with these steps: (1) know your key and parent scale, (2) review which diatonic chords function as home/release points, and (3) evaluate which function as away/tension points. Also consider your melodic and rhythmic options.

Step 1

Write the parent scale
Choose a major key and notate its parent major scale.

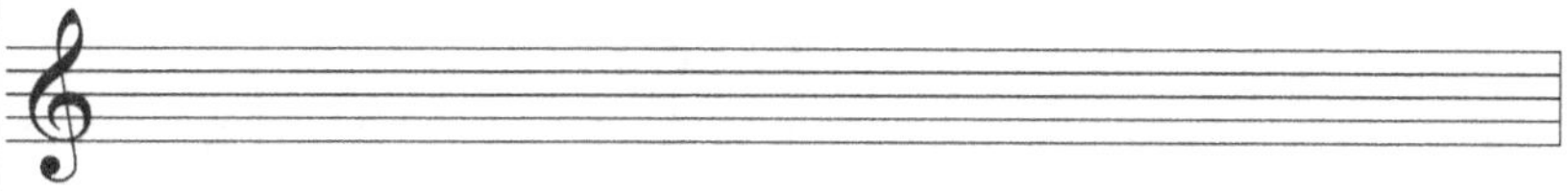

Step 2

Write "home" chords
Write out the chords I, iii, and vi. All provide points of release.

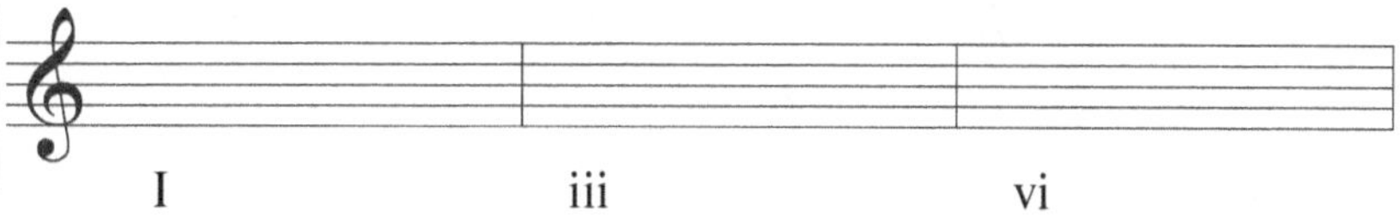

I   iii   vi

Step 3

Write "away" chords
Write out the chords ii, IV, V, and vii°, which all provide points of tension.

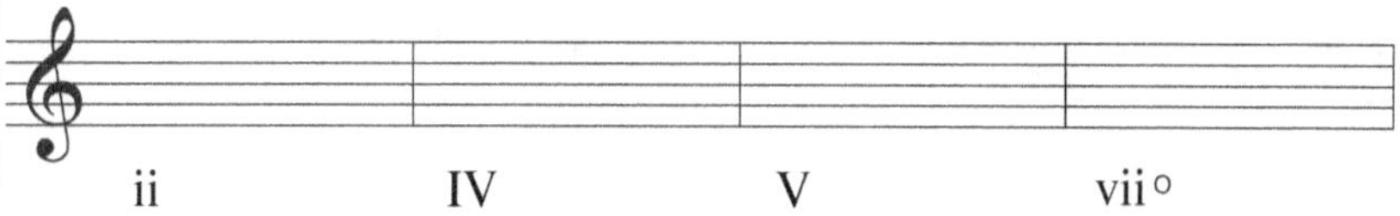

ii   IV   V   vii°

EX. 4.44
Composition example, using only diatonic chords and their chord tones (key of C major)

Study the following composition example, noticing the movement between home/away harmonies in the key of C major.

C   Em7   F   C

I   iii   IV   I

Using only diatonic chords, compose a chord progression and melody in the key of your choice.

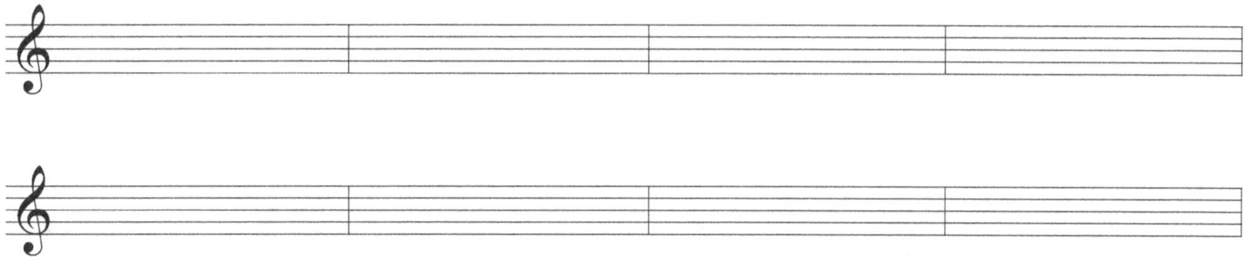

How will you **choose to begin** composing?

- Start with a melody then add chords that match.
- Start with chords then add a matching melody.
- Compose both the chords and melody simultaneously.

Targeted Tension
page 1 of 2

Consider the works of great impressionist painters, especially the way they mixed colors to make line and light interact, all helping to create a dynamic canvas. In music, while chord tone targets are a viable and artistic option, the whole musical canvas allows for more choices. Dissonance increases when a non-chord tone targets a strong beat and such a *targeted tension* may then either move to another dissonance or to a point of resolution and release. Melody need not adhere exactly to harmonic movement, which is nearly always resolved on beat 1. In fact, a targeted tension is often exactly what the music needs most.

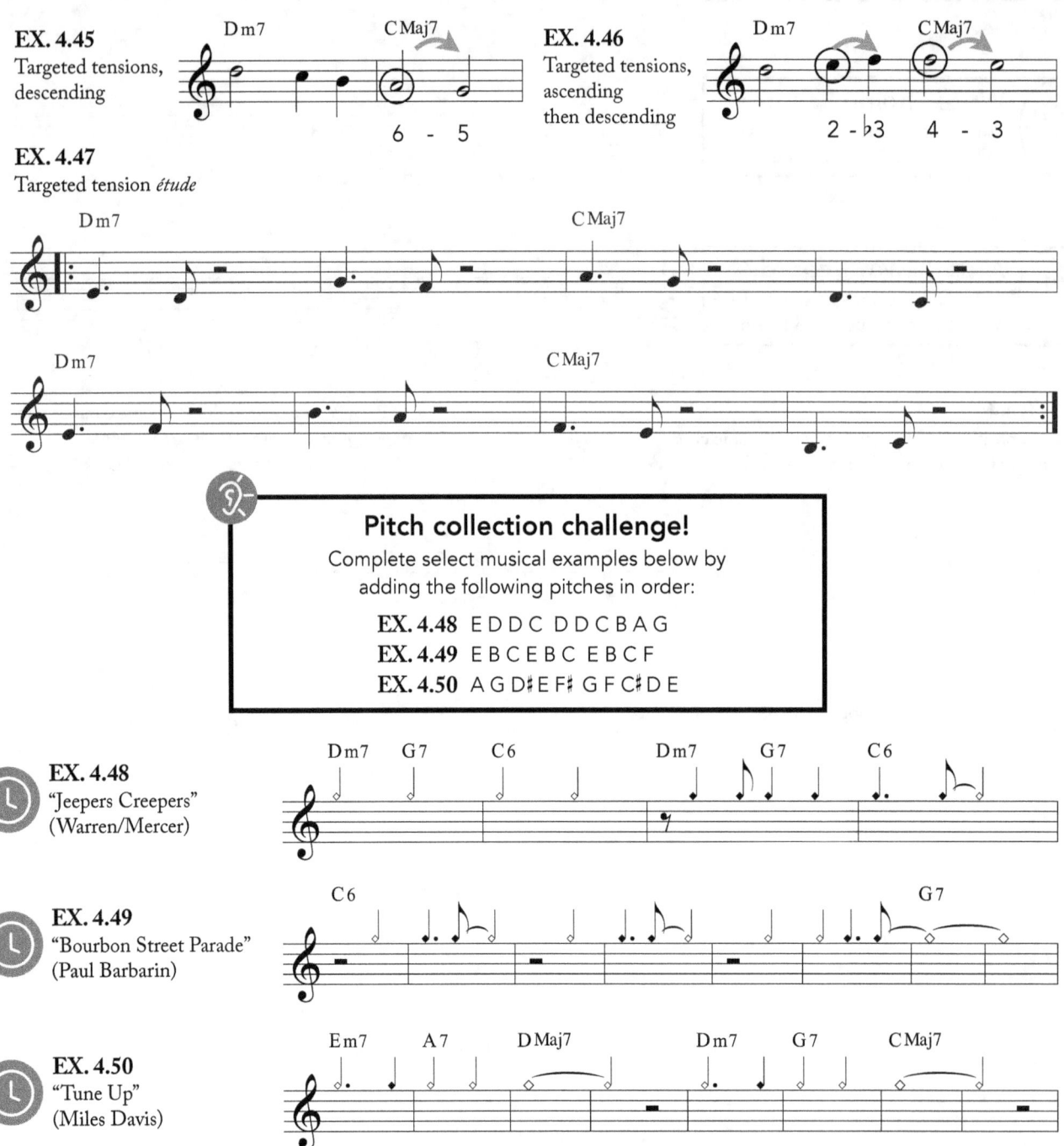

EX. 4.45 Targeted tensions, descending

EX. 4.46 Targeted tensions, ascending then descending

EX. 4.47 Targeted tension *étude*

Pitch collection challenge!
Complete select musical examples below by adding the following pitches in order:

EX. 4.48 E D D C D D C B A G
EX. 4.49 E B C E B C E B C F
EX. 4.50 A G D♯ E F♯ G F C♯ D E

EX. 4.48 "Jeepers Creepers" (Warren/Mercer)

EX. 4.49 "Bourbon Street Parade" (Paul Barbarin)

EX. 4.50 "Tune Up" (Miles Davis)

Targeted Tension
page 2 of 2

The use of targeted tensions can help add color and depth to melody. Characterized by a non-chord tone placed firmly on a downbeat, these tensions eventually resolve, usually within the same measure.

Pitch collection challenge!
Complete select musical examples below by
adding the following pitches in order:

EX. 4.51 G C D D E G C D E♭ F B♭ C C D F B♭ C D♭
EX. 4.52 F♯ G D D C B B♭ G♯ A E E D D♭ C

EX. 4.51
"How High The Moon"
(Lewis/Hamilton)

Draw an arrow connecting each circled
targeted tension to its chord tone
resolution in the following examples.

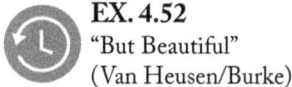

EX. 4.52
"But Beautiful"
(Van Heusen/Burke)

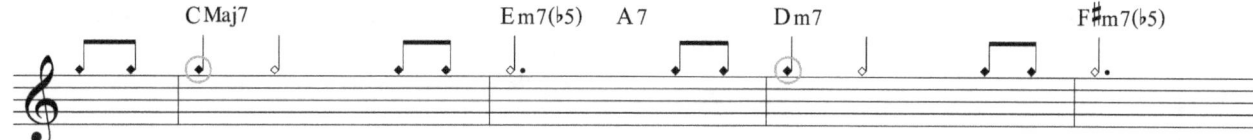

EX. 4.53
John Coltrane tenor sax solo
"All the Things You Are"

To hear targeted tensions clearly, play **whole note
bass chord tone roots** on a piano with the left
hand and the melodic line with the right hand.

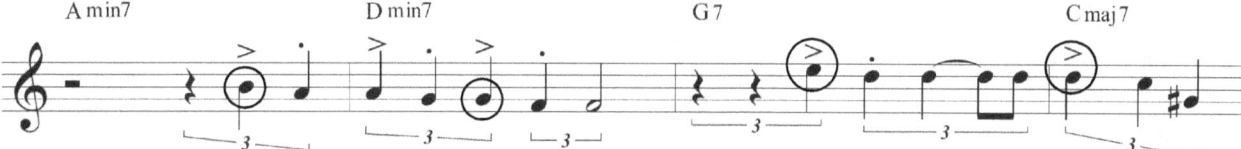

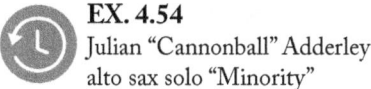

EX. 4.54
Julian "Cannonball" Adderley
alto sax solo "Minority"

Non-Chord Tone Resolutions & Rhythmic Displacement

As the creator of your melodic line, you can determine when or where to place this moment of tension and release. The *non-chord tone* placed on beat 1 can resolve mid-phrase on beat 3, at which point the melodic line may then continue. In the exercises below, the line extends and resolves on the second measure of each phrase. Each final resolution point is circled.

| NCT | non-chord tone tension/dissonance |
| RES | chord tone resolution/consonance |

EX. 4.55
Dorian minor non-chord tone exercise (targets are circled)

Write in the scale degrees for the Dorian minor scale exercise below. Notice how melodic targets are chord tones 1 and 3.

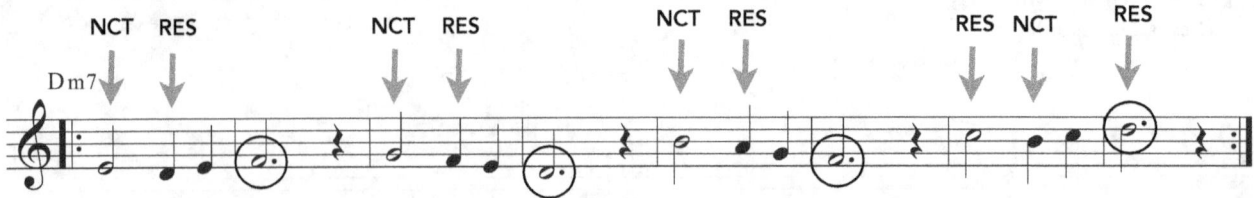

The exercise below uses **rhythmic displacement** to soften the dissonance by resting on beat 1 and placing the non-chord tone on beat 2. The displacement very nearly removes any sign of dissonance since the non-chord tone sounds very much like a passing tone on beat 2, a naturally weak beat.

EX. 4.56
Rhythmic displacement exercise, rest on beat 1, resolve on beat 3

IMPROVISE
Improvise your own rhythms for the melodic line above.
Included below is an example, with some added syncopation.

In a new key of your choice, write out one version of the Dorian minor exercises above. Use your ears and scale degree numbering as two tools in your process.

Appoggiaturas

The more you listen to jazz, the more you'll notice that many of the most memorable melodies use more than just chord tones on strong beats. Placing a non-chord tone on a strong beat adds extra tension while embellishing the melodic line. A common embellishment, called an *appoggiatura*, originated long ago as a non-chord tone placed on a strong beat, usually preceded by skip or leap and followed by stepwise resolution to a chord tone. It is sometimes defined as simply any non-chord tone placed on a downbeat, followed by a stepwise resolution to a chord tone.

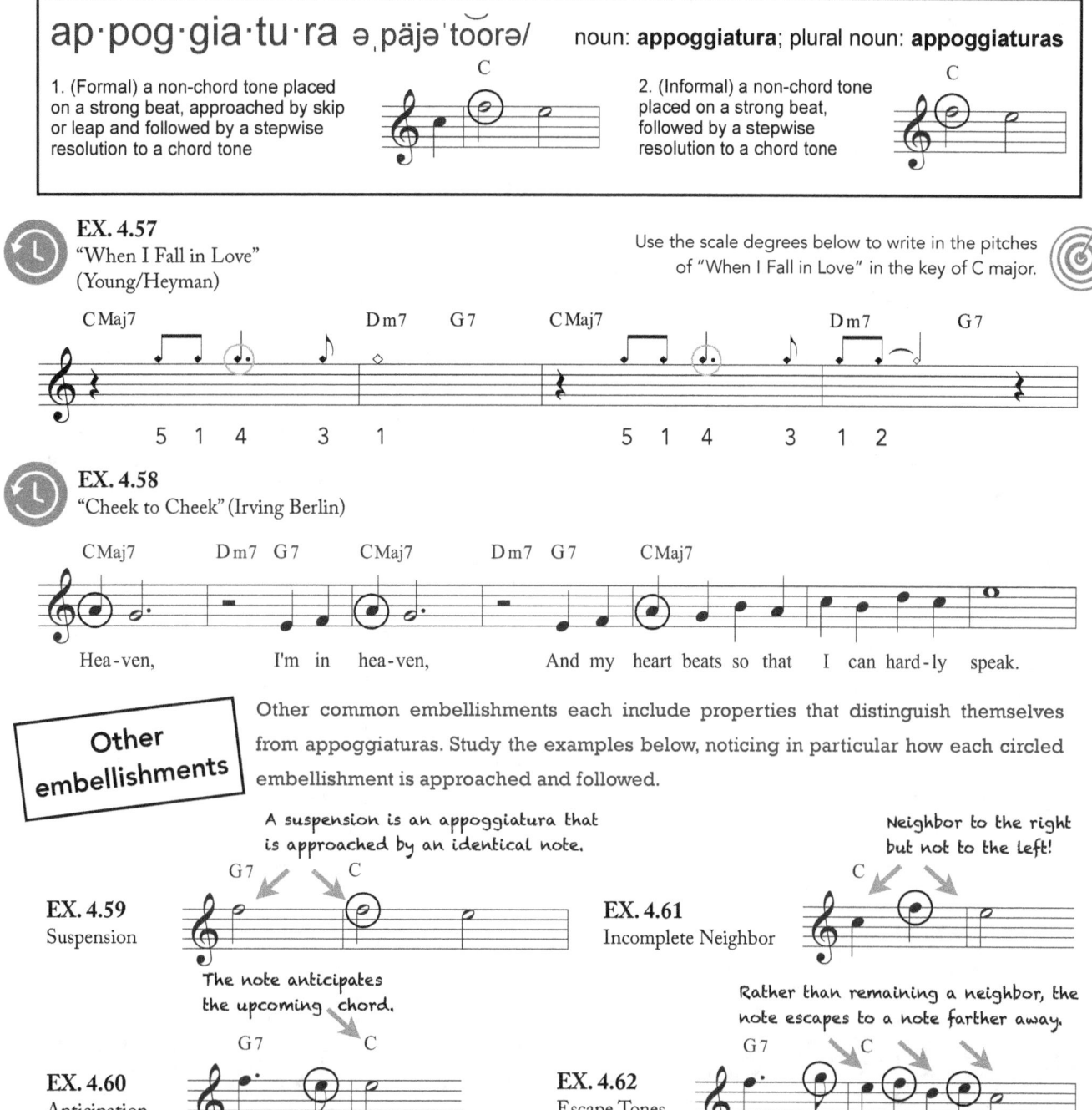

ap·pog·gia·tu·ra ə͵päjə'tŏŏrə/   noun: **appoggiatura**; plural noun: **appoggiaturas**

1. (Formal) a non-chord tone placed on a strong beat, approached by skip or leap and followed by a stepwise resolution to a chord tone

2. (Informal) a non-chord tone placed on a strong beat, followed by a stepwise resolution to a chord tone

EX. 4.57
"When I Fall in Love"
(Young/Heyman)

Use the scale degrees below to write in the pitches of "When I Fall in Love" in the key of C major.

5 1 4   3   1   5 1 4   3   1 2

EX. 4.58
"Cheek to Cheek" (Irving Berlin)

Hea-ven,   I'm in hea-ven,   And my heart beats so that   I can hard-ly   speak.

Other embellishments

Other common embellishments each include properties that distinguish themselves from appoggiaturas. Study the examples below, noticing in particular how each circled embellishment is approached and followed.

A suspension is an appoggiatura that is approached by an identical note.

Neighbor to the right but not to the left!

EX. 4.59
Suspension

EX. 4.61
Incomplete Neighbor

The note anticipates the upcoming chord.

Rather than remaining a neighbor, the note escapes to a note farther away.

EX. 4.60
Anticipation

EX. 4.62
Escape Tones

Parallel Motion and Contrary Motion

Two voices interact in one of three ways: (1) they move in the same direction, in *parallel motion*, (2) they move in opposite directions, in *contrary motion*, or (3) one (or both) remains *stationary* and does not move at all. When improvising, choosing to move in contrary motion from the root movement of a chord can often create more interest but simply choosing how to move — whether parallel, contrary, or stationary — will help give the melodic line greater definition and purpose. Below are examples of parallel and contrary melodic movements.

EX. 4.63
CMaj7 arpeggios in parallel
then contrary motion

EX. 4.64
Diatonic patterns in parallel
then contrary motion

EX. 4.65
Parallel thirds

EX. 4.66
Parallel tenths

Parallel fifths — two voices moving in the same direction while separated by a perfect fifth interval — are rarely used when composing multi-part harmony. When parallel fifths occur between two voices, the second voice sounds almost identical to the first voice, leading the ear to suddenly hear both voices as one. A solution that allows the two voices to continue as separate interacting entities is to avoid parallel fifths altogether and aim for an alternative, including contrary motion or parallel tenths. Parallel fifths can nevertheless be used to great artistic effect in blues, pop, and rock genres, where many find the sound attractive.

Parallel fifths

EX. 4.67
Blues V to IV chord
(key of C major)

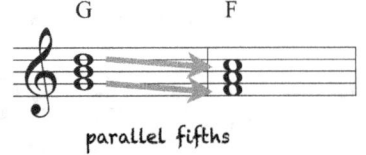

EX. 4.68
Rock power chords

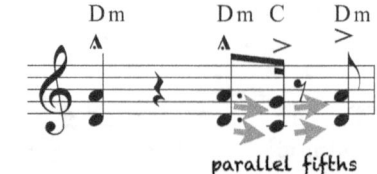

Sequence and the Rule of Three

A melodic phrase that repeats and moves up or down in its entirety is called a *sequence*. Ubiquitous in both composition and improvisation, sequences provide familiarity via this repetition while also adding momentum and thematic interest to melodic development.

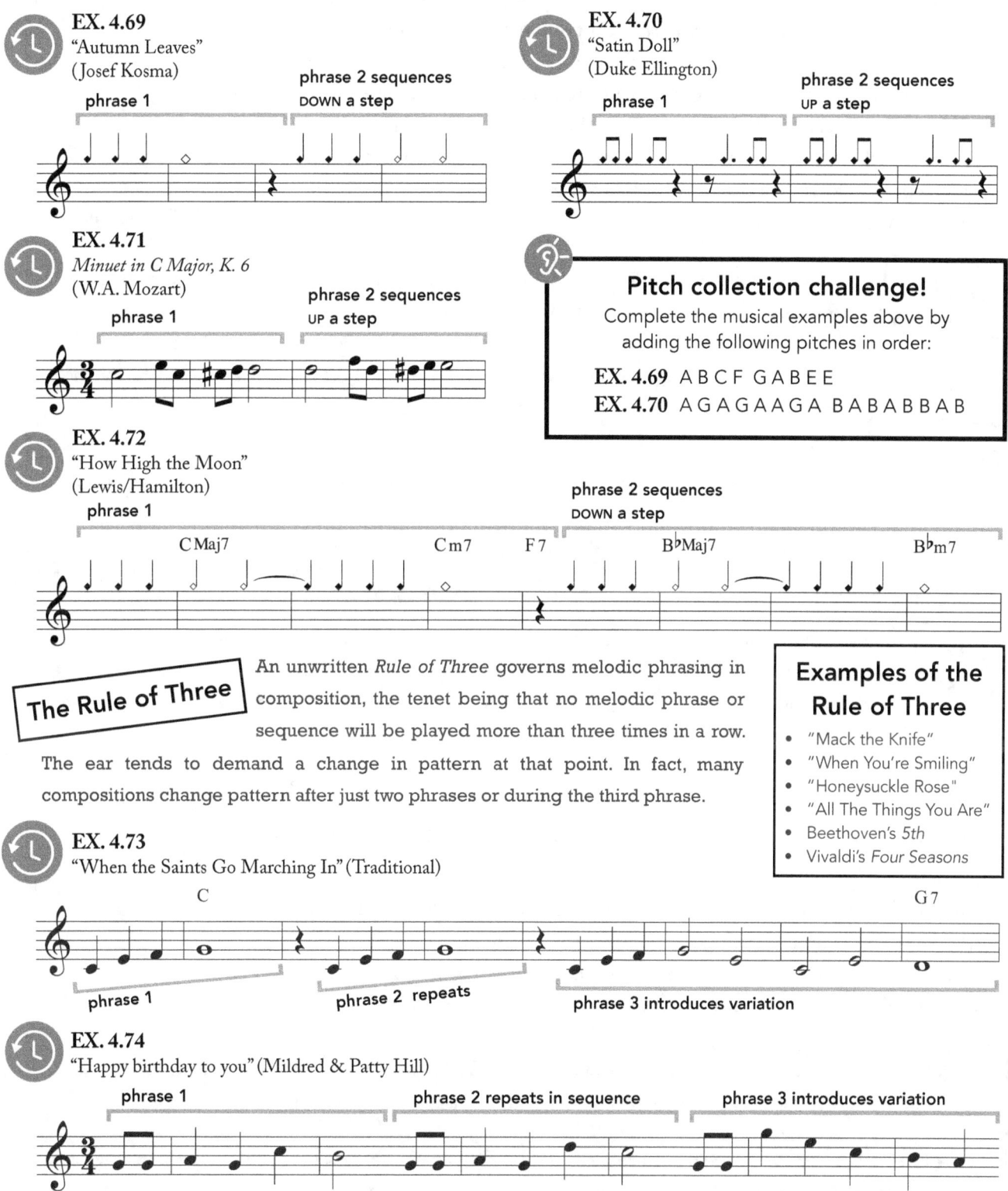

EX. 4.69
"Autumn Leaves"
(Josef Kosma)

phrase 2 sequences DOWN a step

phrase 1

EX. 4.70
"Satin Doll"
(Duke Ellington)

phrase 2 sequences UP a step

phrase 1

EX. 4.71
Minuet in C Major, K. 6
(W.A. Mozart)

phrase 2 sequences UP a step

phrase 1

Pitch collection challenge!

Complete the musical examples above by adding the following pitches in order:

EX. 4.69 A B C F G A B E E

EX. 4.70 A G A G A A G A   B A B A B B A B

EX. 4.72
"How High the Moon"
(Lewis/Hamilton)

phrase 2 sequences DOWN a step

phrase 1

C Maj7   Cm7   F 7   B♭Maj7   B♭m7

The Rule of Three

An unwritten *Rule of Three* governs melodic phrasing in composition, the tenet being that no melodic phrase or sequence will be played more than three times in a row.

The ear tends to demand a change in pattern at that point. In fact, many compositions change pattern after just two phrases or during the third phrase.

Examples of the Rule of Three

- "Mack the Knife"
- "When You're Smiling"
- "Honeysuckle Rose"
- "All The Things You Are"
- Beethoven's *5th*
- Vivaldi's *Four Seasons*

EX. 4.73
"When the Saints Go Marching In" (Traditional)

C   G 7

phrase 1   phrase 2 repeats   phrase 3 introduces variation

EX. 4.74
"Happy birthday to you" (Mildred & Patty Hill)

phrase 1   phrase 2 repeats in sequence   phrase 3 introduces variation

Masterclass   Practical Interpretation
page 1 of 2
of a Lead Sheet

When working out most short-form jazz compositions, players are either rehearsing and performing by ear or from a lead sheet. Every musician tends to be handed the same *lead sheet*, containing not much more than a single staff (usually in treble clef) with the song melody, sometimes the lyrics, and usually a chord progression printed directly above. In any jazz band, each musician's role in interpreting the composition is vital. Check out how each member of a small jazz group typically functions over the same repeated four measures in the following examples. How does your part fit in with the ensemble?

"Oh, lady be good!" lead sheet

What ALL PLAYERS see and hear

In the example below, *all players* follows the specific form of four repeated measures and most players tend to adhere to the given chord progression, albeit with some artistic variation. The slash notation, while not commonly included in a lead sheet, indicates that each player may hear and interpret the lead sheet in a different way, as the remaining examples illustrate.

EX. 4.75
The chord progression that ALL PLAYERS hear and see

Slash notation tends to be included in lead sheets at times when there is no specific composed melody. It is also common in big band parts, indicating specifically where a player should improvise.

What the SOLOIST plays

Soloists follow the chord progression and create a melodic and rhythm line entirely from their own imaginations. Soloists can elevate the artistic quality by listening carefully to the entire ensemble, making solo statements that speak with immediacy and relevance to the whole ensemble's performance.

EX. 4.76
Billy Tipton piano solo "Perdido"

What gets added to a lead sheet ARRANGEMENT

The following elements can transform a simple lead sheet into a more complete and full *arrangement*. Although they can be added in rehearsal, the *intro*, *interlude*, *backgrounds*, and *tag* are often added spontaneously during performance. With experience, musicians know how to communicate these details on the bandstand.

• **INTRO** typically four measures played by the rhythm section before the melody begins.

• **BACKGROUNDS** typically played by horns behind any soloist, lasting no longer than one chorus.

• **INTERLUDE** a melody added in between soloists to help break up the stream of solos.

• **TAG** typically 2-4 measures added to help end the song, usually involving repeating two of the last four bars.

Masterclass   Practical Interpretation
page 2 of 2
of a Lead Sheet

The role of rhythm section players is particularly complex in jazz. The frontline soloist, whether the vocalist or horn player, typically must perform the melody, the *head*, and then improvise a solo at some point. The rhythm section, including the pianist, guitarist, bassist, and drummer, must first offer a foundation for the head and then support every soloist throughout the performance.

What the PIANIST or GUITARIST plays

The chordal musician — *pianist* or *guitarist* — *comps* behind the soloist, actually complementing the soloist's ideas. The simple chords below show the voicings that a pianist might comp. A guitarist or pianist might choose voicings that are less tertiary in concept as combinations of thirds and fourths are particularly idiomatic on the guitar. The rhythms played are carefully chosen, potentially including combinations of rests, accents, and syncopations.

EX. 4.77
What the PIANIST plays
(sample comping phrase)

In an ensemble with both a pianist and guitarist, the two instruments **do not usually comp at the same time**. When comping at the same time, the patterns should be complementary although this can be confusing for the soloist.

What the BASSIST plays

The bassist's role changes depending on style. Sometimes the bassist plays a fixed bass line but quite often the bassist plays a *walking bass line* (presented below in bass clef of course!). When the bassist walks, the line tends to outline the given harmony and is played in quarter notes. There are exceptions to the rhythmic structure and certainly a bassist might take risks, adding to the harmonic depth of the piece.

EX. 4.78
What the BASSIST plays
(sample walking bass line)

The *drummer* is not the only time-keeper in the band. In fact, the role of time-keeper should be shared by every musician in a performance, ensuring that good music has good time. Fundamentally, the drummer provides a rhythmic foundation, syncing up with the bassist, very commonly building a swing foundation from quarter notes on the ride cymbal, *feathering* the bass drum, using the snare drum (S.D.) and toms for occasional fills and accents, and keeping a hi-hat cymbal pair (H.H.) on beats 2 and 4.

EX. 4.79
What the DRUMMER plays
(sample swing pattern)

Investigate   Chord Inversions

A chord may be voiced in root position, starting with 1 on the bottom, but chord tones also can be ordered in any formation. *Chord inversions* are identified according to which chord tone is placed on the bottom. Improvisers tend to invert chords freely even when the chord symbol suggests root position.

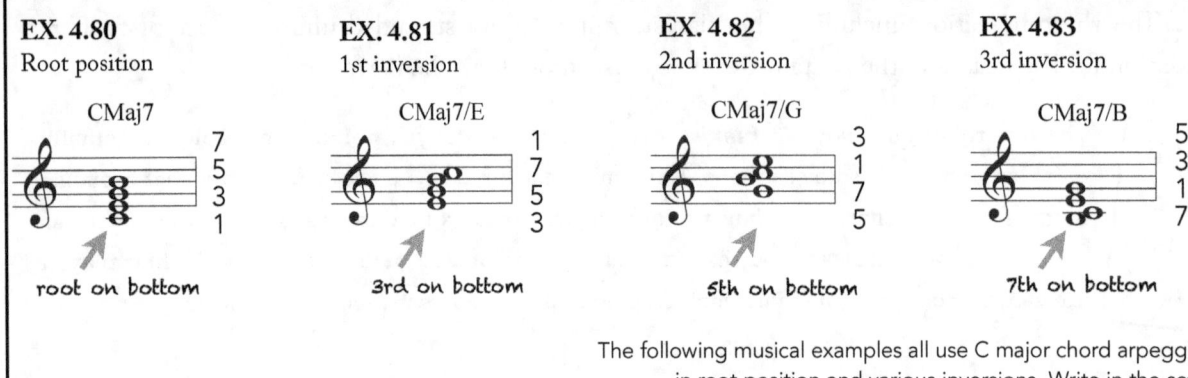

EX. 4.80
Root position

CMaj7

root on bottom

EX. 4.81
1st inversion

CMaj7/E

3rd on bottom

EX. 4.82
2nd inversion

CMaj7/G

5th on bottom

EX. 4.83
3rd inversion

CMaj7/B

7th on bottom

The following musical examples all use C major chord arpeggios in root position and various inversions. Write in the scale degrees for each example and notice the inversion for each.

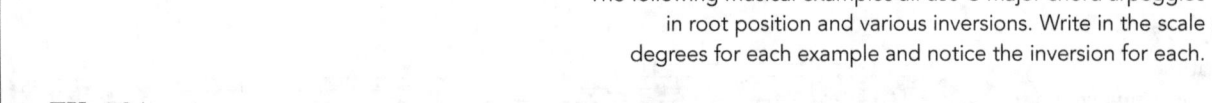

EX. 4.84
"Michael, row the boat ashore" (Traditional)

Mic-hael row the boat

EX. 4.85
"The Star-Spangled Banner" (Key/Smith)

Oh__ say can you see

EX. 4.86
"Amazing Grace" (Traditional)

A - maz - ing grace

EX. 4.87
"Goodnight, ladies" (Edwin Pearce Christy)

Good - night   lad - ies

EX. 4.88
"When You're Smiling" (Shay/Fisher/Goodwin)

When you're smil - ing

EX. 4.89
"Struttin' with Some Barbecue" (Lil Hardin Armstrong)

Struttin' with some barbecue

Slash chords vs. polychords

A *slash chord*, written with a diagonal slash (/), indicates a chord with a specific note in the bass. The bass note can be a chord tone or non-chord tone. A *polychord*, written with a horizontal line (—), indicates two chords stacked on top of each other.

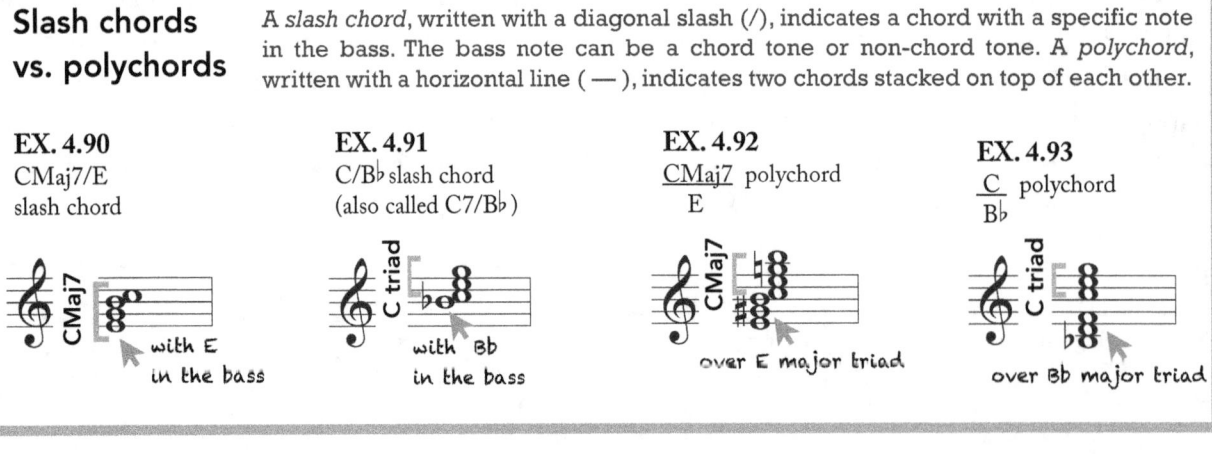

EX. 4.90
CMaj7/E
slash chord

with E
in the bass

EX. 4.91
C/B♭ slash chord
(also called C7/B♭)

with B♭
in the bass

EX. 4.92
CMaj7 polychord
E

over E major triad

EX. 4.93
C polychord
B♭

over B♭ major triad

Solo 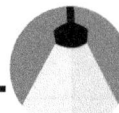 Spotlight

Peggy Lee, vocals · Miles Davis, trumpet
Lee Konitz, alto sax "Bye Bye Blackbird"

Like most jazz classics, "Bye Bye Blackbird" is rarely played exactly the way the rhythms are printed on a lead sheet. Compare versions by Peggy Lee and Miles Davis, both of whom change the rhythm considerably, adding a variety of syncopations. Lee Konitz completely alters the melody in moments too, adding a layer of surprise. Even when performing the melody, all three artists blur the lines between head and improvised solo.

 EX. 4.94
Peggy Lee vocals "Bye Bye Blackbird"

Write in all the rhythmic counts in each version below.
The first two measures' counts are already written.

 EX. 4.95
Miles Davis trumpet "Bye Bye Blackbird"

 EX. 4.96
Lee Konitz alto sax "Bye Bye Blackbird"

Trust your ear and try basing your
own solo off the song melody.

Transpose all three versions above
to three new keys of your choice.

Song Study   "Bye Bye Blackbird"

— page 1 of 2 —

"Bye Bye Blackbird" is widely performed and recorded in jazz circles, engaging and effective at multiple tempos, from slow swing to fast bebop. Its melody is filled with targeted tensions and appoggiaturas placed in nearly every bar. Its form is 32-bar ABA; the first A covering an extended 16 measures.

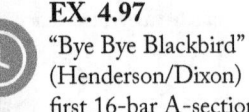

EX. 4.97
"Bye Bye Blackbird"
(Henderson/Dixon)
first 16-bar A-section

Musicians frequently **change the chords** in "Bye Bye Blackbird," to the point where there is no definitive version of the song. A great way to learn how to add variations is to listen to different versions played by jazz greats.

Geometric shifts

"Bye Bye Blackbird" shifts from the I chord to the ii chord, much as if each harmony were on a separate *geometric plane*. The exact moment for this shift is enigmatic though. A ii chord is introduced in measures 2 and 4 but those ii chord occurrences are fleeting and the actual geometric shift to ii7 does not occur until measure 7, followed by a more defined shift up in measure 9. This is reinforced by a melodic shift in bar 9, the melody sequencing up a step. The shift back down to the I chord occurs at measure 15, giving the A-section complete resolution.

EX. 4.98
Geometric shifts,
"Bye Bye Blackbird" A-section

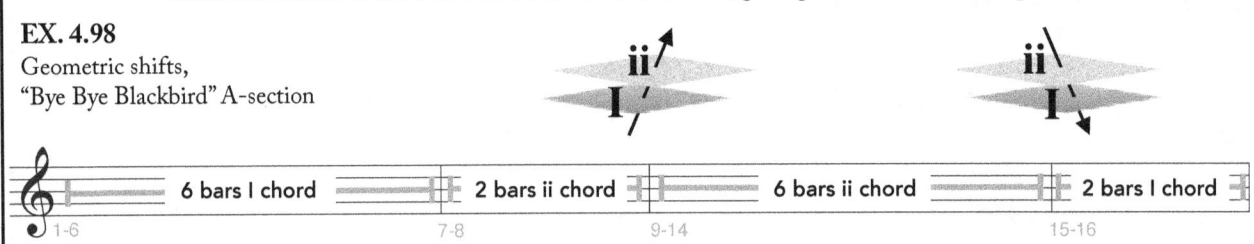

I to ii is a very common harmonic shift. Check out "When You're Smiling" as another example of this movement back and forth from the I to the ii chord.

While the above illustration of I-ii chord geometric shifts is helpful for internalizing harmonic movement and rhythm, it is **a gross simplification**. A deeper understanding of all other harmonic details here is also essential.

Song Study — "Bye Bye Blackbird"

page 2 of 2

The B-section, or bridge, of "Bye Bye Blackbird" is eight measures long and largely alters some diatonic chords. Using a simple approach for learning each bridge harmony, consider which accidentals are added to the parent major scale. For example, learn the chord tones for the first chord of the bridge — Em7(♭5) — then use the C major scale, changing the 7th scale degree to B-flat.

EX. 4.99
"Bye Bye Blackbird" (Henderson/Dixon)
8-bar B-section (bars 17-24)

New improvisers might want to skip the bridge of "Bye Bye Blackbird," which is not easy! Take time to **learn the details and be patient.**

EX. 4.100
Select B-section harmonies:
chord, arpeggio, scale (altered from C major)

The above chords are variants of diatonic chords since they include some **chromatic chord tones.**

Em7(♭5) looks complex but it simply uses the C major scale with a Bb.

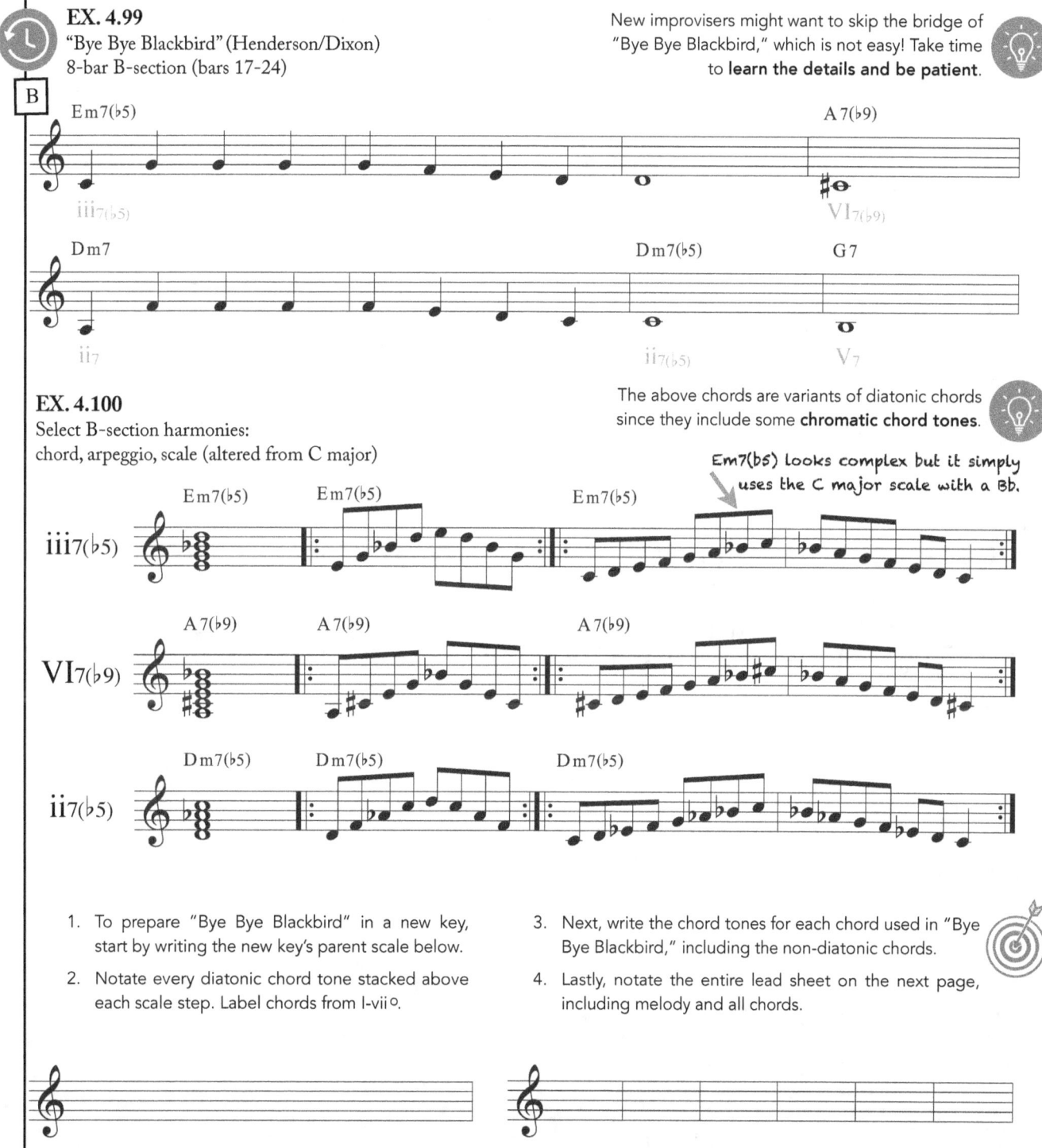

1. To prepare "Bye Bye Blackbird" in a new key, start by writing the new key's parent scale below.

2. Notate every diatonic chord tone stacked above each scale step. Label chords from I-vii°.

3. Next, write the chord tones for each chord used in "Bye Bye Blackbird," including the non-diatonic chords.

4. Lastly, notate the entire lead sheet on the next page, including melody and all chords.

I_{Maj7} ii_7 V_7 $iii_{7(♭5)}$ $VI_{7(♭9)}$ $ii_{7(♭5)}$

Improvise   "Bye Bye Blackbird"

Create a "Bye Bye Blackbird" lead sheet in a new key by notating the melody and chords below. Then improvise in the new key over the first 16 bars of the form. For an added challenge, include bars 17-32, improvising over the entire 32-bar form. Use historical recordings for helpful reference. Repeat the first 16 bars, the full 32 bars, or any smaller sections of the form while improvising.

IMPROVISE
"Bye Bye Blackbird" (bars 1-16)
(Henderson/Dixon)

To keep it even simpler, **improvise only on the first 16 bars**. Remove the iii and VI chords, replacing measure 6 with the I chord and measure 10 with the ii chord. This creates more of a folk/children's music sound, making for an easier entry point for improvisation and harmonic study.

IMPROVISE
"Bye Bye Blackbird" (bars 17-32)
(Henderson/Dixon)

The last A-section, bars 25-32, is quite **similar to the opening A-section** and should be learned and notated by ear.

Zen Jazz Master says:

Tell a story!

One way to build a dynamic and memorable solo is to think of yourself as a storyteller. These are some of the basic elements that shape any good story along with suggestions for conveying them in a solo.

Setting/Mood...

Start your solo by setting a mood. Perhaps slow and mysterious or quick and jumpy.

Characters...

Introduce a couple of contrasting ideas. Maybe one low line and one medium-range line.

Plot...

Now is the time to develop each of your characters. Are the lines going to get more intricate?
Or perhaps the rhythm will evolve from slow and lyrical to something more punctuated.

Conflict...

If you can keep track of the characters you have introduced (easier said than done!), you could try pitting them against each other (maybe a battle between the low line and the medium-range line).

Climax...

You'll probably want to save something for the high point
which could be higher, faster, or louder than the rest of the solo
(although a traditional high point is not always needed for every story).

Resolution...

Saving some time to wind down can be a really good idea.
A wind down might take a couple measures, a final A-section, or maybe even longer.

Chapter 4 Achievements

Congratulations!

You are one step closer to jazz nirvana.

Here is a partial list of what you've achieved:

- Hearing the difference between a "home" chord and an "away" chord
- Visualizing the I and ii chord in a key as being on two different geometric planes
- Using scale fragments while improvising over a 2-chord harmonic progression
- Distinguishing between gaps and transitions while improvising between two chords
- Creating temporary moments of tension and release within your melodic line with suspensions and appoggiaturas
- Understanding differences between parallel and contrary motion

Are you ready for the next chapter?

Answer these questions to determine whether you are prepared to continue to the next chapter:

- **Do you understand** the difference between major and Dorian minor scale fragments, and can you change scale fragments while improvising over simple I-ii chord progressions?

  If "Yes," move to the next chapter.
  If "No," review this chapter.

- **Can you hear the difference between** most non-chord tones and chord tones within the I chord and ii chord?

  If "Yes," move to the next chapter.
  If "No," review this chapter.

- **Do you want** to learn about the most pervasive and perhaps most significant harmonic pairing in all of music?

  If "Yes," move to the next chapter.
  If "No," you have two choices: (1) move to the next chapter anyway and see what piques your interest, or (2) quit now and never be able to play more than major and Dorian, you noodler!

5 Leaps and Bounds
Dominant Harmony, Cadences, and Major Pentatonics

There is an old story of a nobleman who used a live string quartet as his alarm clock. Every morning, the quartet would play a C major scale, starting on C and progressing all the way up to B. The nobleman would so badly need to hear the scale resolve that he would leap out of bed and race to his piano, breathing a sigh of relief only after he had pounded out that high C, thus resolving the scale. There is such a gravitational pull from the leading tone B to tonic C that the tension is palpable. This oppositional force also dominates tonal harmony, particularly the relationship between the dominant V and tonic I chords. An understanding of dominant harmony helps lead to an exploration of phrase endings and cadences. This chapter also delves into the major pentatonic scale, a ubiquitous melodic entity that proves immensely valuable across multiple musical genres.

— Contents —

TOPICS
- Dominant V_7 Harmony
- V_7-I Scale Fragments
- The ii and V_7 chord share two chord tones
- V_7-I Scale Fragment Exercise
- V_7-I Melodic Transitions
- Cadences
- Phrase Pairings (Antecedent/Consequent)
- V_7-I Details and Intent
- Is the 7th really a functional chord tone?
- Verse vs. Chorus
- The Major Pentatonic Scale
- Digital Patterns
- Major Pentatonic Scale Patterns
- Tempo Slider
- Major Pentatonic Scale Manipulation
- Major Pentatonic Scale Examples
- Pedal Points

EAR TRAINING
- Sing I-V chord tone roots
- Rhythmic Chord Tone Exercise
- "My Girl" Guitar Riff in 12 Keys
- Learn "Limbo Jazz" by ear

MASTERCLASS
- Quartal Harmony
- Tertiary vs. Quartal Harmony

INVESTIGATE
- Overtones

SONG STUDY
- "Iko Iko" (Traditional)
- "Limbo Jazz" (Duke Ellington)

HISTORICAL EXAMPLES
- "Going Home" Theme From *New World Symphony* (Antonin Dvořák)
- "It's only a paper moon" (Arlen/Rose/Harburg)
- "The water is wide" (Traditional)
- John Coltrane tenor sax solo "Giant Steps"
- "My Girl" Guitar Riff
- "Old MacDonald had a farm" (Traditional)
- "Cherokee" (Ray Noble)
- Illinois Jacquet tenor sax solo "Flying Home"
- Johnny Griffin tenor sax solo "Autumn Leaves"

SOLO SPOTLIGHT
- Louis Armstrong trumpet solo "When the Saints Go Marching in"
- J.C. Higginbotham trombone solo "When the Saints Go Marching in"
- Johnny Hodges alto sax solo "Limbo Jazz"
- Ray Nance cornet solo "Limbo Jazz"

IMPROVISE
- V-I Target Notes
- "Iko Iko" (Traditional)
- Digital Patterns over ii-V-I
- Major Pentatonic Scale over I-IV
- Pedal Point Improvisation over ii-V-I
- "Limbo Jazz" (Duke Ellington)

LISTENING GUIDE
- Songs with Half Cadences
- "Iko Iko"
- "Limbo Jazz"

ZEN JAZZ MASTER SAYS
- Stay in charge!

Dominant V₇ Harmony

— page 1 of 2 —

Every chord built on each note in a major key's parent scale functions in a specific way. These chords are diatonic since they include only notes within a particular key, each labeled with a Roman numeral, from I through vii. The V chord is termed "dominant" in part because it so effectively dominates the tonal landscape, calling clearly for a resolution, a return "home" to the the tonic I chord. A firm grasp of these two harmonies — *dominant* and *tonic* — is fundamental to understanding every other harmony in music. Their relationship is that significant!

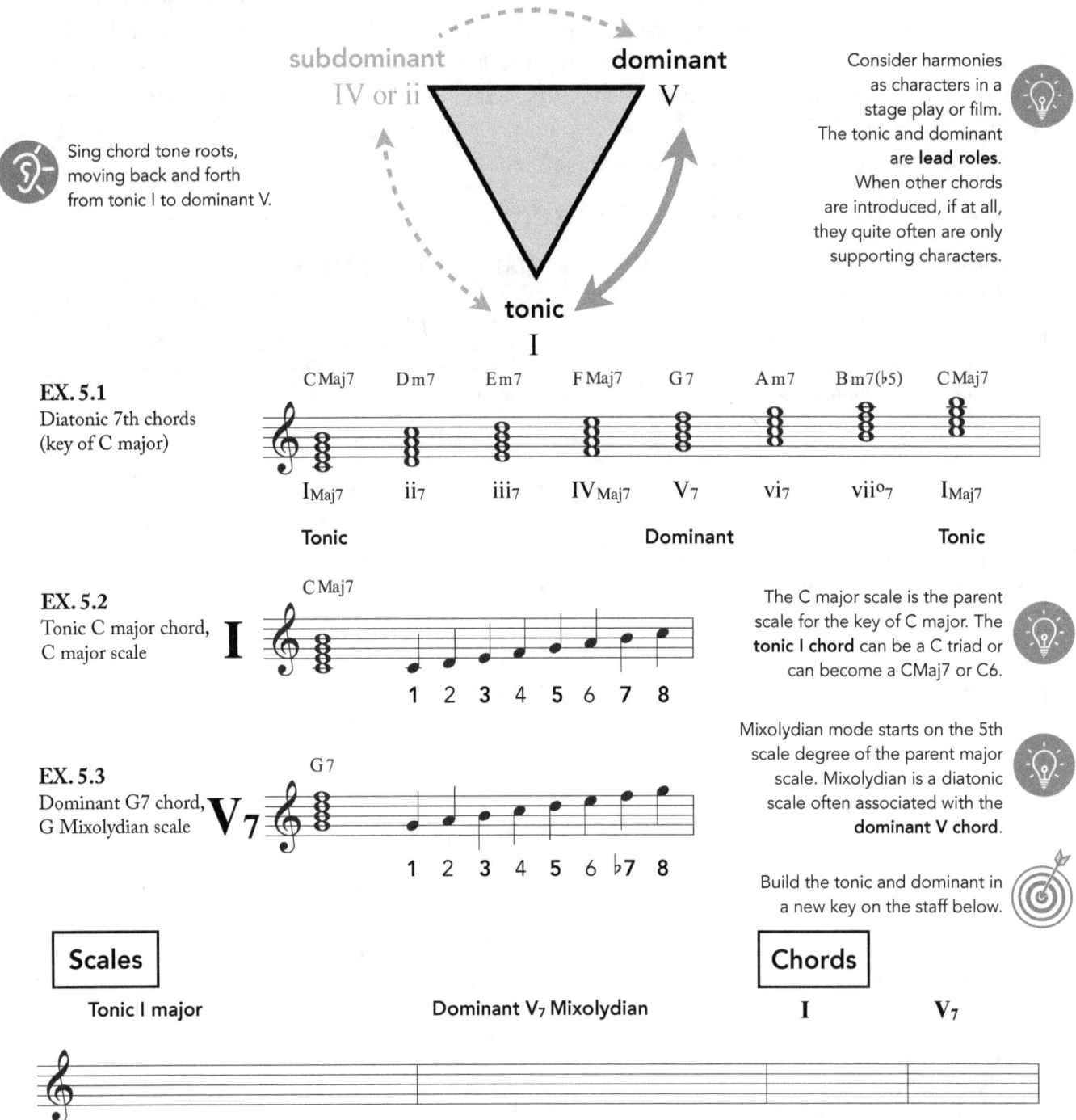

Sing chord tone roots, moving back and forth from tonic I to dominant V.

Consider harmonies as characters in a stage play or film. The tonic and dominant are **lead roles**. When other chords are introduced, if at all, they quite often are only supporting characters.

EX. 5.1
Diatonic 7th chords
(key of C major)

CMaj7   Dm7   Em7   FMaj7   G7   Am7   Bm7(♭5)   CMaj7

I Maj7   ii₇   iii₇   IV Maj7   V₇   vi₇   vii°₇   I Maj7

Tonic   **Dominant**   **Tonic**

EX. 5.2
Tonic C major chord,
C major scale

I   CMaj7

1 2 3 4 5 6 7 8

The C major scale is the parent scale for the key of C major. The **tonic I chord** can be a C triad or can become a CMaj7 or C6.

EX. 5.3
Dominant G7 chord,
G Mixolydian scale

V₇   G7

1 2 3 4 5 6 ♭7 8

Mixolydian mode starts on the 5th scale degree of the parent major scale. Mixolydian is a diatonic scale often associated with the **dominant V chord**.

Build the tonic and dominant in a new key on the staff below.

Scales

Tonic I major   Dominant V₇ Mixolydian

Chords

I   V₇

Dominant V₇ Harmony
page 2 of 2

Each chord tone within the dominant V_7 plays a role in resolving to the tonic I chord. For example, the 3rd of the dominant V resolves to the tonic I root, but the root, or 1, of the V_7 remains as a common tone, becoming the 5th of the tonic. The tendencies of each chord tone are collectively termed *voice-leading*. They play a pivotal role in melodic construction, whether reaching a point of resolution when moving from I to V_7, or creating tension by moving from away from I and arriving at V_7.

EX. 5.4
G7 (V chord) resolving to C (I chord)

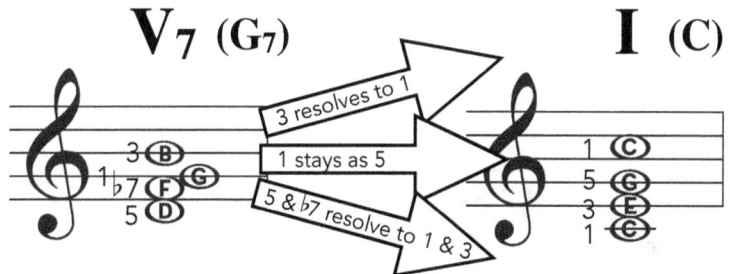

The dominant G7 is presented here in **second inversion**, starting with the note D at the bottom, since this inversion allows its chord tones to resolve stepwise to a root position tonic C triad.

EX. 5.5
V-I chord tone resolutions

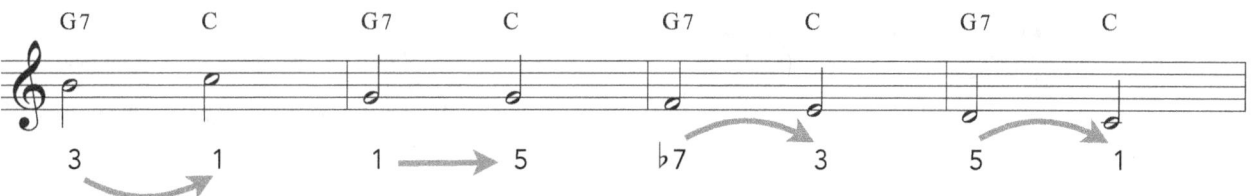

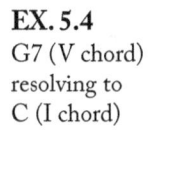 **Rhythmic chord tone exercise:** Tap foot on a chosen beat (e.g. beat 3 only) while playing or singing each line below, first using the printed whole notes the using the printed quarter note rhythm.

V₇-I Scale Fragments

Melody can be developed easily by applying focus and limits. Rather than using both dominant and tonic scales all at once, limit the pitch options to two small scale fragments, chosen from among many. Both of the dominant V_7 scale fragments below help move the melody from chord tones on V_7 to chord tones on I. One dominant G7 fragment, using notes D-E-F, resolves to tonic C major fragment C-D-E from above. The other G7 fragment, B-C-D, resolves to C-D-E from below.

EX. 5.6
Scale fragments moving from dominant (V) to tonic (I)

Scale fragments		
G_7	➜	**C_{Maj7}**
DEF	➜	CDE or EFG
BCD	➜	CDE or GAB
GAB	➜	CDE or GAB
FG	➜	EFG or CDE

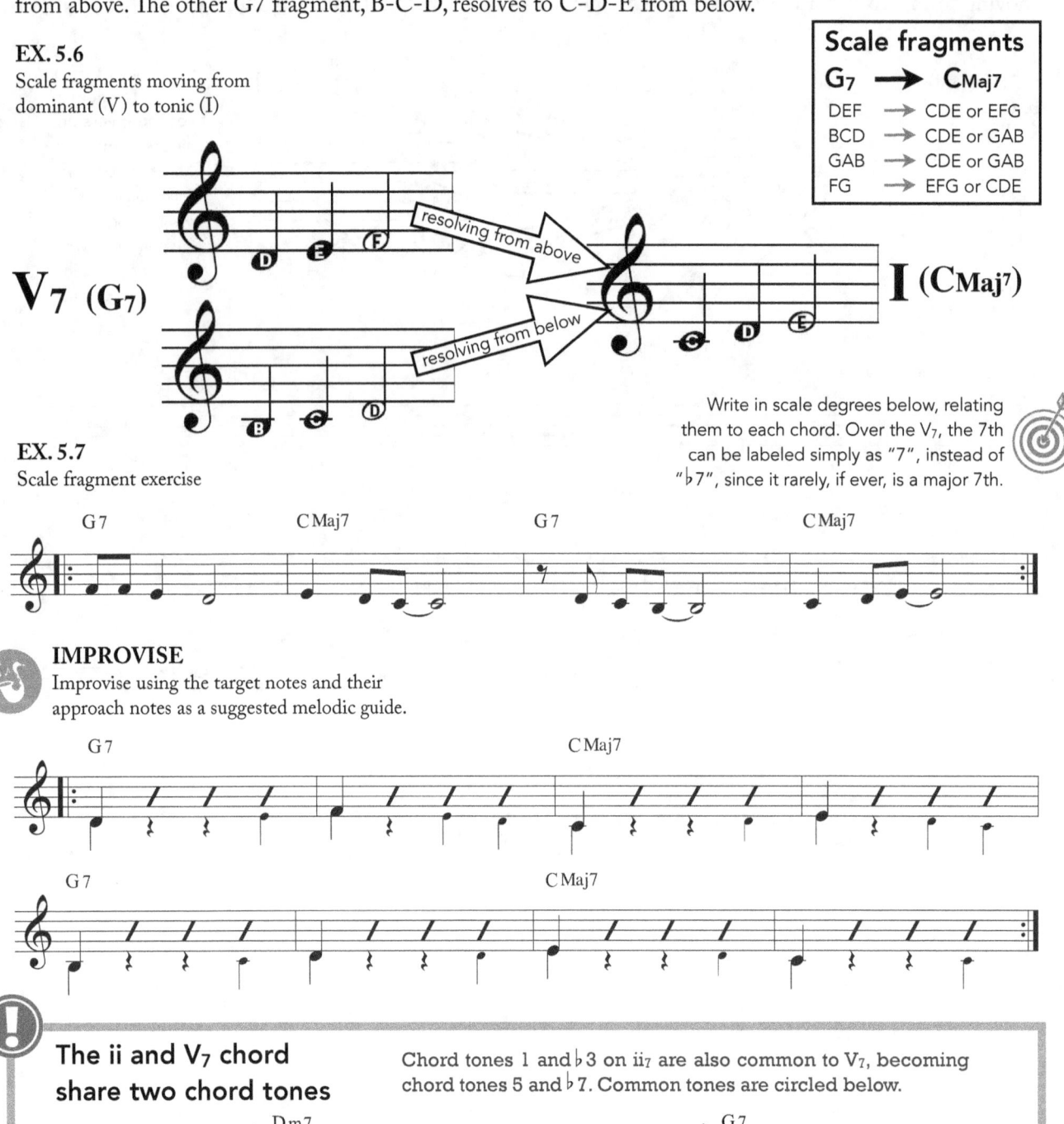

Write in scale degrees below, relating them to each chord. Over the V_7, the 7th can be labeled simply as "7", instead of "♭7", since it rarely, if ever, is a major 7th.

EX. 5.7
Scale fragment exercise

IMPROVISE
Improvise using the target notes and their approach notes as a suggested melodic guide.

The ii and V₇ chord share two chord tones

Chord tones 1 and ♭3 on ii₇ are also common to V_7, becoming chord tones 5 and ♭7. Common tones are circled below.

EX. 5.8
ii₇ vs. V_7

V₇-I Scale Fragment Exercise

In the V₇-I scale fragment exercise below, consider which scale fragment is used in each phrase. Notice the specific appearances of skips vs. steps and why one might be used instead of the other. Consider also why each phrase is rhythmically displaced, starting on beat 2 instead of beat 1.

EX. 5.9
V-I scale fragment exercise

Transpose this exercise to
two keys of your choosing.

Relative minor study

When moving to relative minor, consider two harmonies: (1) the relative minor tonic (i) and (2) the relative dominant (V₇). Then begin to move through small scale fragments that connect each chord tone.

EX. 5.10
Relative minor V₇-i harmonies

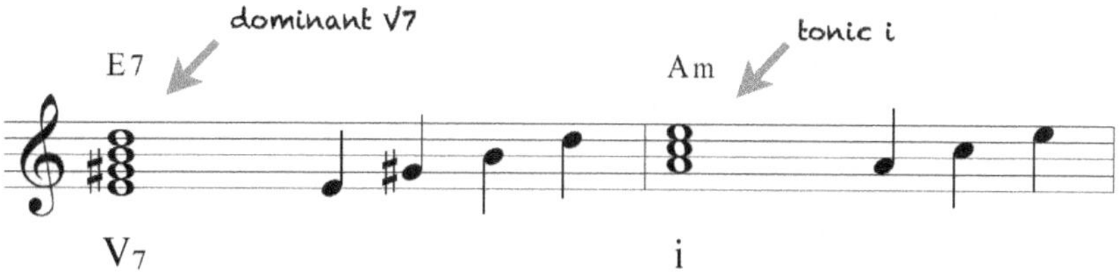

dominant V7

tonic i

E7   Am

V₇   i

EX. 5.11
Relative minor V₇-i
scale fragment exercise

Am   E7   Am   E7

i   V₇   i   V₇

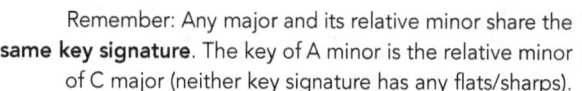

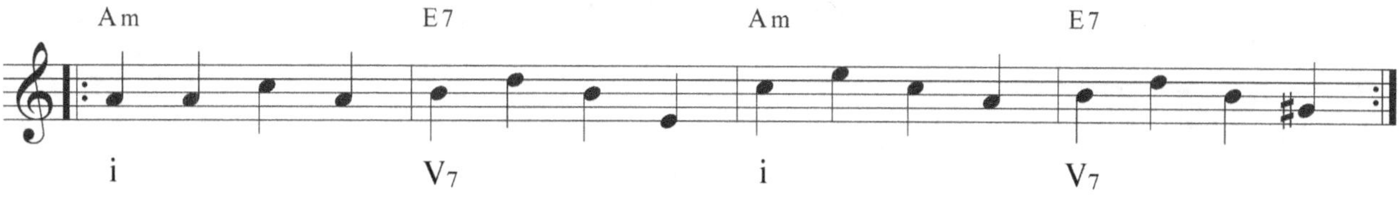

Remember: Any major and its relative minor share the **same key signature**. The key of A minor is the relative minor of C major (neither key signature has any flats/sharps).

V₇-I Melodic Transitions

A melodic phrase composed solely of whole notes usually produces very little melodic momentum. To add musical interest and motion, *melodic transitions* are added to help erase any audible gaps between measures while providing connectivity and movement toward the next target.

EX. 5.12
Whole notes,
no transitions

EX. 5.13
Melodic transitions
étude

Consider style in the *étude* above: Does it matter HOW the strong beat arrival is played? Will it sound better at a slow tempo, fast tempo, straightened eighth note, softened landing, accented landing, etc.?

Relative minor study

To become more familiar with A minor, the relative minor of C major, use the A harmonic minor scale, basing it on two starting points. For the relative minor i chord (Am), start on scale degree 1 (A). For the V₇ chord E7(♭9), start on scale degree 5 (E) then notice specifically how and when the chord tones of both chords target downbeats.

EX. 5.14
A harmonic minor scale, emphasizing
tonic i then dominant V_7(♭9)

Investigate   Overtones

Every sound in nature produces a series of *overtones*. This includes sounds made by musical instruments, the human voice, birds, barking dogs, crashing ocean waves, the wind, even rotating planets. In each soundwave, the main pitch emitted, the fundamental, or 1st harmonic partial, contains overtone frequencies that rise above it. These overtones always follow the same series, with the 1st overtone (also called the 2nd harmonic partial) sounding one octave higher, the 2nd overtone sounding an octave plus a perfect 5th interval above the fundamental, and so on.

Fundamental   1st Overtone   2nd Overtone
(Octave)   (Perfect 5th)

EX. 5.15
Overtone series (based on a C fundamental)

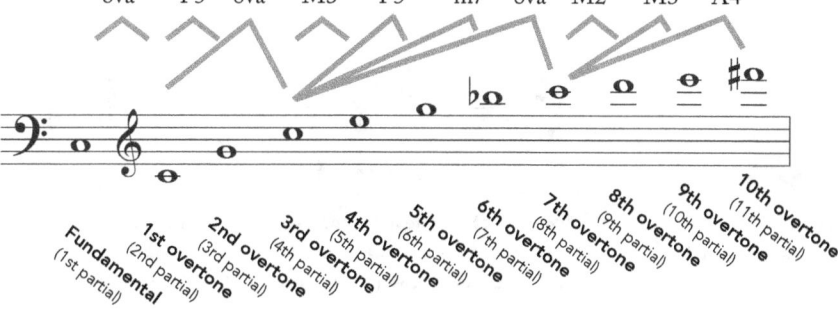

Do you ever wonder how it is that birdsong often sounds entirely tonal as if that meadowlark chirping its tune somehow took music classes? If you take a close look at the C overtone series above, you will see, embedded within the first four overtones, a C major triad. This is what the music theorist Heinrich Schenker termed the "chord of nature."[5] This ubiquitous harmonic presence in the sounds of everyday life provides a clue as to why music around the world shares many traits, including tonal tendencies and gravitation toward key centers.

EX. 5.16
"Chord of nature": C major triad is found within the C overtone series

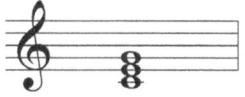

Consider why so many music compositions seem to need to return to a parent key center, the tonic I chord. Jazz theorist George Russell described this phenomenon as **tonal gravity**,[6] observing that musical forces tend to yearn to return to a governing key center. The reasons for this may be rooted in overtone structures and the constant presence of a tonal "chord of nature."

Music and mathematics

The ancient Greek philosopher and mathematician Pythagoras (mid-6th century BCE) revealed how entire scale structures could be built from overtones.[7] Every overtone can be represented by a different numerical ratio. A starting pitch (this could be any note) has the ratio 1:1. Assuming this fundamental pitch vibrates at a speed of 200 cycles per second, the octave above this pitch vibrates at 400 cycles and has the ratio 2:1. The perfect fifth interval vibrates at 300 cycles and has the ratio 3:2. Many composers and performers use these mathematical concepts to improve their intonation while deepening their understanding of harmony.

C major scale and its ratios	
C	2:1
B	15:8
A	5:3
G	3:2
F	4:3
E	5:4
D	9:8
C	1:1

Cadences

Musical phrases mimic speech patterns in any spoken or written language. The cadence of a language often refers to its general rhythmic pulse and feel but, in music, the musical term *cadence* is even more precise as it also refers to the specific ending of a phrase. Some phrases end much like a question, moving to the dominant V chord (*half cadence*), while others end with a requisite answer, resolving to the tonic I chord (*full cadence*).

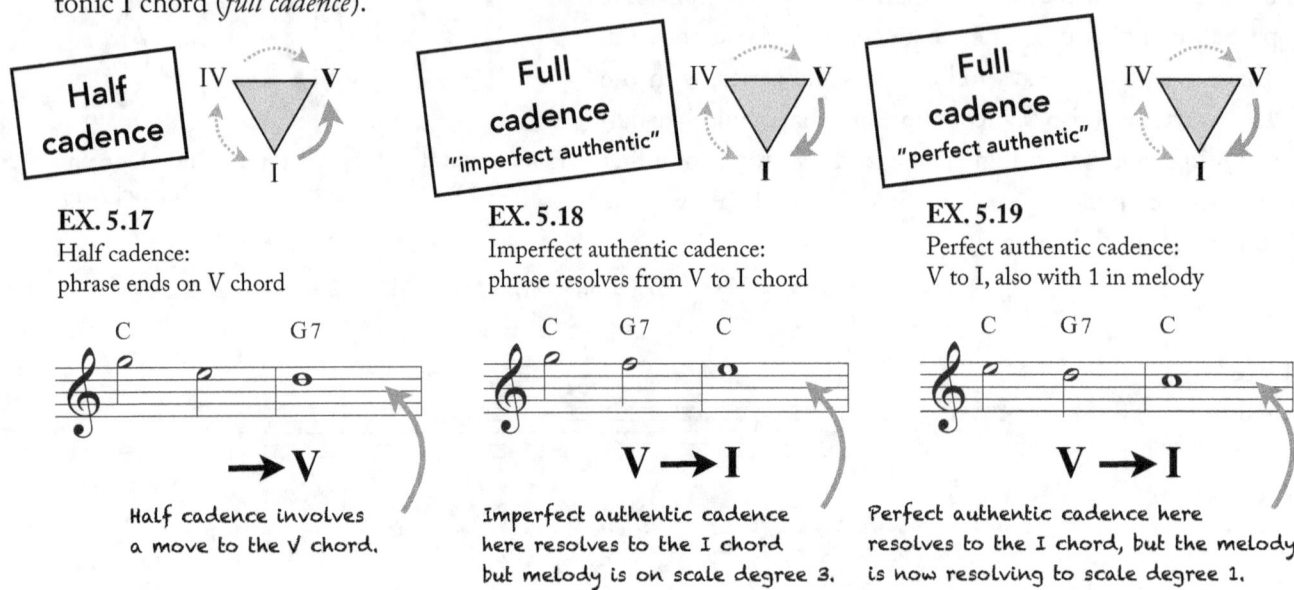

EX. 5.17
Half cadence:
phrase ends on V chord

Half cadence involves
a move to the V chord.

EX. 5.18
Imperfect authentic cadence:
phrase resolves from V to I chord

Imperfect authentic cadence
here resolves to the I chord
but melody is on scale degree 3.

EX. 5.19
Perfect authentic cadence:
V to I, also with 1 in melody

Perfect authentic cadence here
resolves to the I chord, but the melody
is now resolving to scale degree 1.

EX. 5.20
"Going Home" theme from *Symphony No. 9 in E minor, From the New World, II. Largo*"(Antonín Dvořák)

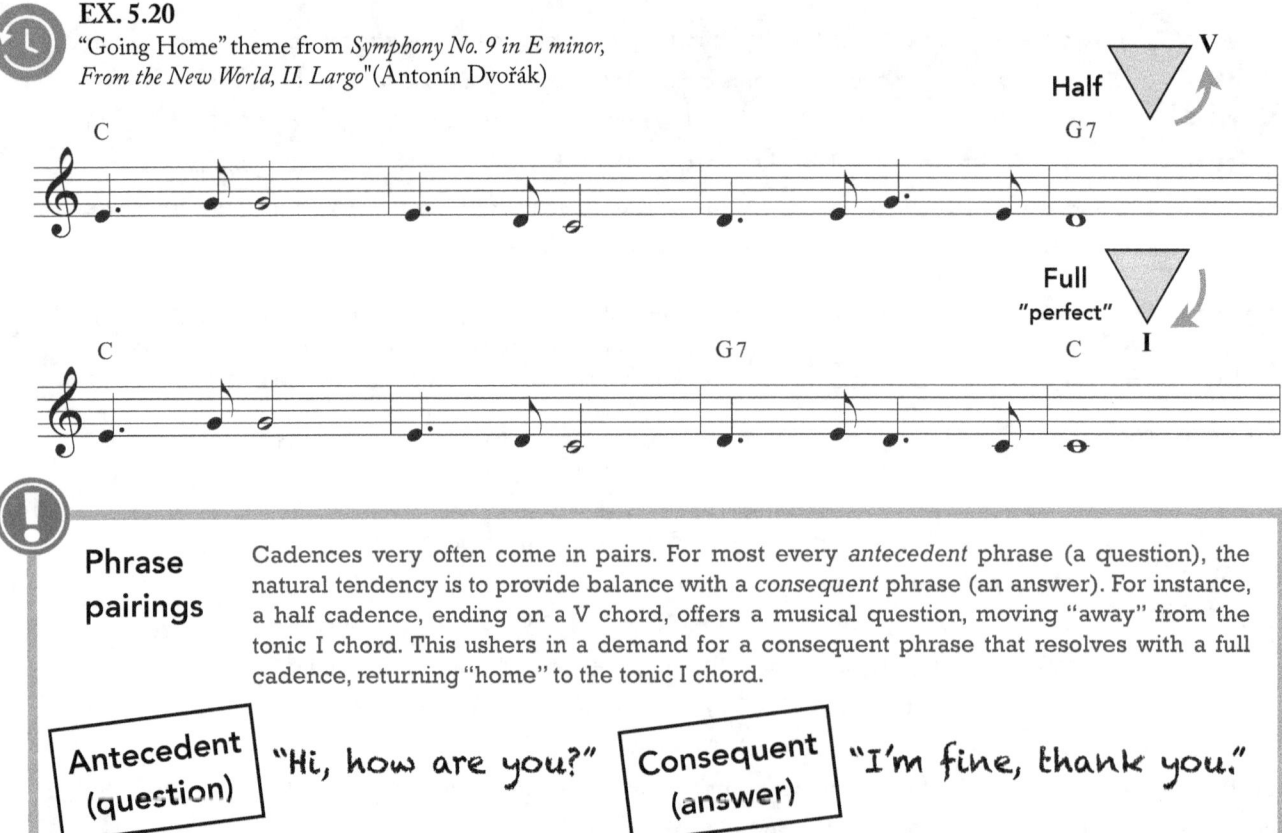

Phrase pairings

Cadences very often come in pairs. For most every *antecedent* phrase (a question), the natural tendency is to provide balance with a *consequent* phrase (an answer). For instance, a half cadence, ending on a V chord, offers a musical question, moving "away" from the tonic I chord. This ushers in a demand for a consequent phrase that resolves with a full cadence, returning "home" to the tonic I chord.

Antecedent (question)   "Hi, how are you?"   Consequent (answer)   "I'm fine, thank you."

Cadences
— page 2 of 3 —

The following excerpt of "It's only a paper moon" involves three cadential moments. Since cadences come at the ends of phrases, it can be deduced that there are a total of three phrases below. Measures 1-2 end with a *half cadence* (to V), measures 3-4 end with an *imperfect authentic cadence* (V to I, with scale degree 3 in the melody), and measures 5-8 end with a *perfect authentic cadence* (V to I, with scale degree 1 in the melody).

In each 4-bar phrase below, notice how a melodic arrival on tonic $\hat{1}$ is delayed until the end of the phrase. This helps build melodic interest, allowing the story to unfold **without resolving too quickly**.

EX. 5.21
"It's only a paper moon"
(Arlen/Rose/Harburg)
cadences and motivic
scale fragments

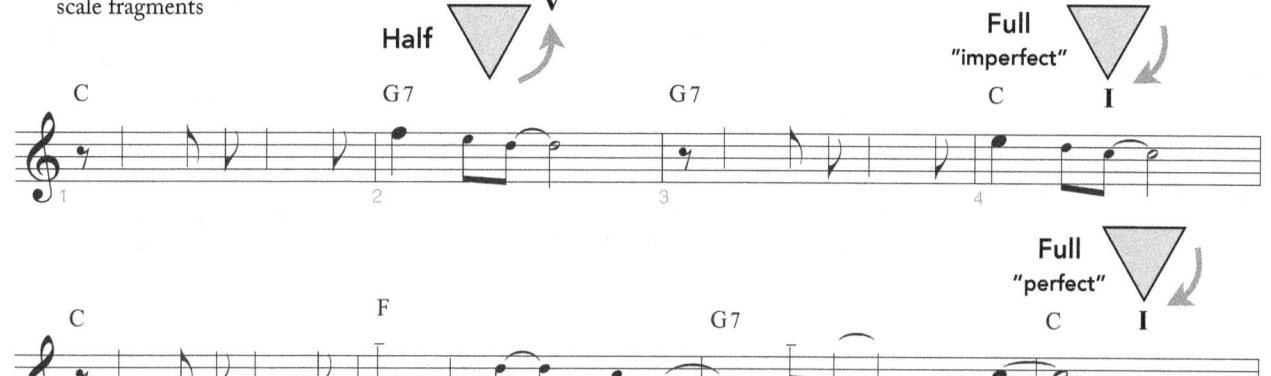

Pitch collection challenge!
Complete the melody above by adding in the following missing scale degrees (key of C major):

5 5 5 5 5   5 5 4 4 4   5 5 5 5 5 6 4   6 5

Consider **octave jumps** throughout.

Songs with half cadences:

- "All of Me"
- "All of You"
- "April in Paris"
- "Bewitched"
- "But Beautiful"
- "Call me irresponsible"
- "Cherokee"
- "A child is born"
- "I could write a book"
- "I got rhythm"
- "Recorda-me"

- "Seven Steps to Heaven"
- "Take Five"
- "There is no greater love"
- "There will never be another you"
- "Triste"
- "Up Jumped Spring"
- "We'll be together again"
- "Well, you needn't"
- "When I Fall in Love"
- "When the Saints Go Marching in"
- "You don't know what love is"

For each song listed here, take ample time to **begin hearing exactly** where half cadences appear. These songs also involve other cadences. Listen, in particular, for authentic cadences throughout.

From this song list, write out a song melody in two keys each and identify and label any cadences.

Cadences
— page 3 of 3 —

Another common cadence is called a *plagal cadence*, which resolves to I from the IV chord. Sometimes referred to as the "Amen" cadence, the plagal cadence took root in gospel and church music and is now used in many genres, including jazz, pop, and R&B. The *deceptive cadence*, mysterious cousin to the more prominent full and half cadences, packs quite a surprise. Just when it seems the progression is going to resolve from V to I, the harmony takes an unexpected turn, resolving to vi instead. Now that's deceptive!

At a piano, play the melody and chords for "The water is wide" below. Notice half and full cadences in the traditional version of the song then exchange the last two measures with alternate endings using plagal and deceptive cadences.

Plagal cadence

EX. 5.22
Plagal cadence (IV - I)

IV → I

Deceptive cadence

EX. 5.23
Deceptive cadence (V - vi)

V → vi

EX. 5.24
"The water is wide"
(Traditional)

The wa-ter is wide,   I can-not cross o'er,

And nei - ther have   I wings to ___ fly,   Half   V

Give me a boat   that can car - ry two,

And both shall row,   My love and I.   Full "perfect"   I

EX. 5.25
Alternate ending with plagal cadence

My love and I.   Plagal   IV → I

EX. 5.26
Alternate ending with deceptive cadence

My love and I.   Deceptive   V → vi

V-I Details and Intent

When weaving a melody through chords, the melodic details really matter. An essential skill to develop is the ability to target chord tones at every chord change. Consider the three melodies below, each moving from tonic I on beat 1 to dominant V on beat 3. The first melody uses an enclosure to ensure a strong beat 3 arrival on a chord tone. The second and third melodies land firmly on a non-chord tone on beat 3 but only the third melody resolves to a chord tone on beat 4. Whether it is truly wrong to sustain that note on beats 3 and 4 all depends on context, including what happens before and after this isolated measure. For each melody, ask, "What was the *intent* behind the note placed on beat 3 of each measure?"

EX. 5.27
Three distinct melodic
approaches, from I to V

Keep in mind that the most fundamental objective —
to develop **fluency with matching** melody to harmony —
is achieved only in the first of these three examples.

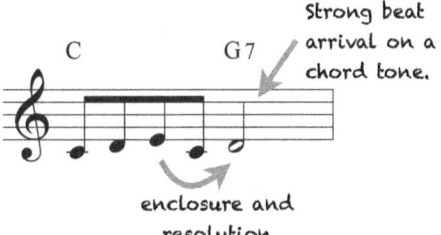

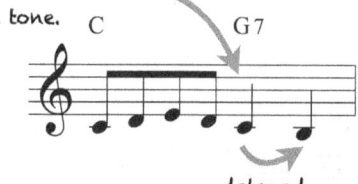

EX. 5.28
Details and
intent exercise

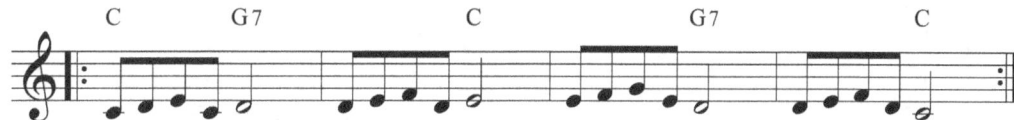

EX. 5.29
Details and
intent exercise

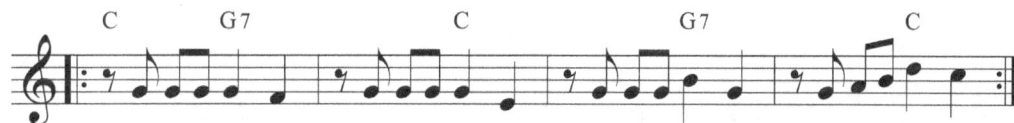

Circle the one moment among the above two exercises where a non-chord tone is
placed on a strong beat. Is this note a mistake — a wrong note? Why, or why not?

Is the 7th really a functional chord tone?

The 7th is a special chord tone. It can double as a passing tone moving from 7 to 1, and if it's used as a target note, it can steer the direction of an entire phrase. Compare the function and tendency of the 7ths of CMaj7, Dm7, and G7. The 7th of the G7 chord very much drives resolution from the dominant V_7 to tonic I, the note F pulling toward E. In contrast, the 7ths of CMaj7 and Dm7 are more ornamental and not as significantly functional.

EX. 5.30
CMaj7 (tonic I)
and Dm7 (ii) chords

EX. 5.31
G7 chord (dominant V_7),
resolving to C (tonic I)

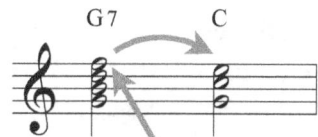

Song Study   "Iko Iko"

"Iko Iko" is rooted in New Orleans blues, Zydeco, Cajun, and American indigenous cultures. Rhythmically, it is based on an infectious 3-2 *clave* rhythm. Melodically, it centers on a single major scale while alternating between half and full cadences, using only tonic and dominant harmonies.

EX. 5.32
"Iko Iko" (Traditional)

*These lyrics comprise the 3rd verse of "Iko Iko." Each verse vividly describes elements of a turf war between families.

First internalize how the parent C major scale is used throughout "Iko Iko." Notice, in particular, which **target notes** are used for each phrase ending and how they match the given chord.

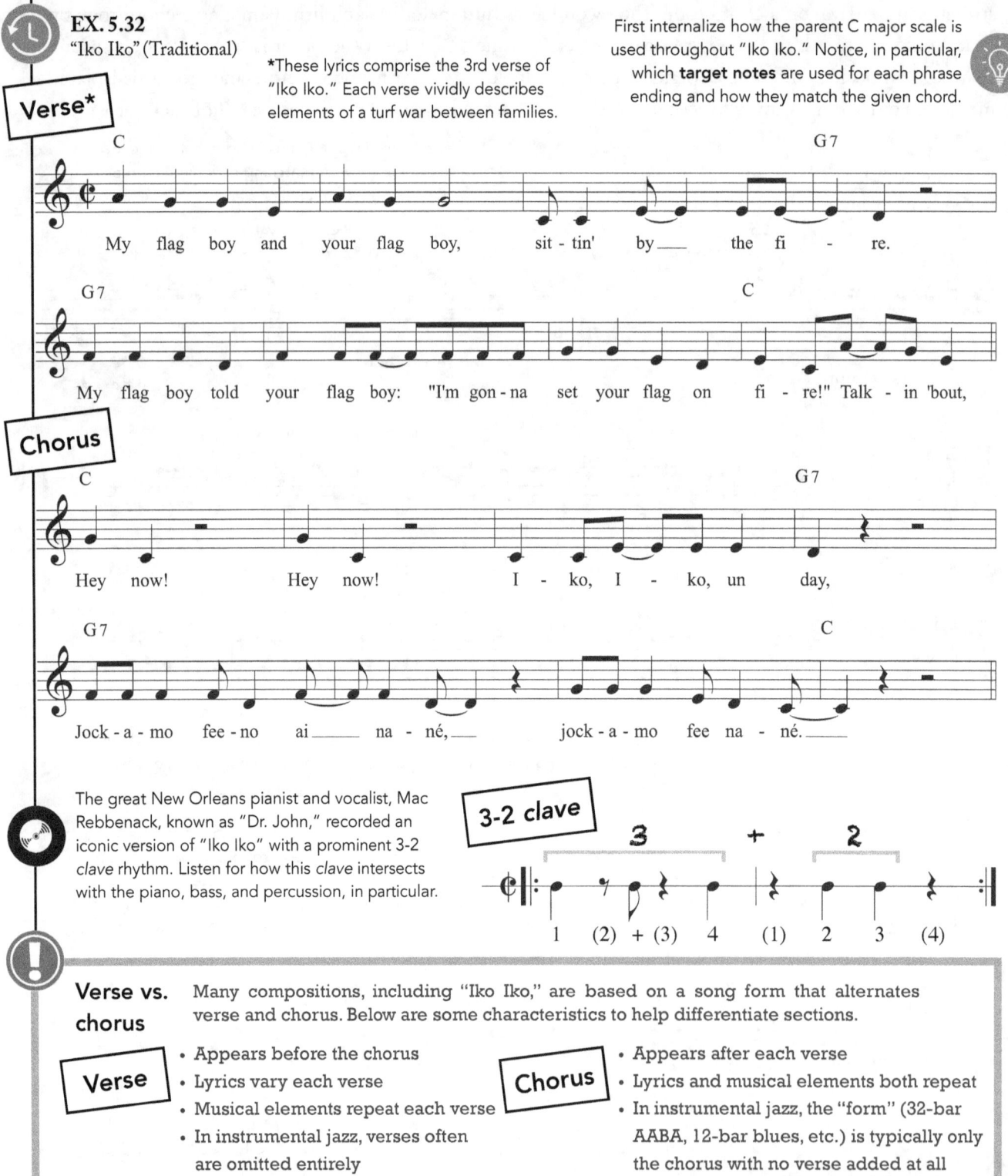

The great New Orleans pianist and vocalist, Mac Rebbenack, known as "Dr. John," recorded an iconic version of "Iko Iko" with a prominent 3-2 *clave* rhythm. Listen for how this *clave* intersects with the piano, bass, and percussion, in particular.

3-2 clave

Verse vs. chorus   Many compositions, including "Iko Iko," are based on a song form that alternates verse and chorus. Below are some characteristics to help differentiate sections.

Verse
- Appears before the chorus
- Lyrics vary each verse
- Musical elements repeat each verse
- In instrumental jazz, verses often are omitted entirely

Chorus
- Appears after each verse
- Lyrics and musical elements both repeat
- In instrumental jazz, the "form" (32-bar AABA, 12-bar blues, etc.) is typically only the chorus with no verse added at all

Improvise   "Iko Iko"

The solo form of "Iko Iko" is really just eight measures long. The first 4-bar phrase of "Iko Iko" starts with 3 bars of the I chord then ends with 1 bar of the V chord (a half cadence). The second 4-bar phrase starts with 3 bars of the V chord then ends with 1 bar of the I chord (an authentic cadence). Become familiar with this harmonic rhythm by improvising first with chord tone pairings then using other options, including additional chord tone pairings and scale fragments.

EX. 5.33
Tonic I to dominant V chord, including chord tone pairings

EX. 5.34
Chord tone pairing across "Iko Iko" (using option #1)

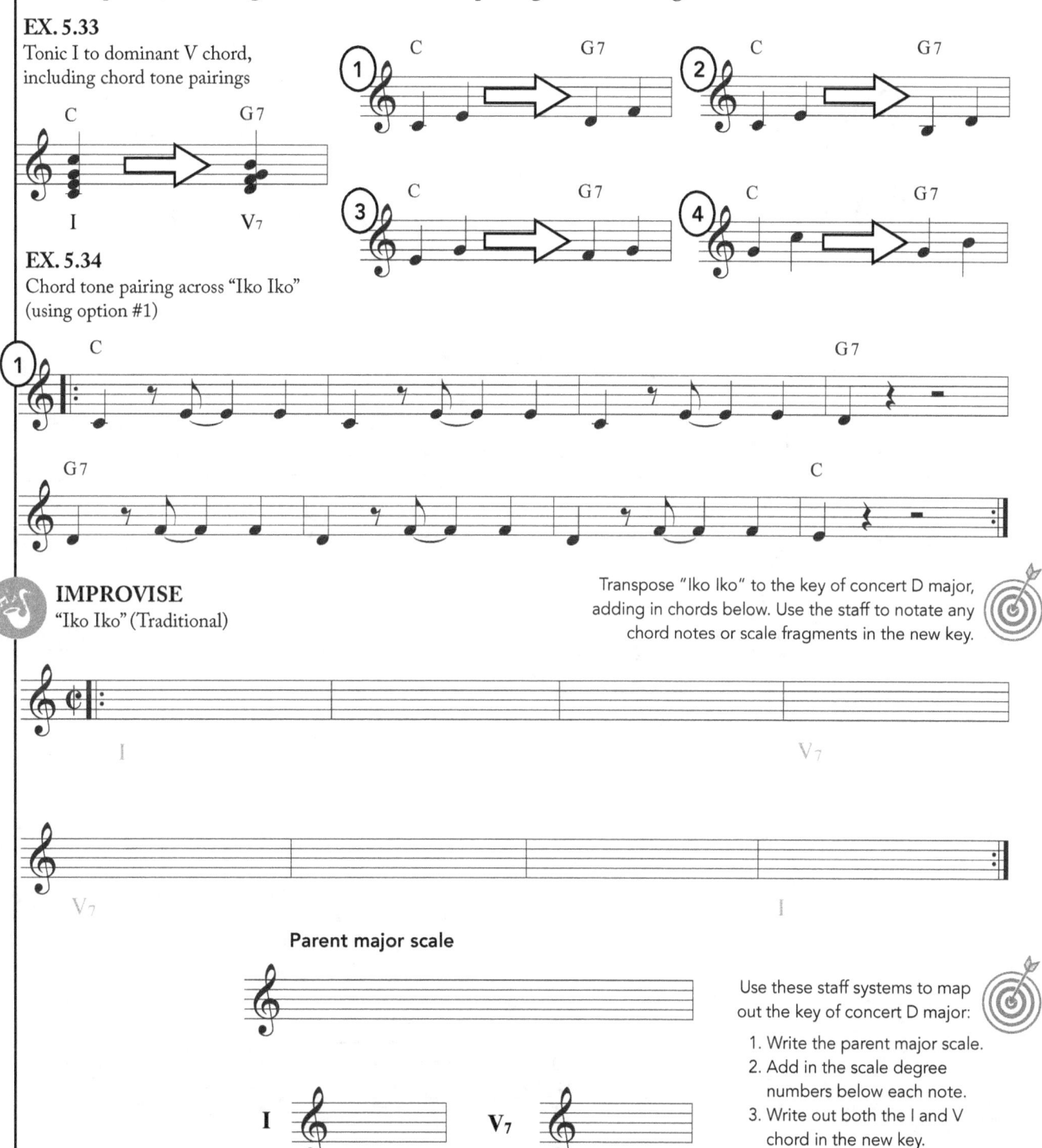

IMPROVISE
"Iko Iko" (Traditional)

Transpose "Iko Iko" to the key of concert D major, adding in chords below. Use the staff to notate any chord notes or scale fragments in the new key.

Parent major scale

Use these staff systems to map out the key of concert D major:

1. Write the parent major scale.
2. Add in the scale degree numbers below each note.
3. Write out both the I and V chord in the new key.

The Major Pentatonic Scale

With pentatonic scales, there are no "wrong notes"! This might seem too good to be true but the simple reason is that its intervallic combination of steps and skips gives the *major pentatonic scale* a distinct and independent melodic strength so that it can easily be played across multiple harmonies. In fact, merely playing the scale up and down produces an attractive and balanced sound. Comprised of only five notes, the major pentatonic scale holds a universal appeal that transcends styles, from jazz and classical to folk, pop, rock, and other genres.

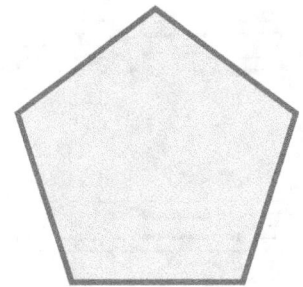

EX. 5.35
C major pentatonic scale, scale degrees, and intervals

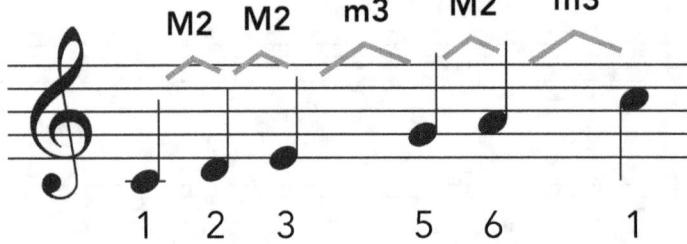

| M2 major second |
| m3 minor third |

EX. 5.36
C major scale and scale degrees

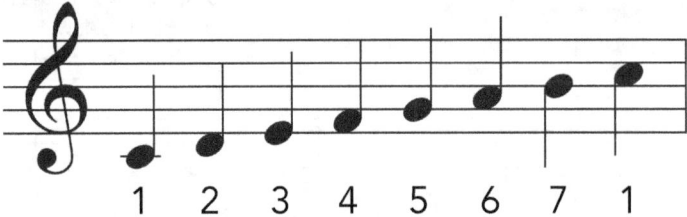

 The major pentatonic is **missing major scale degrees 4 and 7**.

 Hiding in plain sight, the pentatonic scale is embedded in the iconic guitar riff in "My Girl." Instead of practicing each scale in isolation, play the "My Girl" guitar riff by ear to quickly learn all 12 major pentatonics.

1. Write out the F major scale on the blank staff below.
2. Add scale degree numbers below each note.
3. Circle each note of the F major pentatonic scale.
4. Write out the "My Girl" guitar riff, bar 1 in C, bar 2 in F.

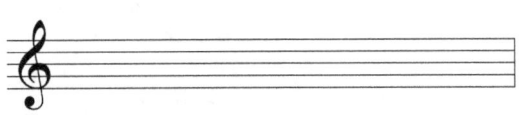

Digital Patterns

Digital patterns are small sets of note combinations, typically only three or four at a time, that are repeated or played with subtle variation. Think of "digital" patterns as notes that can be labeled with scale numbers (digits) and counted on our fingers (our digits!).

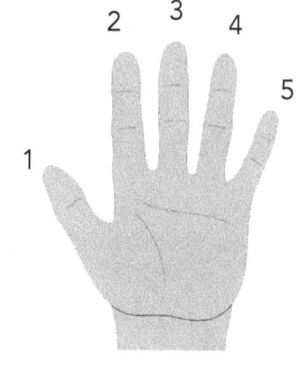

EX. 5.37
Digital pattern 1235 + variations (C major)

1 2 3 5   5 3 2 1   5 3 1 2   3 5 2 1

EX. 5.38
Digital pattern 1235 + variations (G Mixolydian)

EX. 5.39
Rhythmic variations on a
1325 digital pattern

1 2 3 5   5 3 2 1   5 3 1 2   3 5 2 1

1 3 2   5   1 3 2 5

EX. 5.40
Digital pattern 3521 across a ii-V-I (C major)

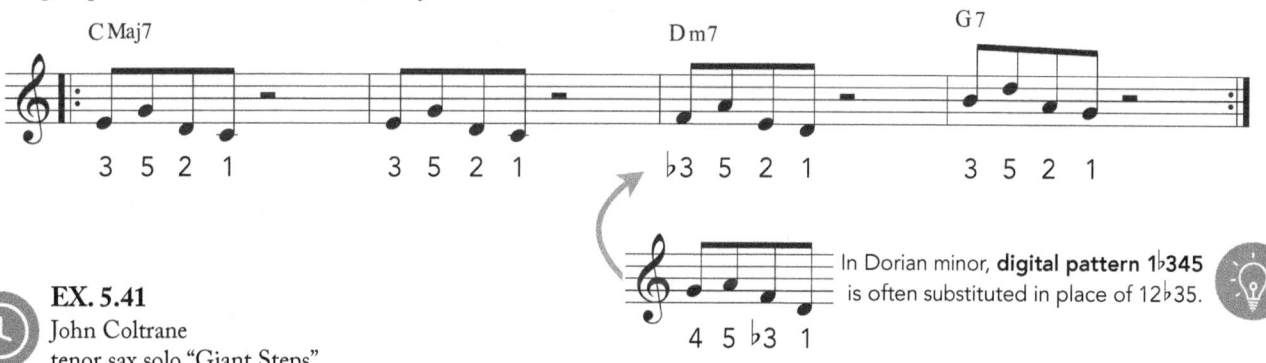

3   5   2   1   3   5   2   1   ♭3 5 2 1   3 5 2 1

In Dorian minor, **digital pattern 1♭345**
is often substituted in place of 12♭35.

4 5 ♭3 1

EX. 5.41
John Coltrane
tenor sax solo "Giant Steps"

1   2   3   5   1   2   3   5   1 5 3 1   9 ♭7 6 5   1 2 3 4   5 6 7 9

IMPROVISE
1. Choose a digital pattern and a rhythm to start with then keep them intact for each measure.
2. Continue improvising, including new patterns and variations.

Dm7   G7   C Maj7

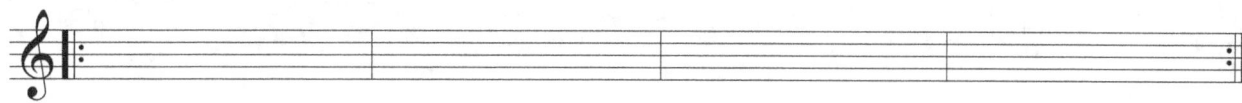

Major Pentatonic Scale Patterns

The following major pentatonic scale patterns will help you learn how to use pentatonics across the full range of your instrument. Practice them to gain agility on each and every fragment within your pentatonics. Only one octave is presented for each pattern here and all notes are numbered according to scale degrees. Learn these patterns across multiple octaves through your entire range.

EX. 5.42
C major pentatonic fragments, looped

5 6 1 2 3 2 1 6   3 5 6 1 2 1 6 5   2 3 5 6 1 6 5 3

1 2 3 5 6 5 3 2   6 1 2 3 5 3 2 1

The C major pentatonic scale uses **exactly the same notes** as the A minor pentatonic scale.

EX. 5.43
Classic C major pentatonic scale pattern

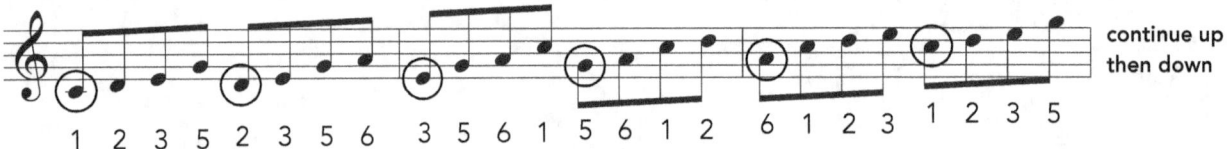

1 2 3 5   2 3 5 6   3 5 6 1   5 6 1 2   6 1 2 3   1 2 3 5

continue up then down

EX. 5.44
C major pentatonic scale pattern

1   2 1 2   3 2 3   5 3 5   6 5 6   1 6 1

continue up then down

TEMPO SLIDER

Can you learn your pentatonic at any speed? Consider playing each pattern using a different note value, from half notes to sixteenth notes. Your goal is to move between rhythmic values seamlessly while in the middle of a pattern. Practice the exercise below to develop this skill as if you are moving a dial — a *tempo slider* — up or down, all while playing through a pentatonic pattern. Own your tempo!

EX. 5.45
Changing rhythmic values within a C major pentatonic scale pattern

Major Pentatonic Scale Manipulation

Major pentatonic scale manipulation can involve simple alterations, where even the smallest change can have a large effect on a pattern. In the examples below, notice how the original classic pentatonic pattern is varied in subsequent iterations, either sometimes melodically by replacing a step with a skip or rhythmically by replacing an eighth note with a quarter note.

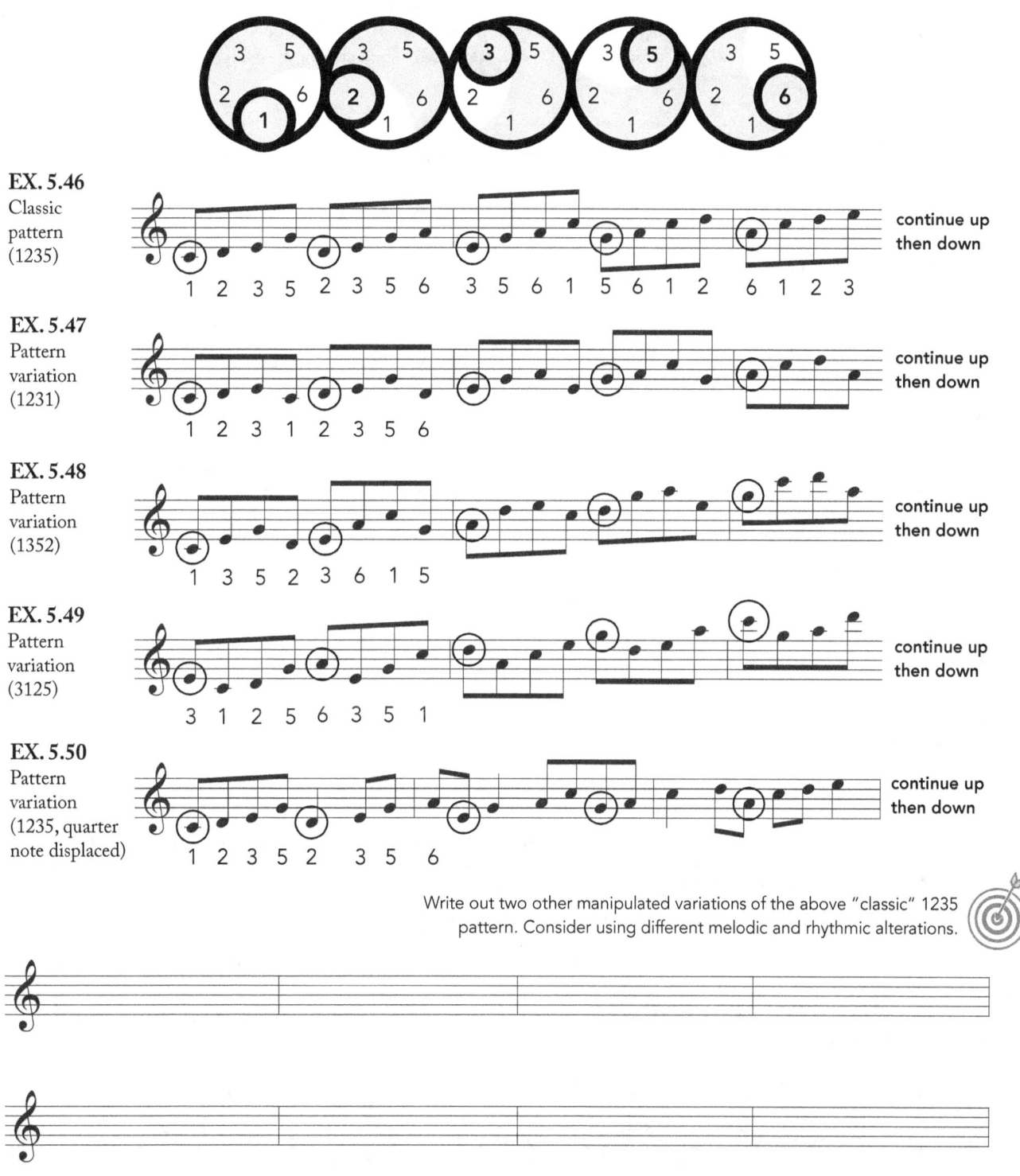

EX. 5.46
Classic pattern (1235)

continue up then down

1 2 3 5 2 3 5 6 3 5 6 1 5 6 1 2 6 1 2 3

EX. 5.47
Pattern variation (1231)

continue up then down

1 2 3 1 2 3 5 6

EX. 5.48
Pattern variation (1352)

continue up then down

1 3 5 2 3 6 1 5

EX. 5.49
Pattern variation (3125)

continue up then down

3 1 2 5 6 3 5 1

EX. 5.50
Pattern variation (1235, quarter note displaced)

continue up then down

1 2 3 5 2 3 5 6

Write out two other manipulated variations of the above "classic" 1235 pattern. Consider using different melodic and rhythmic alterations.

Major Pentatonic Scale Examples

Major pentatonic scales are ubiquitous in classic melodies. Below are two examples, certainly polar opposites, with "Old MacDonald had a farm" being one of the easiest folk song melodies and "Cherokee" a notorious burner that only the bravest attempt. At their core though is a simple 5-note scale.

EX. 5.51
"Old MacDonald had a farm"
(Traditional)
(key of C major)

Notice how the **C major pentatonic is reversed** in "Old MacDonald." The melody starts with the scale's upper fragment (G-A-C) then continues with the scale's lower fragment (C-D-E), displaced to a higher octave, placed above the upper fragment.

EX. 5.52
"Cherokee" (Ray Noble),
2nd A-section rhythm
(key of C major)

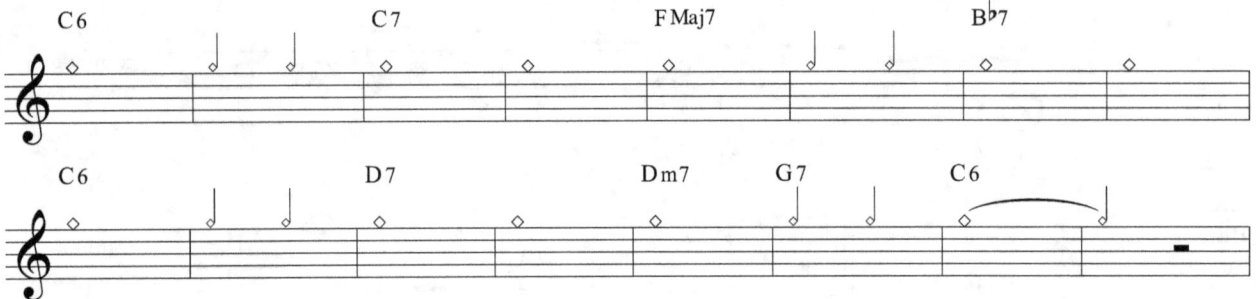

EX. 5.53
"Cherokee" exercise,
constant quarter notes
(key of C major)

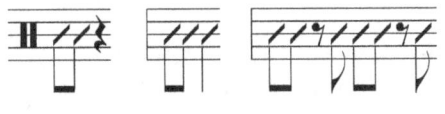

Apply any of these three rhythms to the "Cherokee" exercise above, keeping the original pitches but repeating the new rhythm in a loop.

One of the great challenges in jazz is to learn "Cherokee" in all 12 keys. Knowing now that the A-section melody is simply a single major pentatonic scale, learning it in all 12 keys will be easier. Give it a try!

IMPROVISE
Improvise using the I major pentatonic scale over both the I and IV chords.

Solo 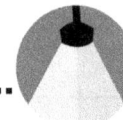 Spotlight

Louis Armstrong, trumpet
J.C. Higginbotham, trombone
"When the Saints Go Marching in"

The great trumpeter Louis "Satchmo" Armstrong played with remarkable rhythmic clarity, placing every note confidently and carefully. He also took many risks as an improviser. In his solo below on "When the Saints Go Marching in," notice which target notes he uses, including when he targets non-chord tones instead of chord tones. In an effort to completely understand his solo, also take time to listen to the original recording and to observe Satchmo's dynamics, articulations, and other stylistic nuances.

 EX. 5.54
Louis Armstrong trumpet solo
"When the Saints Go Marching in"

In the following solo excerpt, Armstrong uses the major pentatonic scale nearly exclusively. Circle every occurrence of the one note that is not part of C major pentatonic.

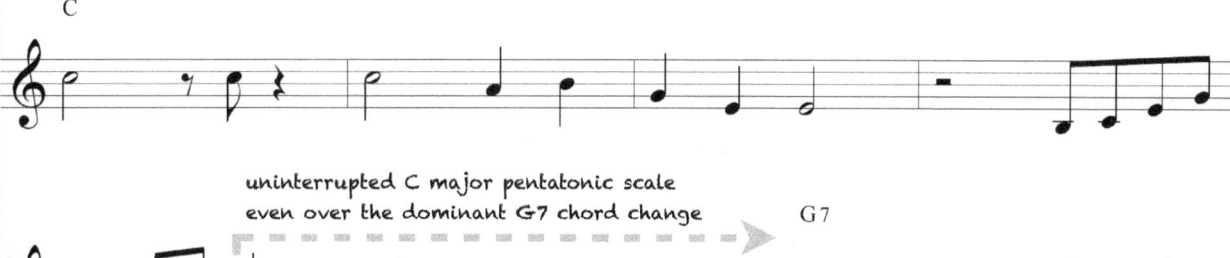

Trombonist J.C. Higginbotham, a contemporary of Satchmo's, improvises a solo on "When the Saints Go Marching in" that integrates both the major scale and the major pentatonic scale. Notice, in particular, the few times Higginbotham uses major scale degrees 4 and 7. Both notes, always absent from the major pentatonic scale, help highlight the appearance of the major scale.

 EX. 5.55
J.C. Higginbotham trombone solo
"When the Saints Go Marching in"

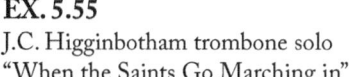

While the printed chord is C, implying a simple C major triad, Higginbotham plays the moment as a C6 then ornaments with an additional major 7th.

Like Satchmo, Higginbotham also outlines chords that differ from the given harmony. Circle these moments in both solos. Why would these alternate harmonies be outlined?

Pedal Points

— page 1 of 2 —

A *pedal point* is a note that is played continuously even while chords change. In jazz, this note can be played by the bassist as a *bass pedal point* but it can also be a tool used by the improvising soloist. The note chosen as a pedal point tends to be common to most or all the chords in the progression. Common pedal points are the root of the tonic (pedal point C in the key of C major) and the fifth note of the tonic (pedal point G in the key of C major).

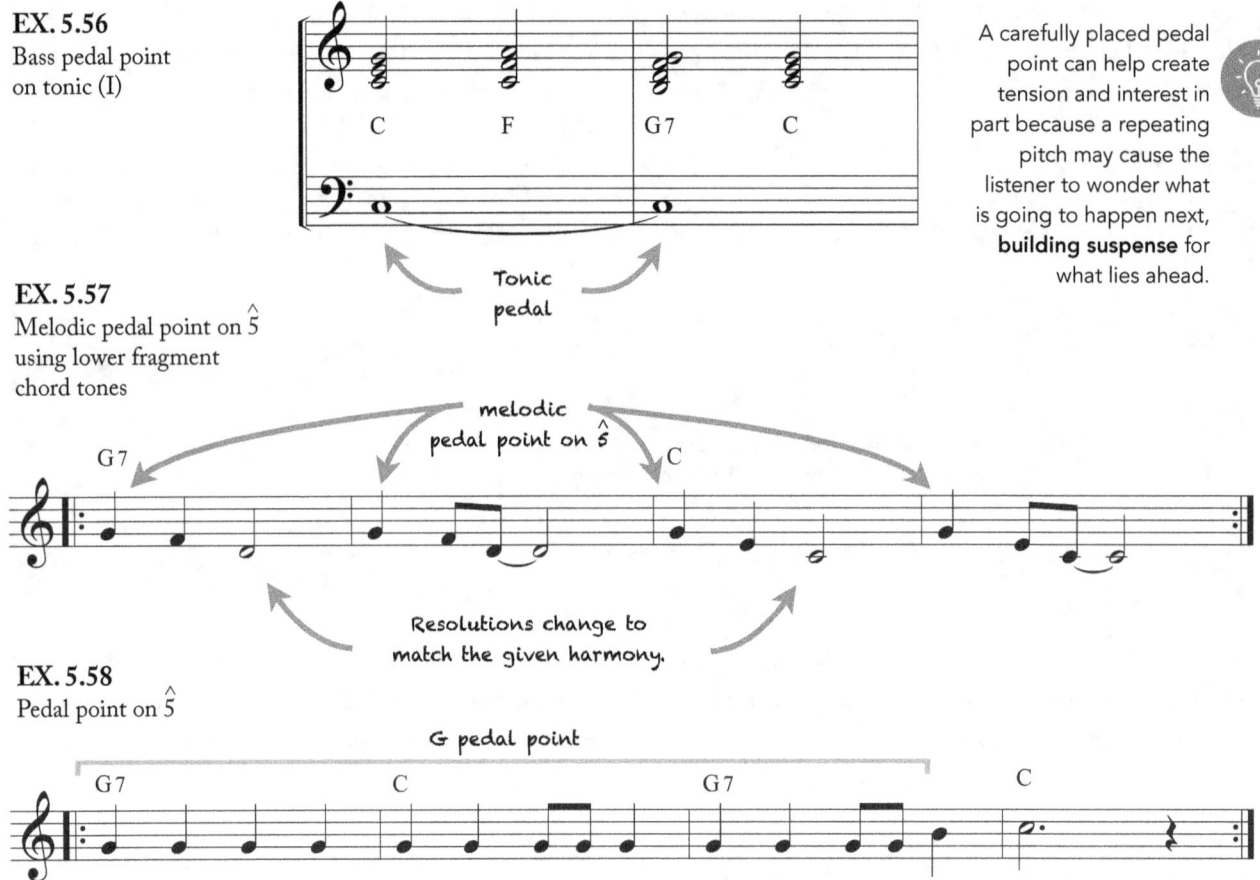

EX. 5.56
Bass pedal point on tonic (I)

A carefully placed pedal point can help create tension and interest in part because a repeating pitch may cause the listener to wonder what is going to happen next, **building suspense** for what lies ahead.

EX. 5.57
Melodic pedal point on $\hat{5}$ using lower fragment chord tones

EX. 5.58
Pedal point on $\hat{5}$

The great tenor saxophonist Johnny Griffin anchors the following phrase on "Autumn Leaves" with a pedal point on $\hat{5}$ (E in the key of A minor), ornamenting this fifth with a D-sharp, its chromatic lower neighbor. The contrast between the low pedal point and the higher melodic punctuation builds interest and tension.

EX. 5.59
Johnny Griffin tenor sax solo "Autumn Leaves,"
with pedal point on 5 (key of A minor)

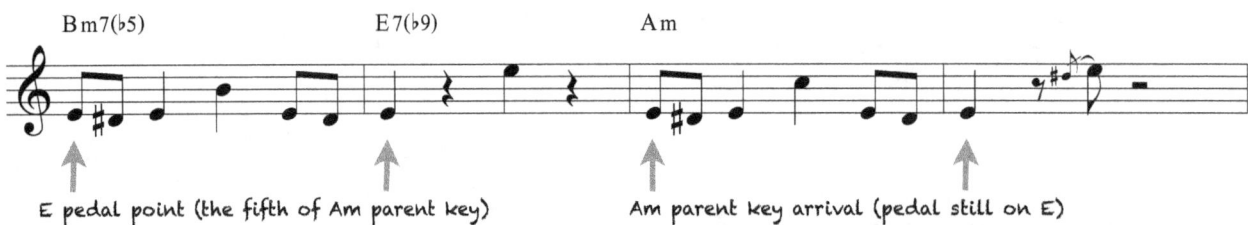

Pedal Points

— page 2 of 2 —

The first exercise below introduces a pedal point on $\hat{5}$, contrasted with a rising melody. It culminates in measure 7, where the melody reaches its highest point and the pedal point ceases in favor of a melodic resolution to tonic. The second example features tenor saxophonist Illinois Jacquet's "Flying Home" solo, with his iconic tonic pedal point creating anticipation and excitement, a series of repeated notes played with a particularly impassioned sense of style.

EX. 5.60
Pedal point and
rising melody

Transpose these examples
to two other keys.

EX. 5.61
Illinois Jacquet tenor sax solo
"Flying Home"

IMPROVISE
Use pedal points while improvising
over the following chord progression.

Keep in mind that, while $\hat{1}$ and $\hat{5}$
are common pedal points, **a
pedal point can be any note**.

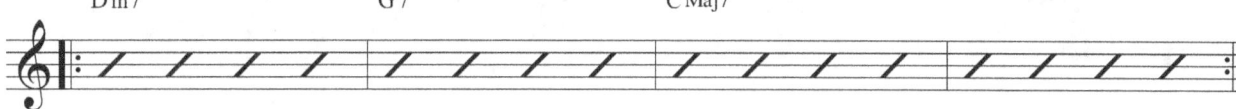

Masterclass   Quartal Harmony

Quartal harmony is music based on fourth intervals. The perfect fourth interval is found in major and minor scales and it also may be built from any note in the chromatic scale. The tritone, also called "augmented 4th" or "diminished 5th," is also a fourth interval. Whether used melodically or harmonically, fourths create a distinct sound.

P4 and P5 are considered **octave complements** since every perfect 4th interval pairs with another perfect 5th interval to add up to a full octave interval (P8). Augmented 4ths complement each other, since they split the octave at a mid-point.

EX. 5.62
Quartal interval types, including perfect 4th (P4) and augmented 4th (A4)

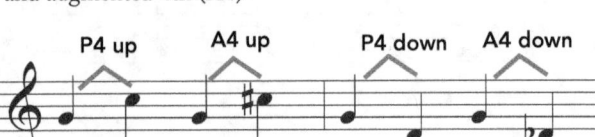

EX. 5.63
Octave complements

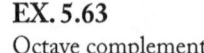

EX. 5.64
C major scale in 4ths

EX. 5.65
Chromatic 4th examples

Compose a short piece using quartal melody and/or harmony, choosing mostly 4th intervals (P4, A4, d5, P5). Choose between diatonic or chromatics.

Songs featuring melody using fourths:

- "Freedom Jazz Dance" (Eddie Harris)
- "Witch Hunt" (Wayne Shorter)
- "Maiden Voyage" (Herbie Hancock)

Tertiary vs. quartal harmony

Tertiary harmony is built on thirds while *quartal harmony* is built on fourths. The sound of a chord can change drastically, depending on whether it is built using thirds or fourths.

EX. 5.66
CMaj9, using stacked 3rds

EX. 5.67
CMaj9, including stacked 4ths

EX. 5.68
Dm13, using stacked 3rds

EX. 5.69
Dm13, using stacked 4ths

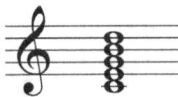

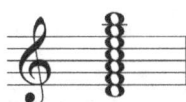
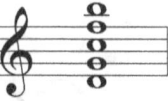

Song Study

"Limbo Jazz"
page 1 of 2

In part because of the underlying groove with its eighth-note pulse, sounding equal parts swing and straight eighths, Duke Ellington's "Limbo Jazz" toes the line between Caribbean music and classic jazz. Follow the directions below to prepare a "Limbo Jazz" lead sheet.

These melodic phrases are out of order! Write them in the correct order in this "Limbo Jazz" lead sheet and label them from 2-8. Phrases 1 and 4 have already been labeled.

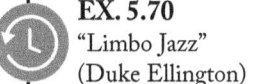

EX. 5.70
"Limbo Jazz"
(Duke Ellington)

"Limbo Jazz" melodic phrases tend to use chord tones and clear target notes. Use the chord symbols below to help guide your placements.

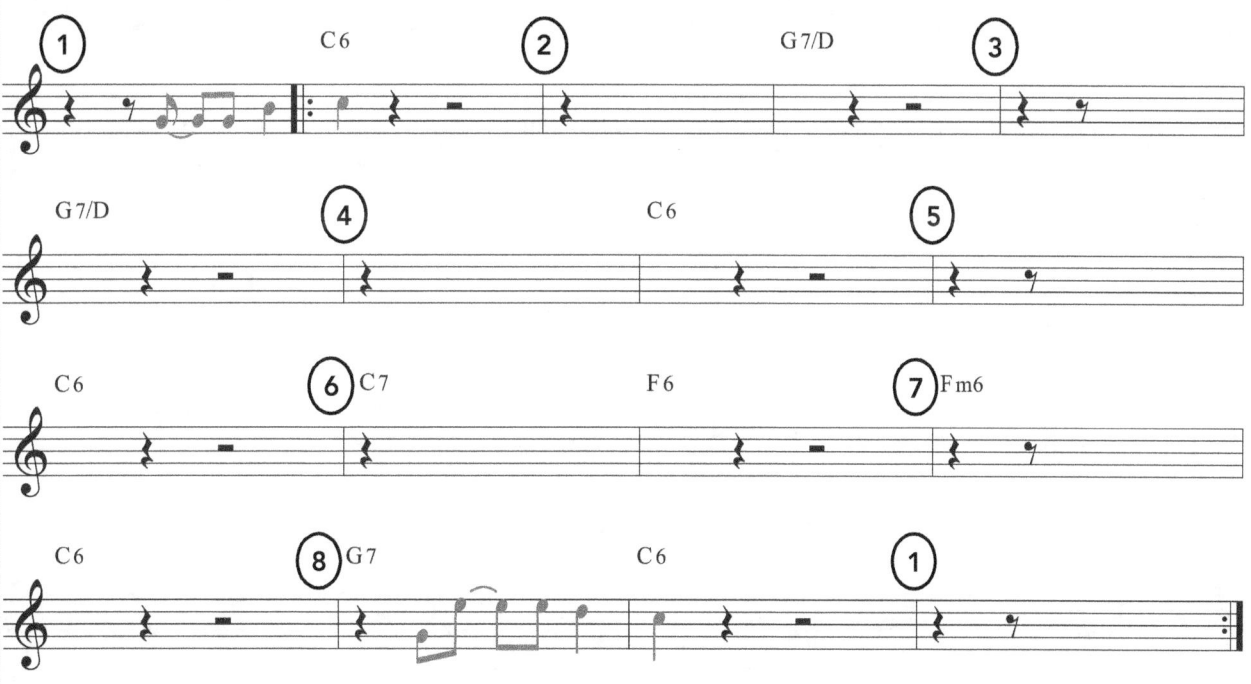

 Learning the melody and harmony by ear before studying notation can help with memorization.

"Limbo Jazz" is presented above in the key of C major. How many I chords do you count? How many V chords do you count (including slash chords)?

Song Study

"Limbo Jazz"
page 2 of 2

"Limbo Jazz" can be played at any speed, from slow to very fast, so establish a tempo before beginning to improvise. Use the exercises below to help learn the chord progression. If choosing to improvise in a key other than C major, take time to internalize the melody and harmony in the new key.

EX. 5.71
"Limbo Jazz" harmony exercise, first eight bars,
using 2 chord tones per chord + motivic rhythms

Alter this exercise by playing just **one chord tone per chord**. This will develop focus, and each note will matter immensely.

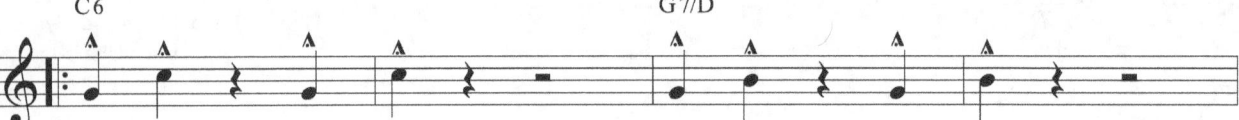

"down down   up   up"

EX. 5.72
"Limbo Jazz" harmony exercise, last eight bars,
using chord tone arpeggios

The example above uses what is called a **"down-down, up-up" rhythm**, describing the combination of downbeats and upbeat syncopations.

EX. 5.73
"Limbo Jazz" harmony exercise, last eight bars,
using select chord tones to create a melodic line

Try **keeping the notes while changing the rhythm**. Alternatively, keep the rhythm but change the notes.

An iconic recording of "Limbo Jazz" appears on the album *Duke Ellington Meets Coleman Hawkins*. Check out drummer Sam Woodyard, in particular, singing gleefully for much of the performance.

The original recording of "Limbo Jazz" is in the **key of A-flat major**. Another common key for this song is E-flat major, which sits a bit more easily for many instrument ranges.

Solo Spotlight

Johnny Hodges, alto sax
Ray Nance, cornet
"Limbo Jazz"

Johnny Hodges and Ray Nance were two of the Duke Ellington Orchestra's premiere performers. On "Limbo Jazz," they both improvise brilliant solos. Hodges' solo is actually ornamental and complementary, played while the rest of the ensemble plays the melody.

 EX. 5.74
Johnny Hodges alto sax solo "Limbo Jazz"

In both solos, circle the last note of each phrase and determine whether the phrase ends on a chord tone or a non-chord tone.

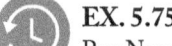 **EX. 5.75**
Ray Nance cornet solo "Limbo Jazz"

Notice creative use of **syncopations and rests** throughout each solo.

Improvise

"Limbo Jazz"

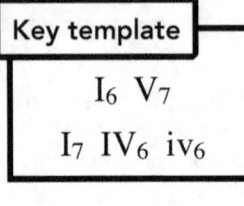

Using chord collection boxes

"Limbo Jazz" includes only five chords in total for the entire composition. Gather them into a "chord collection box" to help facilitate learning the song in new keys. Use the chord collection boxes below, each in a different key, and begin transposing.

Key template

I_6 V_7

I_7 IV_6 iv_6

Key of C major

C_6 G_7

C_7 F_6 F_{m6}

Key of A♭ major

$A\flat_6$ $E\flat_7$

$A\flat_7$ $D\flat_6$ $D\flat_{m6}$

Key of B♭ major

$B\flat_6$ F_7

$B\flat_7$ $E\flat_6$ $E\flat_{m6}$

Key of E♭ major

$E\flat_6$ $B\flat_7$

$E\flat_7$ $A\flat_6$ $A\flat_{m6}$

Key of F major

F_6 C_7

F_7 $B\flat_6$ $B\flat_{m6}$

Parent major scale

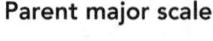

IMPROVISE
"Limbo Jazz"
(Duke Ellington)

Choose a new key from the options above then write in the matching "Limbo Jazz" chords and melody below, using your ear and the Roman numeral chord symbols as your guides. Also write out the parent scale on the blank staff above.

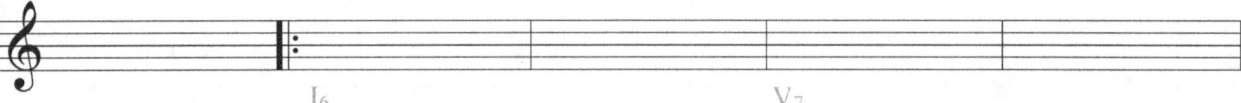

I_6 V_7

V_7 I_6

I_6 I_7 IV_6 iv_6

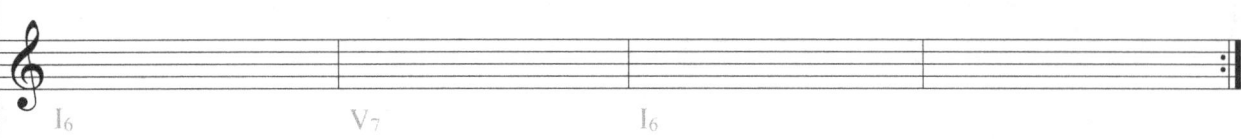

I_6 V_7 I_6

Develop more effectively by focusing only on **one phrase at a time**. Also spend time learning the chords in isolation and in small groups. The melody can also be internalized on its own before it is combined with the chord progression.

Zen Jazz Master says:

Stay in charge!

Below are a few tips to help you keep your confidence and stay in charge while soloing.

Prepare well.

Nerves won't get in the way as easily if you are prepared so study up and practice hard before you stand up to take a solo.

Think first.

Don't just play without thinking about what you are doing. Know your chord progression and song form well enough to be able to choose what notes best tell your story.

Keep track of where you are.

The quickest way to get lost while soloing is to play too much. This simple three-step process should help you stay on track:

1. **Play simply.**
2. **Stop and listen to the rhythm section.**
3. **Repeat.**

Remain confident.

During a solo, the drummer might throw a different groove at you or the pianist might strike an unusual voicing. There is no need to panic or stop playing. If you are not sure how to handle a situation, keep playing with confidence and you will be through the tough spot before you know it. The element of surprise, for the players and for those lucky enough to notice, is part of what makes jazz so thrilling.

Chapter 5 Achievements

Congratulations!

You are one step closer to jazz nirvana.

Here is a partial list of what you've achieved:

- Hearing the details in pitch resolutions between the V and I chord
- Understanding differences between ii and V chords
- Noticing the difference between antecedent and consequent phrases
- Using pedal points while improvising on a V-I chord progression
- Differentiating Dorian, Mixolydian, and major pentatonic scales

Are you ready for the next chapter?

Answer these questions to determine whether you are prepared to continue to the next chapter:

- **Can you target** the arrival of a V chord when approached from a I chord?

  If "Yes," move to the next chapter.
  If "No," review this chapter.

- **Do you understand** the difference between half and full cadences?

  If "Yes," move to the next chapter.
  If "No," review this chapter.

- **Can you play** major pentatonic scale patterns in multiple keys?

  If "Yes," move to the next chapter.
  If "No," review this chapter.

- **Do you want** to learn more about minor keys and the blues?

  If "Yes," move to the next chapter.
  If "No,"… wait, what?! You don't want to learn about minor keys and the blues? Getouttahere!!
  (Everyone loves minor keys!)

6 Blues in the Night

Minor Progressions, Minor Pentatonics, and the 12-Bar Blues

Evoking a wide range of imagery — darkness, mystery, sadness, pain, yearning, reflection — minor keys provide a means of expression that is quite different from major keys. Unlike the major scale, which is composed consistently of the same seven distinct notes, minor scales come in various forms. The notes used within a minor key can shift, depending in part on which underlying harmonies are used. Learning which minor scales suit specific minor key chord progressions will help develop some sense of order within each varying minor key landscape. This chapter addresses minor chord progressions, the minor pentatonic scale, and the 12-bar blues — with much of blues melody rooted firmly in minor.

Contents

TOPICS
- Four Minor Chord Progressions
- Minor i to Minor iv
- Why not change scales for every chord?
- Using the Leading Tone in Minor
- Minor i to IV
- Minor i to minor v
- Minor i to $V_7(\flat 9)$
- A Particularly Special Fragment
- Minor Pentatonic Scale
- Minor Pentatonic Scale Patterns
- The Blues Scale
- Blues Scale Additive Exercise
- Major Blues Scale
- New Orleans Blues Scale
- Other Pentatonics
- Introduction to the 12-Bar Blues
- Lyrics and Phrasing
- Form and Harmony
- Targeted Thirds (and when to avoid the major third)
- "Mercy" Exercise
- Tails

EAR TRAINING
- Sing an improvised solo over a i-iv progression
- By ear, improvise on "Song for My Father"
- Learn Melba Liston's "In Memory of" solo by ear
- Learn Illinois Jacquet's "Flying Home" solo by ear
- Learn "Mercy, Mercy, Mercy" in 3 keys by ear
- Play "C Jam Blues" over "Sonnymoon for Two"

MASTERCLASS
- Chord Extensions

INVESTIGATE
- Origins of Diatonic Minor Harmony
- Origins of the "m7($\flat$5)" Chord

SONG STUDY
- "Oye cómo va" (Tito Puente)

SOLO SPOTLIGHT
- John Coltrane tenor sax solo "Pursuance (A Love Supreme)"
- Melba Liston trombone solo "In Memory of"
- Illinois Jacquet tenor sax solo "Flying Home"
- Mary Lou Williams piano solo "St. Louis Blues"
- Kenny Burrell guitar solo "C Jam Blues"

COMPOSE
- "Oye cómo va" Moña

IMPROVISE
- 2-chord Vamps, i-iv
- "Oye cómo va" (Tito Puente)
- 2-chord Vamps, V-i
- "Song for My Father" (Horace Silver)
- C Minor Vamp Using C Minor Pentatonic Scale
- "Mercy, Mercy, Mercy" (Joe Zawinul)
- "Sonnymoon for Two" (Sonny Rollins)

HISTORICAL EXAMPLES
- "Greensleeves" (Traditional)
- Joe Henderson tenor sax solo "Song for My Father"
- Horace Silver piano solo "Song for My Father"
- "A Love Supreme" (John Coltrane)
- King Curtis soprano sax solo "Soul Serenade"
- "Bag's Groove" (Milt Jackson)
- "Blues in the Closet" (Oscar Pettiford)
- "Mercy, Mercy, Mercy" (Joe Zawinul)
- Sonny Rollins tenor sax solo "Sonnymoon for Two"

LISTENING GUIDE
- Use the original recording of "Song for My Father" to notice details
- Learn blues details from recordings
- Use the original recordings of "Bag's Groove" and "Blues in the Closet" to learn stylistic elements and original keys
- Learn the key for "Sonnymoon for Two" from the original recording

ZEN JAZZ MASTER SAYS
- A word of CAUTION regarding blues scales!

Investigate | Origins of Diatonic Minor Harmony

The road to minor harmony starts with a key center. Among the many minor scales, natural minor is the most organically related to the major scale. With the same key signature and shared notes, the only difference is that the natural minor scale starts on the 6th scale degree of its relative major scale. Once the natural minor scale is established, diatonic harmonies can be built on each scale degree, forming a series of chords that function together within the established minor key.

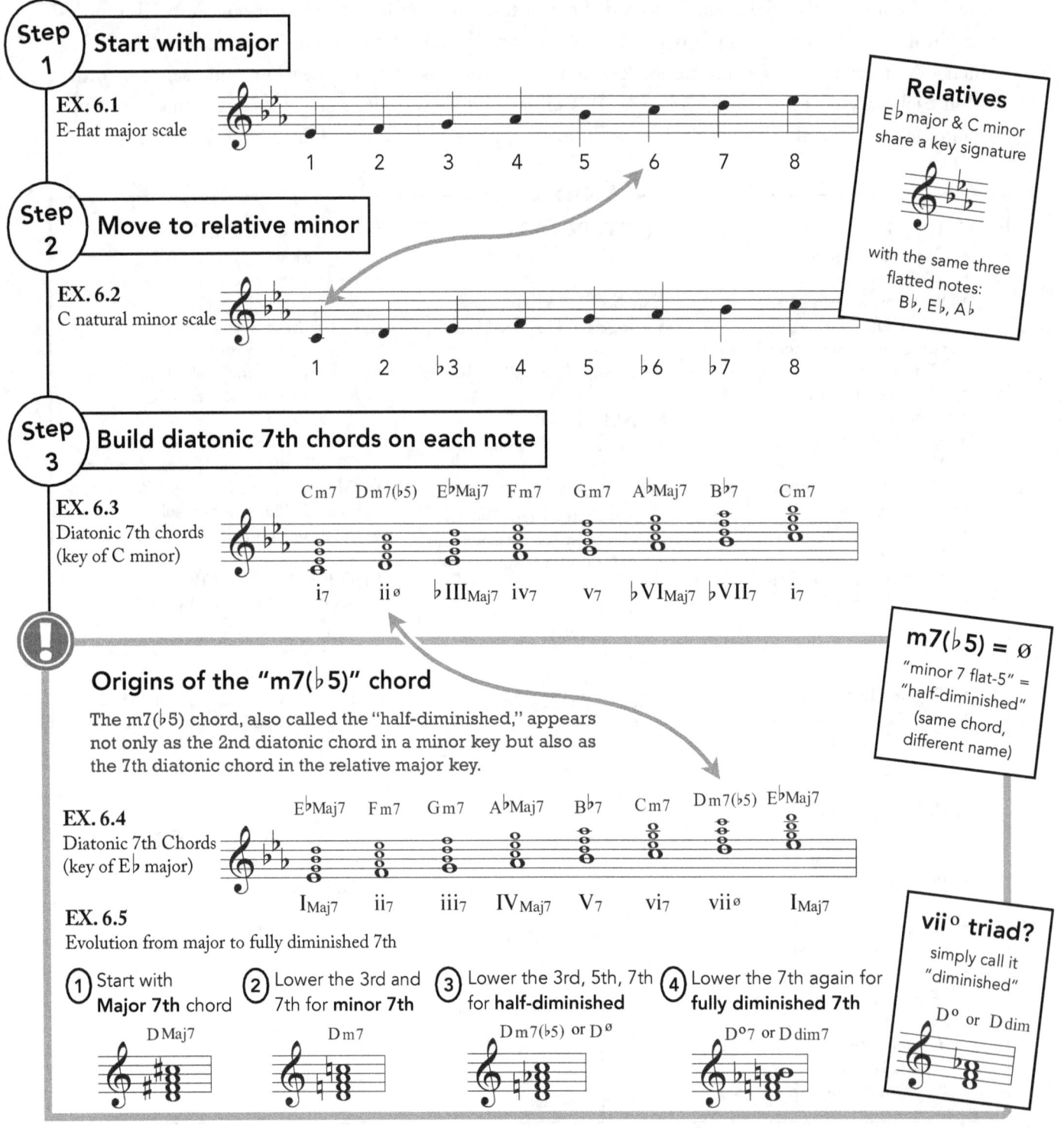

Step 1 Start with major

EX. 6.1
E-flat major scale

1 2 3 4 5 6 7 8

Relatives
E♭ major & C minor share a key signature

with the same three flatted notes:
B♭, E♭, A♭

Step 2 Move to relative minor

EX. 6.2
C natural minor scale

1 2 ♭3 4 5 ♭6 ♭7 8

Step 3 Build diatonic 7th chords on each note

EX. 6.3
Diatonic 7th chords
(key of C minor)

Cm7   Dm7(♭5)   E♭Maj7   Fm7   Gm7   A♭Maj7   B♭7   Cm7

i₇   iiø   ♭IIIMaj7   iv₇   v₇   ♭VIMaj7   ♭VII₇   i₇

m7(♭5) = ø
"minor 7 flat-5" = "half-diminished"
(same chord, different name)

Origins of the "m7(♭5)" chord

The m7(♭5) chord, also called the "half-diminished," appears not only as the 2nd diatonic chord in a minor key but also as the 7th diatonic chord in the relative major key.

EX. 6.4
Diatonic 7th Chords
(key of E♭ major)

E♭Maj7   Fm7   Gm7   A♭Maj7   B♭7   Cm7   Dm7(♭5)   E♭Maj7

IMaj7   ii₇   iii₇   IVMaj7   V₇   vi₇   viiø   IMaj7

EX. 6.5
Evolution from major to fully diminished 7th

1. Start with **Major 7th** chord
2. Lower the 3rd and 7th for **minor 7th**
3. Lower the 3rd, 5th, 7th for **half-diminished**
4. Lower the 7th again for **fully diminished 7th**

DMaj7   Dm7   Dm7(♭5) or Dø   D°7 or Ddim7

vii° triad?
simply call it "diminished"

D° or Ddim

Four Minor Chord Progressions

Listed below are four common two-chord progressions in the key of C minor. Each progression involves pairing the minor i chord with a second chord. Each particular parent minor scale is chosen because it matches the notes for each of the two chords. While other notes are certainly allowed, the chord/scale relationships below offer an approach to simple yet successful melodic structures.

EX. 6.6
Parent scale:
C natural minor

EX. 6.7
Parent scale:
C Dorian minor

EX. 6.8
Parent scale:
C natural minor
(or C Dorian minor)

Raise the 6th (to A-natural)
to change to C Dorian minor.

EX. 6.9
Parent scale:
C harmonic minor

Always keep in mind that these scale relationships are a serious **oversimplification**. Remember that melody is not meant to be kept in some sort of chord/scale "box" and, even when you know the matching scale, exceptions always apply.

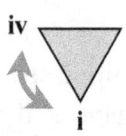

Minor i to Minor iv

page 1 of 2

The minor i chord moves easily to minor iv since both chords are diatonic, originating from the natural minor scale. Consider it an inevitability that the natural minor scale acts as the parent scale here, unifying the progression.

EX. 6.10
Chord arpeggios and C natural minor scales, roots and inversions

Notice which arpeggios and scales below are played from root position and which are played in inversion.
HINT: Notice when chord roots are circled.

EX. 6.11
Simple parent scale melodies (C natural minor)

Of the three melodies below, which does not outline the change to Fm7 as clearly? What harmony is outlined instead?

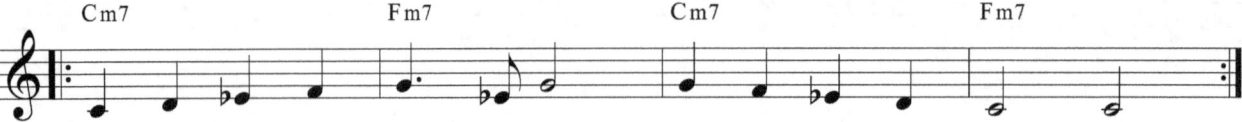

Why not change scales for every chord?

In the key of C minor, the progression from Cm7 to Fm7 involves two harmonies interacting with each other. Since only one C minor parent scale is needed as a unifying melodic element, the interaction helps to maintain a simply and grounded sound.

If you do decide to change scales, **DO NOT change to the F natural minor scale on Fm7** when playing Cm7-Fm7. The upper scale fragment can wreak melodic havoc since D-flat is not a diatonic note in the parent key of C minor.

EX. 6.12
F natural minor scale (in the key of C minor)

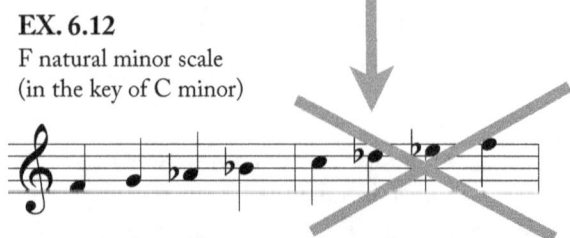

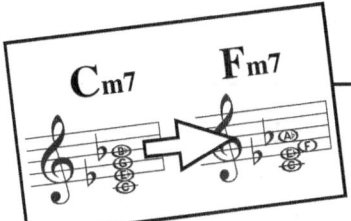

Minor i to Minor iv
— page 2 of 2 —

While the tonic natural minor scale may be played as the parent scale over both the minor i and minor iv chords, other scales — particularly Dorian minor and melodic minor — may be used over the minor i chord. Because the minor i chord is defined mostly by the triad (1-♭3-5), melodies played over the i chord can incorporate variation in the 6th and 7th scale degrees without losing the sound of the key itself. The flatted 6th of the parent scale, however, remains fixed when the progression changes to the iv chord since it is the 3rd of the iv chord — a defining element of that harmony.

Know your scale degrees! This A-flat is both the 3rd of Fm7 and the 6th of the parent C natural minor scale.

EX. 6.13
C melodic minor (over Cm7), C natural minor (over Fm7)

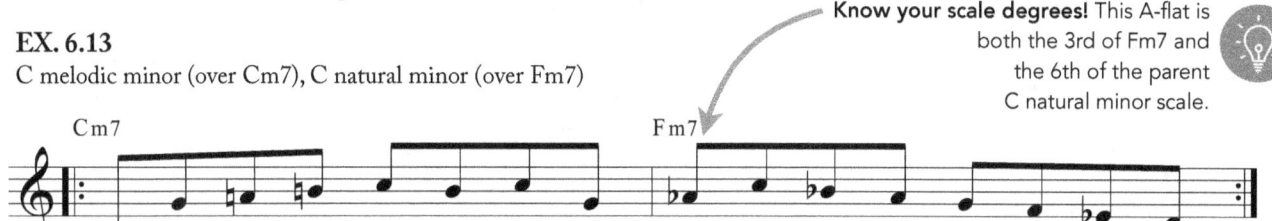

EX. 6.14
Mixing C Dorian and C natural minor scales

IMPROVISE
4-bar vamp: 2 bars i, 2 bars iv

IMPROVISE
2-bar vamp: 1 bar i, 1 bar iv

Using the leading tone in minor

The raised 7th in minor may be used within any minor scale or scale fragment. There's no need to save it for just the harmonic minor scale. The example below uses the lowered 7th (B♭) that belongs to the natural minor scale but it also uses the raised 7th (B), which functions as a leading tone to tonic (C).

EX. 6.15
Mixing in the leading tone

raised 7th AND lowered 7th

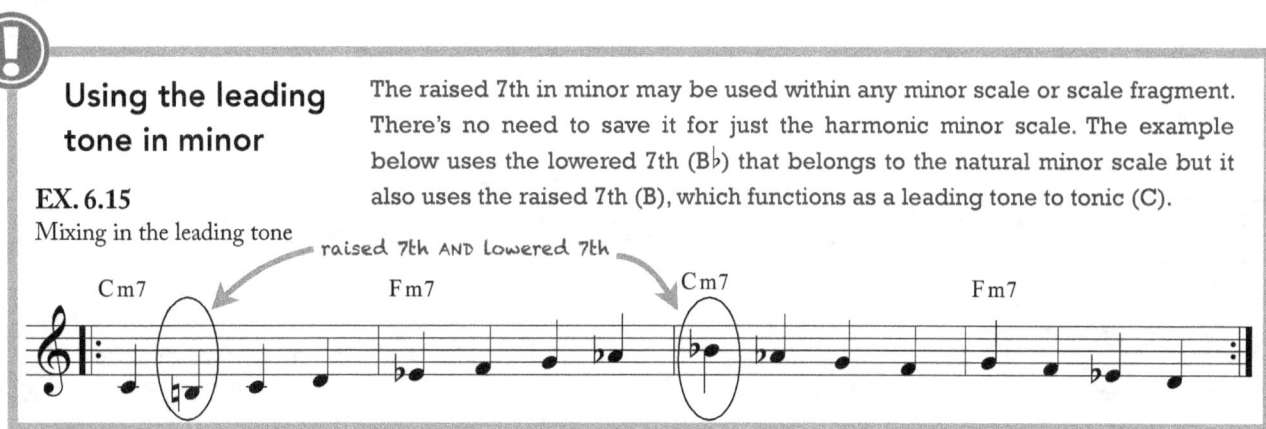

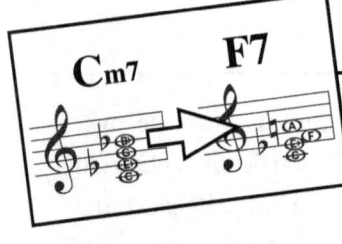

Minor i to IV

When moving between minor i and IV chords, the matching parent scale is Dorian minor. Natural minor can no longer be the unifying scale because the IV chord includes a major third, which is the raised 6 scale degree of the parent minor, and an identifying characteristic within the minor i to IV progression.

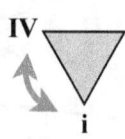

EX. 6.16

Chord arpeggios,
roots and inversions

EX. 6.17

C Dorian minor scale from
roots and across chords

Dorian uses raised 6 of i
(raised 3 of IV).

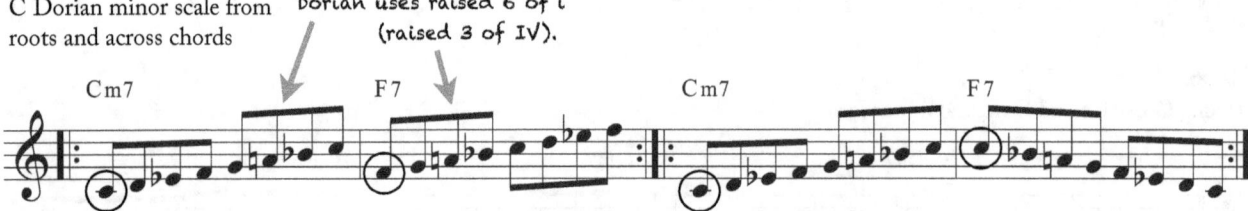

EX. 6.18

C Dorian minor scale
across multiple repetitions of i-IV

EX. 6.19

Simple and independent
parent scale melody (C Dorian minor)

EX. 6.20

Parent scale fragments
(C Dorian minor)

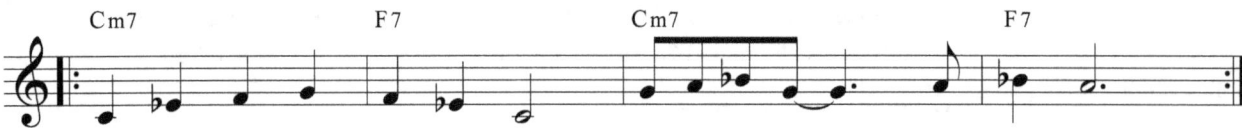

Sing an improvised solo over the above i-IV progression. Aim for pitch accuracy (sing in tune!) on both the 6th and 7th scale degrees.

For variety, **change the rhythms** in these exercises, adding more syncopation.

Song Study   "Oye cómo va"

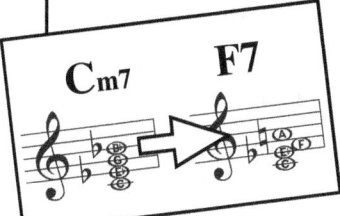

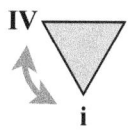

Percussionist Tito Puente's classic "Oye cómo va" transcends genre and is played by performers all over the world. Its central groove can be considered a *cha cha*, featuring a straight-eighth pulse, played at an energetic yet moderately slow tempo. The composition features a two-chord pattern moving between a minor i chord and a IV chord. The song's central melody is based on a minor pentatonic scale. Other riffs (called *moñas*) are introduced and are based on minor pentatonic, Dorian, and blues scales.

EX. 6.21
"Oye cómo va" (Tito Puente)
rhythm only (key of C minor)

Learn the melody to
"Oye cómo va" entirely by ear.

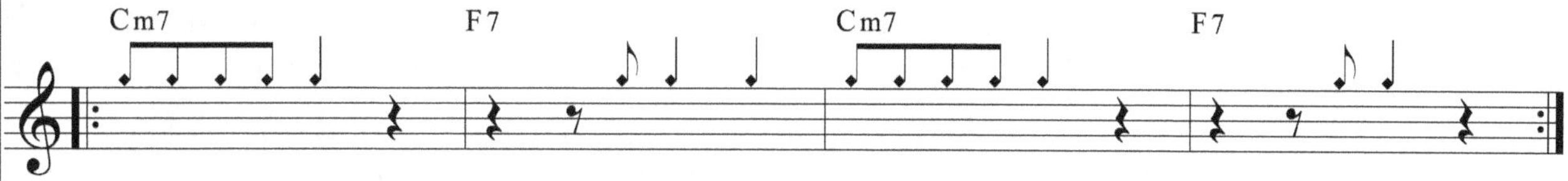

EX. 6.22
Moña 1 "Oye cómo va"

EX. 6.23
Moña 2 "Oye cómo va"

IMPROVISE
"Oye cómo va" (Tito Puente)
(key of C minor)

Does "Oye cómo va" use C Dorian minor or C natural minor?
What is the difference between the two? What are the **context clues**
in the harmony and *moñas* that help determine the scale?

Compose a *moña* over "Oye cómo va"
in a key of your choice.

Transpose "Oye cómo va" to its
original key of A minor.

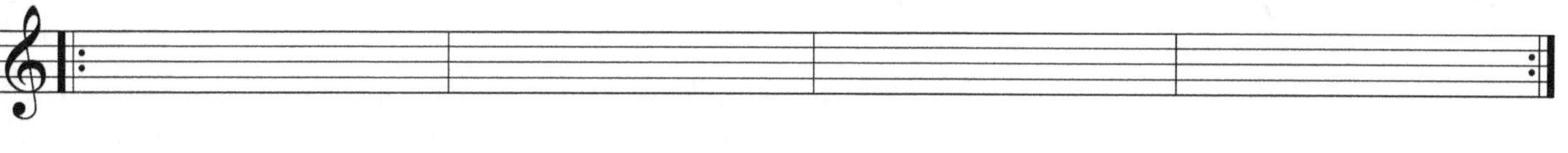

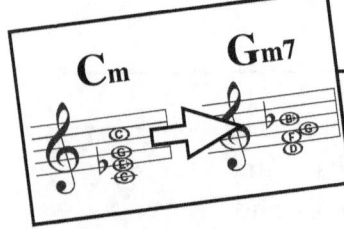

Minor i to Minor v

When building diatonic harmonies on the natural minor scale, the chord built on the 5th note of the scale is a minor v chord, which means that the natural minor scale may be used across minor i and v chord progressions. The Dorian minor scale may also be used, depending on compositional context.

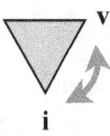

EX. 6.24
C natural minor
parent scale

Compare the **two versions of "Greensleeves"** below. The first uses a minor v chord, keeping every note of the melody within a single parent natural minor scale. The second replaces the minor v chord with a V₇ chord, which establishes a clear tonic-dominant relationship that is missing from the first version, while the melody deviates from natural minor.

EX. 6.25
"Greensleeves (What child is this?)"
(Traditional)

The use of flat-6 and flat-7 in the melody firmly establishes the parent scale as natural minor.

EX. 6.26
"Greensleeves (What child is this?)"
(Traditional)

In this alternate version, the use of raised-6 and flat-7 in the melody establishes C Dorian minor for the first phrase.

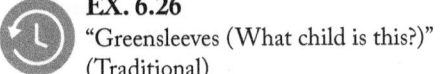

added dominant
V7 chord

IMPROVISE
4-bar vamp: 2 bars i, 2 bars minor v

The raised 7ths at the end of the second phrase match the added dominant V7 chord in this alternate version, suggesting harmonic minor.

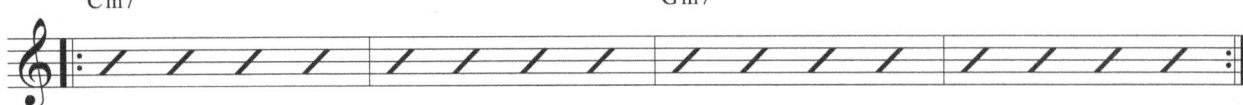

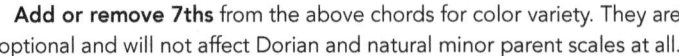

Add or remove 7ths from the above chords for color variety. They are optional and will not affect Dorian and natural minor parent scales at all.

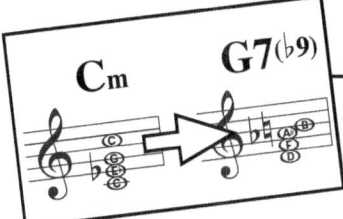

Minor i to V$_{7(\flat9)}$

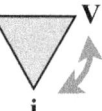

The harmonic minor scale includes all the chord tones of the i and V$_7$ chords. The V$_7$ chord can also include a flat-9 (one half step above the root of the V chord), which is the flat-6 of the parent harmonic minor scale. Use the following exercises to gain fluency with the full harmonic scale but know that rich melodic value also comes from each scale's many smaller fragments.

EX. 6.27
C harmonic minor scale and arpeggios

Understand **scale degrees in relation** to both the minor i chord and the V$_{7(\flat9)}$ chord. For example, in the key of C minor, using the C harmonic scale, the note B is the raised 7th of Cm and the 3rd of G7(♭9).

EX. 6.28
Simple and independent parent scale melody
(C harmonic minor)

Flat-6 of the parent harmonic minor scale is also the flat-9 of the V7 chord.

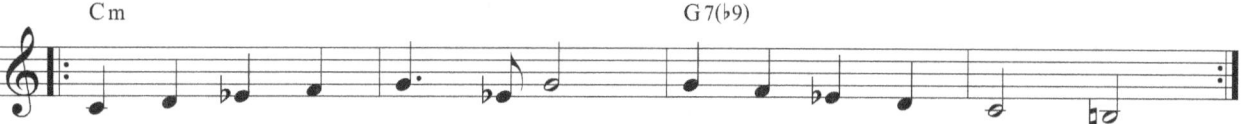

EX. 6.29
Parent scale fragments
(C harmonic minor)

IMPROVISE
C harmonic minor scale,
4-bar vamp: 2 bars V, 2 bars i

A particularly special fragment

The upper fragment of the harmonic minor scale is quite special. Instead of consisting of a series of steps, it also includes a skip — a minor 3rd (m3) interval — bookended by half steps (m2) and offering a particularly intriguing sound.

EX. 6.30
Upper fragment,
C harmonic
minor scale

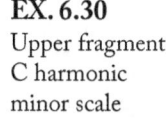

EX. 6.31
Upper fragment
sequence, half
step descent

Masterclass   Chord Extensions

Some of the more common chords and their extensions are listed below. Look for common notes between chords in each row. Also study which notes are unique to specific chords. One fascinating characteristic of *chord extensions* is that they often imply other simple harmonies. For instance, the CMaj13(♯11) chord really is simply a CMaj7 with a D major triad stacked above it — two chords in one! Chords stacked on top of each other are also called *polychords*.

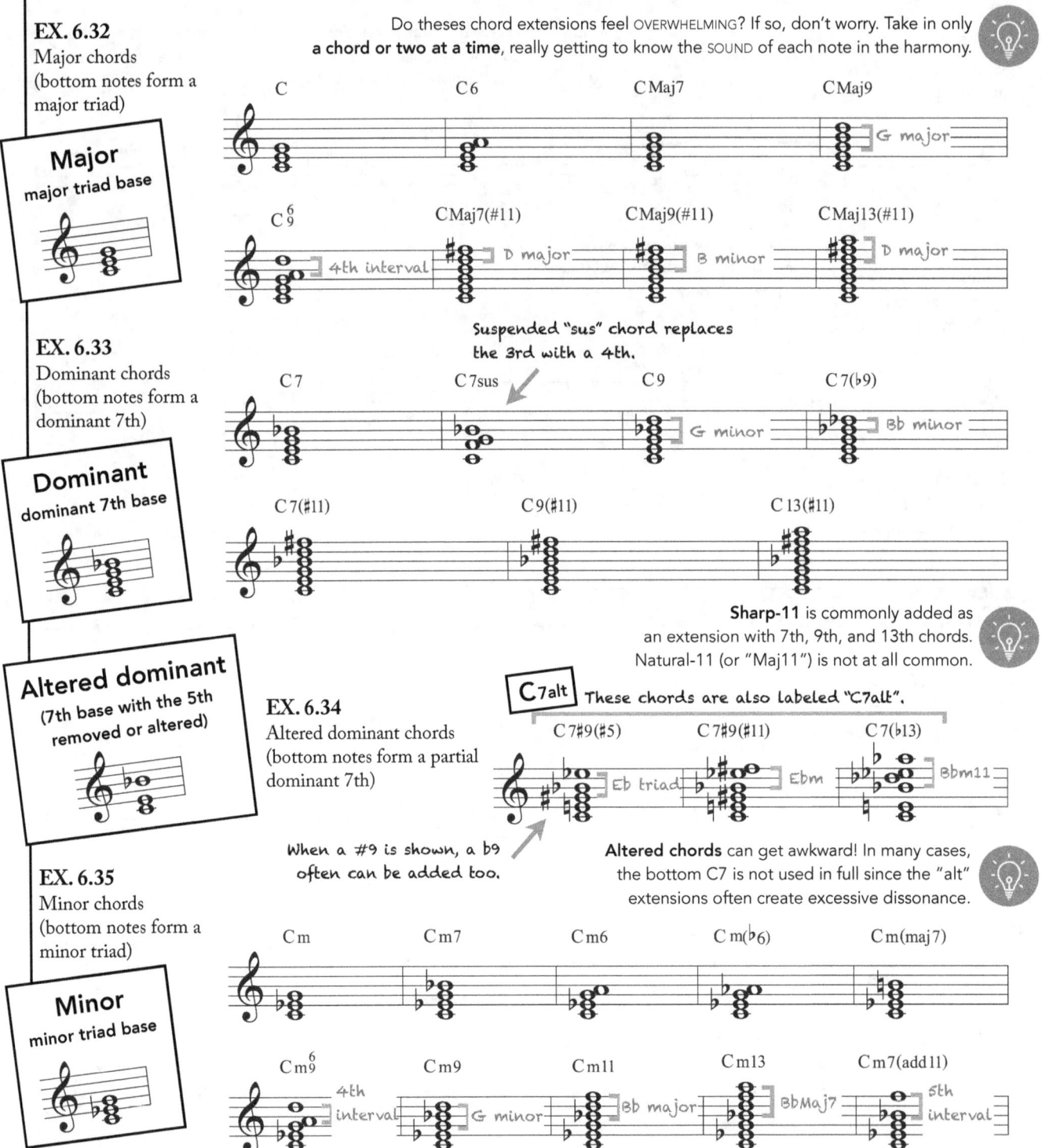

EX. 6.32
Major chords (bottom notes form a major triad)

Do theses chord extensions feel OVERWHELMING? If so, don't worry. Take in only **a chord or two at a time**, really getting to know the SOUND of each note in the harmony.

Major
major triad base

EX. 6.33
Dominant chords (bottom notes form a dominant 7th)

Suspended "sus" chord replaces the 3rd with a 4th.

Dominant
dominant 7th base

Sharp-11 is commonly added as an extension with 7th, 9th, and 13th chords. Natural-11 (or "Maj11") is not at all common.

Altered dominant
(7th base with the 5th removed or altered)

C7alt These chords are also labeled "C7alt".

EX. 6.34
Altered dominant chords (bottom notes form a partial dominant 7th)

When a ♯9 is shown, a ♭9 often can be added too.

Altered chords can get awkward! In many cases, the bottom C7 is not used in full since the "alt" extensions often create excessive dissonance.

EX. 6.35
Minor chords (bottom notes form a minor triad)

Minor
minor triad base

Song Study — "Song for My Father"
— page 1 of 2 —

"Song for My Father" showcases some key characteristics present in pianist Horace Silver's compositions, including an instantly recognizable melody, an engaging chord progression, and an iconic bass line that grounds the composition effectively. Notice how, when the melody is played with ornamentation between notes, the ornaments stem from the natural minor scale. When the ornaments are removed, the melody is played more simply, involving a series of eighth notes. The original recording of "Song for My Father" used ornaments but try it without and notice that the performance works both ways.

EX. 6.36
"Song for My Father"
(Horace Silver)
A-section (key of C minor)

Learn the melody to "Song for My Father" entirely by ear.

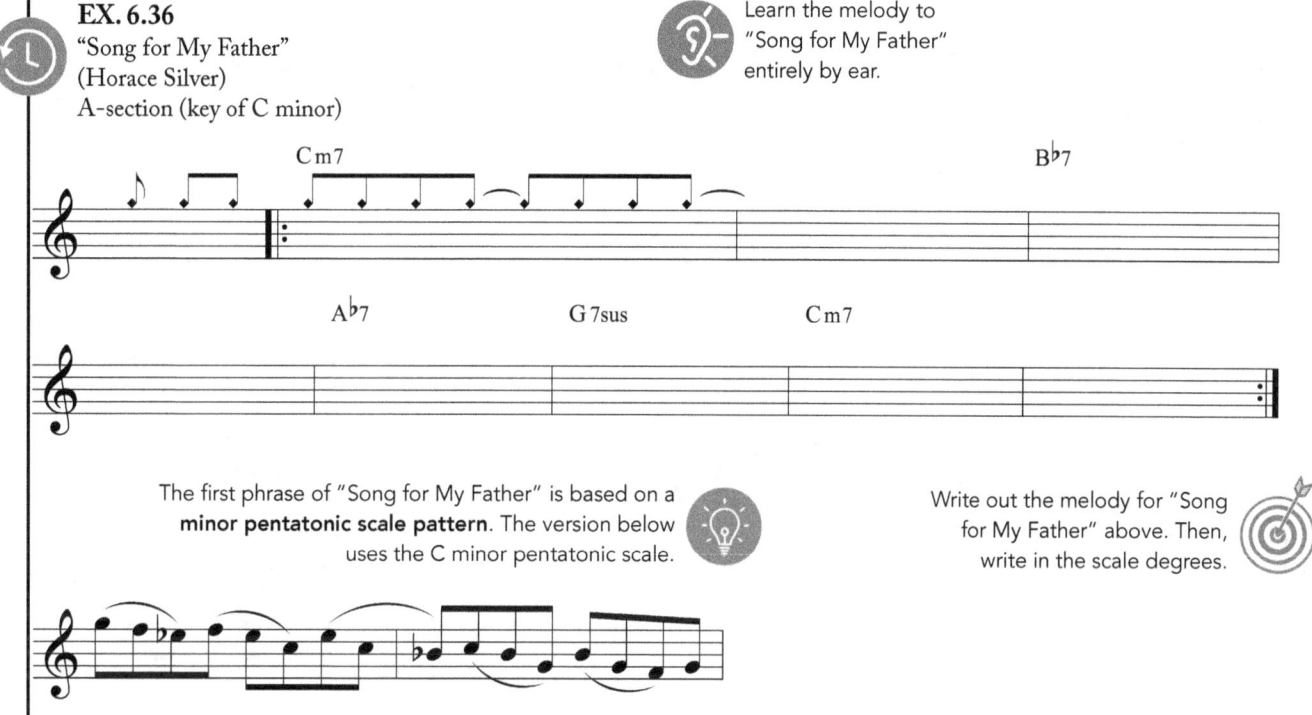

The first phrase of "Song for My Father" is based on a **minor pentatonic scale pattern**. The version below uses the C minor pentatonic scale.

Write out the melody for "Song for My Father" above. Then, write in the scale degrees.

"Song for My Father" bass line

The bass line for "Song for My Father" sets the tone for the piece, ensuring that the underlying groove is established before the melody begins. While the bass line moves through all eight measures of harmony, the exercise below covers only the first 4 measures and is helpful to practice in an ongoing loop.

EX. 6.37
"Song for My Father"
bass line vamp

Still not entirely comfortable with bass clef notation? Make the effort and **learn the bass line** anyway.
HINT: The first pitch here is a low C.

Take extra time to listen to the original recording of "Song for My Father" by Horace Silver and his quintet, featuring tenor saxophonist Joe Henderson, and originally performed in the key of F minor. Do you notice how the music changes from chorus to chorus? Not even the bass line remains constant. Its notes are changing occasionally depending on the creative input of the performers involved.

Song Study — "Song for My Father"
page 2 of 2

In the examples below, saxophonist Joe Henderson and pianist Horace Silver use scale fragments to create effective melodic lines. Knowing the exact chord tones for each chord in "Song for My Father," a soloist can also emphasize non-chord tones and, in their solos, both performers choose to focus occasionally on dissonance instead of resolution.

EX. 6.38
Joe Henderson tenor sax solo
"Song for My Father"

EX. 6.39
Horace Silver piano solo
"Song for My Father"

Horace Silver's solo line here is harmonized in thirds.

1. Practice each harmonized melody separately.
2. Identify which part of the Dorian minor scale each represents.
3. Move each fragment to a new fragment placement within the same scale.

EX. 6.40
"Song for My Father" chord arpeggios
(root position)

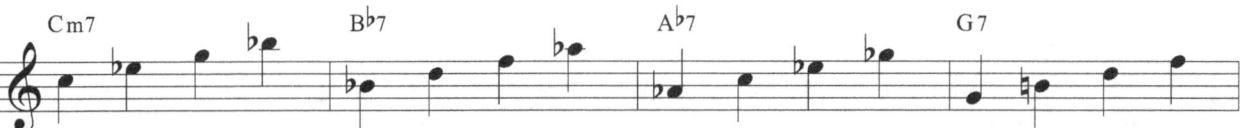

EX. 6.41
"Song for My Father" chord arpeggios
(interlocking up/down)

EX. 6.42
G7sus vs. G7

G7sus is interchangeable with G7 as a dominant V chord in many contexts. One advantage of using a "sus" is that the chord's raised third is also the root of the tonic i chord, which unifies the melodic elements between tonic and dominant harmonies.

Improvise   "Song for My Father"

Using chord collection boxes

"Song for My Father" includes only four chords in total for the entire composition. Gather them into a chord collection box to facilitate learning the song in new keys. Use the chord collection boxes below, each in a different key, and begin transposing.

| i_7 $\flat VII_7$
 $\flat VI_7$ V_7 | C_{m7} $B\flat_7$
 $A\flat_7$ G_7 | A_{m7} G_7
 F_7 E_7 | D_{m7} C_7
 $B\flat_7$ A_7 | F_{m7} $E\flat_7$
 $D\flat_7$ C_7 | G_{m7} F_7
 $E\flat_7$ D_7 |

 **IMPROVISE**
"Song for My Father"
A-section (choose a key)

 Notate the "Song for My Father" A-section below (choose a key).

 "AAB" form

While a 32-bar **AABA** form is common in many songs, the form for "Song for My Father" is AAB. The repeated 8-bar A-section is followed by an 8-bar B-section — the "bridge." Rather than return to a final A-section after the bridge, a new chorus begins, making the total form 24 measures long.

 A term for *AB form* is **binary** form. If there is a return to the A-section, either as AABA or ABA, the form is called **rounded binary**.

 Choose a key and notate the "Song for My Father" bridge below.

1.   Improvise by ear the entire "Song for My Father" bridge in C minor.
2.   Using AAB form in the original key, improvise on the whole song.

Minor Pentatonic Scale

The *minor pentatonic scale* contains only five notes, as the terms *penta* and *tonic* suggest, yet it bears a distinctly different sound from the major pentatonic scale. A defining characteristic includes prominent minor third intervals after scale degrees 1 and 5, caused by an absence of 2nd and 6th major scale degrees. The lower fragment of the scale maintains a shape that includes this minor third interval between 1 and ♭3 and also a major second interval between ♭3-4, a shape that is repeated within the scale's upper fragment, 5-♭7 and ♭7-8, presenting a symmetry of sorts.

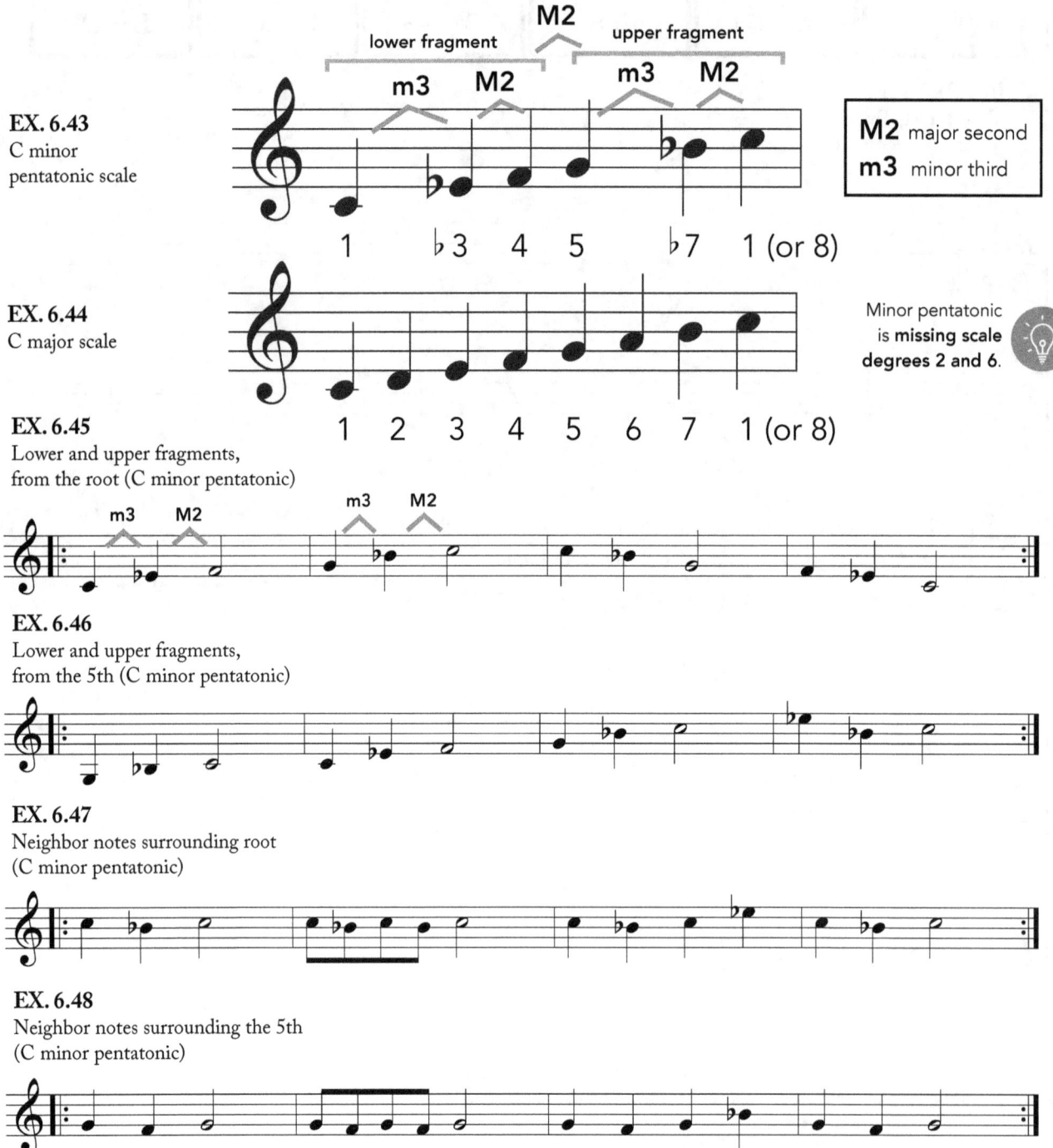

EX. 6.43
C minor
pentatonic scale

EX. 6.44
C major scale

EX. 6.45
Lower and upper fragments,
from the root (C minor pentatonic)

EX. 6.46
Lower and upper fragments,
from the 5th (C minor pentatonic)

EX. 6.47
Neighbor notes surrounding root
(C minor pentatonic)

EX. 6.48
Neighbor notes surrounding the 5th
(C minor pentatonic)

Minor Pentatonic Scale Patterns

Visualizing minor pentatonic scale patterns helps to internalize the scale's implicit intervallic structures, including the frequent appearance of the minor 3rd and major 2nd in addition to perfect 4th and 5th intervals. Pentatonic scale patterns tend also to be quite fun and engaging due in part to this intervallic variety and surprise.

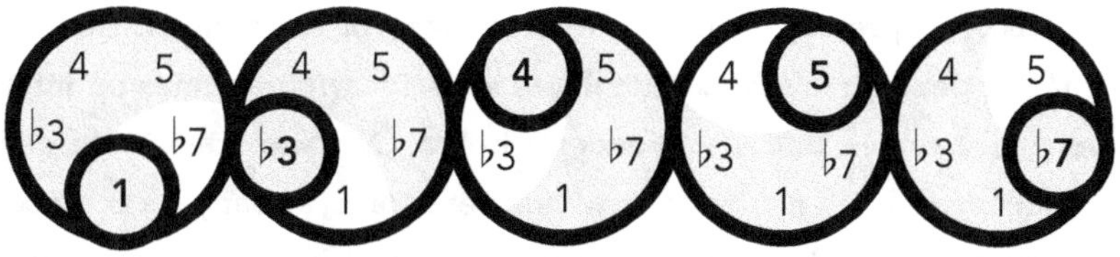

EX. 6.49
Classic
pattern
(1♭345)

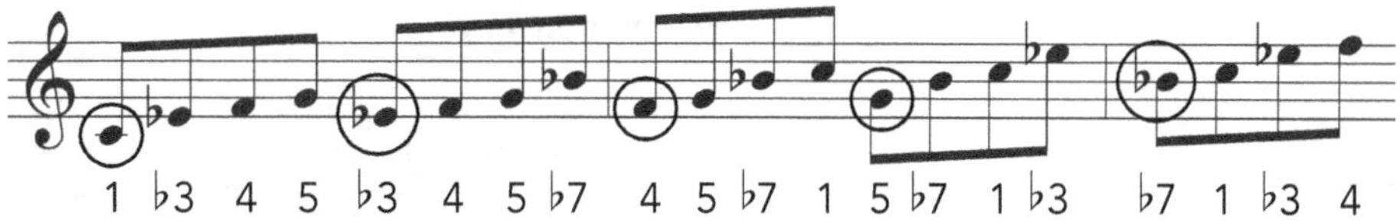

1 ♭3 4 5   ♭3 4 5 ♭7   4 5 ♭7 1   5 ♭7 1 ♭3   ♭7 1 ♭3 4   **continue up then down**

EX. 6.50
Pattern
variation
(14♭35)

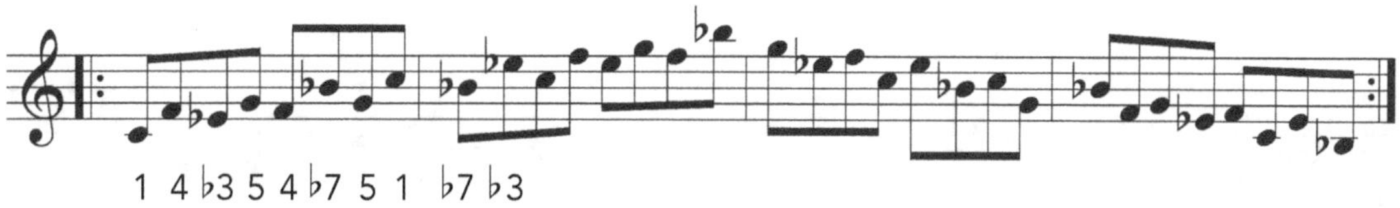

1 4 ♭3 5 4 ♭7 5 1   ♭7 ♭3

EX. 6.51
Pattern
variation
(145♭3)

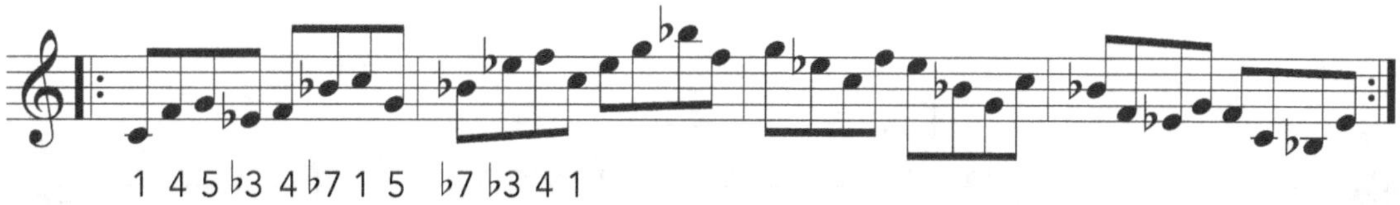

1 4 5 ♭3 4 ♭7 1 5   ♭7 ♭3 4 1

EX. 6.52
Pattern
variation
(1♭341)

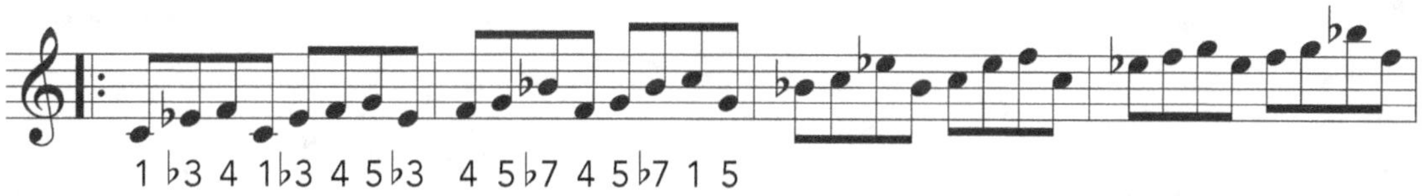

1 ♭3 4 1♭3 4 5♭3   4 5♭7 4 5♭7 1 5

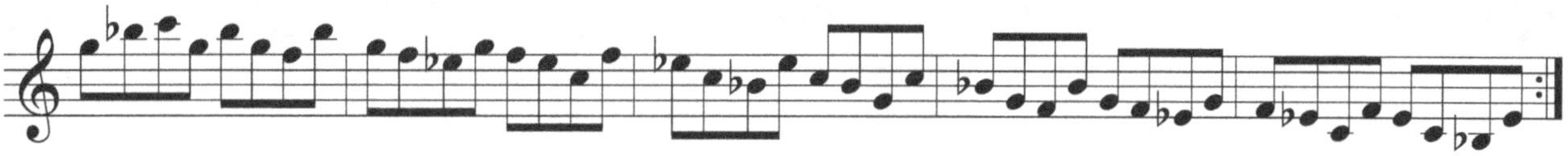

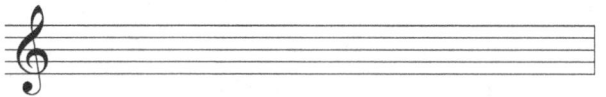

 Really ensure an understanding of skips and steps within the minor pentatonic scale. Use the staff system to the left to sketch out the scale then write in the scale degrees for each pattern.

 IMPROVISE
Improvise using the C minor pentatonic scale over a C minor vamp

Cm

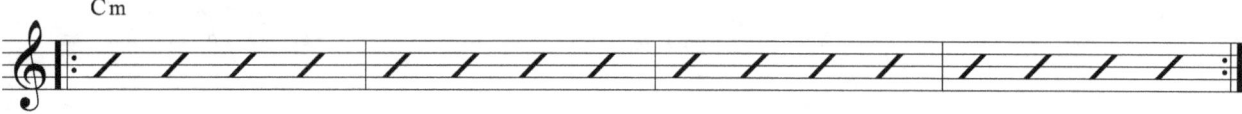

Solo 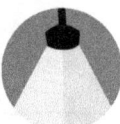 Spotlight

John Coltrane, tenor sax
"Pursuance" (from "A Love Supreme")

Tenor saxophonist John Coltrane, whose contribution to improvised music is vast, continues to influence musicians in all genres, from jazz, rock, and hip-hop to contemporary classical and world music. In his four-part *magnum opus*, "A Love Supreme," Coltrane derives much of his melodic material from pentatonic structures, including minor pentatonic scales in multiple keys, focusing at times on interlocking fragments from within many pentatonic scales. In the solo excerpt below, Coltrane adheres strictly to a single minor pentatonic scale, moving across a full two octaves. Minor pentatonic, already a strong set of melodic notes, becomes even more powerful through a creative combination of skips, leaps, and rests, long tones mixed with flurries of eighth notes and an exceptionally passionate delivery.

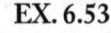

EX. 6.53
John Coltrane tenor sax solo
"Pursuance" (from "A Love Supreme")
(key of C minor)

Coltrane's **pentatonic structures** are so strong and creative that they can be slowed down or sped up. Take time to enjoy each shape he creates.

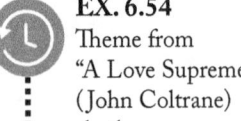

The theme to "A Love Supreme"

The iconic theme to "A Love Supreme" is also based on the minor pentatonic scale. It is played by the bass and piano, at times by the saxophone as a slightly different permutation, and even sung by the band. The chant, a simple repetition of the words "A love supreme," helps the composition and recorded performance transcend jazz music itself — Coltrane presenting it all as a spiritual offering intended to enrich the world for the better.

EX. 6.54
Theme from
"A Love Supreme"
(John Coltrane)
rhythm

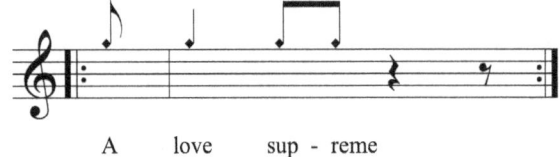

A   love   sup - reme

Learn the four-note theme from "A Love Supreme" entirely by ear, then transpose it into as many keys as possible, playing each key only one at a time.

The Blues Scale

The blues scale is often the first scale that improvisers learn. There are actually two blues scales, sometimes referred to as *minor blues scale* and *major blues scale*. By far, the most common blues scale is the minor blues scale, derived specifically from the minor pentatonic scale. It tends to be used while soloing over major and minor keys but can also be used while soloing over dominant chords.

EX. 6.55
C blues scale (aka *minor blues scale*)

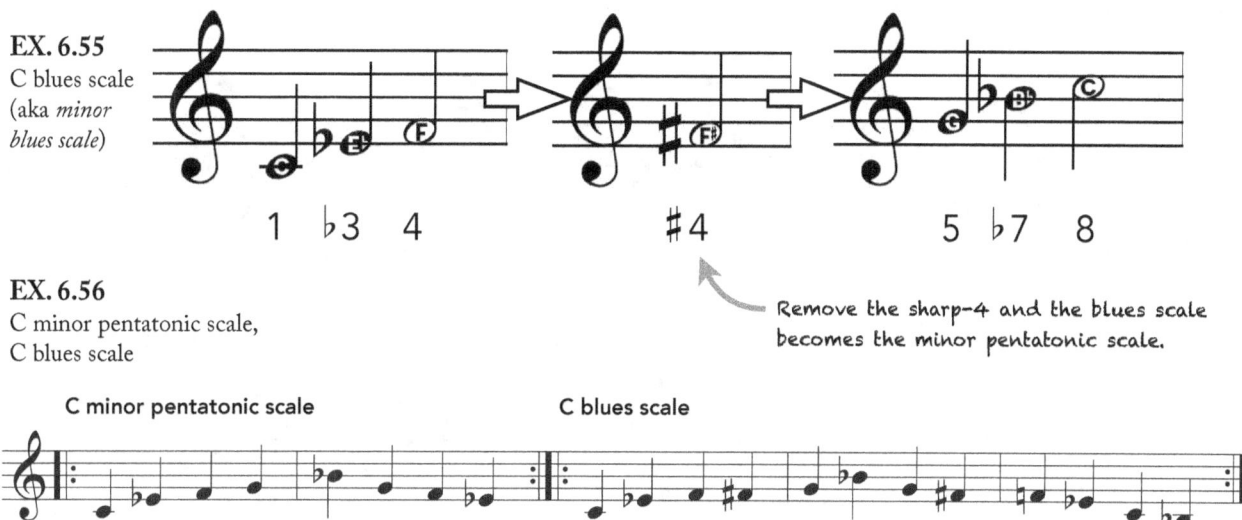

Remove the sharp-4 and the blues scale becomes the minor pentatonic scale.

EX. 6.56
C minor pentatonic scale, C blues scale

Transpose the minor pentatonic and blues scales into at least two more keys to be learned fluently.

Blues scale additive exercise

If you want to get really fluid with your blues scale, try practicing the exercise below at all tempos, from very slow, where you can focus on each interval being played, all the way to very fast, allowing your fingers to develop fluency. You'll also begin to hear exactly where the targets within the scale lie, both rhythmically and melodically.

EX. 6.57
Additive exercise (C blues scale), starting from the root

This is called an **additive exercise** because with each new ascent, a new note of the scale is added until finally all notes are present.

Major Blues Scale

What is fascinating about the minor blues scale is that, while many improvisers are encouraged to use it over the 12-bar blues, it doesn't always sound idiomatic in that context. This might be because the 12-bar blues is usually in a major key. The minor blues scale incorporates only the minor third and does not allow the melody to resolve to the major third. An alternative to the minor blues scale is the *major blues scale*, which incorporates the major 3rd chord tones of both the I and IV chord. The major blues scale is built from the major pentatonic, incorporating all the major pentatonic notes, plus a flatted third.

EX. 6.58
C major blues scale

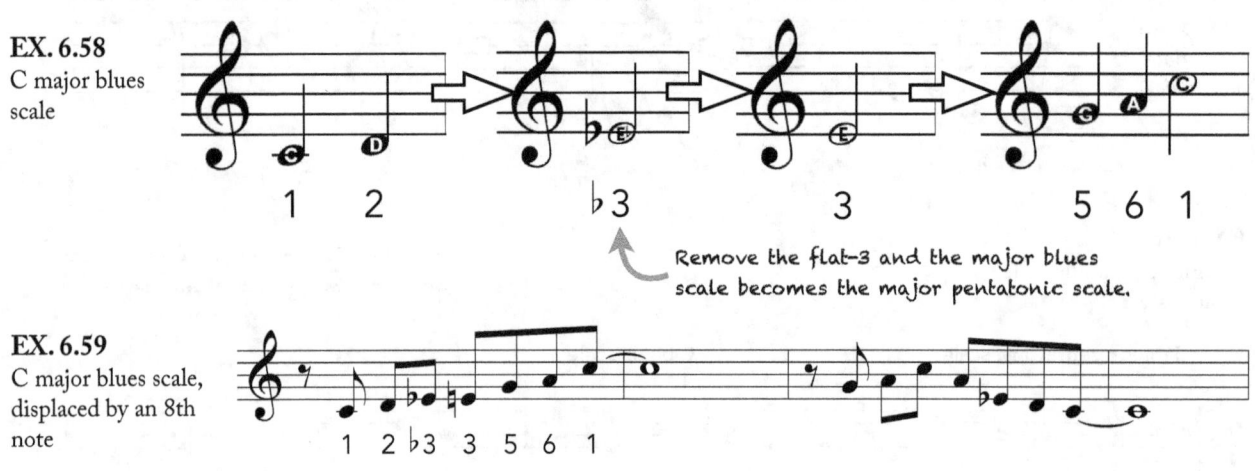

Remove the flat-3 and the major blues scale becomes the major pentatonic scale.

EX. 6.59
C major blues scale, displaced by an 8th note

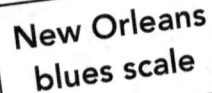

New Orleans blues scale

The *New Orleans blues scale* comprises notes within the major blues scale that sound startlingly great together. While this collection of notes may be played in any order, the descending New Orleans blues scale sounds particularly idiomatic.

EX. 6.60
New Orleans blues scale, ascending

EX. 6.61
New Orleans blues scale, descending

 EX. 6.62
King Curtis soprano sax solo "Soul Serenade"

Other pentatonics

The *major pentatonic* and *minor-6 pentatonic* scale also are quite effective scales to use while playing a blues although the major 3rd scale degree is often used sparingly.

EX. 6.63
Major pentatonic scale

EX. 6.64
Minor-6 pentatonic scale

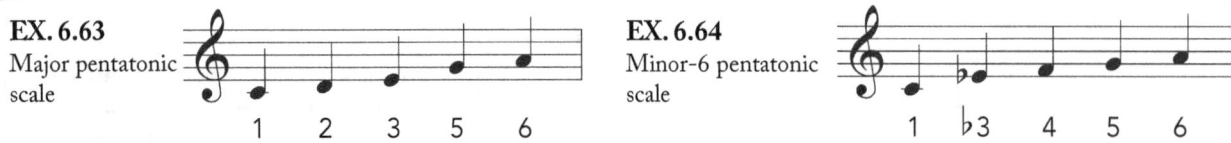

Solo 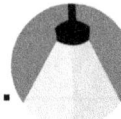 Spotlight

Melba Liston, trombone "In Memory of"
Illinois Jacquet, tenor sax "Flying Home"

Melba Liston and Illinois Jacquet take distinctly different approaches to their solos below. Liston focuses, to powerful effect, exclusively on the minor pentatonic scale and blues scale. Jacquet uses fragments from the major blues scale, major pentatonic scale, and minor pentatonic scales (including the minor-6 pentatonic).

EX. 6.65
Melba Liston trombone solo
"In Memory of" (key of C minor)

Reference Melba Liston's actual performance, internalizing how she expertly delivers the *delayed* phrases below.

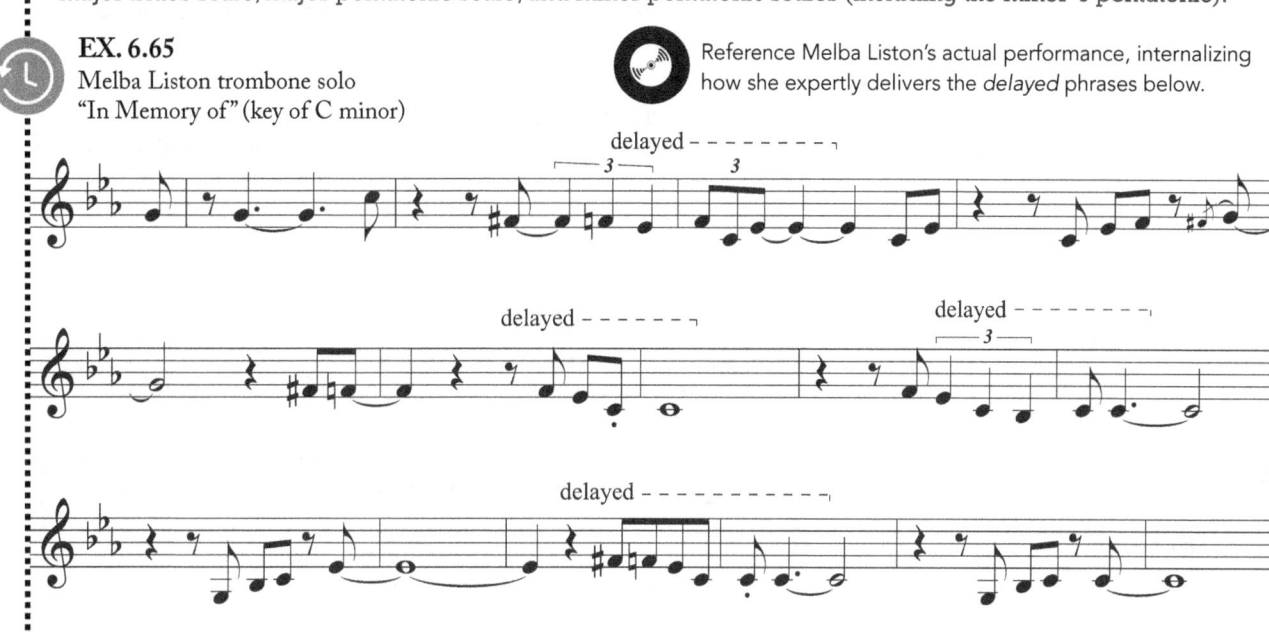

EX. 6.66
Illinois Jacquet tenor sax solo
"Flying Home" (key of C major)

Illinois Jacquet focuses on movement between major 3rd and minor 3rd and uses the **minor-6 pentatonic scale** nearly exclusively.

Learn these solos by ear! Illinois Jacquet might have been small in physical stature but his solos tended to be larger than life. Jacquet's solo on "Flying Home" became instantly iconic and has been studied and emulated by generations of musicians looking to capture the magic of his improvisations.

Introduction to the 12-Bar Blues
— page 1 of 2 —

Blues is a genre, a feeling, and a deep mindset but the blues itself must be understood within its most common context — what is termed the *12-bar blues*. Consider the 12-bar blues in the three 4-bar phrases below, starting first by understanding how lyrics are structured. Next study how chords are placed and then learn how a melody might consist simply of a *riff*, a repeated phrase, over each set of four measures.

	1st phrase (bars 1-4) Theme	**2nd phrase (bars 5-8)** Theme repeated, with emphasis	**3rd phrase (bars 9-12)** Conclusion

Lyrics and phrasing

"My dog Fido, he up and ran."

"My dog Fido, he up and ran!"

"My dog Fido, he up and ran and he's never comin' back again."

Form and harmony

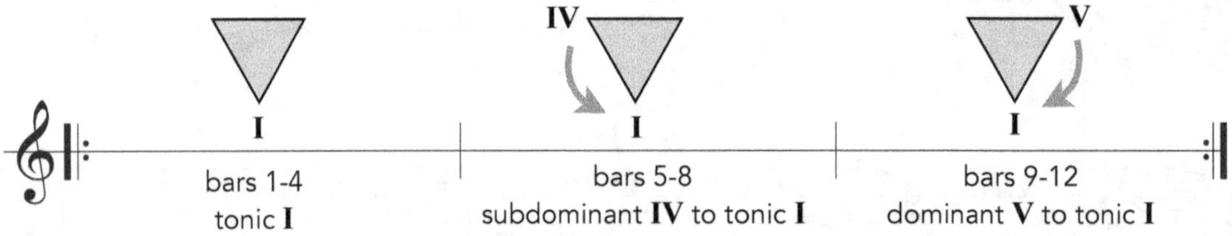

bars 1-4 tonic **I**	bars 5-8 subdominant **IV** to tonic **I**	bars 9-12 dominant **V** to tonic **I**

EX. 6.67
12-bar blues form and chord progression (key of C major)

* The IV chords in bars 2 and 10 are optional but common.

Blues harmony varies frequently but **two elements are constant** in nearly all blues tunes:

1. The third bar of each 4-bar phrase usually resolves back to the I chord.
2. The second 4-bar phrase starts on the IV chord.

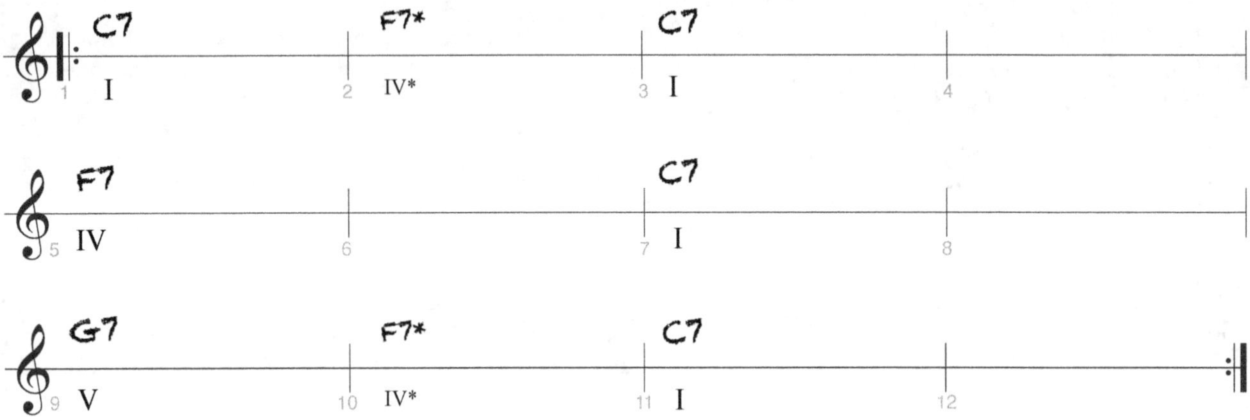

C7	F7*	C7	
1 I	2 IV*	3 I	4

F7		C7	
5 IV	6	7 I	8

G7	F7*	C7	
9 V	10 IV*	11 I	12

EX. 6.68
Alternate chord progression bars 9-12 (last four bars)

Blues chord progressions vary, often involving extra chords and distinct alterations. The last four bars of the 12-bar blues quite often includes the following **ii-V-I variation**.

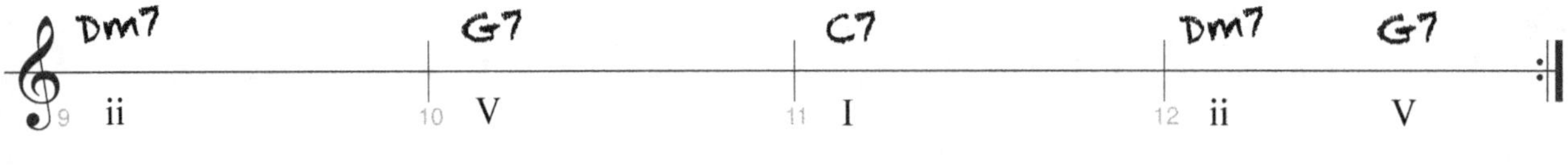

Dm7	G7	C7	Dm7	G7
9 ii	10 V	11 I	12 ii	V

Practice the art of discerning the details of any blues progression via recordings. Not only are the progressions of blues compositions distinct but individual choruses within a performance may vary.

Introduction to the 12-Bar Blues
page 2 of 2

Blues head: "Bag's Groove"

"Bag's Groove" is a riff-based blues, with the same riff repeated every four bars. The rests at the end of each riff give the rhythm section a chance to respond.

"Bag's Groove" uses only the **minor pentatonic scale** throughout. Learn "Bag's Groove" in 12 keys and you've also learned your minor pentatonic in 12 keys!

Choose a key and write in the melody and chords using the numbers as a guide.

EX. 6.69
"Bag's Groove"
(Milt Jackson)

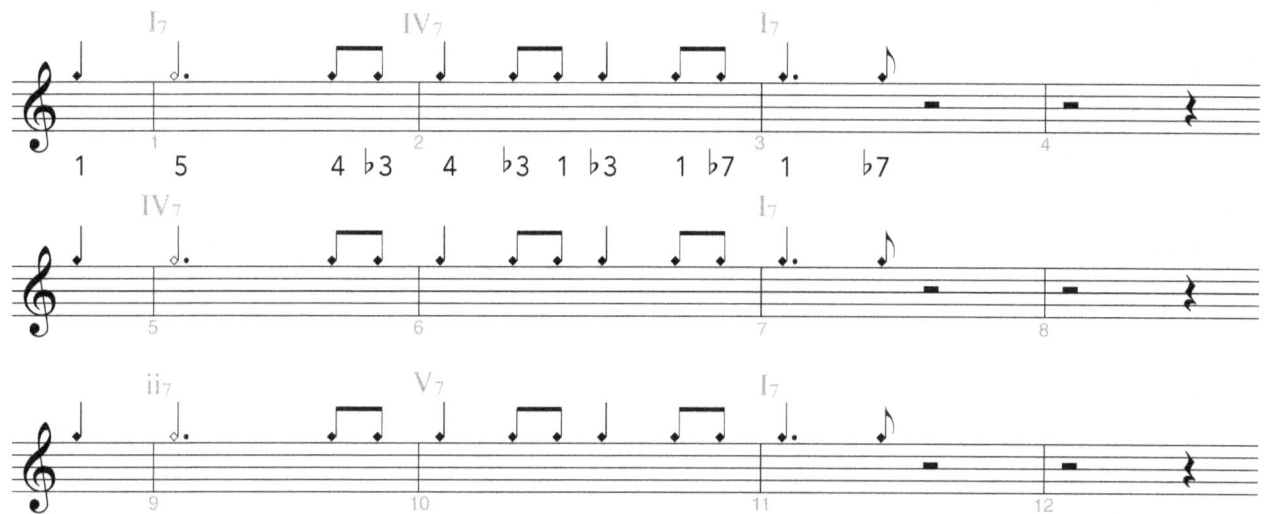

Oscar Pettiford's "Blues in the Closet" is a beloved riff blues with a repeated riff every 4 bars but the riff alters when the chord changes to IV₇ in bars 5-6. Why the alteration? Because the flat-3 of the key ends up matching the flatted 7th of the IV₇ chord perfectly (and the variation sounds great!). Of additional interest is that the riff does not alter for bars 9-10 even though the chords change to ii-V. Perhaps this is because the original riff still matches those harmonies quite well and offers a strong conclusion.

Blues head: "Blues in the Closet"

EX. 6.70
"Blues in the Closet"
(Oscar Pettiford)

Listen to the original recordings of "Bag's Groove" and "Blues in the Closet." Use the source recording to learn stylistic elements and also transpose to their original keys.

Targeted Thirds (and when to avoid the major third)

The minor third of the I chord (the *flatted 3rd*) is a quintessential *blue note* and it can be targeted on both the I and IV chord. The major 3rd of the I chord, however, must be avoided over the IV chord (at all costs!). That's a dissonance attempted only by the most advanced of improvisers. Who knew there were rules when playing the blues?!

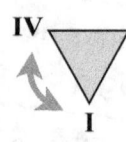

EX. 6.71
Targeted thirds

Right! Minor 3rd is a *blue note*, rubbing against the major 3rd in the I₇ chord.

Right! Same minor 3rd of the I₇ chord is a chord tone (flat-7) of IV₇.

Right! Major 3rd is a chord tone of the I₇ chord.

Avoid! Major 3rd of I₇ tends to sound too dissonant when played over IV₇.

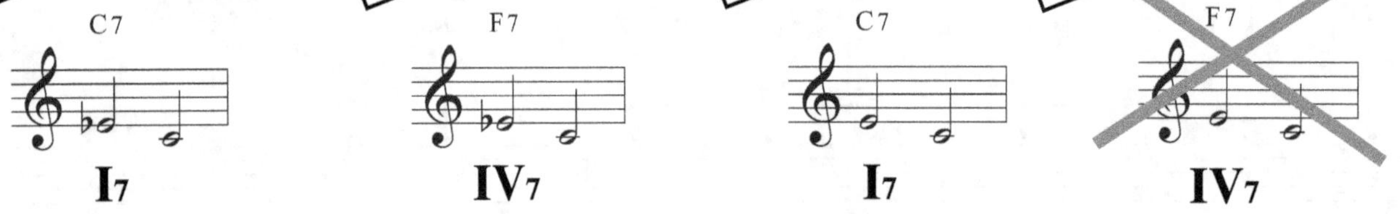

C7 — **I₇**   F7 — **IV₇**   C7 — **I₇**   F7 — **IV₇**

EX. 6.72
Minor 3rd "blue note" over both chords I and IV

C7   F7

EX. 6.73
Major 3rd over I, minor 3rd over IV

C7   F7

"Mercy" exercise

1. Learn to improvise on "Mercy, Mercy, Mercy" in the key of C.
2. Transpose the melody of "Mercy, Mercy, Mercy" into the keys of B-flat and G.
3. Write in each key's I and IV chord symbols above each measure.
4. Write in the minor 3rd blue note for each key in the blank spaces provided.

EX. 6.74
"Mercy, Mercy, Mercy"
(Joe Zawinul)

IMPROVISE
"Mercy, Mercy, Mercy"

I₇   IV₇   I₇   IV₇

6 5   3 1   2 1 1 6 1   2   6 5   3 1   2 1 1 6 1   6

key of B-flat: ____

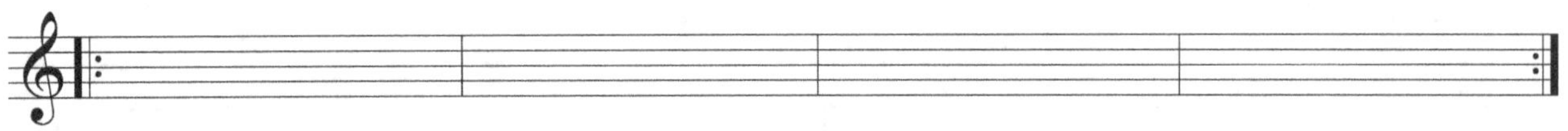

key of G: ____

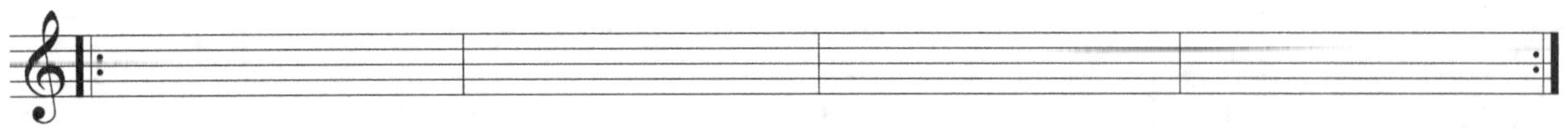

Solo Spotlight

Mary Lou Williams, piano "St. Louis Blues"
Kenny Burrell, guitar "C Jam Blues"

Pianist Mary Lou Williams and guitarist Kenny Burrell take similar approaches to their 12-bar blues solos below. Both soloists combine elements from blues and pentatonic scales while also carefully targeting major and minor thirds. Burrell incorporates some additional chromatics and both use space amply to enhance their masterful phrasing.

EX. 6.75
Mary Lou Williams piano solo
"St. Louis Blues"

Label exactly where Williams and Burrell use targeted thirds. Also label any moments where a soloist uses pentatonic scales or blues scales and specify which type.

EX. 6.76
Kenny Burrell guitar solo
"C Jam Blues"

Notice the **subtle differences in blues chord progressions**. Over "C Jam Blues," Burrell plays the first four bars entirely on the I chord without a move to the IV chord on bar 2. On "St. Louis Blues," the chord in bar 9 is D7, not Dm7.

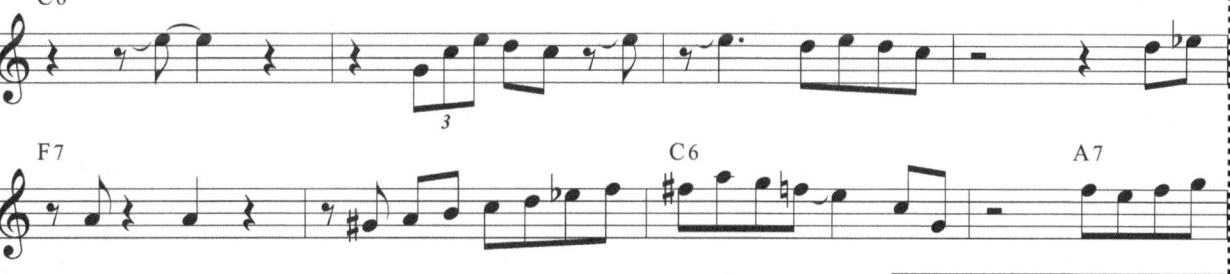

Grace notes

These two types of notation are played the same way, starting with a *grace note* placed a half step below and quickly resolving to the main note.

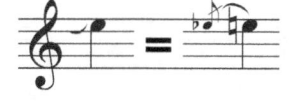

When listening to the recordings of Mary Lou Williams and Kenny Burrell, focus on keeping track of the underlying tempo and 12-bar blues form. Since both solos here are relatively fast, feel the pulse in cut time. Achieve this either by tapping your hands or feet in half notes.

Song Study	"Sonnymoon for Two"

page 1 of 2

Tenor saxophonist Sonny Rollins' "Sonnymoon for Two" is a traditional riff-based 12-bar blues. In its simplest form, its melody consists entirely of notes from the minor pentatonic scale, starting from the octave and descending downward for the first two bars of each 4-bar riff. Rollins also played a version of "Sonnymoon for Two" with a more complex melody that included some major thirds in addition to bringing ornamental variety to each riff statement. In all versions, the chords establish a progression that anchors the blues form with the melody coasting across the top of the chord changes.

EX. 6.77

"Sonnymoon for Two"
(Sonny Rollins)

Choose a key and write in the melody and chords using the numbers as a guide.

Bars 1-2 perfectly outline the chord tones in each measure.

Bars 3-4 definitely do not outline the I chord. That the melody still works so well is a testament to the strength of the minor pentatonic scale.

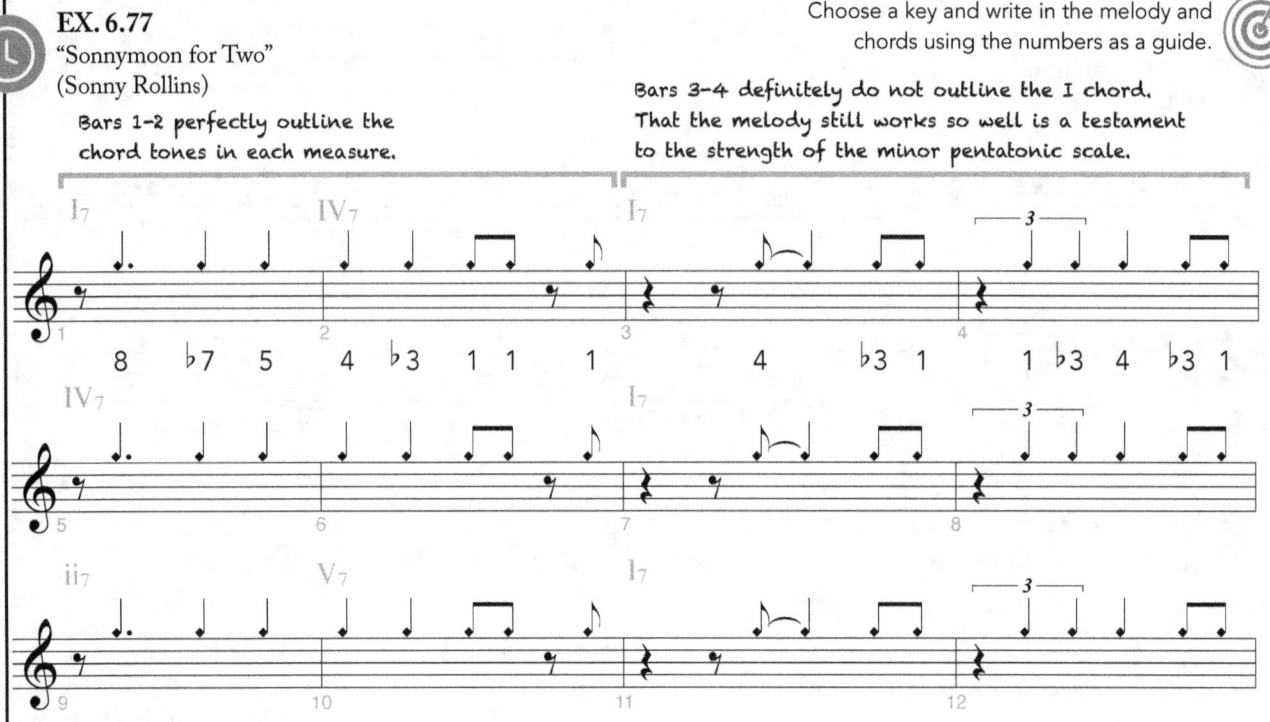

Every chord tone must be internalized even when only a simple pentatonic or blues scale ultimately is played as melodic material. The goal is to learn each arpeggio in any tempo, rhythm, and inversion. Each harmony must be learned in relation to every other harmony.

Blues chord arpeggios

EX. 6.78

Four basic chords for the blues, using root position arpeggios

Below is a set of all four central blues harmonies (I, IV, ii, and V) and select chord inversions. Extrapolate from the exercises below and apply the arpeggios and permutations to the chords as they appear in the 12-bar blues form.

EX. 6.79

Four basic chords for the blues, using chord inversions

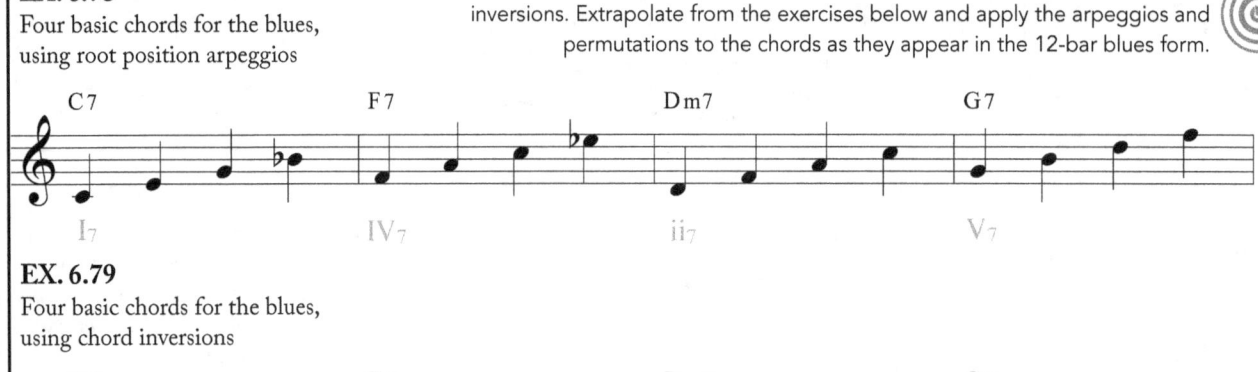

Song Study   "Sonnymoon for Two"

page 2 of 2

Targeted thirds

The third of each chord varies within the 12-bar blues. The following targeted thirds exercise addresses the subtle changes from chord to chord while also highlighting common tones between chords, as evidenced in the beat 3 resolution in each measure.

Develop this targeted thirds exercise:

1. Change the rhythm.
2. Add passing tones and neighbor notes.

EX. 6.80
Targeted thirds exercise

Sonny Rollins opens his iconic "Sonnymoon for Two" solo by emphasizing common tones and targeted thirds. His solo continues for many more choruses and several are devoted to developing the motifs he establishes in this first chorus.

EX. 6.81
Sonny Rollins tenor sax solo
"Sonnymoon for Two"

If this solo makes you laugh a bit, it's intentional. Rollins is someone who improvises with **a great sense of humor**.

P5

Why does a **repeated 5th interval** work so well here even though the note C is not part of the underlying G7 chord? C is the root of the key of the song itself and functions as a tonic pedal point. Quite often, blues melody is rooted in the key, more so than it is in the individual chords.

Improvise   "Sonnymoon for Two"

IMPROVISE
"Sonnymoon for Two" (Sonny Rollins)
in its original key

Reference the original recording of Sonny Rollins playing "Sonnymoon for Two" to learn the original key then write it out below.

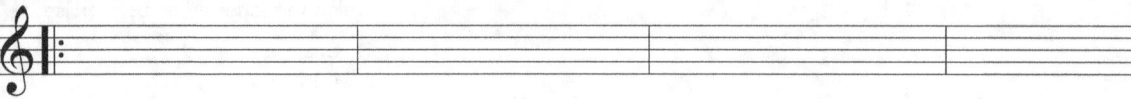

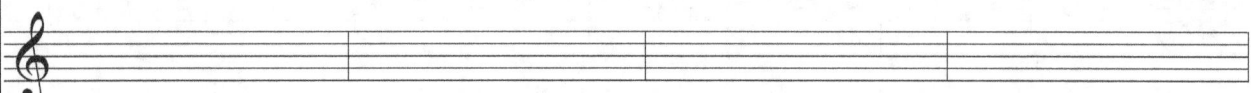

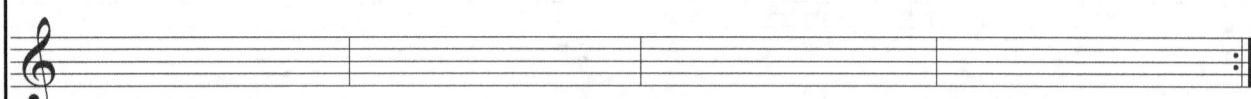

When learning a blues, it is essential to know the form, the chords within the chosen key, and the melody of the blues itself. The soloist must also become equipped with knowing three essential scale options: (1) the minor pentatonic scale, (2) the minor blues scale, and (3) the major blues scale. Internalizing even the smallest 2- and 3-note fragments within each scale will become helpful when constructing melodic themes as an improvising soloist.

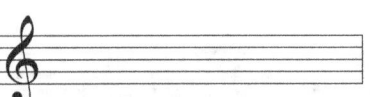

Scale options
1. Minor pentatonic scale
2. Minor blues scale
3. Major blues scale

EX. 6.82
Minor pentatonic scale

EX. 6.83
Minor blues scale

EX. 6.84
Major blues scale (sometimes)

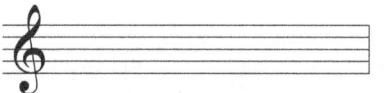

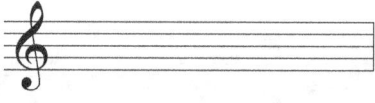

Over the chord changes of "Sonnymoon for Two" in its original key, play the melody for "C Jam Blues."

After writing in the major blues scale above, circle the following notes to get the New Orleans blues scale: 1-2-♭3-5-6.

Tails

Tail is a fanciful name for a lower neighbor, typically directly under the root of a scale or key. A tail can be the raised 7th leading tone, minor 7th, or major 6th. Tails are often used in melodies even when the chord symbol does not specify it as a chord tone. For example, the major 7th tail below can be used over a Cm7 or C7 even though the chord does not include a B natural.

EX. 6.85
Major 7th tail
(key of C)

1   7   1

EX. 6.86
Minor 7th tail
(key of C)

1 ♭7 1

EX. 6.87
Major 6th tail
(key of C)

1   6   1

Zen Jazz Master says:

A word of CAUTION regarding blues scales!

Don't overuse the blues scale. Many musicians first learn to improvise by being assigned a blues scale and using it exclusively during a solo. Even if they manage to play only the notes in that scale, without mistakenly hitting any notes outside of the scale, they still almost always sound really "green." This is largely because the ear grows tired of hearing the sharped-4th scale degree. To help avoid ear fatigue, use the blues scale sparingly. Instead, choose the minor pentatonic!

Chapter 6 Achievements

Congratulations!

You are one step closer to jazz nirvana.

Here is a partial list of what you've achieved:

- Choosing when to use Dorian vs. natural minor scales on a i-iv or i-IV chord progression
- Hearing the differences between iv and V chords
- Understanding basic use of minor pentatonic scales and related blues scales
- Knowing where to use the tonic major third in a 12-bar blues form
- Being able to play the head of "Sonnymoon for Two" in a few keys

Are you ready for the next chapter?

Answer these questions to determine whether you are prepared to continue to the next chapter:

- **Do you clearly understand** why parent scales differ when approaching i-iv and i-IV chord progressions?

  If "Yes," move to the next chapter.
  If "No," review this chapter.

- **Can you distinguish** minor blues scales from major blues scales?

  If "Yes," move to the next chapter.
  If "No," take some time to review the 12-bar blues.

- **Can you explain** the basic harmony of a 12-bar blues?

  If "Yes," move to the next chapter.
  If "No," take some time to review the 12-bar blues but also move on to the next chapter. It can take some time to process the elements of the 12-bar blues.

- **Do you want** to learn about the mightiest of all jazz chord progressions?

  If "Yes," move to the next chapter.
  If "No,"…move to the next chapter anyway. Jazz is not jazz without the ii-V-I chord progression and it's now time that you dip into the deep end!

UNIT THREE

Unity and Purpose

- Voice-leading across jazz standards
- Upper structure harmony
- Bebop vocabulary and nuance

**From a 1954 Boston radio interview,
featuring alto saxophonists Charlie Parker and Paul Desmond
with radio DJ John McClellan:**

C.P. — "Since I've ever heard music I've thought it should be very clean, very precise — as clean as possible … something that was beautiful, you know. There's definitely stories and stories and stories that can be told. Music is basically melody, harmony and rhythm — but I mean people can do much more with music than that. It can be very descriptive in all kinds of ways, you know, all walks of life. Don't you agree, Paul?"

P.D. — "Yeah, and you always do have a story to tell. It's one of the most impressive things about everything I've ever heard of yours."

C.P. — "That's more or less the object. That's what I thought it should be."

P.D. — "Another thing that's been a major factor in your playing is this fantastic technique, that nobody's quite equaled. I've always wondered about that, too — whether there was — whether that came behind practicing or whether that was just from playing, whether it evolved gradually."

C.P. — "Well, you make it so hard for me to answer you, you know, I can't see where there's anything fantastic about it all. I put quite a bit of study into the horn, that's true. In fact the neighbors threatened to ask my mother to move once when we were living out west. She said I was driving them crazy with the horn. I used to put in at least 11 to 15 hours a day."

P.D. — "Yes, that's what I wondered."

C.P. — "That's true, yes. I did that for over a period of three to four years."

P.D. — "Oh … yeah. I guess that's the answer."

C.P. — "That's the facts anyway. [chuckle]"

P.D. — "I heard a record of yours a couple of months ago that somehow I've missed up to date and I heard a little 2-bar quote from the Klose book that was like an echo from home…"

C.P. — "Yeah, yeah. Well that was all done with books, you know. Naturally, it wasn't done with mirrors, this time it was done with books."

P.D. — "Well that's very reassuring to hear because somehow I got the idea that you were just born with that technique and you never had to worry too much about it, about keeping it working."

J.M. — "You know, I'm very glad that he's bringing up this point because I think that a lot of young musicians tend to think that…"

P.D. — "Yeah, they do. They just go out…"

J.M. — "It isn't necessary to do this."

P.D. — "And make those sessions and live the life but they don't put in those 11 hours a day with any of the books."

C.P. — "Oh definitely, study is absolutely necessary, in all forms. It's just like any talent that's born within somebody. It's like a good pair of shoes when you put a shine on it, you know. Schooling brings out the polish of any talent that happens anywhere in the world. Einstein had schooling but he has a definite genius, you know, within himself, schooling is one of the most wonderful things there's ever been, you know." [8]

7 Trinity

ii-V-I Voice-leading and Linear Improvisation

The Holy Trinity — the ii-V-I. If there ever were a jazz "bible," the ii-V-I would be central to the book. No other chord progression is as ubiquitous … and for good reason. The ii-V-I encapsulates all facets of tonality, providing a template rich with detail — ready to support and enhance endless melodic possibilities. It is through the ii-V-I that much of jazz music has evolved since the progression is foundational for bebop harmony and chromaticism. The ii-V-I progression also serves as a perfect launching pad for the study of voice-leading and guide tone lines, two components central to improvisation and composition. This chapter delves into approaches to the ii-V-I and also explores its intersection with linear improvisation and motivic development.

Contents

TOPICS
- ii-V-I Voice-leading and Functional Harmony
- ii-V-I Exercises
- ii-V-I Common Tones
- Guide Tone Lines
- ii-V-I Line Examples
- Development Between Target Notes
- Why Details Matter
- Turnarounds
- Linear Improvisation
- Make a decision!
- Why Motifs Work (and why they shouldn't!)
- Hemiola Rhythms
- Quick-study Guide to the Genius of Charlie Parker
- Beware the lead sheet!
- "Oh lady be good" Turnarounds

EAR TRAINING
- Sing ii-V-I chord roots
- "Mack the Knife" Rhythm

MASTERCLASS
- Compound Melody

INVESTIGATE
- Secondary Dominants

SONG STUDY
- "Mack the Knife" (Kurt Weill)
- "Oh, lady be good!" (Gershwin)

SOLO SPOTLIGHT
- Louis Armstrong trumpet solo "Mack the Knife"
- Ella Fitzgerald vocal solo "Mack the Knife"
- Art Blakey drum solo "A Night in Tunisia"
- Charlie Parker alto sax solo "Oh, lady be good!"

COMPOSE
- ii-V-I Line
- Chord Progression + 3-note Fragments

IMPROVISE
- ii-V-I Improvisation Workouts
- "Mack the Knife" (Kurt Weill)
- "Oh, lady be good!" (Gershwin)

LISTENING GUIDE
- Sonny Rollins' "Moritat" & Ella Fitzgerald's "Mack the Knife"

ZEN JAZZ MASTER SAYS
- Rules are made to be broken!

HISTORICAL EXAMPLES
- "Tea for Two" (Vincent Youmans)
- Dexter Gordon tenor sax solo "Shiny Stockings"
- Sonny Rollins tenor sax solo "Moritat (Mack the Knife)"
- Ben Webster tenor sax solo "Honeysuckle Rose"
- Chet Baker trumpet solo "Autumn Leaves"
- Tommy Flanagan piano solo "Mack the Knife"
- Marian McPartland piano solo "Jeepers Creepers"
- Johnny Griffin tenor sax solo "The Way You Look Tonight"
- Dexter Gordon tenor sax solo "Blow, Mr. Dexter"
- Paul Desmond alto sax solo "Pennies From Heaven"
- Miles Davis trumpet solo "Autumn Leaves"
- J. J. Johnson trombone solo "Just Friends"
- George Coleman tenor sax solo "There is no greater love"
- Dexter Gordon tenor sax solo "It's you or no one"
- Joe Henderson tenor sax solo "Recorda-me"
- "Autumn Leaves" (Josef Kosma)
- Charlie Parker alto sax solo "Anthropology"
- "Perhaps" (Charlie Parker)
- *Violin Partita No. 2 in D minor* (J. S. Bach)
- Lester Young tenor sax solo "Oh, lady be good!

ii-V-I Voice-leading and Functional Harmony
— page 1 of 2 —

The *ii-V-I chord progression* tells a complete harmonic story, moving from subdominant to dominant before returning home to tonic. Along the way, the voice-leading between each chord tone is purposeful, adding layers of detail. A common phrase length for the ii-V-I is four measures. While the ii and V chords bring tension to bars 1-2, the I chord balances out the remaining half of the phrase by releasing this tension for bars 3-4. The examples below help illustrate ii-V-I form and *harmonic function*.

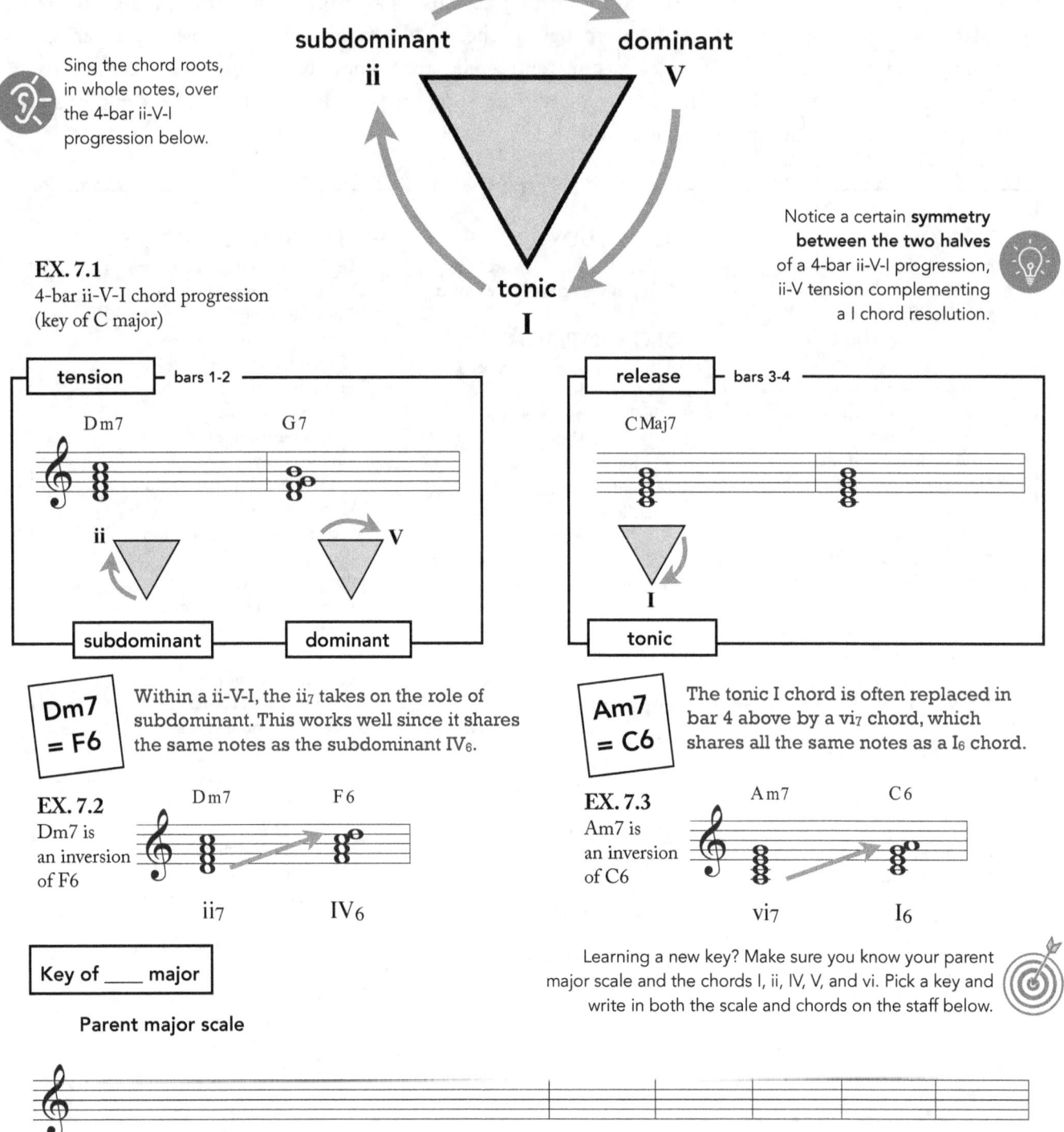

Sing the chord roots, in whole notes, over the 4-bar ii-V-I progression below.

Notice a certain **symmetry between the two halves** of a 4-bar ii-V-I progression, ii-V tension complementing a I chord resolution.

EX. 7.1
4-bar ii-V-I chord progression
(key of C major)

Dm7 = F6   Within a ii-V-I, the ii$_7$ takes on the role of subdominant. This works well since it shares the same notes as the subdominant IV$_6$.

Am7 = C6   The tonic I chord is often replaced in bar 4 above by a vi$_7$ chord, which shares all the same notes as a I$_6$ chord.

EX. 7.2
Dm7 is an inversion of F6

EX. 7.3
Am7 is an inversion of C6

Key of ____ major

Parent major scale

Learning a new key? Make sure you know your parent major scale and the chords I, ii, IV, V, and vi. Pick a key and write in both the scale and chords on the staff below.

I_{Maj7} ii_7 IV_7 V_7 vi_7

ii-V-I Voice-leading and Functional Harmony
page 2 of 2

Each note within each chord is considered a *voice* that *leads* to a voice within the chord that is next in line. While a chord tone might leap to a note in the next harmony, it is more likely that the voice-leading will be smooth, either moving up or down by step or not moving at all, remaining as a common tone between chords.

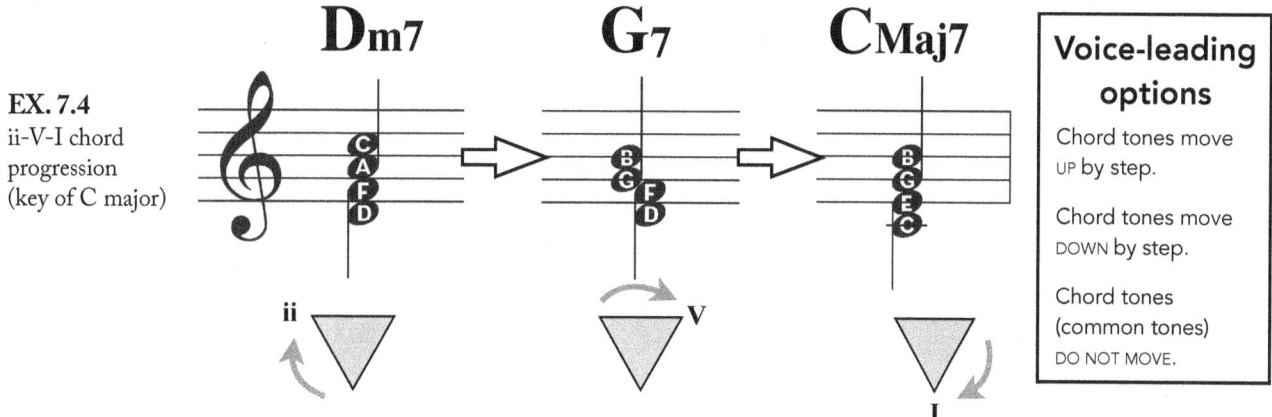

EX. 7.4
ii-V-I chord progression (key of C major)

Voice-leading options

Chord tones move UP by step.

Chord tones move DOWN by step.

Chord tones (common tones) DO NOT MOVE.

EX. 7.5
ii-V-I arpeggios, interlocking

Arpeggios may be played from root position in parallel motion. **Interlocking arpeggios** are played in contrary motion, alternating up and down, allowing the last and first notes of each chord to touch, as if they are pieces of a puzzle *locking* into place.

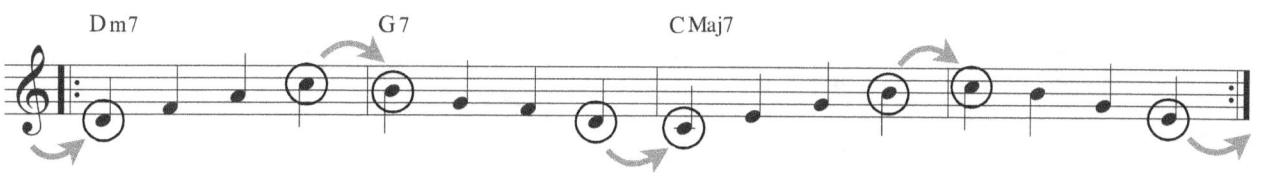

Mix it up: Switch the chord tones on beats 2 & 3 in each measure above. The example to the left illustrates this, changing measure 1 from D-F-A-C to D-A-F-C.

EX. 7.6
ii-V-I voice-leading options (key of C major)

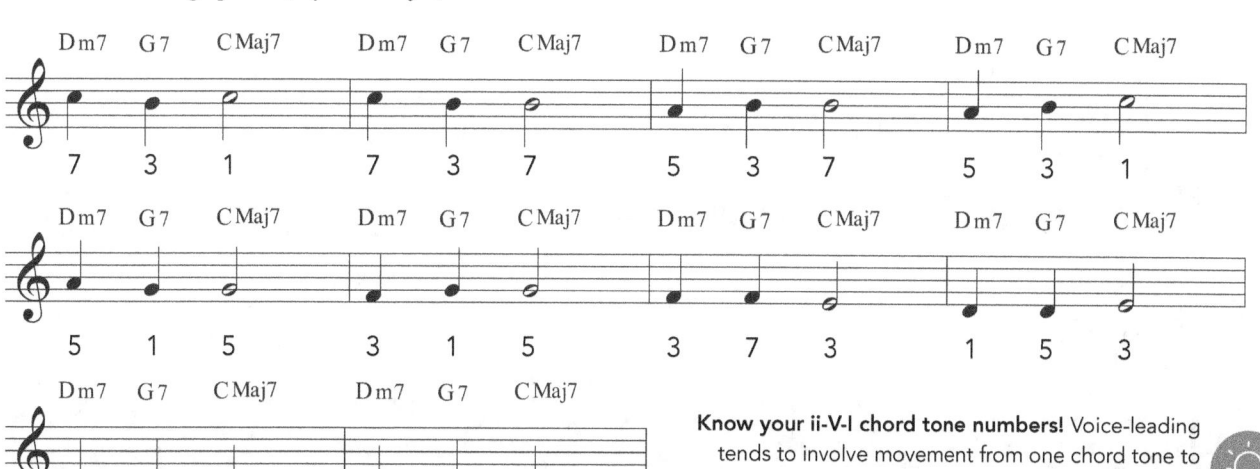

Know your ii-V-I chord tone numbers! Voice-leading tends to involve movement from one chord tone to another whether it's the 7-3-1 in bar 1 above or another combination of chord tones across the harmony.

ii-V-I Exercises

Fundamental ii-V-I exercises include arpeggios and scales played from the root of each chord in addition to interlocking arpeggios, alternating ascent and descent. Although improvisers very seldom will create melodies that run arpeggios and scales like the examples below, be sure to master the following exercises. They might sound a bit clinical but the arpeggio exercises will ultimately help solidify your approach to the harmony. The ear will also benefit from the contrast between root movement arpeggios and scales and the smoother voice-leading inherent in interlocking arpeggios.

EX. 7.7
ii-V-I arpeggios from the root of
each chord, parallel motion

Write in the scale degrees for all the exercises below.
Then, either by ear or on a separate piece of paper,
transpose the exercises to a new key of your choice.

EX. 7.8
ii-V-I scales from the root of
each chord, parallel motion

EX. 7.9
Interlocking arpeggios
first ascending then descending

EX. 7.10
Interlocking arpeggios,
first descending then ascending

EX. 7.11
Doubling up the halves of each arpeggio

ii-V-I Common Tones

Each chord arpeggio of the ii-V-I includes a lower and upper set of chord tones. For example, an ascending Dm7 arpeggio begins with lower fragment notes D and F, which are then followed by upper fragment notes A and C. When the lower fragment becomes the melodic focus, ii-V common tones emerge since D and F are common to both Dm7 and G7. Choosing a melodic fragment at the start of your melodic line will help predetermine the melodic track. In the case of lower fragment D to F, this track eventually resolves, descending stepwise to C and E, the lower fragment of CMaj7. Understanding the upper and lower melodic track for any fragment, including knowing when and where common tones are involved, will help with harmonic navigation.

EX. 7.12
Note which chord tones are common to Dm7, G7, and CMaj7 (both upper and lower fragments)

Follow the arrows!
(and stay on the
upper or lower track)

Fragment **chord tone targets** either:

1. move by step OR
2. are common tones so they do not move.

EX. 7.13
Common
ii-V-I upper
fragments

EX. 7.14
Common
ii-V-I lower
fragments

EX. 7.15
Lower fragment
exercise (ii-V-I)

EX. 7.16
Upper fragment
exercise (ii-V-I)

Guide Tone Lines

A *guide tone line* provides a rich layer of melodic color by complementing the root movement in the chord progression while also helping define the major and minor sounds and melodic tendency of each harmony. Guide tone lines are created by interlocking the 3rds and 7ths of chords. Across a ii-V-I, these guide tone lines follow the rule that either they only move by step or they remain static as common tones between harmonies.

EX. 7.17
Guide tone line exercise
(targeting 7ths and 3rds)

The 3rd and 7th of each chord can start a guide tone line. Across a ii-V-I progression, notice whether the line adheres to an **upper or lower track**.

upper track (starting on 7)

lower track (starting on 3)

EX. 7.18
Combining upper and lower fragments,
targeting guide tones

Transpose the examples on this page to a new key of your choice.

EX. 7.19
Voice-leading exercise,
targeting guide tones

EX. 7.20
"Tea for Two"
(Vincent Youmans)

This one extra target note, the A in these examples, suggests both C6 and Am7.

C6 = Am7

ii-V-I Line Examples

In creative contexts, guide tone lines are often obvious, clearly targeting each 3rd and 7th. When they are obscured, it is due to various harmonic and rhythmic displacements. The following ii-V-I examples showcase real-world cases of guide tone line application.

EX. 7.21
Dexter Gordon tenor sax solo "Shiny Stockings"

EX. 7.22
Dexter Gordon tenor sax solo "Shiny Stockings"

EX. 7.23
Sonny Rollins tenor sax solo "Moritat (Mack the Knife)"

Mix it up! Instead of targeting the V every time you see or hear a V chord, try playing a ii chord followed by the V chord. Ben Webster and Sonny Rollins both improvise a ii chord arpeggio over the V chord in their solos. The end result is a less abrupt arrival on the V chord as well as a more focused melody.

EX. 7.24
Ben Webster tenor sax solo "Honeysuckle Rose"

EX. 7.25
Chet Baker trumpet solo "Autumn Leaves"

EX. 7.26
Tommy Flanagan piano solo "Moritat (Mack the Knife)"

EX. 7.27
Marian McPartland piano solo "Jeepers Creepers"

Trace any guide tone lines in the examples above, labeling the 3rds and 7ths.

Development Between Target Notes

Since there are countless ways to approach any chord tone target, a melodic line may even develop between target notes. In the examples below, notice how the same targets are reached at each chord although the approaches are different — some using quarter notes and others using eighths. *Pivots*, where scalar lines are displaced by an octave, can also be used as a tool for development to help balance stepwise movement with wider intervals, adding shape to the line.

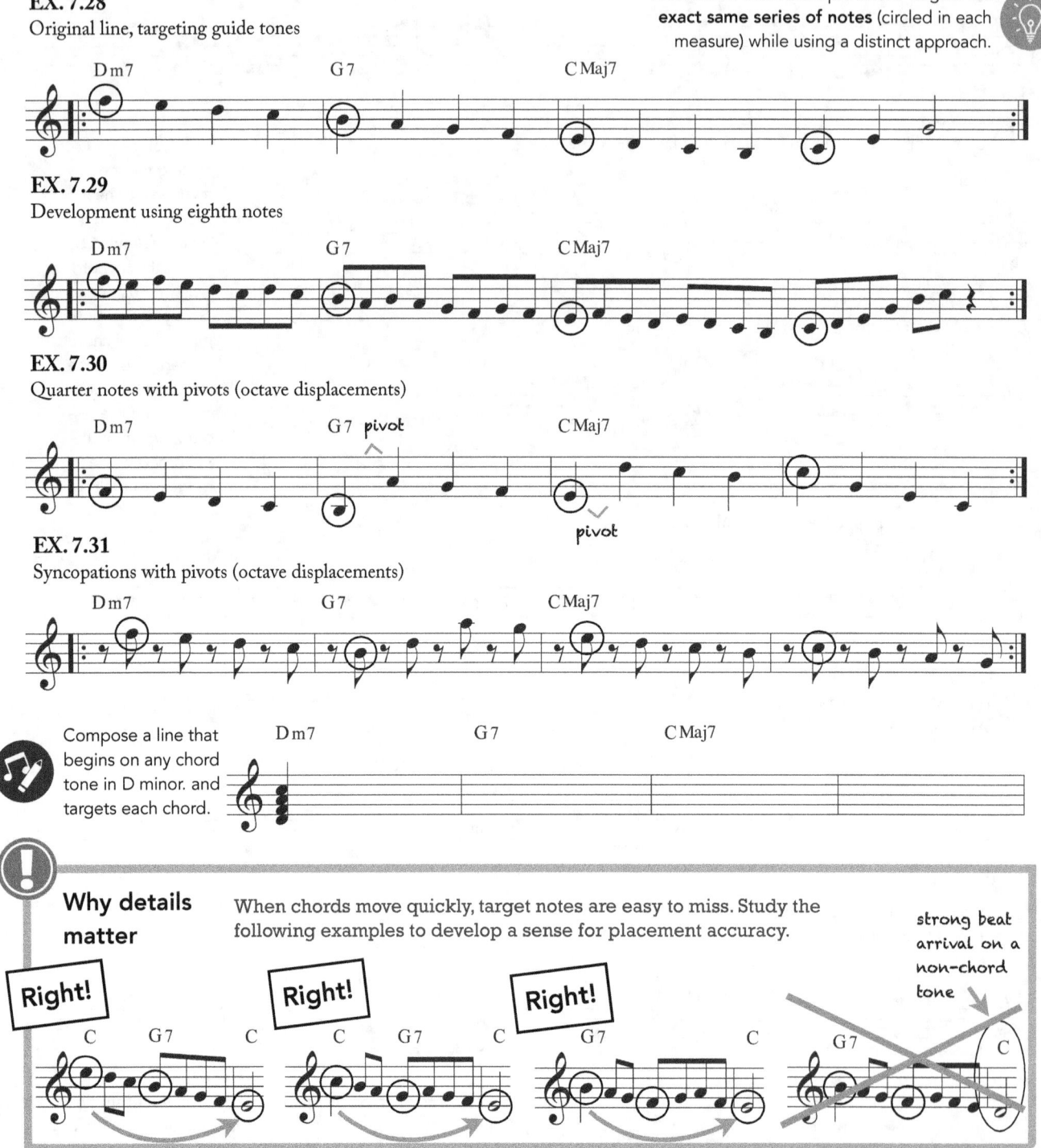

EX. 7.28
Original line, targeting guide tones

Notice how each example below targets the **exact same series of notes** (circled in each measure) while using a distinct approach.

EX. 7.29
Development using eighth notes

EX. 7.30
Quarter notes with pivots (octave displacements)

EX. 7.31
Syncopations with pivots (octave displacements)

Compose a line that begins on any chord tone in D minor. and targets each chord.

Why details matter

When chords move quickly, target notes are easy to miss. Study the following examples to develop a sense for placement accuracy.

strong beat arrival on a non-chord tone

Right!

Right!

Right!

Investigate   Secondary Dominants

A dominant V chord resolves to the I chord in any key. For example, G7 is the dominant V_7 chord of CMaj7 in the parent key of C. A *secondary dominant*, also known as an *applied dominant*, can approach any chord as its dominant, adding chromatic color and variation to the chord progression. For example, in the parent key of C major, an A7 chord can function as a secondary dominant of Dm7 and is called a "five of two" or "five-seven of two" (written as "V_7/ii").

EX. 7.32
I to V/ii to ii
(key of C)

EX. 7.33
Secondary dominants
(key of C)

Learn the sound of secondary dominants by using arpeggios, playing only one voice at a time.

EX. 7.34
4-bar ii-V-I progression with a secondary dominant (VI) on bar 4

In the key of C major, A7 is the V/ii since it moves to Dm7 although it is more commonly known as a **VI chord**. It often is used in bar 4 of a 4-bar ii-V-I.

Turnarounds   While most song forms end with two measures of a tonic I chord, the common insertion of a *turnaround* in the last measure or two contributes momentum for a strong return to the top of the form and the next chorus. The distinct chord sequence of a turnaround can double the harmonic rhythm of a song. A common 1-bar turnaround is ii-V and for 2 bars it's I-VI-ii-V (or iii-VI-ii-V), each leading to tonic I.

EX. 7.35
"Bye Bye Blackbird"
turnaround (1-bar)

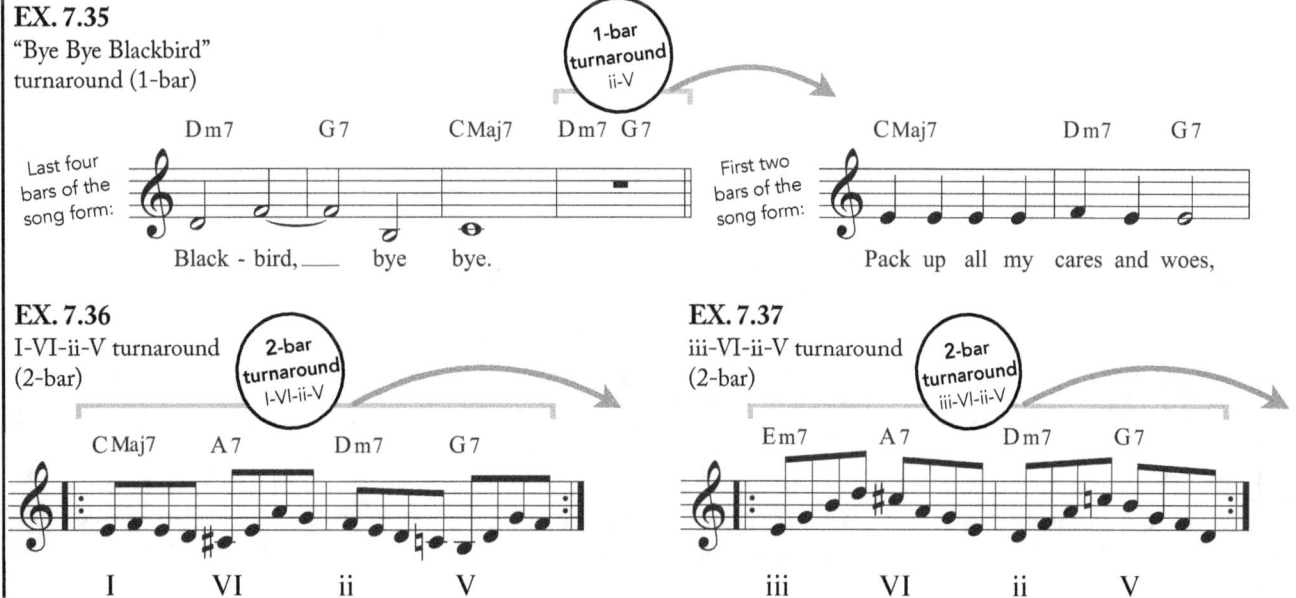

EX. 7.36
I-VI-ii-V turnaround
(2-bar)

EX. 7.37
iii-VI-ii-V turnaround
(2-bar)

Song Study   "Mack the Knife"

Like so many jazz standards, "Mack the Knife" was not written as a jazz vehicle. This song, originally from Bertold Brecht's *Threepenny Opera*, became a hit among jazz musicians and audiences because of its clever lyrics, rhythmic drive, and irresistible melody. The motifs are simple and there is plenty of space for internalizing each melodic statement. Particularly fascinating is the use of common tones across chords. The melody tells a story that begins with a targeted major 6th (bar 1, beat 1) that moves to an eventual resolution with the targeted root at the end of the composition (bar 31, beat 1).

EX. 7.38
"Mack the Knife"
(Kurt Weill)

Follow the circled targets and annotations below and get to know **how the story unfolds.**

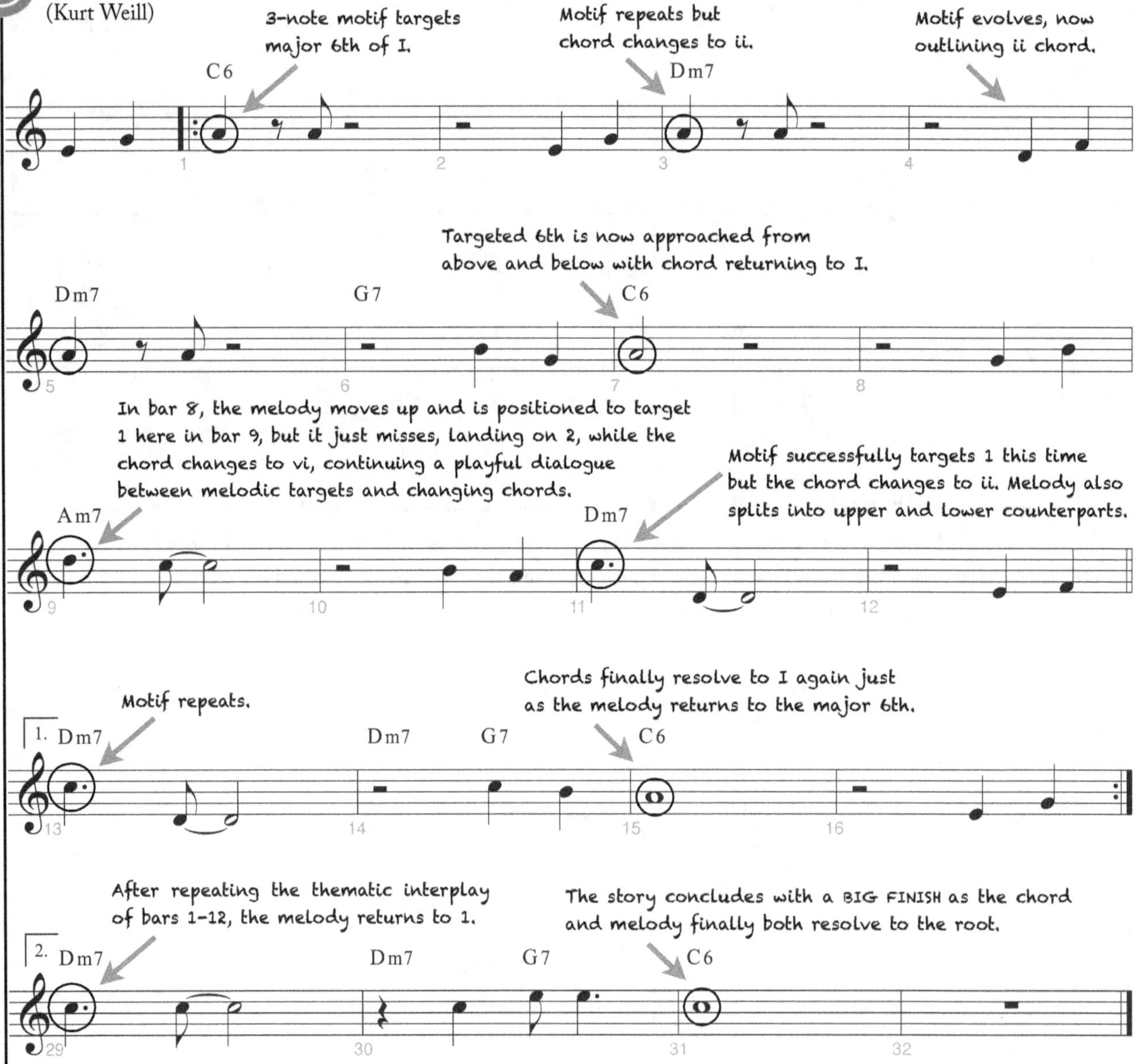

3-note motif targets major 6th of I.

Motif repeats but chord changes to ii.

Motif evolves, now outlining ii chord.

Targeted 6th is now approached from above and below with chord returning to I.

In bar 8, the melody moves up and is positioned to target 1 here in bar 9, but it just misses, landing on 2, while the chord changes to vi, continuing a playful dialogue between melodic targets and changing chords.

Motif successfully targets 1 this time but the chord changes to ii. Melody also splits into upper and lower counterparts.

Motif repeats.

Chords finally resolve to I again just as the melody returns to the major 6th.

After repeating the thematic interplay of bars 1-12, the melody returns to 1.

The story concludes with a BIG FINISH as the chord and melody finally both resolve to the root.

Tap the rhythm to the melody of "Mack the Knife" while counting, out loud, "1,2,3,4" in each measure, all at a slow-medium tempo.

Write in the scale degree numbers for each chord above.

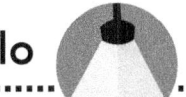

Solo Spotlight

Louis Armstrong, trumpet · Ella Fitzgerald, vocals
"Mack the Knife"

Riffing on "6"

One clear path to a successful solo is to base the improvisation on the melody of the composition. In the solo examples below, trumpeter Louis Armstrong and vocalist Ella Fitzgerald both use the major 6th target note as a continued motif that stems originally from its prominence in the song's melody. This persistent use of a pitch or phrase is called *riffing*. In this specific case, it is termed *riffing on "6"*. While Fitzgerald's improvisation is part of a solo chorus, here Armstrong showcases a masterful interpretation of the song's melody at the end of the arrangement (known as playing the *head* out).

EX. 7.39
Louis Armstrong trumpet solo
"Mack the Knife"

Notice exactly when the major 6th is targeted as well as **its matching chord** at each moment. Then determine which scale steps and arpeggios surround the major 6th motif.

Major 6th introduced in original melody.

Major 6th continues as theme, now syncopated.

C6   Dm7

Dm7   G7   C6

Repeated 6ths — simple, swinging, and memorable.

Chord is G7 but melody toggles between C and A, keeping the riff on 6 focused on the tonic C6 chord.

REVIEW!
C6 = CMaj7
Among musicians, even when a chord is labeled C6, the chord symbol tends to be interpreted as interchangeable with CMaj7, CMaj9, and even a simple C major triad.

EX. 7.40
Ella Fitzgerald vocal solo
"Mack the Knife"

Major 6th is introduced as a series of repetitions in a pickup measure.

Arpeggio outline of CMaj7 leads back to 6th target, followed by a descent to lower octave 6th.

C6   Dm7

Dm7   G7   C6

6th keeps a focused return to the original octave.

The melody again first approaches the original major 6th before descending to the lower octave 6th.

Improvise

"Mack the Knife"
page 1 of 2

"Mack the Knife," like every jazz classic, may be performed in any key and the improviser's goal is to be able to transpose freely from key to key. Use the tools below to begin learning "Mack the Knife" fluidly enough to solo in various keys.

Transposition

Steps to transposing "Mack the Knife" into new keys

Try this out with the four keys below.

(Some parts have already been filled in.)

1. Write out the parent major scale of the new key.
2. Write the numbers for each scale degree under each note.
3. Write out the four main chords.
4. Label these four chords with Roman numerals.
5. Write out the major pentatonic scale of the new key.

In any key, the chords to "Mack the Knife" will include the following: **I, ii, V, vi**. If you review these four chords, you will be able to start soloing in any key.

Key of C

Key of F

Key of E

Key of E♭

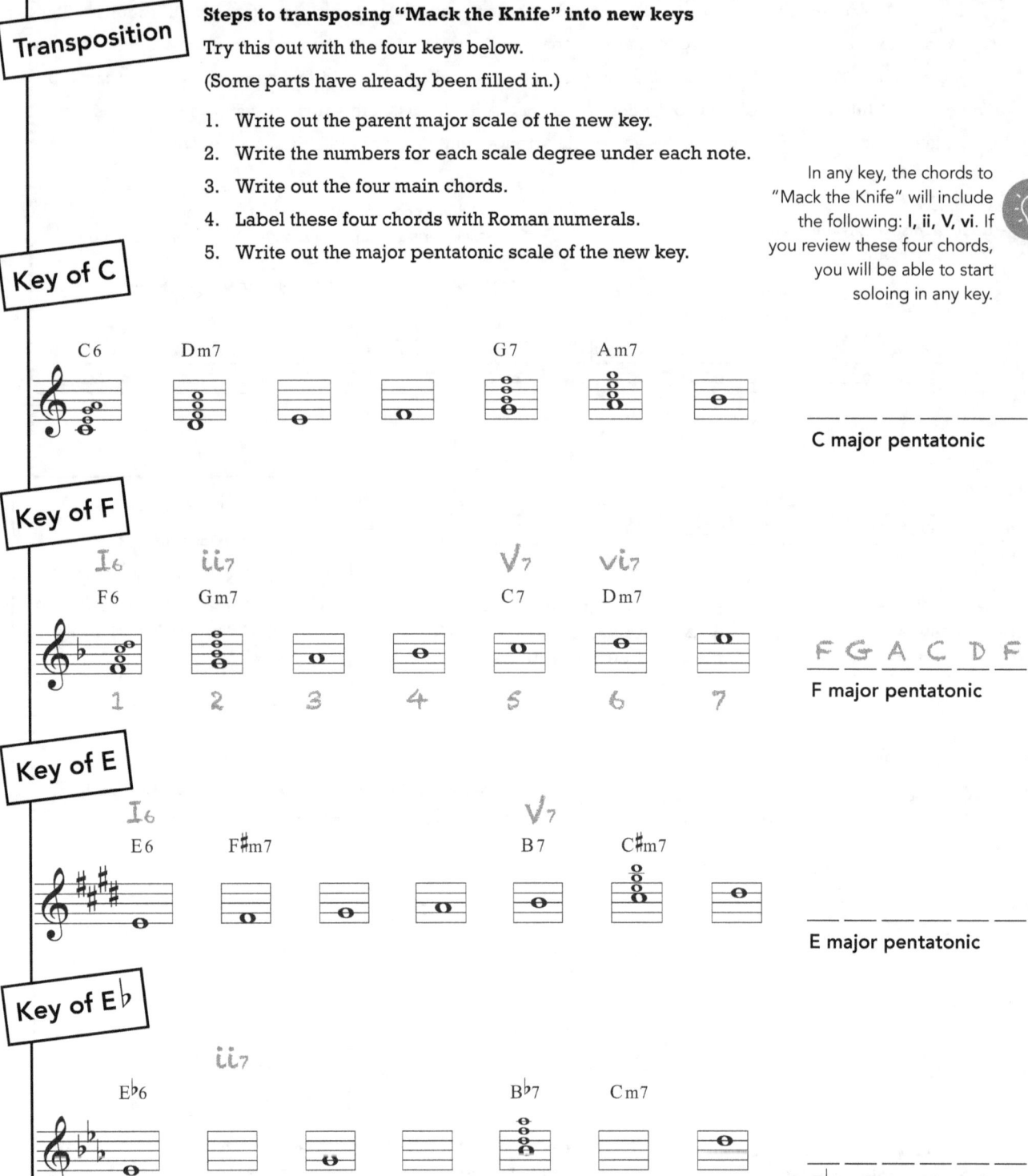

Improvise

"Mack the Knife"

IMPROVISE
"Mack the Knife" (Kurt Weill)
in a key of your choice

 Listen to early recordings of "Mack the Knife." What was its original key?

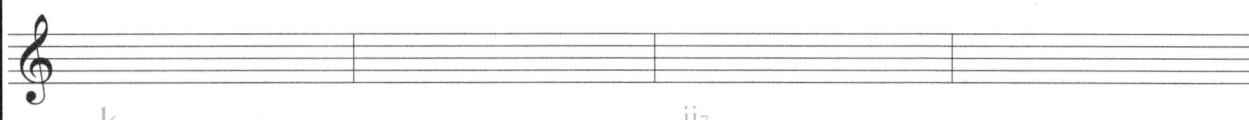

I_6 ii_7

ii_7 ii_7 V_7 I_6

vi_7 ii_7

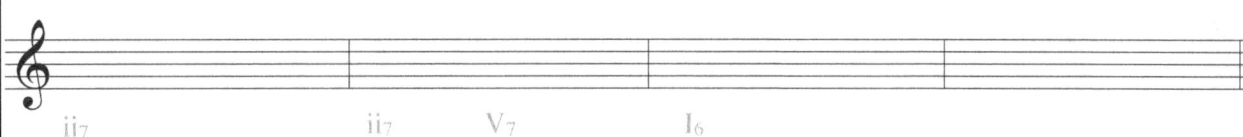

ii_7 ii_7 V_7 I_6

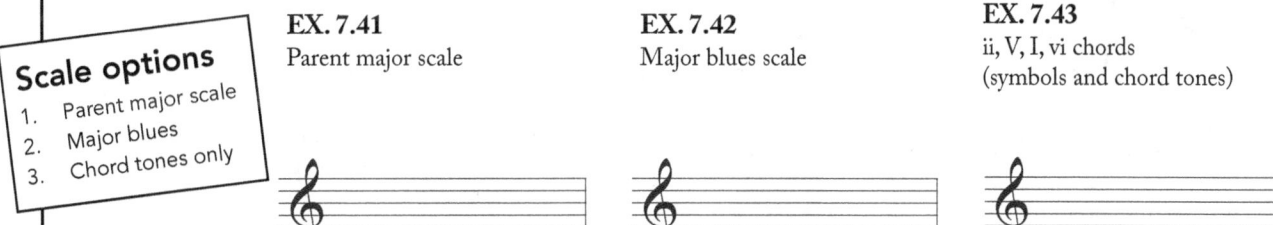

EX. 7.41
Parent major scale

EX. 7.42
Major blues scale

EX. 7.43
ii, V, I, vi chords
(symbols and chord tones)

Scale options
1. Parent major scale
2. Major blues
3. Chord tones only

Add a secondary dominant in bar 8

For additional chromatic color, add a V_7/vi in measure 8. This secondary dominant leads to the vi_7 in measure 9.

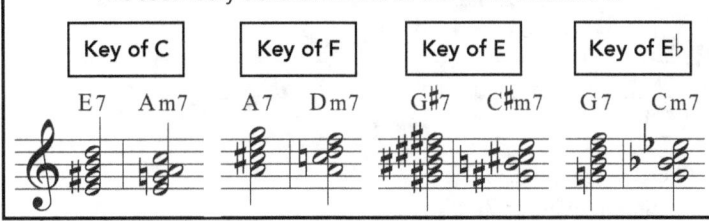

| Key of C | Key of F | Key of E | Key of E♭ |
| E7 Am7 | A7 Dm7 | G#7 C#m7 | G7 Cm7 |

 Refer to both the Sonny Rollins performance on "Mack the Knife", renamed "Moritat," on his album *Saxophone Colossus* and the Ella Fitzgerald live recording from her album *Live in Berlin*.

 Once you start getting the hang of the chord progression, try moving up chromatically in all keys (*à la* Ella Fitzgerald).

Linear Improvisation
— page 1 of 2 —

Linear improvisation involves keeping a focus on motivic development across a chord progression. This can include the use of scales, arpeggios, and many other melodic devices. A tool for linear development can be the use of a central melodic structure to anchor the improvisation. This can be something as simple as a melodic pedal point with all other notes relating to the single pedal. It can also involve a single chord (quite often this will be the parent tonic I chord), a single scale, or scale fragment.

Using parent major scale

EX. 7.44
Johnny Griffin tenor sax solo "The Way You Look Tonight"

Rather than outlining each chord through the progression, Johnny Griffin allows a **repeated parent major scale** to govern his line.

Using parent pentatonic scale

EX. 7.45
Dexter Gordon tenor sax solo "Blow, Mr. Dexter"

Circle each time a non-chord tone is targeted in Dexter Gordon's blues solo below. Why does the single minor pentatonic scale work across all chords here?

Sometimes linear (sometimes not!)

A musician may craft a solo that is linear for only a moment. On "Pennies from Heaven," Paul Desmond improvises linearly over bars 1-6. Rather than adhering strictly to the chord tone voice-leading of each harmony, he uses the parent major scale and floats across the progression. This ceases for bars 7-8 as the focus moves to chord tones and a guide tone line.

EX. 7.46
Paul Desmond alto sax solo "Pennies from Heaven"

These chords are passing chords. Desmond focuses more intently on C major tonic harmony instead.

Follow the circled notes below and notice a fascinating and hidden melodic development. Desmond's two 4-bar phrases **target the same notes** (circled) with the first phrase ending on C and the second resolving to B.

Linear (bars 1-6)

Target notes stretch across two measures.

C resolves to B, the 7th and 3rd of a guide tone line.

Resolution(?) to tonic C, distinctly NOT a G7 chord tone.

Vertical (bars 7-8)

Target notes compress into one measure.

Chord tones outlined, starting here in bar 7.

Linear Improvisation

page 2 of 2

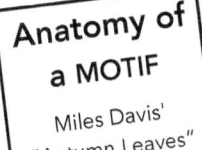

Anatomy of a MOTIF

Miles Davis' "Autumn Leaves" solo

Motivic development and linear improvisation frequently intertwine. In his classic "Autumn Leaves" solo, Miles Davis introduces a simple and memorable rhythmic motif which he then develops. Davis keeps to linear improvisation by sticking to parent major and minor scales, only occasionally outlining specific chord tones.

The rhythmic motif and first two variations are labeled below. Label all remaining variations.

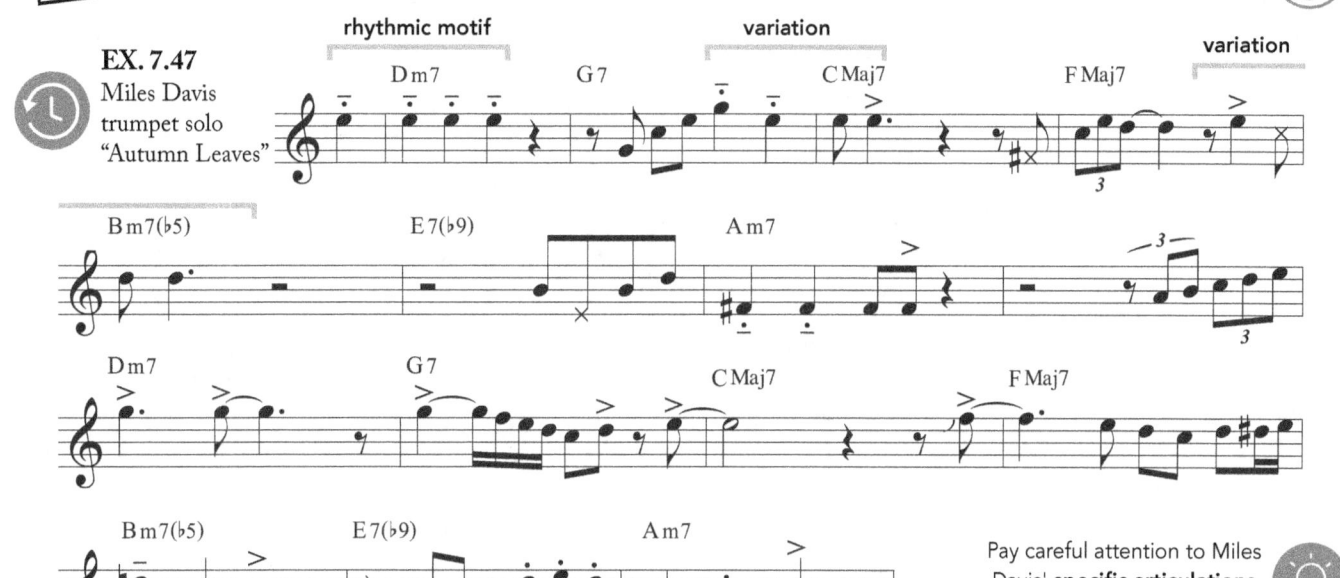

EX. 7.47
Miles Davis trumpet solo "Autumn Leaves"

Pay careful attention to Miles Davis' **specific articulations.** They are motivic!

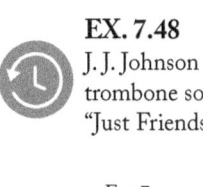

Anatomy of a MOTIF

J. J. Johnson's "Just Friends" solo

J. J. Johnson introduces a rhythmic cliché in his second solo measure on "Just Friends," a solo based on a rhythmic variation of this cliché. Rather than outlining specific chords, he glides across the progression, allowing his scalar and linear path to remain the focal point.

A "cliché" can be a famous and popular rhythm or short melodic fragment. It tends to be played frivolously.

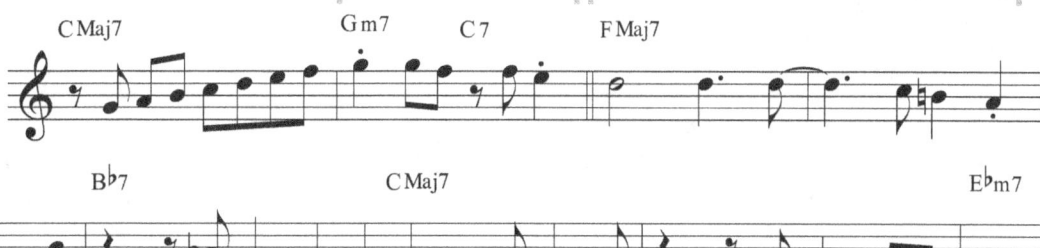

EX. 7.48
J. J. Johnson trombone solo "Just Friends"

Make a decision!

Who's in control? You are! Decide what type of solo line you are creating. Blues scale, pedal point, parent scale floating over the chord changes, motivic development, rhythmic structure, common chord tones, guide tone lines, silence — each builds a clear direction for your musical statement.

Why Motifs Work (and why they shouldn't!)

A solo may use a scale pattern as motif to govern the solo line, which can quickly gain melodic independence, no longer targeting underlying chord tones. In each of the following examples, (1) notice the motif, (2) consider why it shouldn't work, and (3) discover why it actually works.

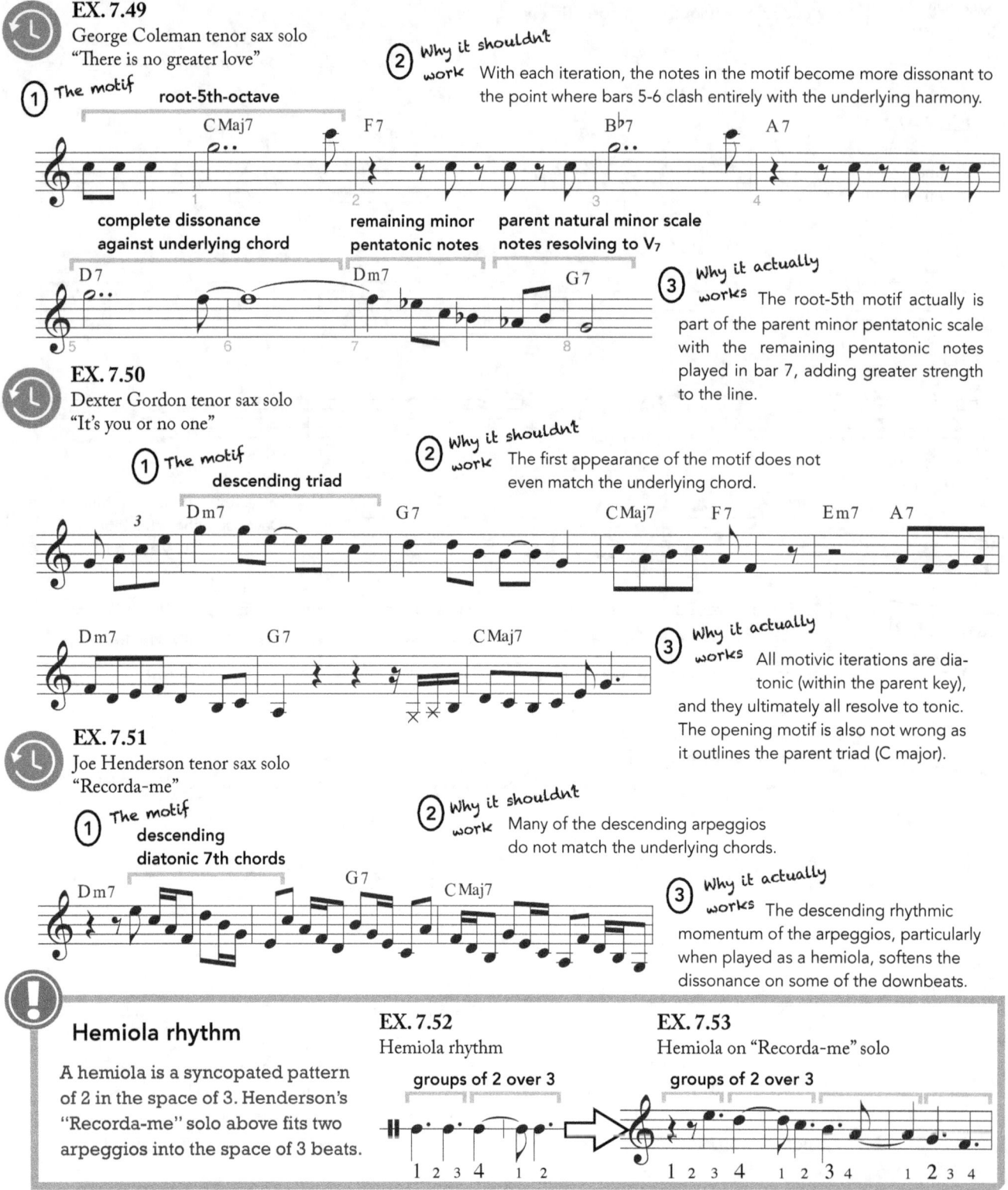

EX. 7.49

George Coleman tenor sax solo
"There is no greater love"

① The motif — root-5th-octave

② Why it shouldn't work With each iteration, the notes in the motif become more dissonant to the point where bars 5-6 clash entirely with the underlying harmony.

complete dissonance against underlying chord

remaining minor pentatonic notes

parent natural minor scale notes resolving to V_7

③ Why it actually works The root-5th motif actually is part of the parent minor pentatonic scale with the remaining pentatonic notes played in bar 7, adding greater strength to the line.

EX. 7.50

Dexter Gordon tenor sax solo
"It's you or no one"

① The motif — descending triad

② Why it shouldn't work The first appearance of the motif does not even match the underlying chord.

③ Why it actually works All motivic iterations are diatonic (within the parent key), and they ultimately all resolve to tonic. The opening motif is also not wrong as it outlines the parent triad (C major).

EX. 7.51

Joe Henderson tenor sax solo
"Recorda-me"

① The motif — descending diatonic 7th chords

② Why it shouldn't work Many of the descending arpeggios do not match the underlying chords.

③ Why it actually works The descending rhythmic momentum of the arpeggios, particularly when played as a hemiola, softens the dissonance on some of the downbeats.

Hemiola rhythm

A hemiola is a syncopated pattern of 2 in the space of 3. Henderson's "Recorda-me" solo above fits two arpeggios into the space of 3 beats.

EX. 7.52
Hemiola rhythm

groups of 2 over 3

EX. 7.53
Hemiola on "Recorda-me" solo

groups of 2 over 3

Solo Spotlight

Art Blakey, drums "A Night in Tunisia"

The great bandleader and drummer, Art Blakey, was a master of development, crafting artistic solos filled with an abundance of striking rhythmic themes. His solo on "A Night in Tunisia," while focusing on the toms, is also structured so that the form of the composition is quite clear. On a macrolevel, the initial triplet theme is developed over the A-sections and then the B-section introduces a contrasting motif based on a slower eighth-note pattern. On a microlevel, every phrase builds on and complements the previous. In the first four measures, the initial triplet theme is a punctuated five notes, repeated, before turning into a steady stream of triplets grouped in six, analogous to an engine building momentum at the start of a road race.

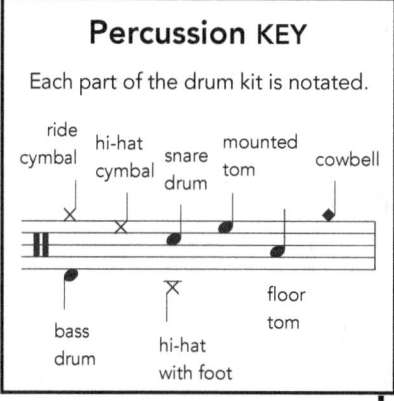

EX. 7.54
Art Blakey drum solo
"A Night in Tunisia"

Learn from drummers! This Blakey solo provides a masterful example of motivic development based entirely on rhythms.

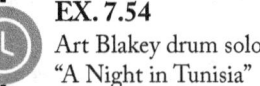

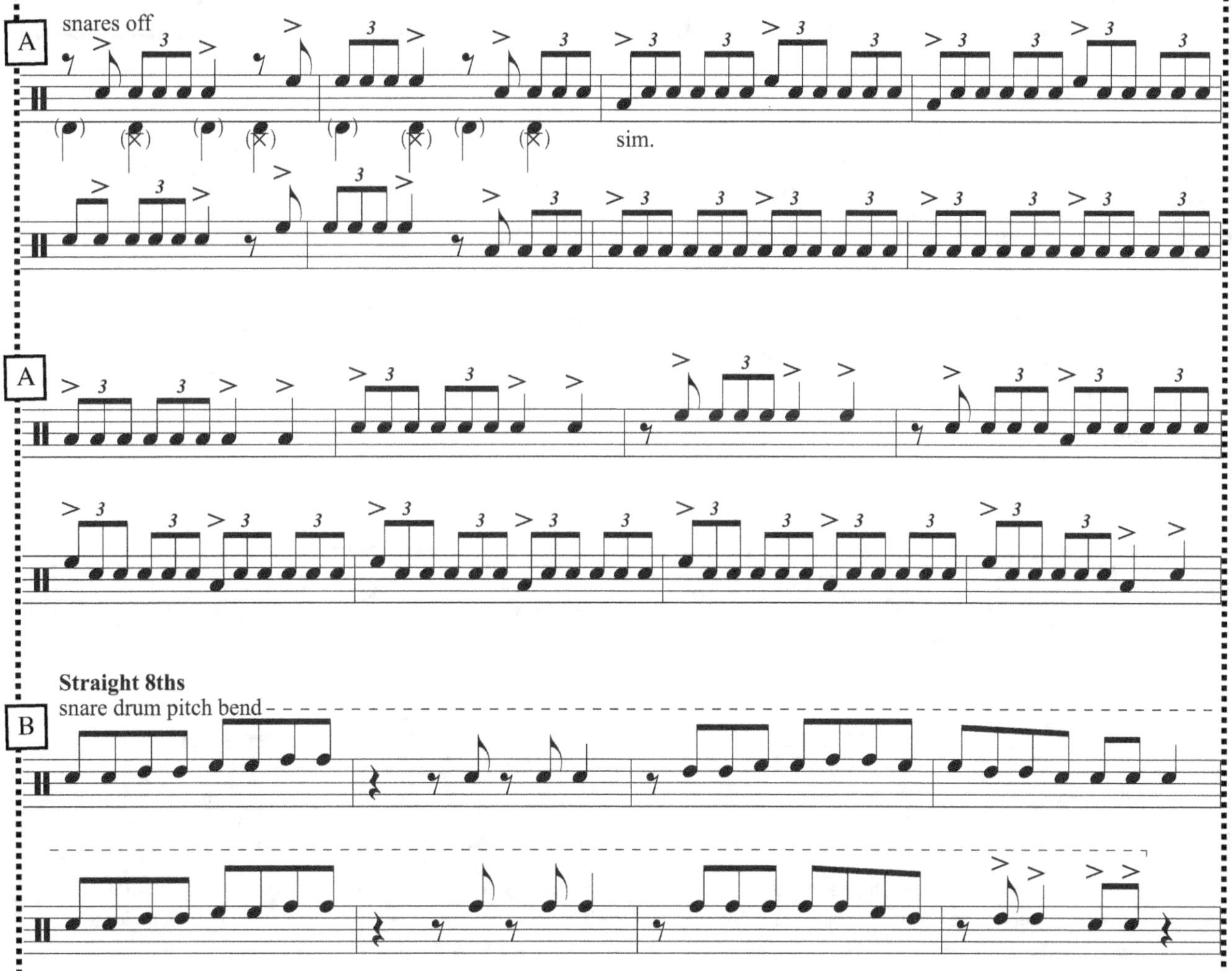

Masterclass

Compound Melody
page 1 of 2

While a melodic line might at first sound like just one melody, closer listening reveals at least TWO simultaneous melodies. The highest voice of a *compound melody* tends to be easiest to hear. A lower voice often creates a new melody that may be more subtle. Careful analysis offers a better understanding of the way compound melodies are regularly used by composers and improvisers.

EX. 7.55
"Autumn Leaves" (Josef Kosma)
melody and countermelody

Trace the upper and lower voices
in each example below.

[musical notation: upper voice melody, chords Dm7, G7, CMaj7, FMaj7, Bm7(b5), E7(b9), Am7; lower voice countermelody circled]

EX. 7.56
Creative compound melody using
scale fragments on "Autumn Leaves"

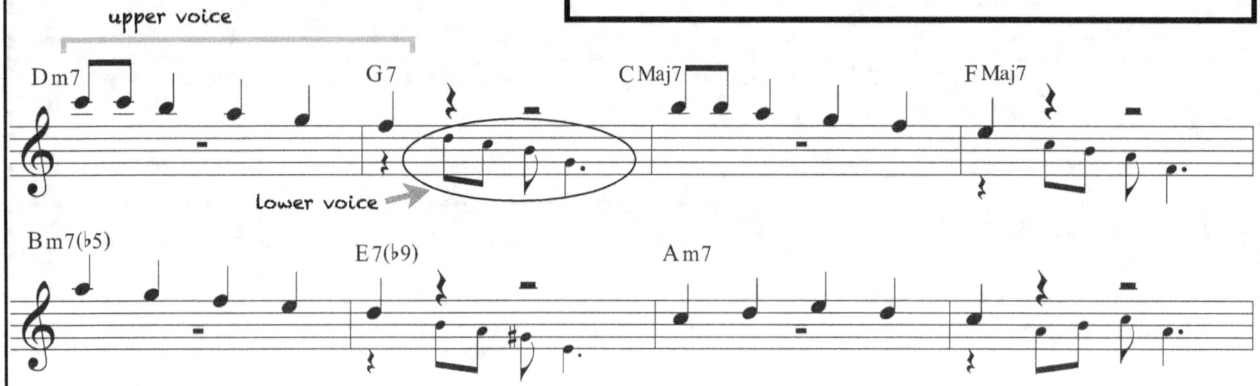

Pitch collection challenge!
Complete "Autumn Leaves" by adding the following pitches:
A B C F G A B E F G A D E F♯ G♯ C

[musical notation: upper voice, chords Dm7, G7, CMaj7, FMaj7; lower voice circled; second line Bm7(b5), E7(b9), Am7]

EX. 7.57
Charlie Parker alto sax solo
"Anthropology"

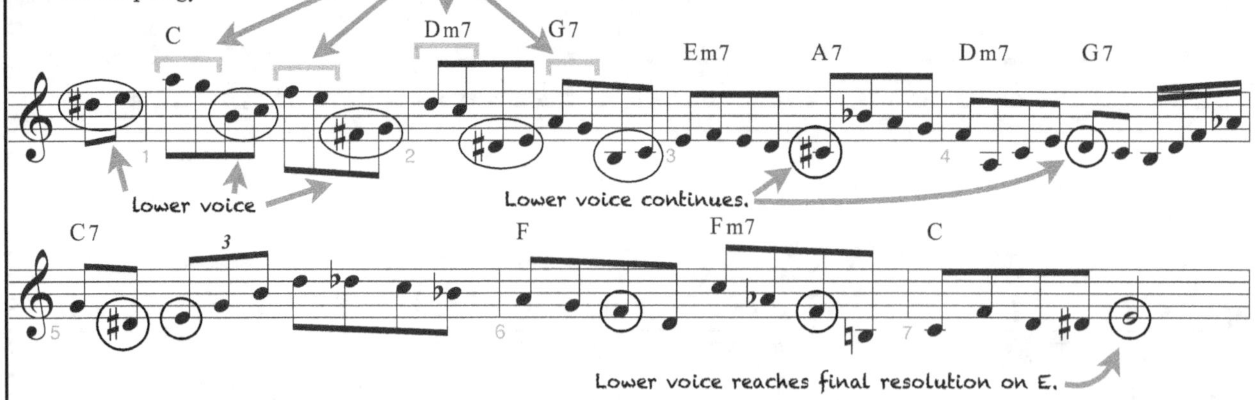

[musical notation: upper voice, chords C, Dm7, G7, Em7, A7, Dm7, G7; lower voice, Lower voice continues; second line C7, F, Fm7, C; Lower voice reaches final resolution on E.]

The first two bars of this Charlie Parker solo excerpt form a clear compound melody involving two sets of neighbor groups outlining the parent C major triad. The upper voice is highlighted with brackets. The lower voice, highlighted with circles, continues beyond bar 2, forming a steady chromatic ascent leading to a final resolution on the note E in measure 7. This sort of **melody within a melody**, expertly intertwined, is found throughout Parker's improvisations.

Masterclass   Compound Melody
page 2 of 2

One way to understand compound melody is to use various bracket/stem techniques and harmonic or melodic *reductions*, all of which help distinguish between upper and lower melodic voices. Quite often, great artists like J. S. Bach and Charlie Parker created melodies that included 3-4 melodic lines occurring simultaneously. They certainly set the bar high for melodic ingenuity!

Quick-study guide to the genius of Charlie "Bird" Parker

When Charlie Parker introduces a new voice, he constantly keeps track of it, guiding it stepwise over time. In the example below, notice that three voices are analyzed.

Both the upper voice and lowest voice are stemmed and bracketed. The middle voice (circled below) remains static, acting throughout as a constant pedal point.

EX. 7.58
Reduction on "Perhaps" (Charlie Parker)

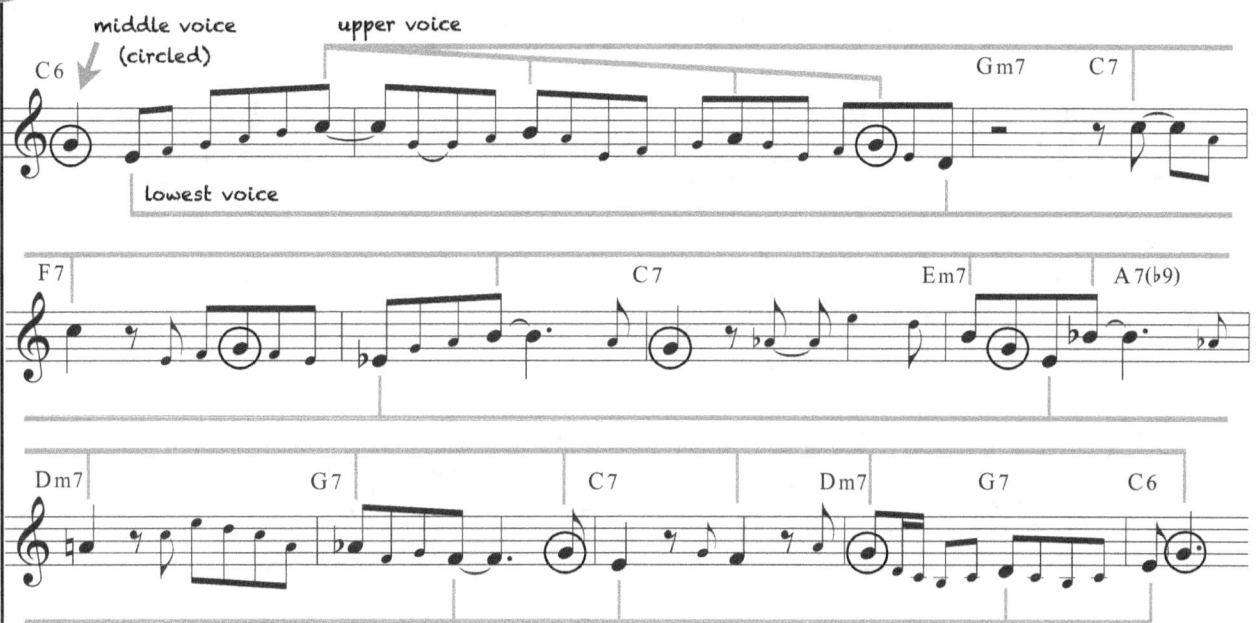

The concept of compound melody existed even before J. S. Bach, yet the approach Bach took as a composer in the 1600s had a particularly profound impact on jazz music. Notice below how Bach creates a melodic pathway for each of the four voices he introduces, illustrated by the reduction under the score.

Compound melody origins

EX. 7.59
Violin Partita No. 2 in D minor (J. S. Bach)

The smaller second staff system is a **reduction** that illustrates how each voice in the partita moves from measure to measure.

ii-V-I Improvisation Workouts

The following improvisation workouts just might be the most valuable in this entire study of the ii-V-I. Get creative with applying different ideas and parameters to your improvisations. Below are some specific ideas to be taken one at a time:

- Consider oppositions at all times (loud-soft, short-long, play-rest, step-leap, etc.)
- Rest in the middle of each measure, focusing on the transitions connecting to beat 1 of each new bar.
- Delay your entrance, resting on beat 1 before playing the first note of the phrase.
- Syncopate your arrival, targeting the upbeat "and" of beat 4, instead of beat 1.
- Play simply, adding only one or two new notes to each measure.
- Play more complexly but still try to land on your target note, whether it's the "and" of beat 4 or beat 1.

Use pre-determined notes for voice-leading

Workout #1

Adhere to the voice-leading targets below or write out your own set of notes per measure. Notice how the pre-determined notes below are all chord tones but even that parameter can change if you choose.

IMPROVISE
Use the voice-leading notes below as your targets, approaching your targets any way you choose. Targets may be placed on beats other than beat 1.

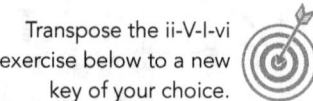

Transpose the ii-V-I-vi exercise below to a new key of your choice.

Change the focus to linear improvisation

Workout #2

Your linear improvisation might be based on a parent scale, a rhythmic motif, interval, or other device. Develop your line, prioritizing this over specific chord tone targets.

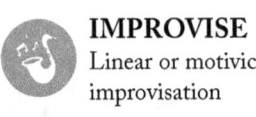

IMPROVISE
Linear or motivic improvisation

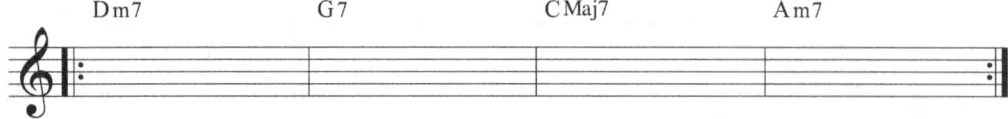

ii-V-I Improvisation Workouts
page 2 of 2

Workout #3

Cerebral challenge

Label every numerical relation for the notes of the C major scale over Dm G7 CMaj7. In the first measure below, the note C is labeled as the root (1) of CMaj7 and the 7th of Dm7.

CMaj7: <u>1</u>   <u>7</u>   __   __   __   __   __   __

Dm7: <u>7</u>   <u>6</u>   __   __   __   __   __   __

G7: __   __   __   __   __   __   __   __

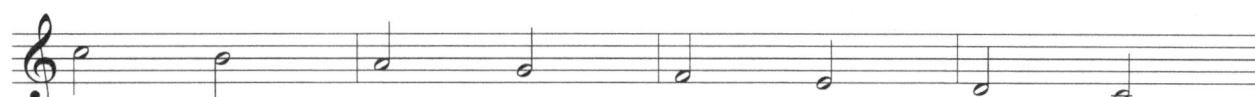

Workout #4

Compose your own chord progression, then improvise

All major scale fragments fit into the ii-V-I. Every set of 3-note fragments within the major scale belongs to either the ii, the V, or the I chord, in addition to matching other diatonic 7th chords.

EX. 7.60

Every 3-note stepwise fragment in the C major scale
and every matching diatonic 7th chord

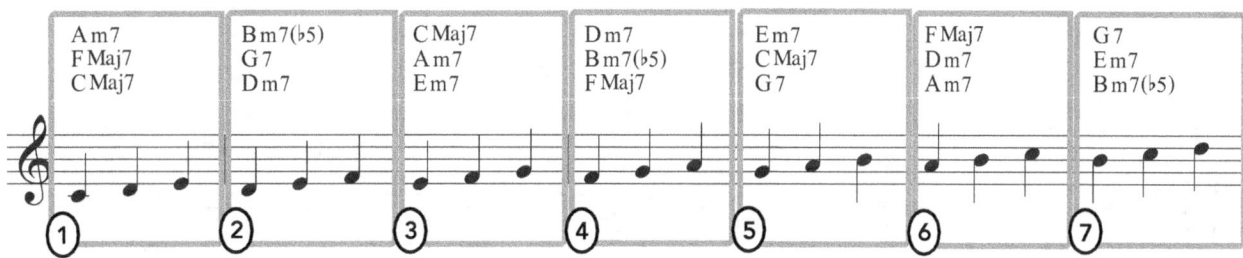

Am7	Bm7(♭5)	CMaj7	Dm7	Em7	FMaj7	G7
FMaj7	G7	Am7	Bm7(♭5)	CMaj7	Dm7	Em7
CMaj7	Dm7	Em7	FMaj7	G7	Am7	Bm7(♭5)
①	②	③	④	⑤	⑥	⑦

 Compose eight measures of chord symbols, one chord per measure below, choosing from chords in boxes 1-7 above.

 IMPROVISE
Improvise a solo over your new chord progression, using a designated scale fragment for each box.

Workout #4 composition example

Song Study — "Oh, lady be good!"

Gershwin's "Oh, lady be good!", popularized by Lester Young and others, is a wonderful solo vehicle. "Oh, lady be good!" follows a 32-bar AABA form and its A-section consists primarily of a ii-V-I progression. Use the segments below to build the full 32-bar form.

EX. 7.61
"Oh, lady be good!" (Gershwin)
(key of C major)

Internalize the remarkably creative and varied rhythms throughout "Oh, lady be good!" by tapping out the notes (or playing them all on one pitch).

When listening to various performances of "Oh, lady be good!", notice how the chord progression varies depending on the performance. Some chords change entirely (bar 18 is often played as iv7 instead of ♯iv°7), and other chords are omitted entirely (bar 2 often stays on tonic I instead of moving to the IV chord).

Solo 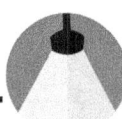 Spotlight

Charlie Parker, alto sax "Oh, lady be good!"

Alto saxophonist Charlie Parker perfectly demonstrates numerous melodic devices while soloing on "Oh, lady be good!" These include using guide tone lines when voice-leading through ii–V–I progressions, arpeggiating, using neighbor notes, focusing on a single blues scale, and adding rhythmic variety to develop an engaging melodic line.

EX. 7.62
Charlie Parker, alto sax solo
"Oh, lady be good!"
1946 (age 26)
(key of C major)

Charlie Parker's solos sound great at any tempo. Practice them slowly, taking extra care to count the rests and **play each rhythm accurately.**

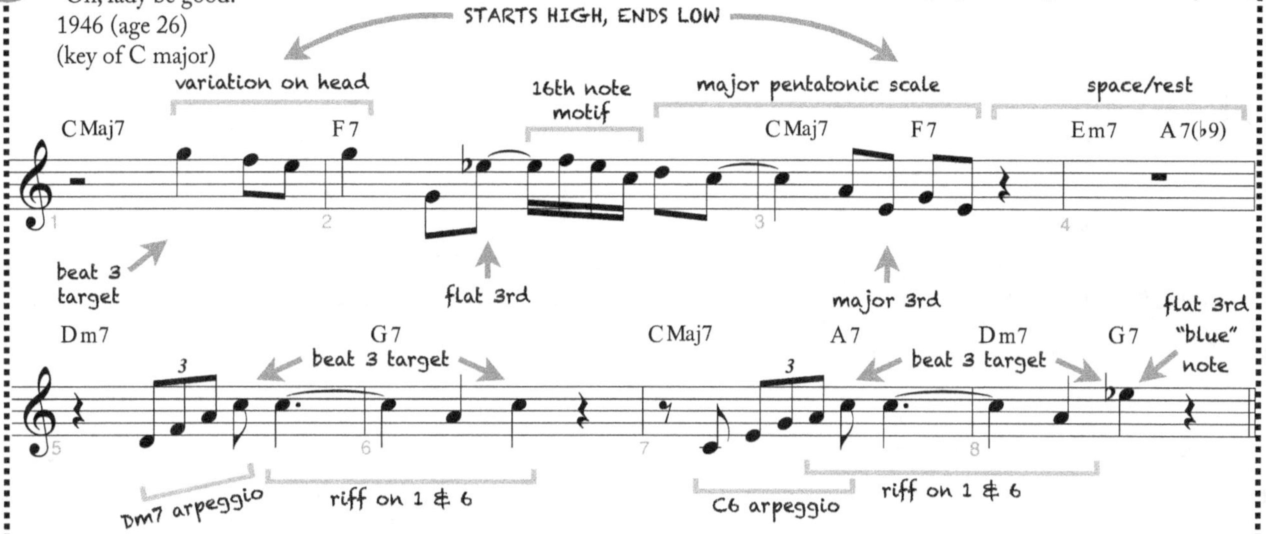

EX. 7.63
Charlie Parker, alto sax solo
"Oh, lady be good!"
1940 (age 20)
(key of C major)

Charlie Parker was only 20 years old when he recorded "Oh, lady be good!" in 1940 with the Jay McShann Orchestra, and saxophonist Lester Young's influence was palpable.

Label the scale degrees and chord arpeggios in the solo example below.

EX. 7.64
Charlie Parker, alto sax solo
"Oh, lady be good!"
reduction

The top voice in Charlie Parker's solo, illustrated in the reduction below, carves a descent from **scale degree 5 down to 1**, a melody within a melody.

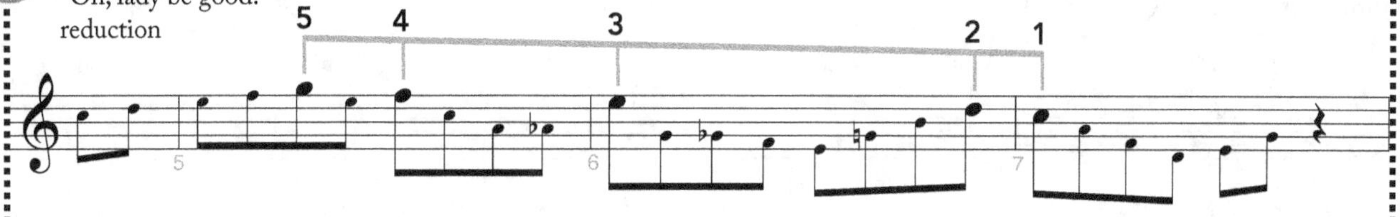

Improvise

"Oh, lady be good!"
page 1 of 3

The following two improvisation exercises are templates to use over the A-section of "Oh, lady be good!" in the key of C major. Use the guide tones and voices below to help shape improvised lines.

If adding extra pitches feels a bit daunting, first try **adding rhythms**, including some syncopations, while sticking largely to only the pitch content presented here.

IMPROVISE
"Oh, lady be good!" A-section, guide tone line from the 3rd

IMPROVISE
"Oh, lady be good!" A-section, guide tone line from the 7th

Lester Young's solo below touches on very few guide tones. Label any guide tones, then also label COMMON TONES, which he uses often.

EX. 7.65
Lester Young tenor sax solo "Oh, lady be good!" 2nd A-section (bars 9-16)

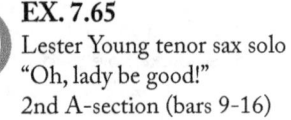

Listen to Lester Young's solo. Why do think that some notes sound good, even though they don't always match the chord tones?

The A-section of "Oh, lady be good!" includes two turnarounds: I-IV-iii-VI (resolving to the ii chord in measure 5) and I-VI-ii-V (resolving to the I chord in measure 1). Both these turnarounds are designed to help the harmony arrive organically at either the ii or I chord, and they are ubiquitous throughout jazz.

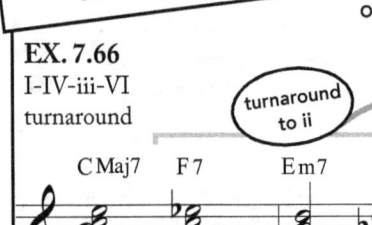

"Oh, lady be good!" turnarounds

EX. 7.66
I-IV-iii-VI turnaround

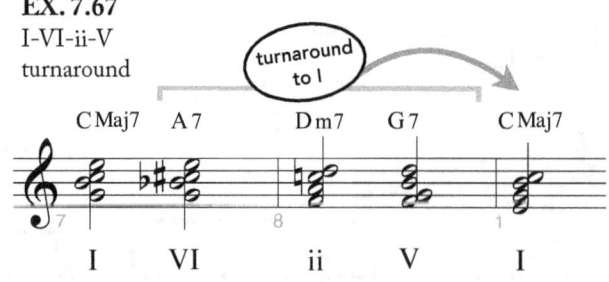

EX. 7.67
I-VI-ii-V turnaround

Improvise

"Oh, lady be good!"
page 2 of 3

Bridge (B-section)

The "Oh, lady be good!" B-section, or the bridge, provides a welcome harmonic break from the tonic-heavy "Oh, lady be good!" A-section. Totaling eight measures — bars 17-24 of each 32-bar chorus — the bridge includes four primary harmonies — IV_{Maj7} I_{Maj7} II_7 V_7 — with other passing chords shaping the B-section's harmonic rhythm and detail.

EX. 7.68
"Oh, lady be good!"
B-section *étude*

The four primary harmonies are circled.

Don't miss F♯! In the key of C, perhaps the most distinct note on the bridge is F♯, the major 3rd of D7.

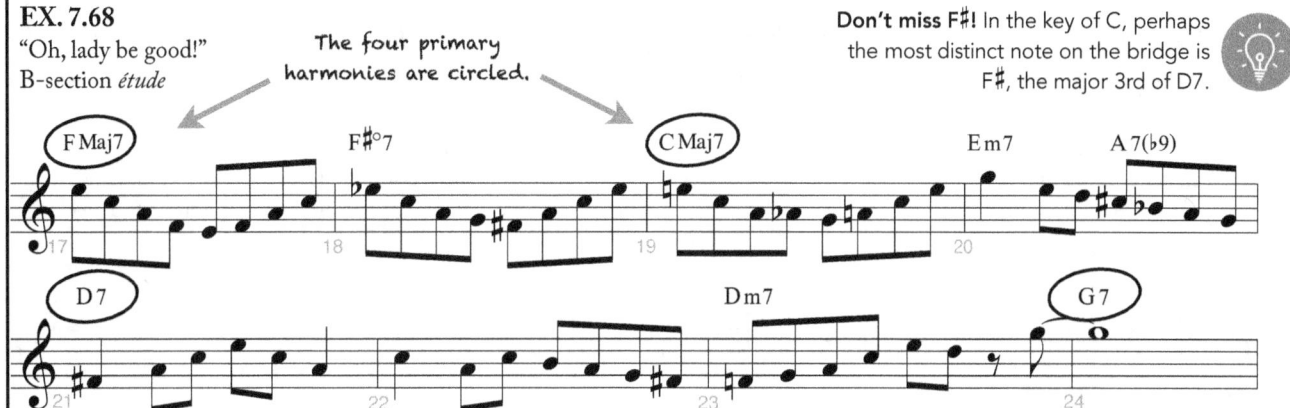

EX. 7.69
Lester Young tenor sax solo
"Oh, lady be good!" B-section

Lester Young does not play every chord tone while weaving his melody through the bridge. Label the COMMON TONES he uses below.

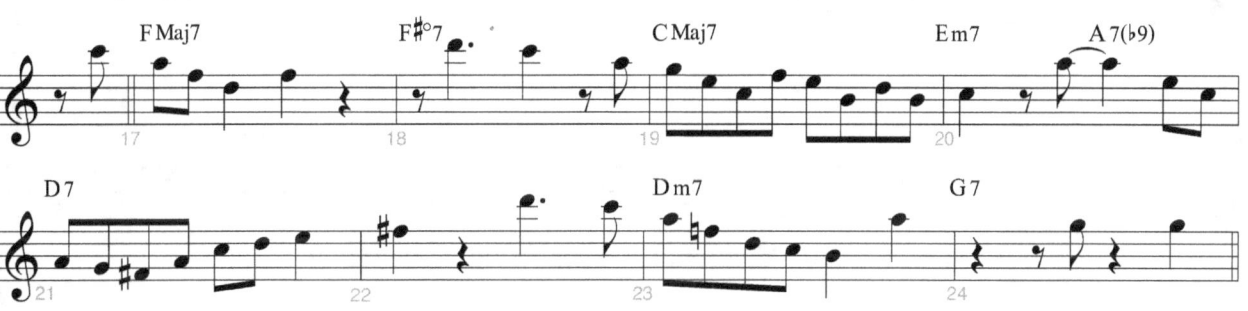

Learn Lester Young's iconic "Oh, lady be good!" solo entirely by ear. Start with the first 8 bars.

BEWARE the lead sheet!

Jazz cannot, and should not, be reduced to a "fake book" lead sheet. It is not meant to be a series of chords that we decipher then match up as we follow each line, four bars at a time. Chords are dynamic and meant to be ever-changing, subject to creative input and development. Study the alternate changes for the B-section of "Oh, lady be good!" below for an example of this variability.

EX. 7.70
"Oh, lady be good!" B-section
alternate chord changes

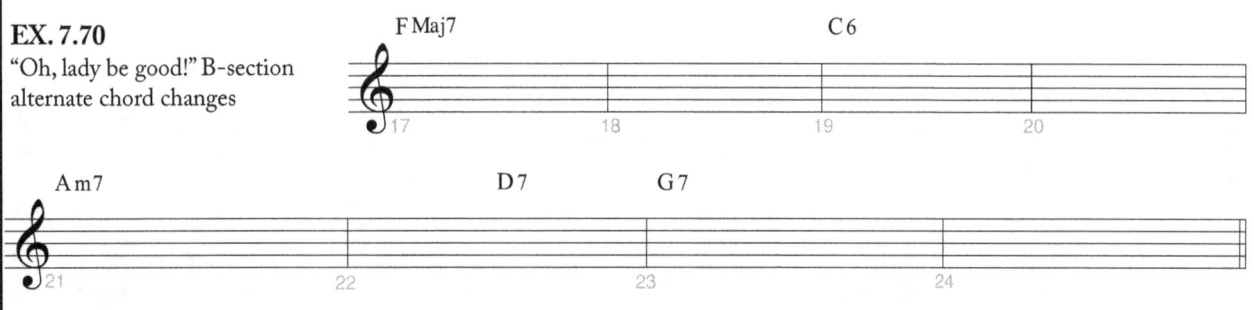

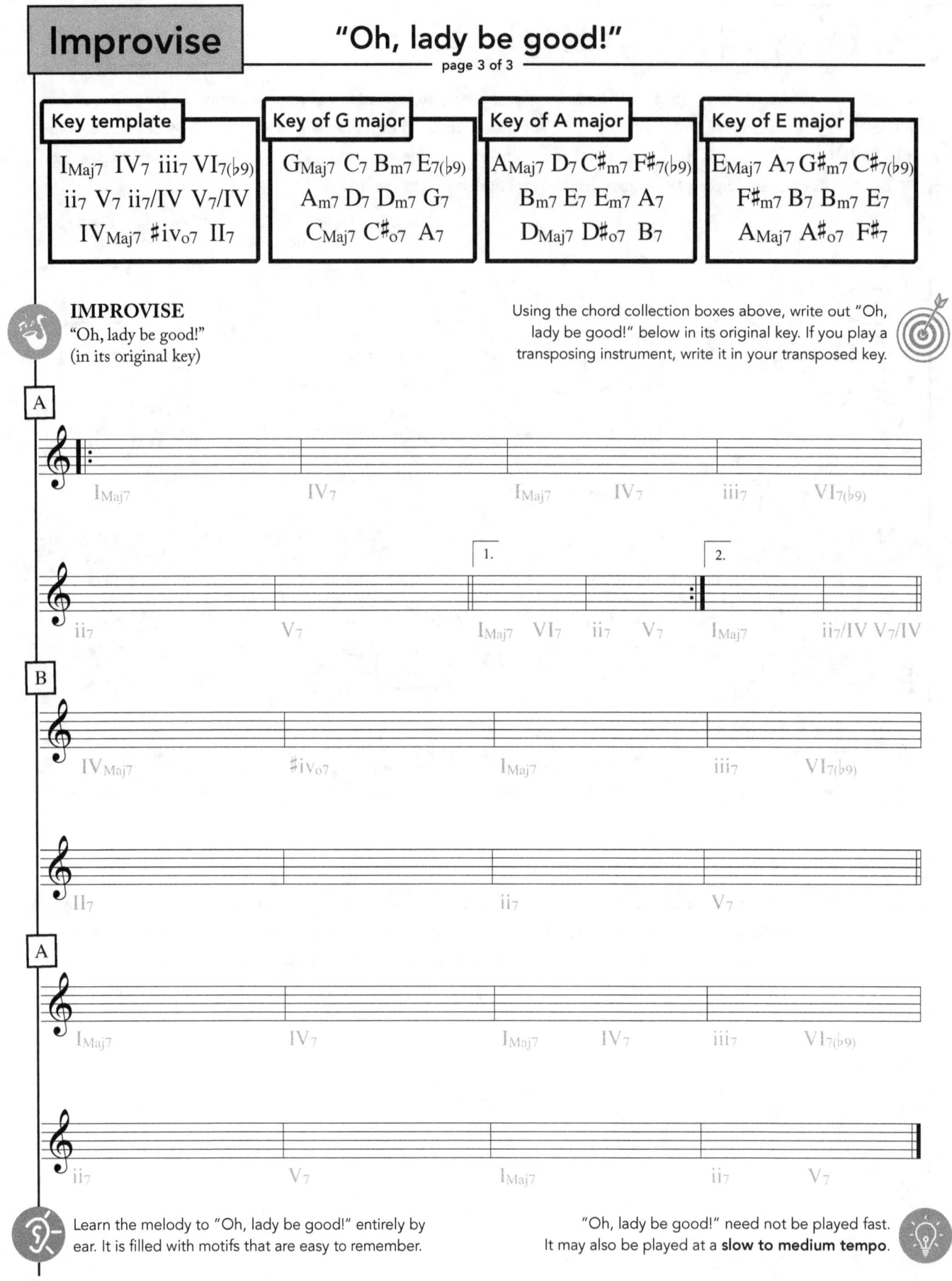

Zen Jazz Master says:

Rules are made to be broken!

The improviser can make a great melody even without a balance of opposites. Some solos are filled nearly entirely with dissonances. Some melodies consist predominantly of fast notes with only the occasional slow note for balance. "Autumn Leaves" is composed nearly exclusively of legato phrases and there is no need to balance this out with the occasional staccato passage. As long as the improviser retains an awareness of oppositions, the melody will remain deeply purposeful.

Chapter 7 Achievements

Congratulations!

You are one step closer to jazz nirvana.

Here is a partial list of what you've achieved:

- Understanding which scale fragments are common between ii-V-I chords
- Mapping guide tones to develop a longer melodic line
- Using both the vi and VI chords to enhance a ii-V-I progression
- Exploring linear improvisation and how it may be applied over a ii-V-I progression
- Enhancing learning through analysis of improvised solos throughout jazz history

Are you ready for the next chapter?

Answer these questions to determine whether you are prepared to continue to the next chapter:

- **Can you use** guide tones while improvising over a ii-V-I chord progression (in more than one key)?

    If "Yes," move to the next chapter.
    If "No," continue to the next chapter but keep working on your fluency with guide tones and common tones.

- **Can you explain** the basic principles of linear improvisation?

    If "Yes," move to the next chapter.
    If "No," review this chapter.

- **Do you understand** how to use and develop rhythmic motifs while improvising over a ii-V-I?

    If "Yes," move to the next chapter.
    If "No," review this chapter.

- **Do you want** to learn about the minor ii-V-i and the roots of bebop harmony?

    If "Yes," move to the next chapter.
    If "No," … actually, nevermind. You're too committed to this book at this point and you KNOW you want to check out this next chapter. Great job!

8 Night Shift

Minor ii-V-i, Modal Mixture, and the Altered Dominant

An initial step into minor key harmony requires a cursory understanding of the minor ii-V-i chord progression. Yet, unlike major, a small wonder of minor is that its fundamental harmonies are brimming with dynamic details that render it nearly impossible to improvise using any single parent scale. While this chapter does explore parent scale options and various solutions to pitfalls, a deeper dive here includes an exploration of modal mixture, implied harmony, altered dominant chord extensions, and the altered scale, all of which have the power to bring an improviser much closer to demystifying many of the most complex concepts in jazz.

Contents

TOPICS
- Minor Key Harmony
- Minor ii-V-i Chords and the Flat-9
- Natural Minor and the Minor ii-V-i
- Line Clichés
- Deconstructing Harmonic Minor
- Piggy Ear and Tail
- Harmonic Minor Octave Pivots
- Demystifying the Flat-9
- Modal Mixture
- Minor Third Substitutions
- Altered Dominant Chord Extensions
- Modes of Melodic Minor
- Chord Substitution vs. Superimposition
- Altered Scales on "Blue Bossa"
- Hidden Changes in "Blue Bossa"

EAR TRAINING
- Sing Minor Chord Roots
- C Blues Scale
- D-flat Major Scale

MASTERCLASS
- Hidden Changes (Implied Harmony)

INVESTIGATE
- Two Views: Altered Dominant Scale

SONG STUDY
- "Softly, as in a Morning Sunrise" (Romberg/Hammerstein)
- "Blue Bossa" (Kenny Dorham)

HISTORICAL EXAMPLES
- "Summertime" (Gershwin/Heyward)
- Emily Remler guitar solo "Softly, as in a Morning Sunrise"
- Miles Davis trumpet solo "So What"

SOLO SPOTLIGHT
- Bob Brookmeyer valve trombone solo "My Funny Valentine"
- Kenny Barron piano solo "Softly, as in a Morning Sunrise"

IMPROVISE
- Harmonic Minor Scale over Minor ii-V-i
- "Softly, as in a Morning Sunrise" (Romberg/Hammerstein)
- Minor Third Substitutions
- Altered Scale over Minor ii-V-i
- "Blue Bossa" (Kenny Dorham)

SMACKDOWN!
- Half-diminished ii Scales

LISTENING GUIDE
- Pedal Points on "Softly, as in a Morning Sunrise"
- Versions of "Softly, as in a Morning Sunrise"
- Versions of "Blue Bossa"

ZEN JAZZ MASTER SAYS
- Measuring Progress

Minor Key Harmony

Minor key harmony is rich and wonderful, suggesting a world of possibilities. At its core are three distinct functional harmonies — the tonic i, the subdominant iv, and the dominant V_7. In the key of C minor, these chords are Cm, Fm, and G7. In this key of C minor, the parent scale is, not surprisingly, the C harmonic minor scale. It includes every chord tone from each of these chords and may be used to create melodies across minor key progressions.

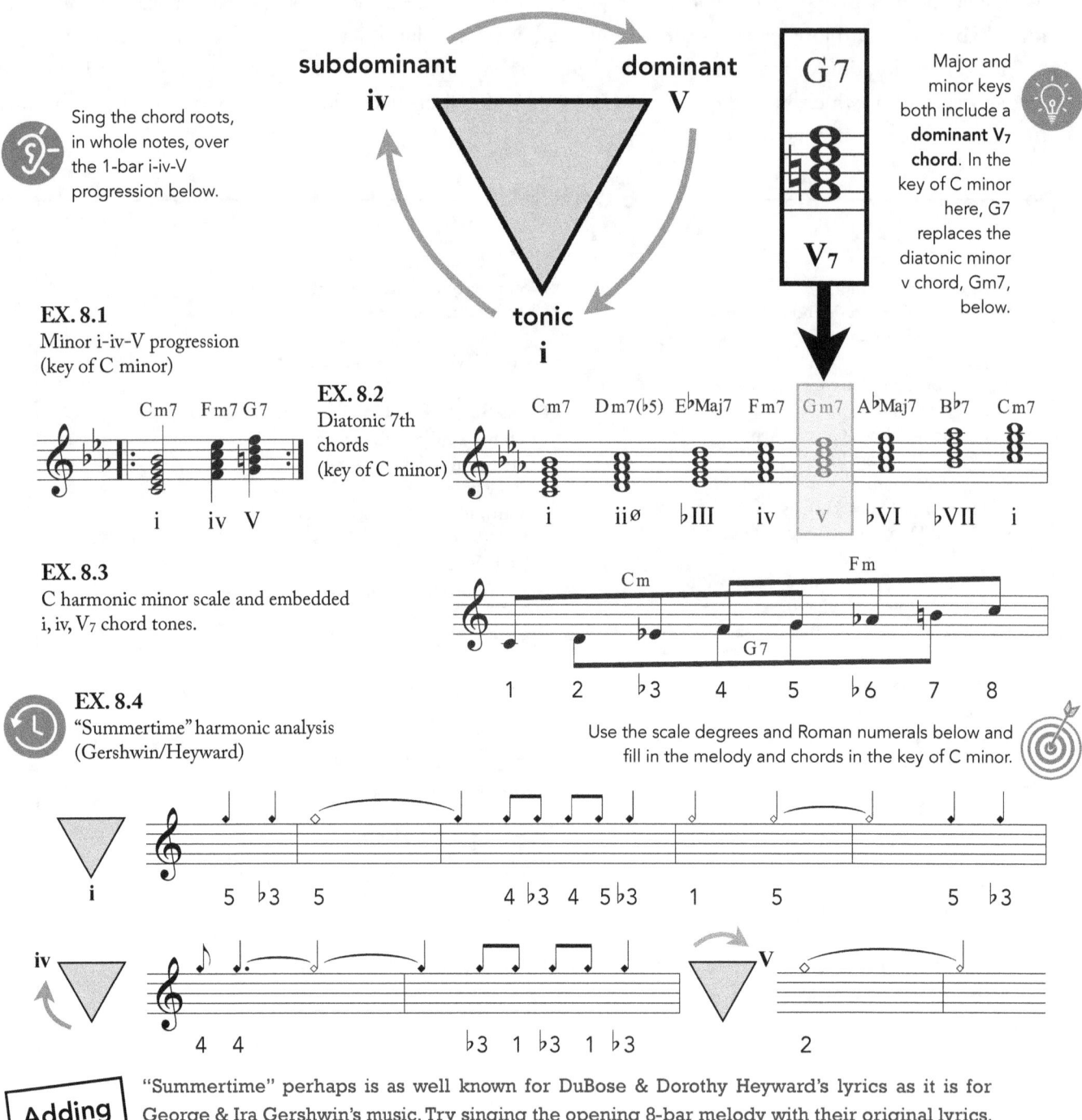

"Summertime" perhaps is as well known for DuBose & Dorothy Heyward's lyrics as it is for George & Ira Gershwin's music. Try singing the opening 8-bar melody with their original lyrics. The three images — *easy living, jumping fish, high cotton* — are each supported by a distinct harmony — minor i, iv, and V.

Minor ii-V-i Chords and the Flat-9

To understand the origins of the *minor ii-V-I chord progression*, it helps to examine how each chord relates within its parent minor key. Both the minor i and half-diminished ii chord are diatonic chords. Minor ii-V-i progressions use a dominant V7 chord. In the key of C minor, the note B-natural is central to the dominant function of G7 even though it is an alteration from the key signature's B♭. A complex and colorful quality of minor keys is that the dominant V7 chord also features prominently a *flat-9*. In the key of C minor, this is the note A♭ and the V7 chord becomes G7(♭9).

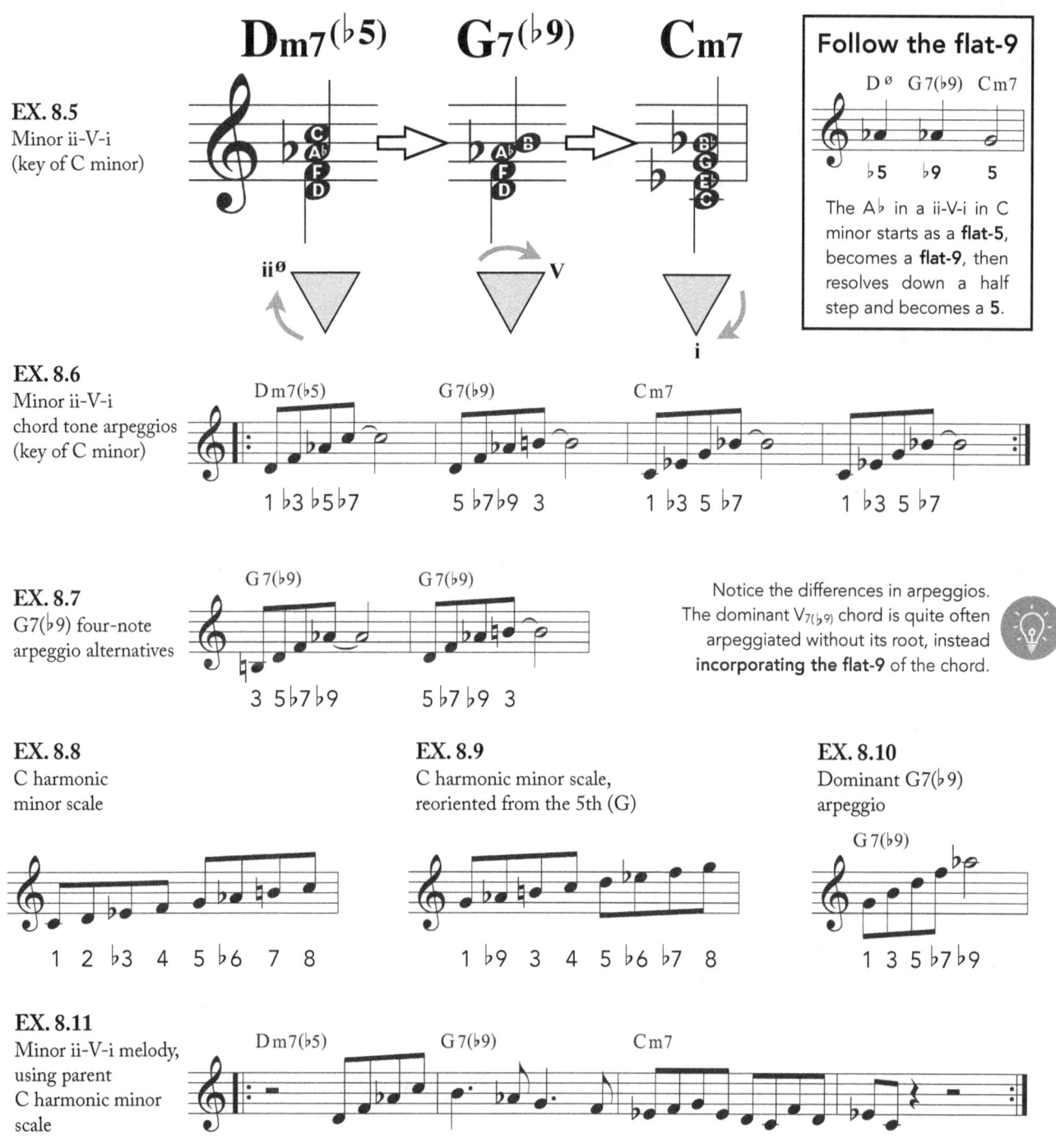

EX. 8.5
Minor ii-V-i
(key of C minor)

Follow the flat-9

The A♭ in a ii-V-i in C minor starts as a **flat-5**, becomes a **flat-9**, then resolves down a half step and becomes a **5**.

EX. 8.6
Minor ii-V-i
chord tone arpeggios
(key of C minor)

EX. 8.7
G7(♭9) four-note
arpeggio alternatives

Notice the differences in arpeggios. The dominant V7(♭9) chord is quite often arpeggiated without its root, instead **incorporating the flat-9** of the chord.

EX. 8.8
C harmonic
minor scale

EX. 8.9
C harmonic minor scale,
reoriented from the 5th (G)

EX. 8.10
Dominant G7(♭9)
arpeggio

EX. 8.11
Minor ii-V-i melody,
using parent
C harmonic minor
scale

Natural Minor and the Minor ii-V-i

The natural minor scale can serve as a parent scale, used exclusively across all three chords of a minor ii-V-i progression. In the examples below, each melody begins with a focus on tonic minor i chord tones (scale degrees 1, ♭3, 5). The melody then moves to a combination of chord tones that match the ii and V chords (circled as parent scale degrees 2, 4, ♭6). While these melodies are clearly dependent on the harmony, there is still freedom within each melodic line. Trace the target notes (circled), where sometimes the melody will start and stay near scale degree 5 rather than starting and ending on the more obvious scale degree 1. Other times, the line will move unexpectedly, forming surprising shapes.

EX. 8.12
C natural minor scale
(parent scale)

Target notes are numbered below. A circled number indicates a chord tone and **all numbers remain related to the parent key.**

EX. 8.13
Only 1, ♭3, 5 and 2, 4, ♭6 outlined, clear and concise

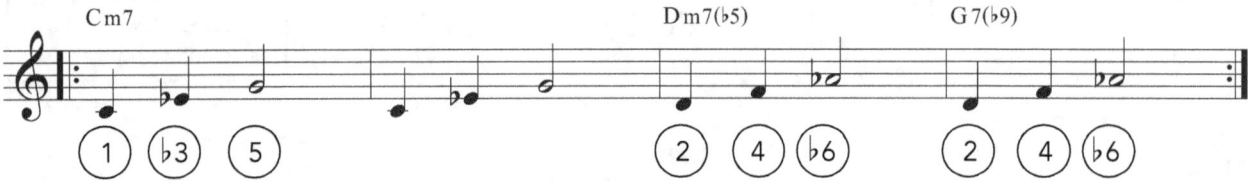

EX. 8.14
Melodic focus limited to chord tones 1, ♭3, 5 and 2, 4, ♭6

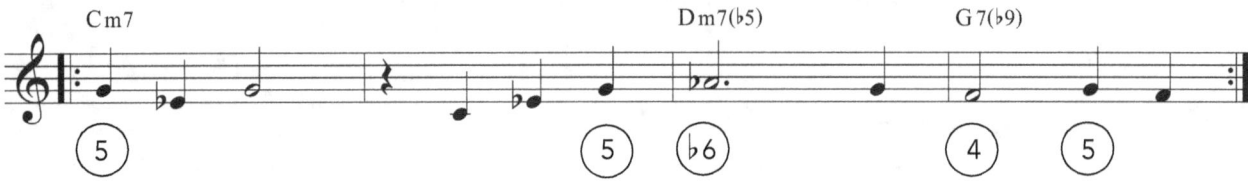

EX. 8.15
Melodic focus on chord tones, including a raised-7 leading tone over V₇

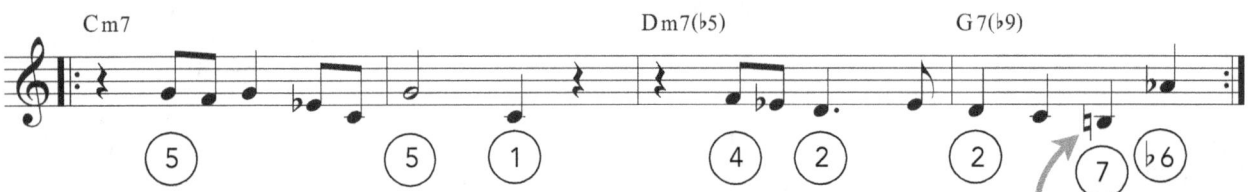

EX. 8.16
Melodic focus on chord tones, introducing a combination of flat-7 and raised-7 leading tone

Incorporate the **leading tone**, the raised 7th of the parent natural minor scale, particularly when targeting the 3rd of the V chord.

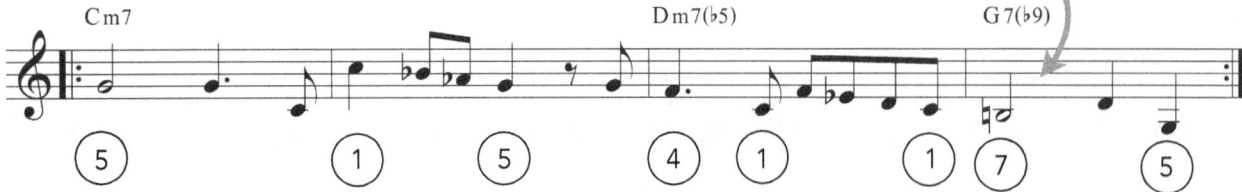

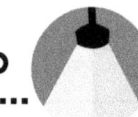

Solo Spotlight

Bob Brookmeyer, valve trombone
"My Funny Valentine"

"My Funny Valentine" involves myriad minor key harmonies yet trombonist Bob Brookmeyer largely incorporates only diatonic pitches across the chord changes, sticking mostly with a single natural minor parent scale. Trace, in particular, how Brookmeyer crafts a C minor melody that consistently returns to the notes G and A-flat throughout his entire solo.

EX. 8.17
Bob Brookmeyer trombone solo
"My Funny Valentine"

Bob Brookmeyer is considered a master of motivic development. Notice how he uses **rhythmic motifs** to develop his improvisation.

Line clichés

Line clichés add to a single minor triad an extra chord tone that moves chromatically, contributing momentum to an otherwise repetitive and static harmonic foundation. One cliché (and its variations) descends from octave root to major 7th, to minor 7th, to major 6th. Another cliché ascends from the 5th.

EX. 8.18
Descending line cliché, from the octave root

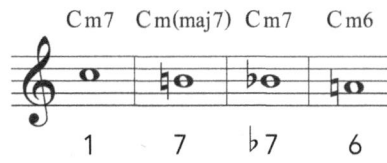

EX. 8.19
Descending line cliché, with chromatic bass descent

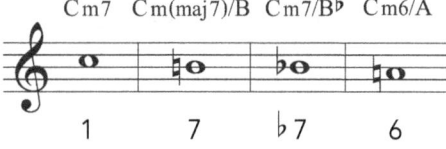

EX. 8.20
Implied descending line cliché, chords no longer static

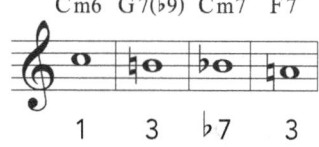

EX. 8.21
Ascending line cliché, from the 5th

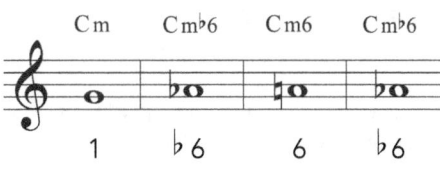

Carefully examine all four line cliché examples. What are the distinguishing characteristics in each? How does Bob Brookmeyer handle the line cliché as a soloist in "My Funny Valentine"?

Deconstructing Harmonic Minor

Rather than considering the harmonic minor scale ascending from scale degrees 1-8, a novel approach deconstructs the harmonic minor scale, reimagining fragments of the scale as a "little piggy" — its body consisting of the scale degrees 1-5, its tail (scale degree 7) wiggling below scale degree 1, and its ears (scale degree ♭6) wiggling up high, an upper neighbor to scale degree 5. This is frequently how the harmonic minor scale is used in actual musical context.

Piggy ear and tail

EX. 8.22
Piggy ear/tail

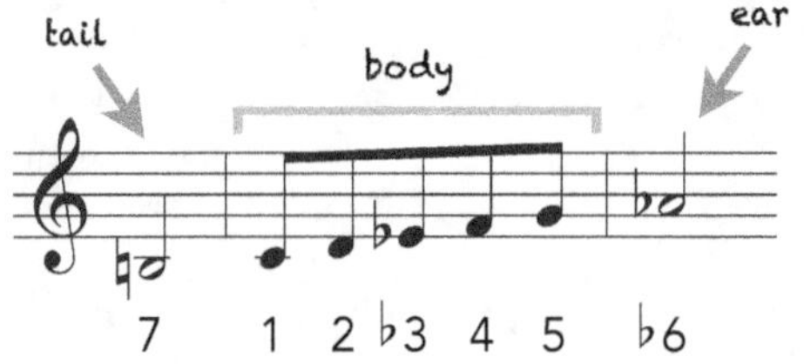

tail | body | ear

7   1 2 ♭3 4 5   ♭6

EX. 8.23
Body, ear, tail
exercise

body | ear | tail

1 2 ♭3 4 5   5 4 ♭3 2 1   5 ♭6 5 ♭6 5   1 7 1 7 1

EX. 8.24
Harmonic minor
scale exercise

Write in the scale degrees for both exercises
below then transpose each to 3 new keys.

Cm7   Dm7(♭5)   G7(♭9)   Cm7   Dm7(♭5)   G7(♭9)

EX. 8.25
Body, ear, tail
extended exercise

Cm7   Dm7(♭5)   G7(♭9)   Cm7   Dm7(♭5)   G7(♭9)

Cm7   Dm7(♭5)   G7(♭9)   Cm7   Dm7(♭5)   G7(♭9)

IMPROVISE
Use the parent harmonic
minor scale and consider
the piggy ear/tail.

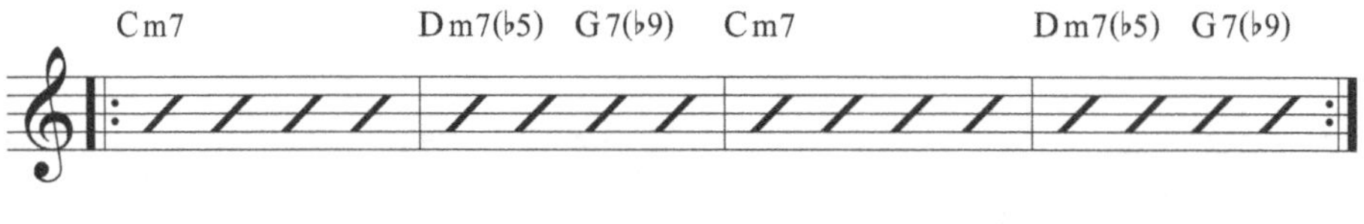

Cm7   Dm7(♭5)   G7(♭9)   Cm7   Dm7(♭5)   G7(♭9)

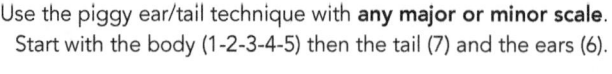

Use the piggy ear/tail technique with **any major or minor scale**.
Start with the body (1-2-3-4-5) then the tail (7) and the ears (6).

Harmonic Minor Octave Pivots

Harmonic minor scale *octave pivots* are a constant across genres throughout history. These pivots, formed by displacing the scale with a sudden leap to a different octave, have been used as melodic devices by Baroque era composer J. S. Bach and bebop jazz pioneer Charlie Parker, among countless others.

EX. 8.26
C harmonic minor, pivots targeting C minor chord tones on beat 1

EX. 8.27
C harmonic minor scale fragments and pivots

Get to know the phrases below. Which pivots **sound best to you?**

Each of the above 9-note phrases may be found in the scale pattern below. Find and circle each phrase.

EX. 8.28
C harmonic minor scale pattern, pivots targeting descending scale steps on beat 1

Demystifying the flat-9

An upper extension of the dominant V chord, the *flat-9* is a feature in jazz, particularly in bebop. It may be used in both major and minor keys, introducing a rich and chromatic palette to any melodic line.

EX. 8.29
Common flat-9 melodic line

Transpose this classic bebop line to a new key of your choice.

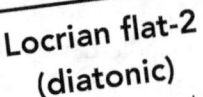 **Half-diminished ii Scales**

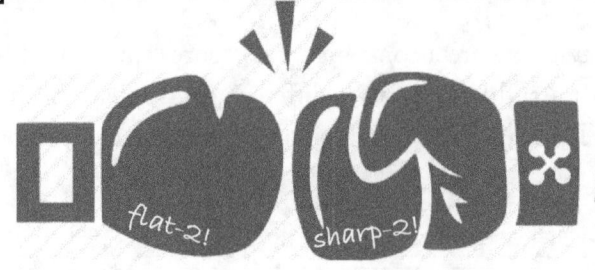

Locrian flat-2 (diatonic)
keeping the parent key signature

Locrian sharp-2 (half-diminished)
raising the 2nd scale degree, adding color to the ii chord

Across a minor ii-V-i, *half-diminished ii chords/scales* are a challenge! Just like the I and V chord, the half-diminished ii chord can involve various scales. Typically notated with a "m7($\flat$5)" or a "ø" symbol, in the key of C minor, the ii chord is Dm7($\flat$5) or D^{ø}. The chord can wreak havoc on melody because its two most common scales — *Locrian flat-2* and *Locrian sharp-2* — are both problematic. Examine below the pitfalls of each scale and determine which solution(s) might be right for you.

EX. 8.30
D Locrian flat-2, the 2nd diatonic
mode of parent C natural minor scale

EX. 8.31
D Locrian sharp-2,
the "half-diminished scale"

THE PROBLEM

At a slow or medium tempo, the *Locrian flat-2 scale* often sounds mismatched in a jazz style perhaps because its flat-2 (E-flat in the key of C minor) does not match the sharp-2 (E) commonly used as a chord extension (the 9th) on the ii^{ø} chord — Dm7($\flat$5). What's more, the *Locrian sharp-2 scale* is difficult to navigate, particularly at faster tempos since its sharp-2 (E) conflicts with the overall minor key (C minor).

EX. 8.32
Unidiomatic voicing,
including flat-2 as a very
dissonant flat-9

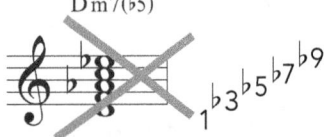

EX. 8.33
Common jazz voicing,
including sharp-2
as a ninth

Right!

THE SOLUTION

F Dorian minor is a perfect scale to use with Dm7($\flat$5), the ii chord in C minor, since it includes the flat-2 (E-flat), part of the parent scale, and it can also easily include the sharp-2 (E) as a leading tone.

EX. 8.34
F Dorian minor,
with leading tone

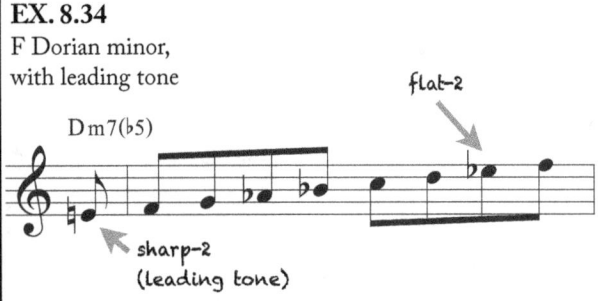

EX. 8.35
F Dorian minor,
with leading tone

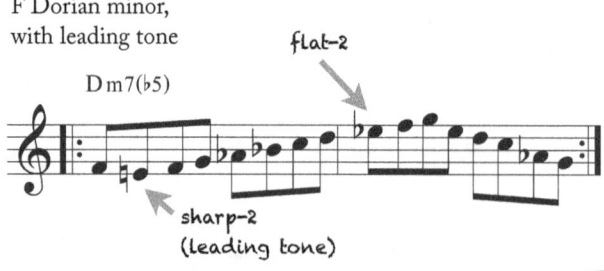

After internalizing the examples above in the
key of C minor, transpose them to other keys.

Solo 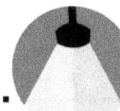 Spotlight

Kenny Barron, piano

"Softly, as in a Morning Sunrise"

Jazz pianist Kenny Barron improvises a chorus on "Softly, as in a Morning Sunrise" filled with inventive use of parent minor scales, development of rhythmic and melodic themes, and creative application of chord arpeggios. While originally performed at a fast tempo, Barron's solo may be practiced slowly.

EX. 8.36
Kenny Barron piano solo
"Softly, as in a Morning Sunrise"

For optimal understanding and fluency, learn only **two to four measures at a time**.

 A careful listen will reveal bassist Buster Williams playing pedal points (G and A-flat) on many chords throughout Kenny Barron's solo. These pedals add a layer of interest while supporting the tonic C minor tonality.

Song Study | "Softly, as in a Morning Sunrise"

"Softly, as in a Morning Sunrise" follows a 32-bar AABA form, with each 8-bar A-section involving a repeated minor ii-V-i progression and a melody based entirely on the parent key's minor scale without incorporating the scale's 7th scale degree at all. Measures alternate between chord tones, presented as both half and whole notes, and faster neighbor note motifs.

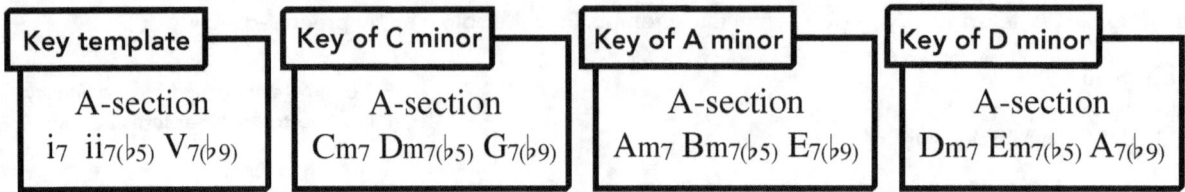

EX. 8.37

"Softly, as in a Morning Sunrise"
(Romberg/Hammerstein)
(key of C minor)

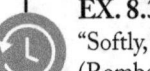 

Learn different parent minor scales by internalizing the melody of "Softly, as in a Morning Sunrise" and the following scale exercises in the other keys presented in the chord collection boxes above.

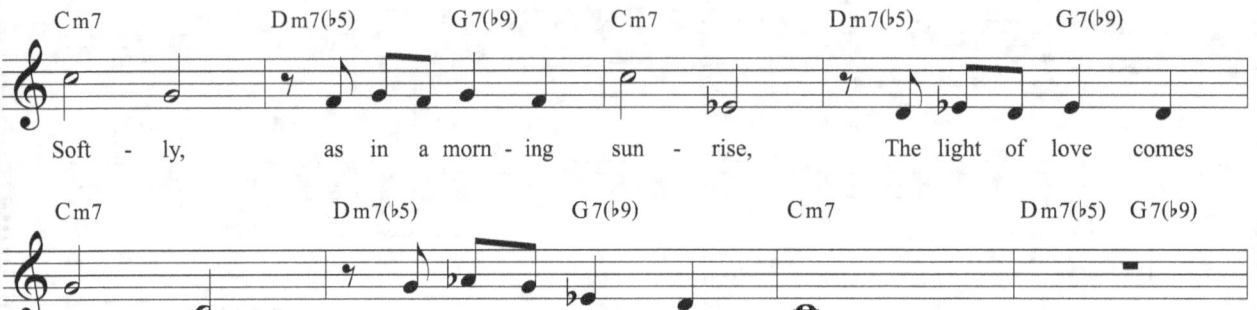

EX. 8.38
Minor i chord tones (C minor triad)

EX. 8.39
Neighbor notes between
tonic and dominant chords

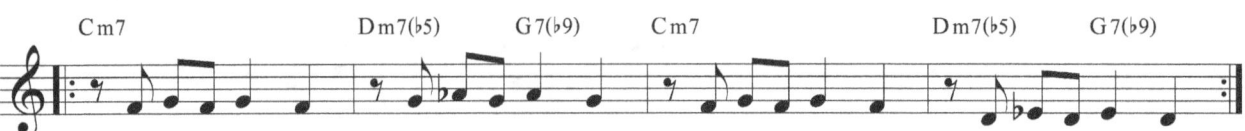

EX. 8.40
Harmonic minor scale exercise (C minor)

Song Study | "Softly, as in a Morning Sunrise"

Bridge (B-section)

On the bridge, or B-section, of "Softly, as in a Morning Sunrise," the key center changes to the relative major of the A-section. In the key of C minor, the bridge moves to E-flat major. This major key contrast provides a welcome change of the scenery before transitioning back to C minor.

Choose your key then write in the melody of the "Softly" bridge, using the placement of the rhythms as your guide.

EX. 8.41
Chord tone arpeggios on the bridge (key of C minor)

EX. 8.42
Common tones on the bridge (key of C minor)

Transpose this page to a new key, using the chord collection boxes above as your guide.

Improvise | "Softly, as in a Morning Sunrise"

Before improvising on "Softly, as in a Morning Sunrise," write out the song's melody and chords in the key of your choice. Take extra time to understand the underlying parent key's harmonic and natural minor scale to review which scale degrees comprise chord tones, which are passing tones, and the difference between raised 7th and lowered 7th scale degrees. Also notice the parent key's minor ii-V-i progression and its relative major key on the bridge of the composition.

IMPROVISE
"Softly, as in a Morning Sunrise"
(Romberg/Hammerstein)

Listen to the following versions of "Softly":

- Abbey Lincoln, *Abbey is Blue*
- Kenny Barron Trio, *Green Chimneys*
- John Coltrane, *Live at the Village Vanguard*
- Sonny Rollins, *Live at the Village Vanguard*

Can you hear and keep track of the 32-bar AABA form of "Softly, as in a Morning Sunrise" even during solo sections?

Write out the parent natural minor scale, circle the 7th scale degree, then circle which scale degree is the root of its relative major.

Improvise | "Softly, as in a Morning Sunrise"

A-section

Know your options when using scales throughout "Softly, as in a Morning Sunrise." Below are a few options for the A-section ii-V-i progression (key of C minor). Notice how common it is to remain on a single scale or, if changing scales, how there might be one or two notes that change.

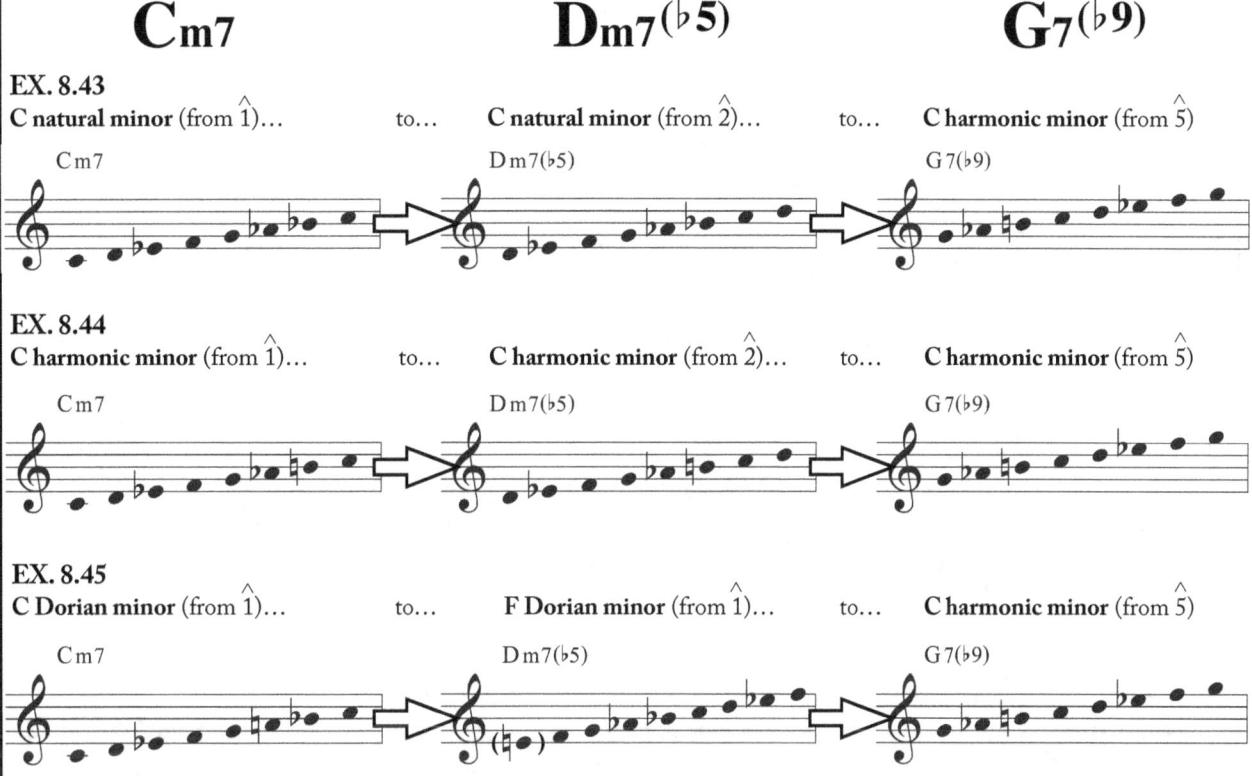

Cm7   Dm7(♭5)   G7(♭9)

EX. 8.43
C natural minor (from 1̂)...   to...   **C natural minor** (from 2̂)...   to...   **C harmonic minor** (from 5̂)

EX. 8.44
C harmonic minor (from 1̂)...   to...   **C harmonic minor** (from 2̂)...   to...   **C harmonic minor** (from 5̂)

EX. 8.45
C Dorian minor (from 1̂)...   to...   **F Dorian minor** (from 1̂)...   to...   **C harmonic minor** (from 5̂)

Bridge (B-section)

On the bridge, or B-section, of "Softly, as in a Morning Sunrise," the key center changes to the relative major of the A-section. In the key of C minor, this is a tonicization to E-flat major. The harmonic rhythm also changes, with bridge chords tending to move only every 1-2 bars.

EX. 8.46
On bar 16, the last measure before the bridge, B♭7 is a transitional harmony, with B♭ Mixolydian as a common scale

Having trouble learning the bridge of "Softly, as in a Morning Sunrise"? **Keep listening** to recordings, giving your ears ample time to adapt.

EX. 8.47
Bridge: **E♭ major** (from 1̂)   to... **F harmonic minor** (from 7̂) to... **F Dorian minor** (from 1̂) to... **G harm. minor** (from 7̂)

On the bridge scales above, circle the chord tones then identify which serve as common tones throughout the bridge.

If learning "Softly, as in a Morning Sunrise" in a key other than C minor, write out the above scales and chords in your key on a separate sheet of paper.

Modal Mixture

Major key chord progressions can include chords from minor keys, helping add color and contrast. A chord progression in the key of C major may include *borrowed chords* originating in C minor, its parallel minor key. This is also known as *modal mixture* or *modal interchange*. These borrowed chords often incorporate the flat-6 scale degree of the parent minor scale. In the key of C minor, the flat-6 scale degree, the note A-flat, can be found within Dm7(♭5), Fm7, A♭Maj7, and B♭7.

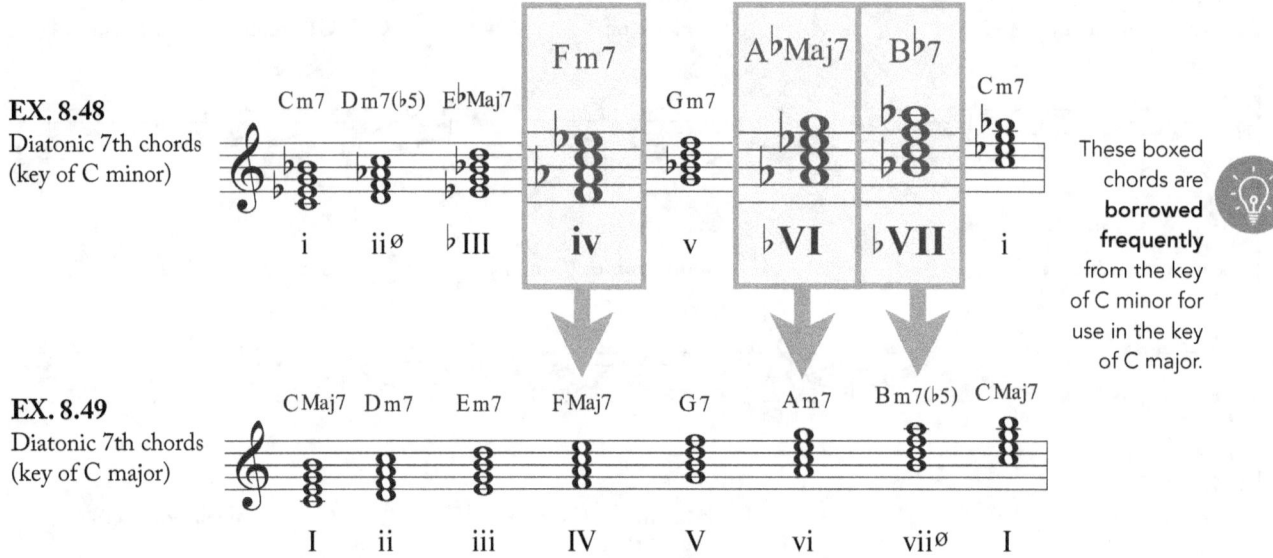

EX. 8.48
Diatonic 7th chords
(key of C minor)

These boxed chords are **borrowed frequently** from the key of C minor for use in the key of C major.

EX. 8.49
Diatonic 7th chords
(key of C major)

Chord progressions that use modal mixture tend to follow a pattern, allowing the flat-6 of the key (the note A-flat in the key of C) to resolve to the 5 (the note G). Study the examples below, tracing the voice-leading of each chord tone across the progression.

Common mixed mode progressions

EX. 8.50
IV-iv-I (C major)

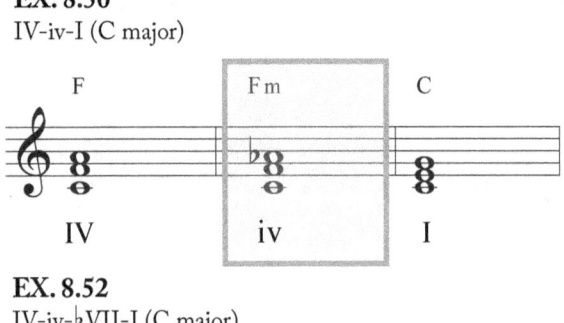

EX. 8.51
IV-iv-I arpeggios
(C major)

Notice the **line cliché** below, moving from 6 to ♭6 to 5.

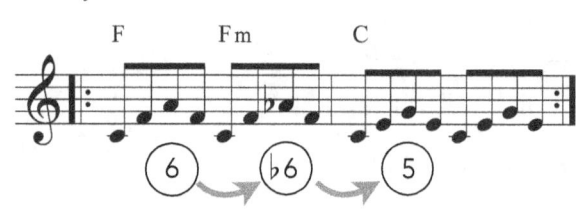
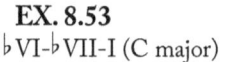

EX. 8.52
IV-iv-♭VII-I (C major)

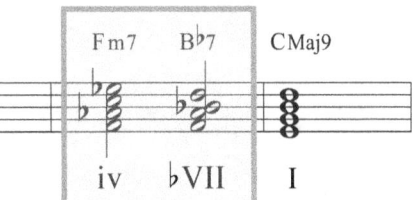

EX. 8.53
♭VI-♭VII-I (C major)

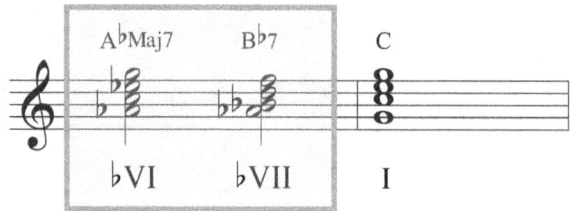

 Cole Porter used modal mixture in many of his compositions, including "Night and Day," "What is This Thing Called Love," and "I Love You."

 Arpeggiate these above progressions in three other keys of your choice.

Minor Third Substitutions

The *minor third substitution*, sometimes called a *back door substitution*, is a common chord substitution that implies a major ii-V a minor third higher than the original minor ii-V. For example, a ii-V in the key of E-flat major — Fm7 B♭7 — may be played in place of a ii-V in the key of C minor — Dm7(♭5) G7(♭9). It directs focus to G7(♭9) chord extensions, including the flat-9 (A-flat) and sharp-9 (B-flat).

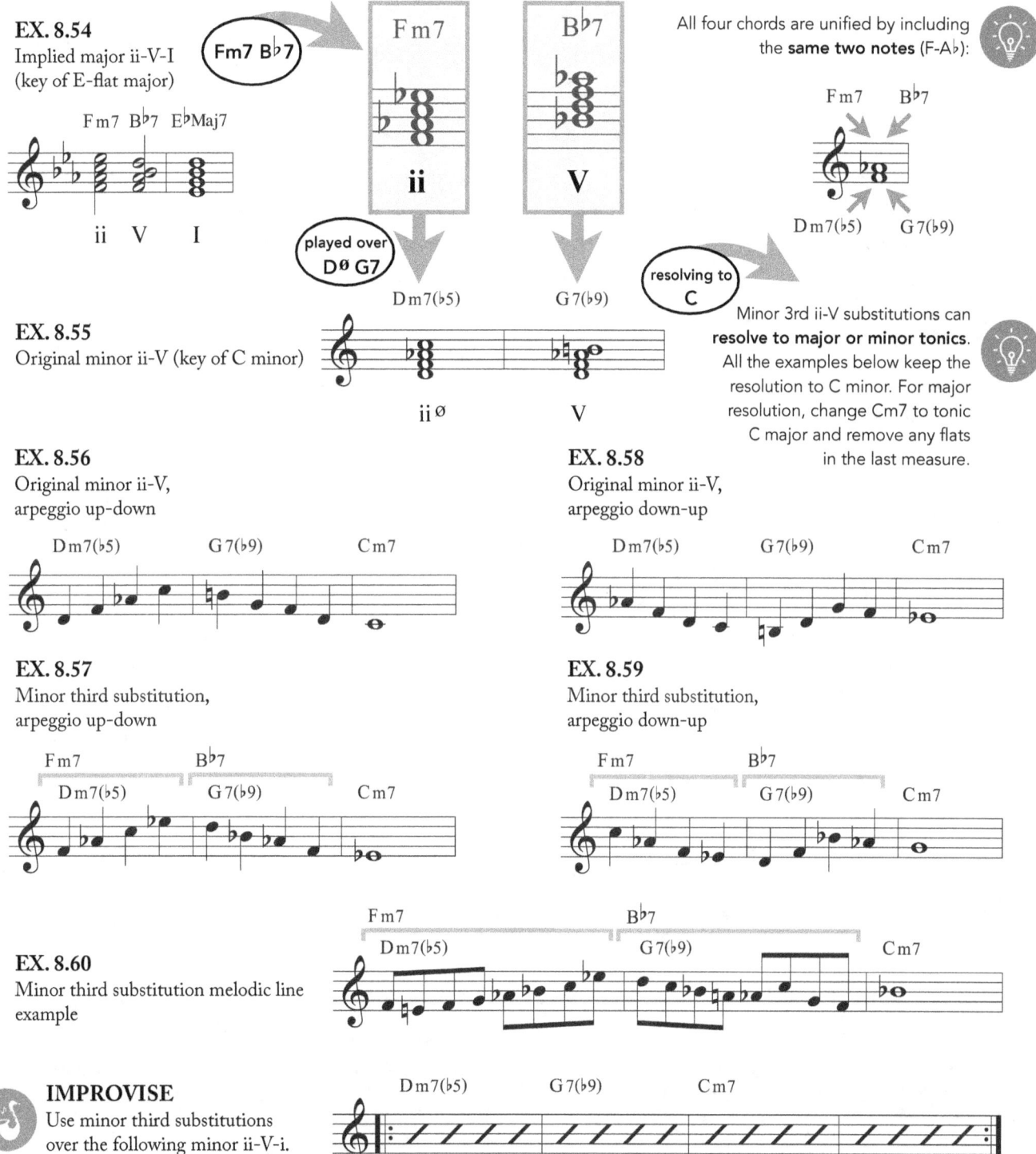

EX. 8.54
Implied major ii-V-I
(key of E-flat major)

All four chords are unified by including the **same two notes** (F-A♭):

EX. 8.55
Original minor ii-V (key of C minor)

Minor 3rd ii-V substitutions can **resolve to major or minor tonics**. All the examples below keep the resolution to C minor. For major resolution, change Cm7 to tonic C major and remove any flats in the last measure.

EX. 8.56
Original minor ii-V,
arpeggio up-down

EX. 8.58
Original minor ii-V,
arpeggio down-up

EX. 8.57
Minor third substitution,
arpeggio up-down

EX. 8.59
Minor third substitution,
arpeggio down-up

EX. 8.60
Minor third substitution melodic line
example

IMPROVISE
Use minor third substitutions
over the following minor ii-V-i.

Altered Dominant Chord Extensions

— page 1 of 2 —

A favorite sound among jazz musicians is the *altered dominant*, wherein various chromatic extensions are added to the typical dominant V_7 chord to give it an altered sound. Below are two approaches to understanding the altered V_7 chord within any ii-V-I (minor or major) as well as some unspoken rules and guidelines followed by examples of the altered dominant in musical context.

EX. 8.61
Various V_7 altered chords
(key of C major or C minor)

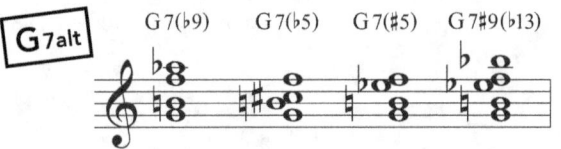

Altered dominants can be labeled simply as **"alt"** or with chord symbols that include specific extensions. These chord symbols all suggest *altered*.

Direct alteration approach
(accidentals relate to dominant V_7 chord)

By numbering the chord tones directly, with chord tone 1 being the root of the dominant V_7, each note relates immediately to the original V_7 Mixolydian mode. This is the most thorough and exact way of understanding altered dominants, making space for every possible chromatic variation, including the flat-9, sharp-11 (or flat-5), sharp-5, etc.

EX. 8.62
G Mixolydian scale

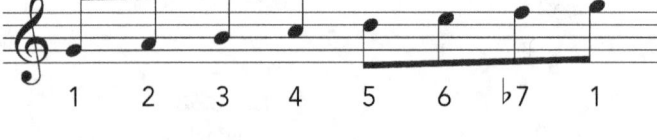

Notice that A and E, the **9th and 13th**, are missing from this group of extensions. This is because, while they might be included in other dominant chords, they are not commonly part of altered dominant harmony.

EX. 8.63
Dominant G7 chord and common altered chord tone extensions

Parallel minor approach
(accidentals relate to parent minor i scale)

Every parent major key has a parallel minor key. The parallel minor scale includes tones — specifically the flat-3, flat-6, and flat-7 — that may be used as altered notes on a dominant V_7 chord, where they are labeled as flat-9, sharp-9, and flat-13. In the example below, the G7 altered sound may be used in either a major or minor key, resolving back to either C major or C minor.

EX. 8.64
C natural minor scale
(parallel minor of C major)

EX. 8.65
C natural minor scale notes typically used in a G altered chord

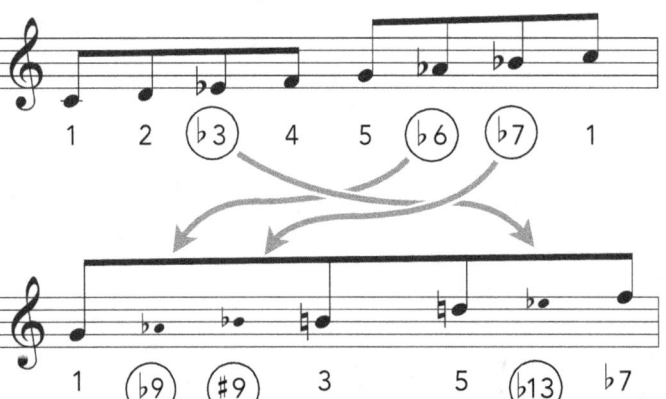

The parallel minor approach is easy and very clear. Although it includes three important altered notes, notice that the **flat-5 (or sharp-11) is missing**, rendering it less detailed than the direct alteration approach above.

Altered Dominant Chord Extensions
page 2 of 2

The language of jazz harmony is passed down from generation to generation, its many details and nuances learned through practical application and experience. Below are some guidelines to consider when using dominant chord extensions. Consider these to be unspoken rules in jazz, each commonly followed by musicians steeped in this idiom. Break these rules at your own risk!

- extensions may be played in any octave

- a plain V₇ often can be treated as a V7alt

- if flat-9, then no natural 9

- "9" is rarely called "2"

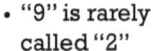

- never call them "10" and "12," always chord tones "3" and "5"

- sharp-11 is rarely called "sharp-4" and flat-5 is interchangeable with sharp-11

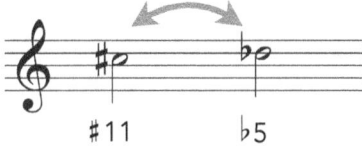

- if sharp-9, then also flat-9

- if "alt" include flat-13 (or sharp-5), not natural-5 or natural-13

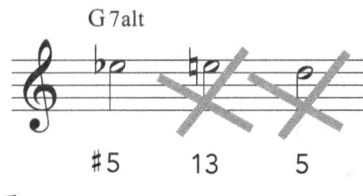

- natural-11 is not added alongside other altered extensions (but 11 can be used melodically)

Altered dominant extensions provide ample color and contrast to chord progressions and melodic lines. In the ii-V-I examples below, notice that the ii introduces a 9th as a chord extension, which helps prepare the progression for altered notes on the V chord.

EX. 8.66
ii-V-I with common chord extensions added

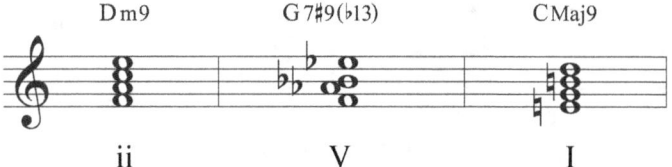

Not every note of the altered G7 chord is used in these examples. Use **artistic judgment** when deciding which notes to include.

EX. 8.67
Bebop line, including flat-9 and sharp-9

Modes of Melodic Minor

The *melodic minor scale* produces *seven modes*, each based on a different scale degree from 1-7. They are used often in jazz improvisation in part because of the distinct chromatic alterations within each mode.

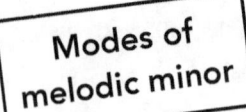

Each of the C melodic minor scale's seven notes marks the start of one of seven modes — *C melodic minor, D Dorian flat-2, E-flat Lydian augmented, F Lydian dominant, G Mixolydian flat-6, A Locrian sharp-2*, and *B Super Locrian*.

EX. 8.68
Modes of the C melodic minor scale

The simplest way to remember the melodic minor scale is to think **"major scale with a flatted 3rd."**

i   Melodic minor
Cm(maj7)

ii   Dorian flat-2
Dm7(b9)

♭III⁺ Lydian augmented
E♭Maj7(#5)

IV Lydian dominant
F 7(#11)

V   Mixolydian flat-6
G 9(♭13)

vi° Locrian sharp-2
("half-diminished" scale)
Am7(♭5)

VII⁺ Super Locrian
("diminished whole tone" or "altered" scale)
B 7alt

Diatonic chords

The seven melodic minor modes each pair with a specific chord. The notes below indicate the 1, 3, 5, and 7 of each chord; many of the chord symbols below describe extensions beyond the 7th.

EX. 8.69
Diatonic 7th chords of the C melodic minor scale

Cm(maj7)	Dm7(b9)	E♭Maj7(#5)	F 7(#11)	G 9(♭13)	Am7(♭5)	B 7alt	Cm(maj7)
i	ii	♭III+	IV	V	vi°	VII+	i

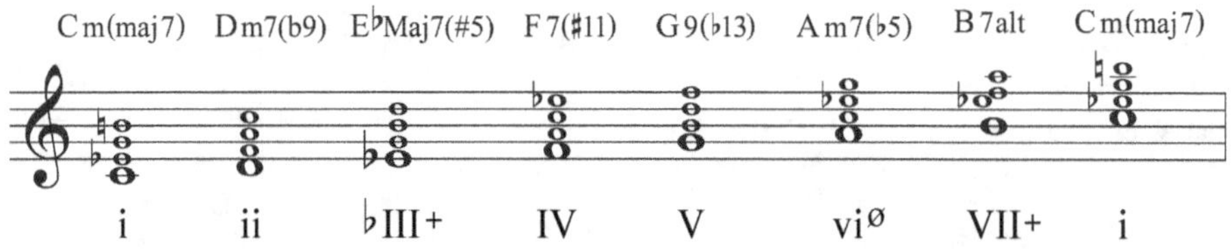

Investigate | Two Views: Altered Dominant Scale

An altered dominant chord — called many names, including G7alt, G7(♭9), G7(♭5), G7(♯5), and G7♯9(♭13) — is created when select dominant V chord extensions are altered and made sharp or flat. In the key of C, a G7, when altered, might include a flat-9 or sharp-9 (or both). The *altered dominant scale*, or simply the *altered scale*, includes many notes that are found in most altered chords, including the flat-9, sharp-9, flat-5, and flat-13. The *Lydian augmented scale* also uses the same set of notes. These scales may create chromatic tension over any dominant V7, whether it is written as altered or not.

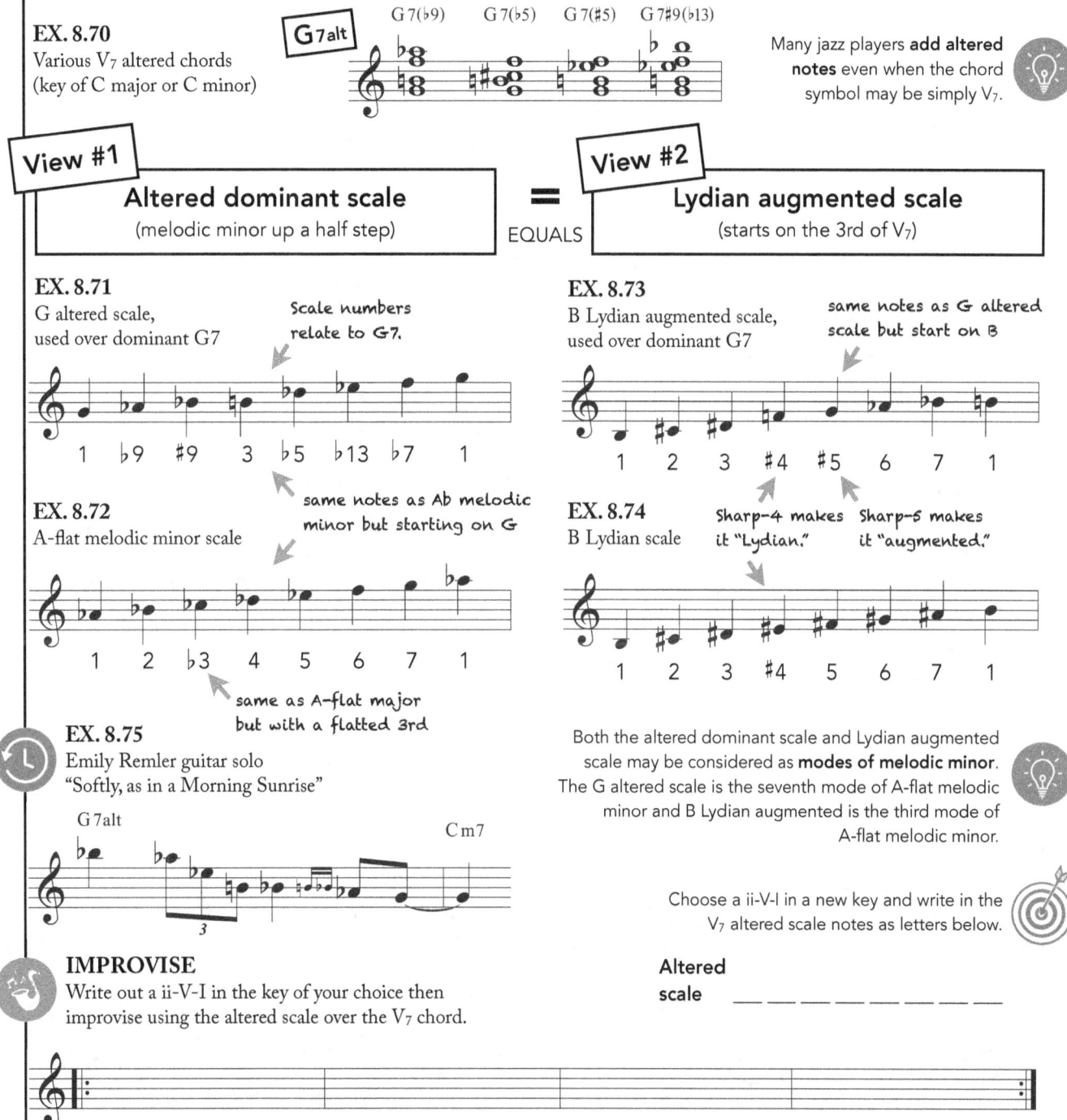

EX. 8.70
Various V7 altered chords
(key of C major or C minor)

G7alt   G7(♭9)   G7(♭5)   G7(♯5)   G7♯9(♭13)

Many jazz players **add altered notes** even when the chord symbol may be simply V7.

View #1

Altered dominant scale
(melodic minor up a half step)

EQUALS

View #2

Lydian augmented scale
(starts on the 3rd of V7)

EX. 8.71
G altered scale,
used over dominant G7

Scale numbers relate to G7.

1   ♭9   ♯9   3   ♭5   ♭13   ♭7   1

same notes as Ab melodic minor but starting on G

EX. 8.72
A-flat melodic minor scale

1   2   ♭3   4   5   6   7   1

same as A-flat major but with a flatted 3rd

EX. 8.73
B Lydian augmented scale,
used over dominant G7

same notes as G altered scale but start on B

1   2   3   ♯4   ♯5   6   7   1

EX. 8.74
B Lydian scale

Sharp-4 makes it "Lydian."   Sharp-5 makes it "augmented."

1   2   3   ♯4   5   6   7   1

EX. 8.75
Emily Remler guitar solo
"Softly, as in a Morning Sunrise"

G7alt   Cm7

Both the altered dominant scale and Lydian augmented scale may be considered as **modes of melodic minor**. The G altered scale is the seventh mode of A-flat melodic minor and B Lydian augmented is the third mode of A-flat melodic minor.

Choose a ii-V-I in a new key and write in the V7 altered scale notes as letters below.

Altered
scale ____ ____ ____ ____ ____ ____ ____

IMPROVISE
Write out a ii-V-I in the key of your choice then improvise using the altered scale over the V7 chord.

Masterclass

Hidden Changes

— page 1 of 2 —

A given chord often can imply additional harmony that may be thought of as *hidden changes*. Many of these *implied harmonies* are simple to identify (in the example below, see the E minor triad hiding inside a CMaj7 chord). Some are a bit harder to find, particularly when hidden within various chord extensions — such as the Fm7(♭5) buried inside the G7♭9(♯11) below.

EX. 8.76
Implied harmony in I, ii, and V chords (key of C major)

As more extensions are added to a chord, the **more hidden changes** result. A CMaj7 chord implies only one hidden chord — E minor — but CMaj13(♯11) implies at least five additional chords.

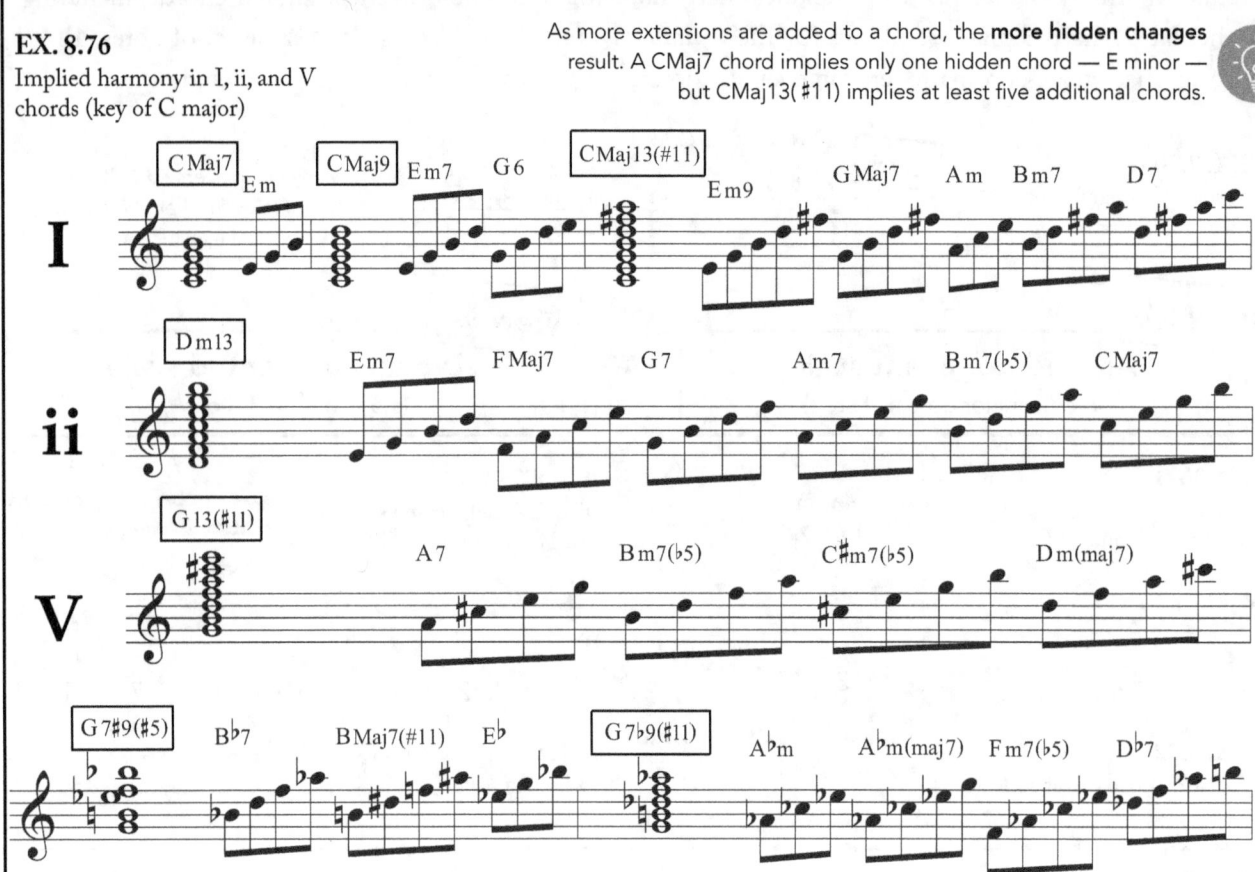

Miles Davis' iconic "So What" solo below suggests added harmonic movement by emphasizing C major, which is already hiding inside the given Dm13 chord, before resolving to a melody based on a D minor triad and D blues scale.

Miles Davis' hidden changes

EX. 8.77
Miles Davis trumpet solo "So What"

Transpose Miles' solo example to two new keys. For each, start by reviewing the key's Dorian minor scale and blues scale.

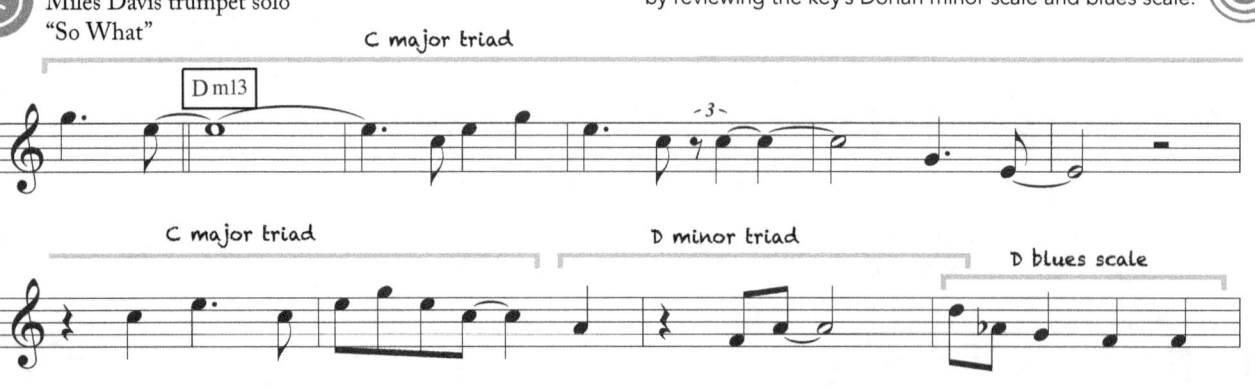

Masterclass

Hidden Changes
page 2 of 2

The use of implied harmony may lead to creative and unpredictable melodic routes. The examples below assume that, even when a dominant 7th chord is written in its simplest form (G7), the melody may imply hidden chord changes within an altered dominant form (G7alt). For example, although the written V₇ chord may read G7, the melody can imply A♭m6, incorporating the ♭9 and ♯5 in a G7♭9(♯5).

EX. 8.78
Implied harmony
over ii-V-I (key of C)

Just as the V chord can incorporate altered notes, notice how **the tonic I chord can imply CMaj13(♯11)** and the upper structure harmonies Am7 and D major.

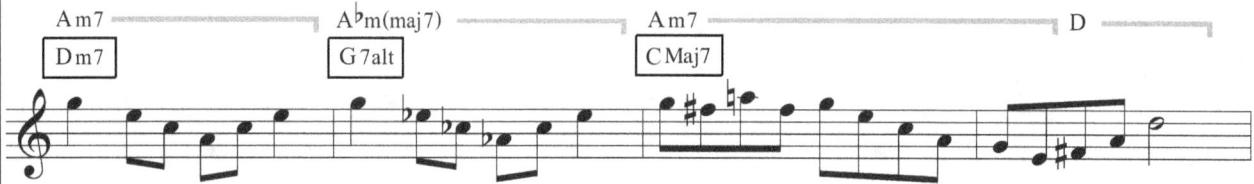

EX. 8.79
Implied harmony over
ii-V-I-VI (key of C)

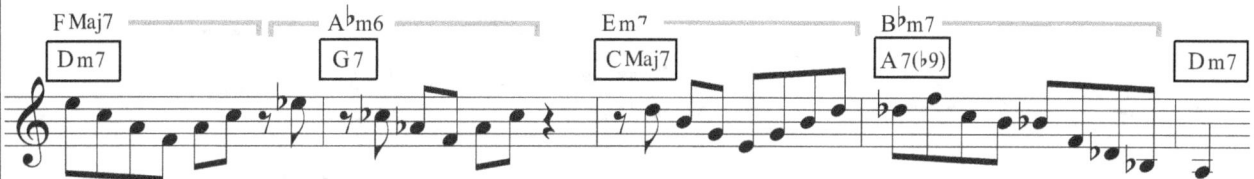

Chord substitution is similar to chord superimposition.

Substitution can involve replacing the underlying chord entirely.

In composition, chord substitution is often referred to as *reharmonization* or *reharm.*

Superimposition is melodic and is placed only over the original set of chords.

Chord substitution vs. superimposition

EX. 8.80
ii-V-I chord substitutions

EX. 8.81
Extreme chord superimposition (quite dissonant)

Hidden changes are chord substitutions but not all chord substitutions are hidden changes. Although chord substitution may imply harmonies not at all related to the underlying harmony, **a hidden change always is always embedded in the original chord.**

Song Study

"Blue Bossa"

Kenny Dorham's "Blue Bossa" follows a 16-bar form, broken into four distinct 4-bar phrases. The first and second phrases (bars 1-8) use notes from a single parent natural minor scale and slightly resemble an A-section. The third phrase (bars 9-12) changes to a major key up a half step from the parent minor key, introducing a new ii-V-I progression and a melody based on the new parent major scale as a B-section of sorts. The fourth phrase (bars 13-16) returns to minor, an A-section recap.

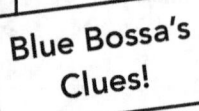

Each of the musical examples below present clues that help construct the melody of "Blue Bossa" in its original key of C minor. Use these clues to write out the head to "Blue Bossa" below. Chord changes and some rhythms are already provided.

EX. 8.82
"Blue Bossa" template
(Kenny Dorham)

Keep on trying! Stick to it! Learning a tune by ear can be a great challenge, but it pays big dividends. It's worth it!

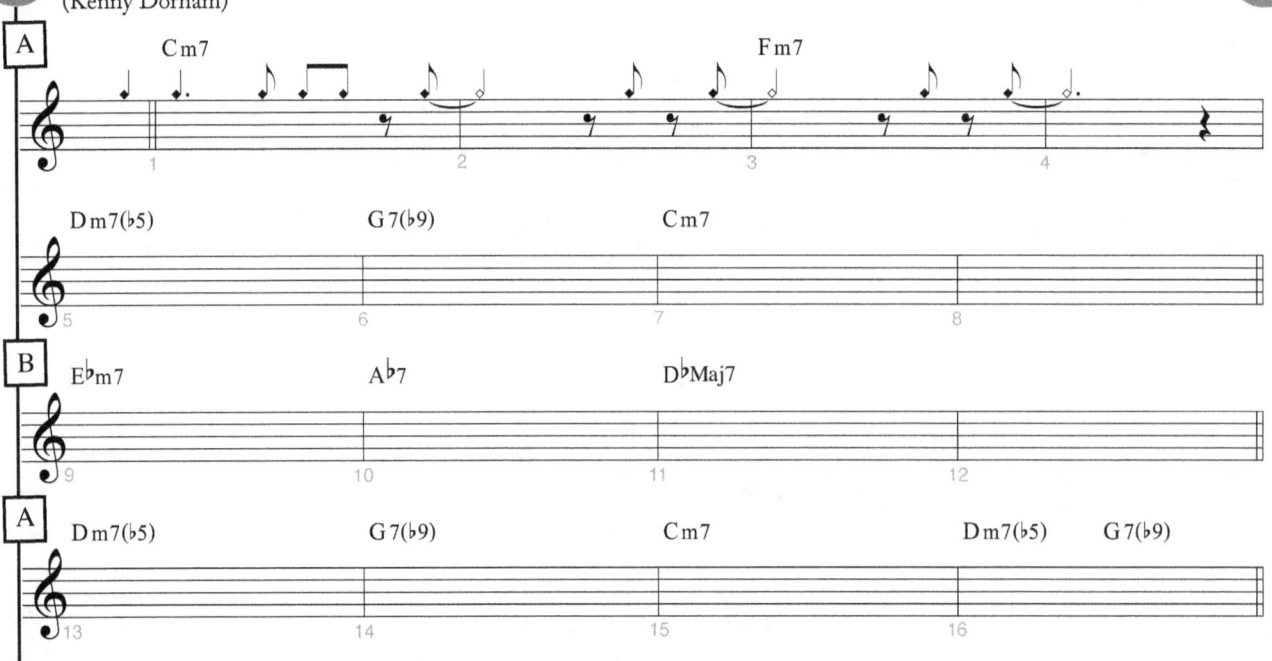

Song Study   "Blue Bossa"
page 2 of 3

Fundamental scale and chord arpeggio exercises help with internalizing melodic and harmonic possibilities on "Blue Bossa." Practice the following examples, then develop more practice material using scales and arpeggios. Consider range, direction, inversions, displacements, voice-leading approaches, common tones, and more.

The A-section of "Blue Bossa" uses the following four chords. **Adapt these and other arpeggio variations** over the entirety of its 8-bar A-section.

EX. 8.83
"Blue Bossa" chords (A-section)

EX. 8.84
"Blue Bossa" chords (B-section)

EX. 8.85
"Blue Bossa"
scale fragments *étude*

Notice in bar 8 below that the ♭3̂-4̂-5̂ scale fragment in C minor happens also to imply 1̂-2̂-3̂ in E-flat major. This connects smoothly to the "Blue Bossa" bridge since the B-section in bar 9 begins simply with a **parallel shift to an E-flat minor chord**.

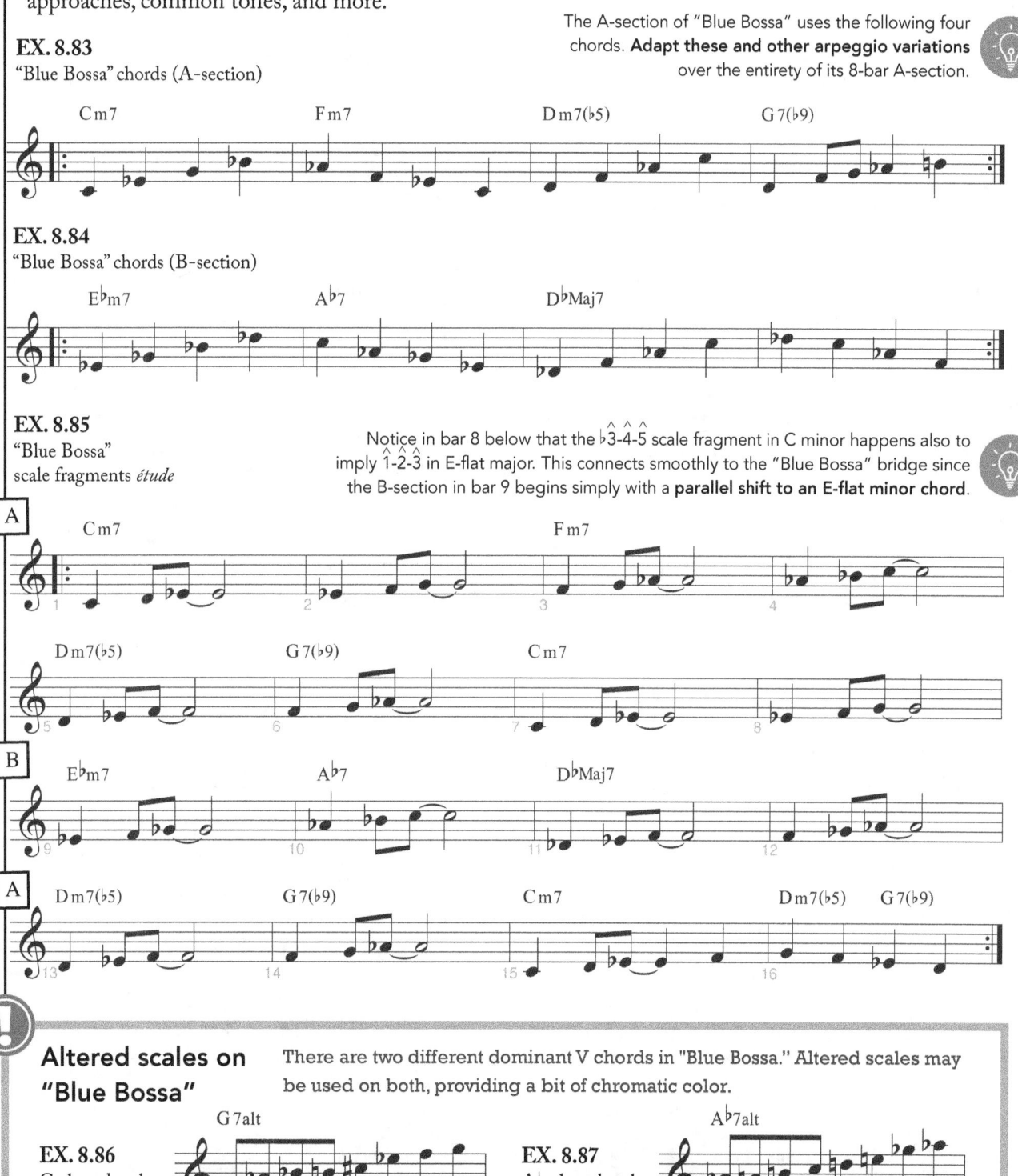

Altered scales on "Blue Bossa"

There are two different dominant V chords in "Blue Bossa." Altered scales may be used on both, providing a bit of chromatic color.

EX. 8.86
G altered scale

EX. 8.87
A♭ altered scale

Song Study

"Blue Bossa"
page 3 of 3

The following "Blue Bossa" *étude* is built using scale fragments, many of which are shared between chords. Practice this slowly to gain fluency while also noting details, including target notes, fragment lengths, leading tones, pivots, and more.

EX. 8.88
"Blue Bossa"
scale fragments *étude*

Consider how each 3-note motif here might be **adapted and applied** during your improvised solo over "Blue Bossa" and other repertoire.

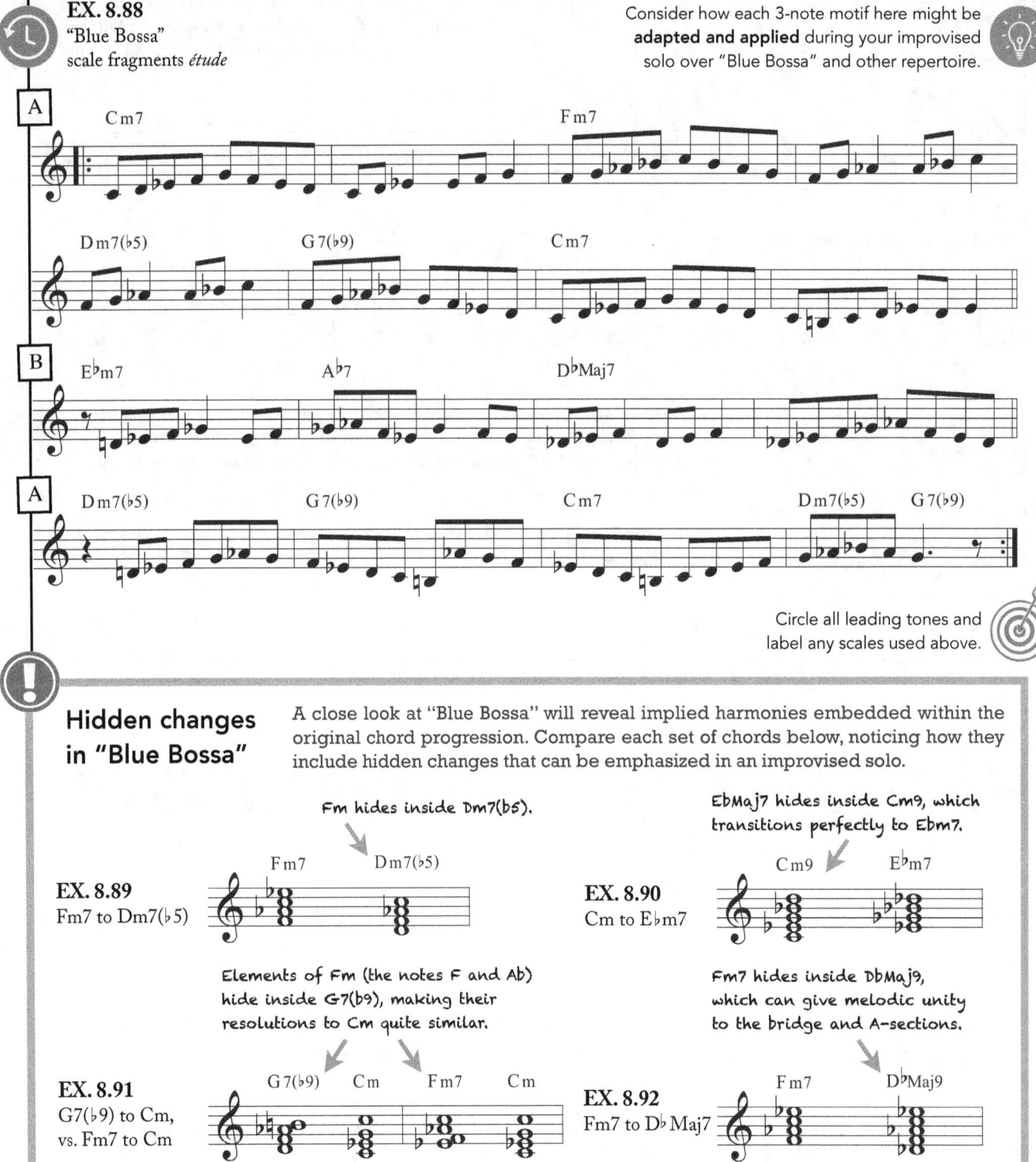

Circle all leading tones and label any scales used above.

Hidden changes in "Blue Bossa"

A close look at "Blue Bossa" will reveal implied harmonies embedded within the original chord progression. Compare each set of chords below, noticing how they include hidden changes that can be emphasized in an improvised solo.

Fm hides inside Dm7(b5).

EX. 8.89
Fm7 to Dm7(b5)

EbMaj7 hides inside Cm9, which transitions perfectly to Ebm7.

EX. 8.90
Cm to Ebm7

Elements of Fm (the notes F and Ab) hide inside G7(b9), making their resolutions to Cm quite similar.

EX. 8.91
G7(b9) to Cm, vs. Fm7 to Cm

Fm7 hides inside DbMaj9, which can give melodic unity to the bridge and A-sections.

EX. 8.92
Fm7 to Db Maj7

Improvise

"Blue Bossa"
page 1 of 2

Internalize every basic chord/scale relationship on "Blue Bossa" below. Notice the relationships among A-section chords and scales and how they differ from the new key and chords on the bridge. Presented below are the chord/scales in the original key of C minor, plus a transposition exercise, moving all the chord/scales to a new key of your choice.

EX. 8.93
"Blue Bossa" diatonic scales
(parent key of C minor)

Consider the B-section to "Blue Bossa" as a **major ii-V-I a half step higher** than the A-section key.

Transpose "Blue Bossa" to another key of your choice, writing down all the above scales in the new key below.

In your new key, also write out the altered dominant scale for the V chords on both the A- and B-sections.

Improvise

"Blue Bossa"
page 2 of 2

An improvisation over "Blue Bossa" can stay quite simple, based on small melodic and rhythmic motifs. Keeping to only two parent scales, sparse melodic content can unify the improvisation, helping the solo take on a memorable and lyrical quality. On the other hand, an abundance of melodic content may be used, including multiple scale types per chord, added harmonies introduced via borrowed chords and chord extensions, and extensive chromaticism. This decidedly more complex approach might help a solo build momentum and interest. Either approach requires careful work to understand how chords relate, which scales include commonalities, and which harmonies can be adapted to include elements of modal mixture and chromaticism.

IMPROVISE
After writing out "Blue Bossa," improvise multiple choruses over the song.

Transpose "Blue Bossa" to your key, writing it all out below. If you play a concert key instrument, then write it out in C minor.

Master, by ear, both the concert C blues scale and the concert D-flat major scale.

The simplest version of "Blue Bossa" (concert key):
Concert C blues scale over the entire A-section.
Concert D-flat major scale over the B-section.

Listen to the following versions of "Blue Bossa."

• Joe Henderson, *Page One*
• Dexter Gordon, *Biting the Apple*
• Pat Martino, *Cream*
• Bobby McFerrin & Chick Corea, *Play*

Write these scales out in your instrument's key.

Concert C blues scale ___ ___ ___ ___ ___ ___

Concert D♭ major scale ___ ___ ___ ___ ___ ___ ___ ___

Zen Jazz Master says:

Measuring Progress

How do you measure progress? Is it in terms of how good you sound? Is it in terms of how bad you sound?

If you are measuring yourself in terms of what you *cannot* play, your road to success will be harder.

Remember that, while good music must have good time, it is also true that, to make good music, you must also have a good time. Try to keep the practice experience positive by making note of your improvements.

These will be small improvements but they make up the building blocks that lead to real achievement.

Of course, continue to work on your weaknesses. Just try not to get too weighed down by them.

Chapter 8 Achievements

Congratulations!

You are one step closer to jazz nirvana.

Here is a partial list of what you've achieved:

- Identifying central differences between major and minor ii-V-i chord progressions
- Understanding which scale fragments are common between minor ii-V-i chords
- Being able to apply minor third substitutions on a minor ii-V-i progression
- Alternating between an understanding of pitches as they relate to the parent minor key and how the same pitches relate to each new chord (for example, flat-6 in the key of C minor is the same as flat-9 in a G7 harmony)
- Using modal mixture by applying minor scale fragments within major key chord progressions

Are you ready for the next chapter?

Answer these questions to determine whether you are prepared to continue to the next chapter:

- **Can you name**, in several keys, the flat-9 of a V chord in a minor ii-V-i?

  If "Yes," move to the next chapter.
  If "No," review this chapter.

- **Can you develop** a coherent solo on the A-section of "Softly, as in a Morning Sunrise," using the "piggy ear/tail" construction?

  If "Yes," move to the next chapter.
  If "No," continue to the next chapter but keep working on your fluency with melodic development.

- **Do you want** to learn more about bebop language and using chromatics in jazz?

  If "Yes," move to the next chapter.
  If "No,"… move to the next chapter anyway. You'll love checking out chromatics and you're on the home stretch here!

9 Next Level

Bebop and Chromatic Linear Improvisation

A goal and passion among musicians is to start with creative imagination, connect the ear and mind to the instrument, and ultimately bring a melodic line to life in performance. Although jazz masters make this sound easy, their fluency comes in part from an understanding and confidence in the deeper intersections of melody, harmony, rhythm, and form. Jazz can move far beyond melodies based on diatonic scales and chords. This chapter journeys into approaches to bebop and chromatic linear improvisation, addressing an influential and artistic language spoken by so many great jazz improvisers.

Contents

TOPICS
- Chromatic Enclosures
- Chromatic Target Note Exercises
- Why Chromatic Details Matter
- Bebop Scales
- Bebop and the Diminished Scale
- Tritone Substitutions
- Chromatic Linear Improvisation
- "Grapes on a Vine"
- Intervals as Motifs
- Chromatic Examples
- Extended Chromatics
- Whole Tone (or not!)

EAR TRAINING
- Learn "Autumn Leaves" melody by ear
- Learn "Take the 'A' Train" melody by ear

MASTERCLASS
- Super Scales

INVESTIGATE
- Whole Tone and Augmented Scales

SONG STUDY
- "Autumn Leaves" (Josef Kosma)
- "Take the 'A' Train" (Ellington/Strayhorn)

SOLO SPOTLIGHT
- Ray Nance trumpet solo "Take the 'A' Train"

COMPOSE
- Simple Bridge Melody on "Take the 'A' Train"

IMPROVISE
- Tritone Substitutions
- "Autumn Leaves" (Josef Kosma)
- "Grapes on a Vine" Concept
- Super Scales on "Take the 'A' Train" A-Section
- "Take the 'A' Train" (Billy Strayhorn)

SMACKDOWN!
- Linear vs. Vertical Improvisation

LISTENING GUIDE
- Pres' "Shoe Shine Boy" and Hawk's "Body and Soul"
- Ray Nance trumpet solo "Take the 'A' Train"

ZEN JAZZ MASTER SAYS
- Individuality (No one plays like you!)

HISTORICAL EXAMPLES
- Dizzy Gillespie trumpet solo "All the Things You Are"
- "Giant Steps" (John Coltrane)
- Don Byas tenor sax solo "I got rhythm"
- Bill Evans piano solo "Someday my prince will come"
- Valaida Snow trumpet solo "I can't give you anything but love"
- Lester Young tenor sax solo "Shoe Shine Boy"
- Coleman Hawkins tenor sax solo "Body and Soul"
- Sonny Stitt tenor sax solo "Avalon"
- Kenny Burrell guitar solo "On the Sunny Side of the Street"
- Vi Redd alto sax solo "All the Things You Are"
- George Coleman tenor sax solo "Autumn Leaves"
- Dexter Gordon tenor sax solo "It's you or no one"
- Stan Getz tenor sax solo "Billie's Bounce"
- Clifford Brown trumpet solo "Cherokee"
- Clora Bryant trumpet solo "Makin' Whoopee"
- John Coltrane tenor sax solo "Crescent"
- Ray Brown bass line "Take the 'A' Train"

Chromatic Enclosures

The examples below chart an evolution from diatonic voice-leading connecting guide tone lines (3rds and 7ths) to using *chromatic enclosures* to connect each chord. Both diatonic and chromatic enclosures start on an upper or lower neighbor to a target note, then skip to its opposite side, and finally resolve to the target itself. Chromatic enclosures can enhance a melody with a bit of chromatic color while still preserving the voice-leading inherent in a harmonic progression.

EX. 9.1
Arpeggios
over ii-V-I

Write in the scale degrees below as they relate to each chord. For example, over a G7, the note B is 3̂. Over a CMaj7, B is 7̂.

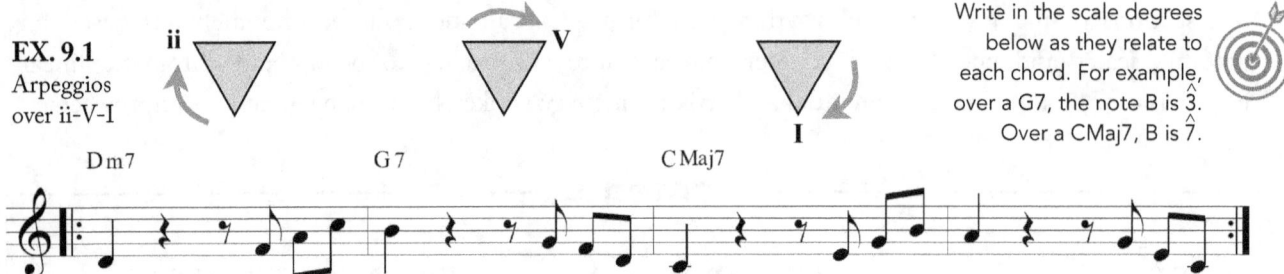

EX. 9.2
Replacing arpeggios with chromatic enclosures

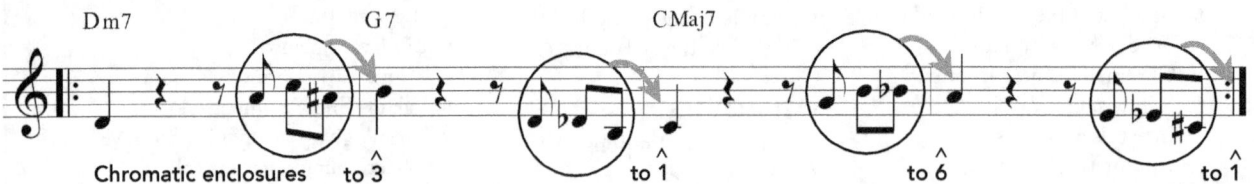

EX. 9.3
2-note chromatic enclosures (over ii-V)
+ sequence down to diatonic enclosure (over I)

While a diatonic enclosure uses only notes within a given key, a chromatic enclosure includes **at least one chromatic note**. Notice which specific chromatics (and how many) are used in each example below.

EX. 9.4
3-note chromatic enclosures,
sequencing down from ii-V to I

EX. 9.5
4-note chromatic enclosures,
sequencing up from ii-V to I

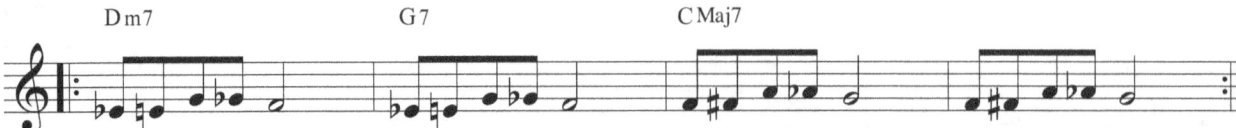

Chromatic Target Note Exercises

Learn how to use the exact number of chromatic notes between chord tones with the following chromatic target note exercises. Each example moves between two chord tones over a ii-V-I in C major but note that each set of chromatics can also be used over other chords.

EX. 9.6
Chromatics from F to A
(major 3rd interval used over Dm7)

Each chromatic target example below **functions over many chords**. For example, C to E can be played over FMaj7 or Dm9 or Am. G to B can also be played over CMaj7, Em, Dm13, or Am9.

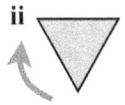

EX. 9.7
Chromatics from G to B
(major 3rd interval used over G7)

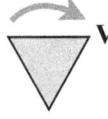

EX. 9.8
Chromatics from C to E
(major 3rd interval used over CMaj7)

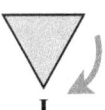

Transpose the ii-V-I chromatics above to three new keys, with the eventual goal of playing them in all 12 keys.

EX. 9.9
Chromatic target permutations

Why chromatic details matter

Consider a blues in C, with F7 as the IV chord. The following example moves from C7 to F7 before resolving back to C7. Switch the order of the last two notes to continue the line over F7 instead.

EX. 9.10
Blues line: I to IV to I

Bebop Scales
— page 1 of 2 —

Bebop scales are hybrids — typically major or minor scales or modes with one or more added chromatic note. Two common scales are the *major bebop scale* (simply the major scale with an added sharped 5th) and the *dominant bebop scale* (Mixolydian with an added raised 7th). The added chromatics help keep chord tones targeting downbeats throughout an eighth-note line.

Major bebop
Major scale with added ♯5 (up) or ♭6 (down)

EX. 9.11
C major bebop scale

Tonic I (C)
Major bebop scales are usually played over a I chord.

EX. 9.12
C major bebop scale, downbeats targeting C6 chord tones (I chord)

Dominant bebop
Mixolydian with added raised 7 OR major scale with added ♭7

EX. 9.13
G dominant bebop scale

Dominant V₇ (G₇)
Dominant bebop scales are usually played over a V₇ chord.

EX. 9.14
G dominant bebop scale, downbeats targeting G7 chord tones (V₇ chord)

Why bebop scales?

Major scales and modes successfully target chord tones for the first measure but, when extended into a second bar, a problem arises as non-chord tones become targets. Bebop scales solve this by adding an extra note, continually aligning chord tones as targets.

EX. 9.15
C major scale

PROBLEM!
non-chord tone targets

1 + 2 + 3 + 4 +   1 + 2 + 3 + 4 +

EX. 9.16
C major bebop scale

SOLUTION!
chord tone targets

1 + 2 + 3 + 4 +   1 + 2 + 3 + 4 +

Bebop Scales
page 2 of 2

Bebop scales can start on any chord tone and can include variations beyond standard dominant and tonic bebop scales. The following examples illustrate bebop scales from the 9th and 13th in addition to their application in conjunction with other melodic devices, including arpeggios and octave pivots, all within the context of ii-V-I chord progressions.

EX. 9.17
Tonic bebop scale, descending from the 3rd, with added chromatics

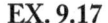

EX. 9.18
Tonic bebop scale, descending from the 9th, with added chromatics

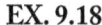

> **be·bop** /ˈbēˌbäp/ noun: **bebop**
>
> Bebop jazz differed from earlier diatonic jazz, based mostly on 7-note major and minor scales, through its use of extended harmonies and added chromaticism giving more opportunities to the jazz soloist. As bebop improvisation evolved in complexity, the genre's rhythmic pulse became more syncopated and double-time elements were introduced to break up any metronomic regularity.

EX. 9.19
Dominant bebop scale, descending from the 13th (used over both the ii and V)

Use the tonic bebop scale over the tonic I chord. **Use the dominant bebop scale over both the ii and V.** Notice in the examples below where arpeggios are added and how chord tones are targeted.

EX. 9.20
Bebop scale variations

Bebop and the Diminished Scale
— page 1 of 2 —

The *diminished scale* helps develop chromatic melody in any genre. Used heavily in bebop, the diminished scale, abbreviated below as *dim*, incorporates notes common to the $V_7(\flat 9)$, a chord that plays a crucial role in bebop language. There are only three diminished scales, each implying multiple harmonies.

EX. 9.21
D diminished scale (whole-half)

W h W h W h W h

The diminished scale is also known as an **octatonic scale** because it includes 8 notes instead of the usual 7 notes found in major scales and minor scales.

EX. 9.22
D fully dim 7th chord tones

EX. 9.23
G7($\flat$9) chord tones

dim 7th chord

1   3   5 $\flat$7 $\flat$9

EX. 9.24
G half-whole diminished scale
(same notes as D diminished scale above)

1   $\flat$9 $\sharp$9   3 $\flat$5 $\natural$5   6 $\flat$7

FOUR scales in ONE!
D dim, F dim, A$\flat$ dim, B dim
are really the same scale, each starting on a different chord tone of D dim

EX. 9.25
F diminished scale, using the same notes as D dim

Play the D dim scale starting on a different chord tone each time.

FOUR keys in ONE!
embedded in D dim are 4 dominant V_7 chords relating to 4 parent keys

G7 → C   B$\flat$7 → E$\flat$
D$\flat$7 → G$\flat$7   E7 → A

EX. 9.26
Implying leading tones for each minor harmony

Fm   Dm   Bm   A$\flat$ m

EX. 9.28
Embedded V_7 chords

E7   D$\flat$7   B$\flat$7   G7

EX. 9.27
Implying minor scale fragments and leading tones

Dm   Fm   Bm   A$\flat$ m

EX. 9.29
"Coltrane" diminished lick

E7($\flat$5)   D$\flat$7($\flat$5)   B$\flat$7($\flat$5)   G7($\flat$5)

Write out the remaining two diminished scales and then identify the four parent keys related to each diminished scale.

C$\sharp$ diminished scale

C$\sharp$ dim relates to the following 4 parent keys: ___ ___ ___ ___

C diminished scale

C dim relates to the following 4 parent keys: ___ ___ ___ ___

Bebop and the Diminished Scale
page 2 of 2

Diminished scales add to a melodic palette on dominant V_7 chords that already includes Mixolydian, tonic harmonic minor, and altered dominant scales. Diminished scales and dominant chords relate to each other quite differently than these other scale types. The diminished scale may be viewed in three ways: (1) as a *half-whole diminished*, wherein the scale begins with a half step, (2) as a *whole-half diminished*, wherein the scale begins with a whole step, or (3) as combined minor scale fragments. When played over a G7 as a V_7 chord, the half-whole diminished may start on G and the whole-half diminished may start on D.

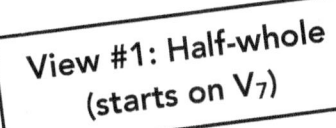

EX. 9.30
G half-whole diminished scale

All 4 notes from G7 are embedded in the scale.

EX. 9.31
D whole-half diminished scale

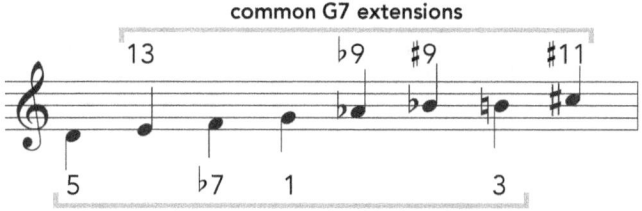

All 4 notes from G7 are embedded in the scale.

View #3: Combined minor scale fragments

EX. 9.32
D Dorian minor vs. D whole-half diminished scale

Dm and Am lower scale fragments form the D Dorian minor scale.

Dm lower fragment

Am lower fragment

A♭m lower fragment

Dropping the top Am fragment to A♭m results in D whole-half diminished.

EX. 9.33
Diminished scale melodic line resolving to tonic I major

EX. 9.34
Diminished scale melodic line resolving to tonic i minor

Want to resolve to C major? Change the final pitch to E.

The diminished scale — always alternating whole steps and half steps — is a **symmetrical scale**. It may be split in two at any point and will maintain its perfect symmetry:

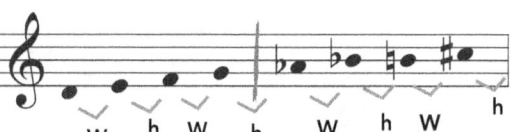

Tritone Substitutions

> "The flatted fifth. When I ran across that in the music, it really hit — boom!
> I played that thing over and again. It adds a hue to your solos."[9] — **Dizzy Gillespie**

Tritone substitutions, also called *tritone subs*, are ubiquitous in jazz because they bring chromatic color, adding altered notes, including the flat-5 and flat-9, to select harmonies. The most common tritone sub replaces the V_7 chord with another dominant 7th chord a flatted 5th — a tritone — away. In the key of C major, the G7 would be replaced with D♭7. Notice how the 3rd and 7th of each chord hold to the same pitch so that the guide tone line over the original ii-V-I can remain intact.

EX. 9.35
G7 and D♭7 are tritone subs, a tritone interval apart from each other

The tritone interval is also known as a diminished 5th (or augmented 4th). It was also known as the **"Devil's interval,"** thought to possess a sinister sound.

EX. 9.36
Original V chord (key of C)

EX. 9.37
Tritone sub of V

EX. 9.38
Original ii-V

EX. 9.39
Tritone sub of ii-V

EX. 9.40
Original ii, tritone sub of V, original I

EX. 9.41
9th extensions, tritone of V

EX. 9.42
Dizzy Gillespie trumpet solo "All the Things You Are"

IMPROVISE
Use the following tritone sub lines as examples, and also improvise your own ideas.

Instead of playing every chord tone of a tritone substitution, **try using only select notes**.

Investigate | Whole Tone and Augmented Scales

Whole tone and augmented scales are *hexatonic* scales, which can often be used over dominant 7th chords. *Whole tone scale 1* uses six notes separated by whole step, including the note C. The only other whole tone scale, *whole tone scale 2*, uses the remaining six notes available. The whole tone scale may also be constructed by pairing two augmented chords separated by whole step. Also used in jazz are four distinct *augmented scales*, formed by pairing two augmented triads separated by half step.

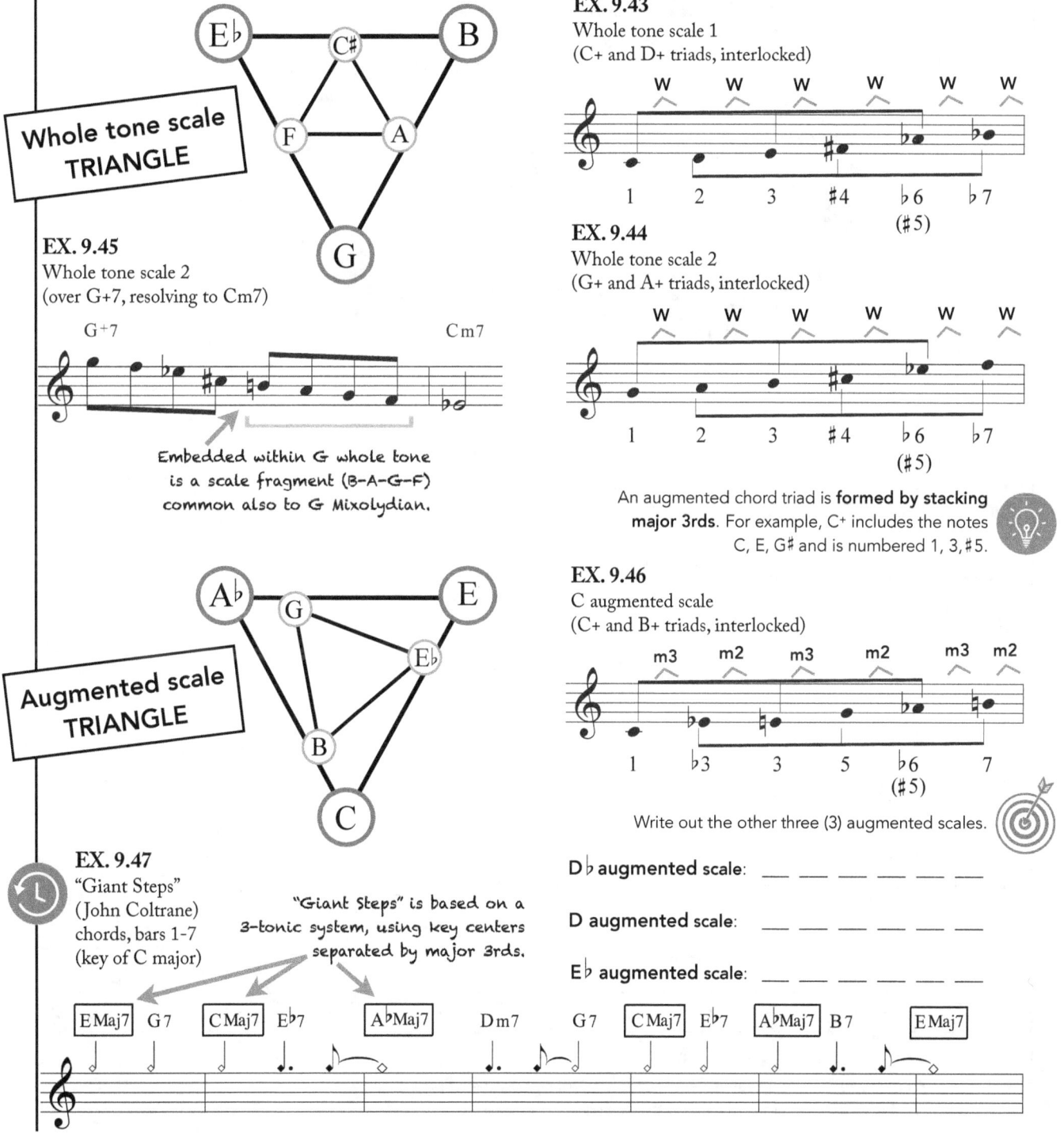

Whole tone scale
TRIANGLE

EX. 9.45
Whole tone scale 2
(over G+7, resolving to Cm7)

Embedded within G whole tone is a scale fragment (B-A-G-F) common also to G Mixolydian.

Augmented scale
TRIANGLE

EX. 9.43
Whole tone scale 1
(C+ and D+ triads, interlocked)

EX. 9.44
Whole tone scale 2
(G+ and A+ triads, interlocked)

An augmented chord triad is **formed by stacking major 3rds.** For example, C+ includes the notes C, E, G♯ and is numbered 1, 3, ♯5.

EX. 9.46
C augmented scale
(C+ and B+ triads, interlocked)

Write out the other three (3) augmented scales.

D♭ augmented scale: __ __ __ __ __ __

D augmented scale: __ __ __ __ __ __

E♭ augmented scale: __ __ __ __ __ __

EX. 9.47
"Giant Steps"
(John Coltrane)
chords, bars 1-7
(key of C major)

"Giant Steps" is based on a 3-tonic system, using key centers separated by major 3rds.

Song Study   "Autumn Leaves"
─────────────── page 1 of 2 ───────────────

"Autumn Leaves" charts a pathway that moves between relative major and minor keys, offering the performer a gorgeous template for crafting something simple or complex. Much like a great work of literature, "Autumn Leaves" may be explored by the improvising musician throughout an entire lifetime. The template is sure to remain the same but the improvisations will continue to change and develop.

EX. 9.48
ii-V-I pathway, major to minor (over bars 1-8 of "Autumn Leaves")

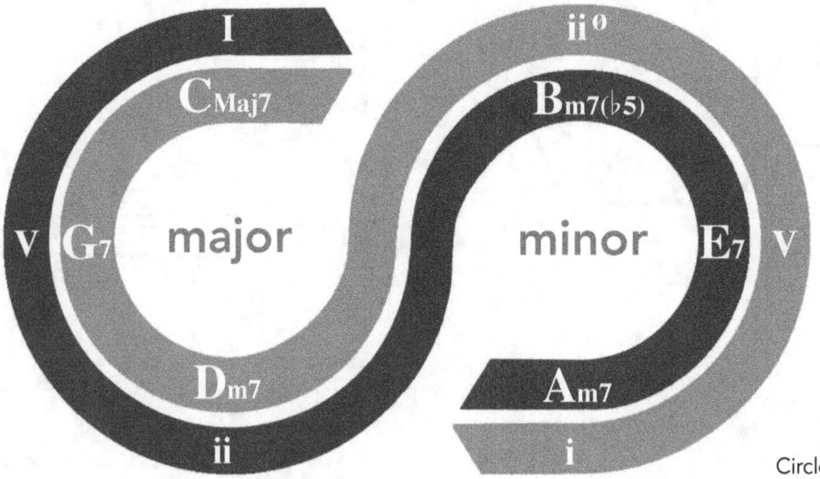

I
C Maj7
V G7   major
Dm7
ii

ii⁰
B m7(♭5)
minor   E7 V
A m7
i

EX. 9.49
Arpeggios from root position (moving from 7th to 3rd)

Circle the target notes throughout this page. Also number each chord tone.

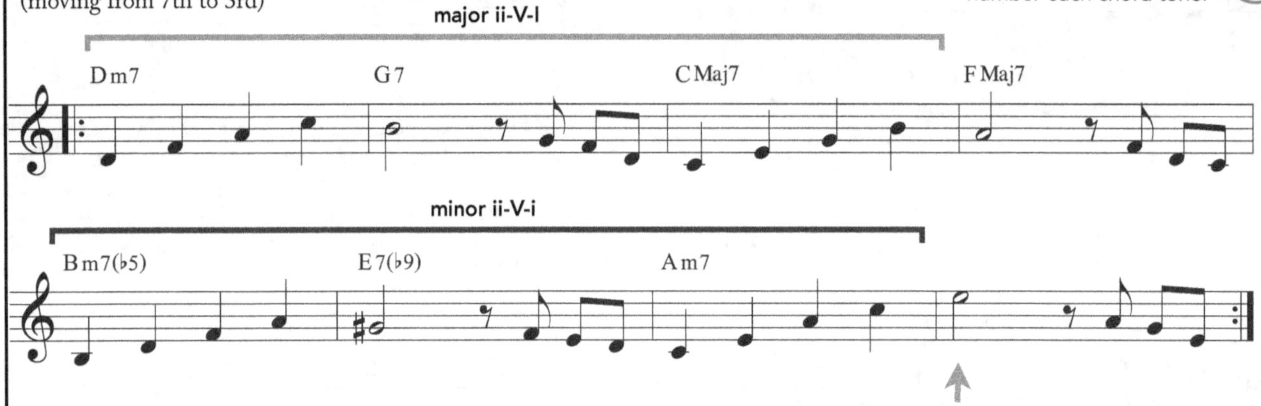

major ii-V-I

Dm7   G7   C Maj7   F Maj7

minor ii-V-i

B m7(♭5)   E 7(♭9)   A m7

An optional chord that is often added to "Autumn Leaves" is a V/ii chord, **A7(♭9)**, in bar 8, which transitions well to the ii chord, Dm7, at bar 1.

EX. 9.50
Descending melodic sequence (moving from the 7th to the 3rd)

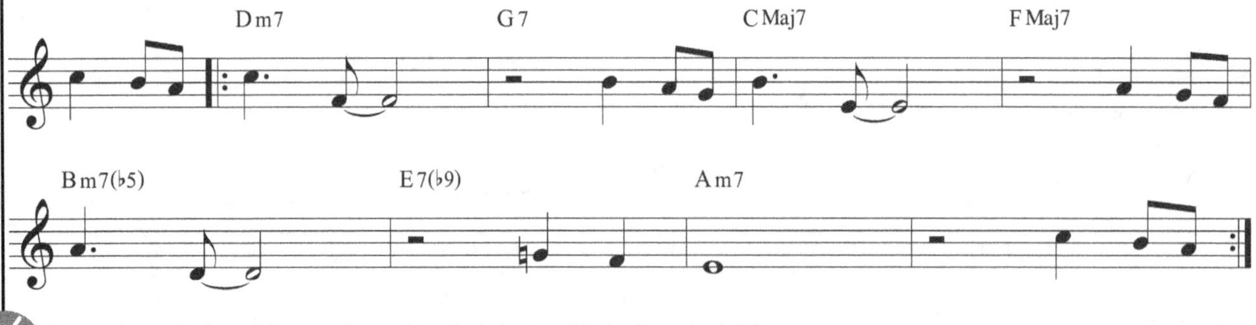

Dm7   G7   C Maj7   F Maj7

B m7(♭5)   E 7(♭9)   A m7

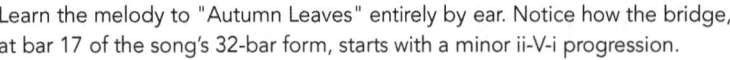
Learn the melody to "Autumn Leaves" entirely by ear. Notice how the bridge, at bar 17 of the song's 32-bar form, starts with a minor ii-V-i progression.

Song Study   "Autumn Leaves"
page 2 of 2

The exercises below include specific approaches to each harmony across "Autumn Leaves," including its major ii-V-I and minor ii-V-i progressions as well as the iii-VI-ii-V chord sequence within bars 27-29 of its 32-bar form. Take your time with these, noting particularly how notes transition to each chord.

EX. 9.51
Scales from the 3rd (circled),
across "Autumn Leaves" (bars 1-8)

When a secondary dominant, A7(♭9), is included on bar 8, **the scale type changes** (the bar 8 example below uses D harmonic minor).

EX. 9.52
Dominant bebop scale resolving
to tonic (bars 1-8)

The following phrase may be played over bars 1-4 and 5-8 of "Autumn Leaves" since the **same dominant bebop scale** can be applied to minor and major ii-V-I progressions.

EX. 9.53
iii-VI-ii-V arpeggio exercises
(bars 27-29)

EX. 9.54
Arpeggios and chromatic enclosures,
including tritone subs (over bars 27-29)

Play this entire page but introduce some rhythmic variations. For example, consider replacing some notes with rests.

"Autumn Leaves" bars 27-29 can also include **tritone substitutions**. Notice (1) which chords are tritone substitutions and (2) the resulting chromatic bass descent across all five chords.

Improvise

"Autumn Leaves"
page 1 of 2

In part because of its harmonic subtleties and inspired form, "Autumn Leaves" offers something for everyone. A beginner might scratch the surface of the composition and the greatest improviser continues to breathe life into "Autumn Leaves" by constantly reaching into the creative imagination. Before improvising, get to know your tools and options. Learn the form of the piece, listen to masters' performances, get to know the lyrics and harmonic rhythm, then dive in.

Improviser's toolkit
Which approach will you choose?

Regardless of level or experience, a musician can take inventory of their ever-expanding musical toolkit, choosing from a variety of approaches in an improvisation. Consider the following approaches as just four of many options that can be used while creating your own statement. These examples are presented over "Autumn Leaves" in the key of A minor.

The following phrases may be played over **both bars 1-4 and 5-8 of "Autumn Leaves"** so the chord progressions for each 4-bar phrase are written over each example.

Pentatonic or blues

EX. 9.55
A minor (or C major) blues scale

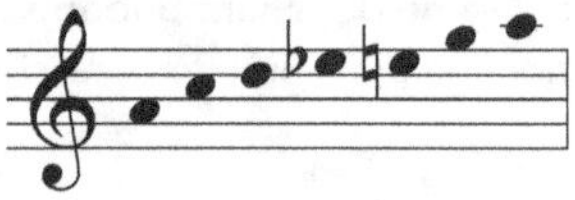

EX. 9.56
C major (or A minor) blues and pentatonic scales

Dm7   G7   C Maj7   F Maj7
Bm7(b5)   E 7(b9)   A m7   A 7(b9)

Rhythmic motif

EX. 9.57
1-bar rhythm as motif

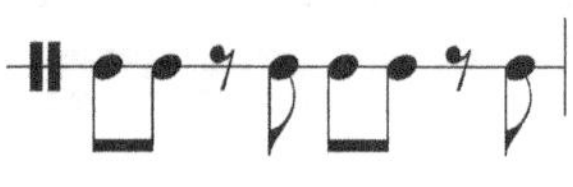

EX. 9.58
Melodic sequence using repeated rhythmic motif

Dm7   G7   C Maj7   F Maj7
Bm7(b5)   E 7(b9)   A m7   A 7(b9)

Parent scale

EX. 9.59
C major scale (or A natural minor) as parent scale

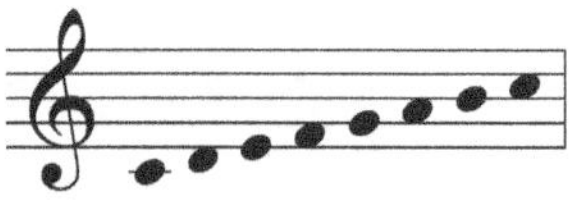

EX. 9.60
C major (or A natural minor) parent scale

Dm7   G7   C Maj7   F Maj7
Bm7(b5)   E 7(b9)   A m7   A 7(b9)

Bebop scales

EX. 9.61
G dominant bebop scale (adds 1 chromatic note to G Mixolydian)

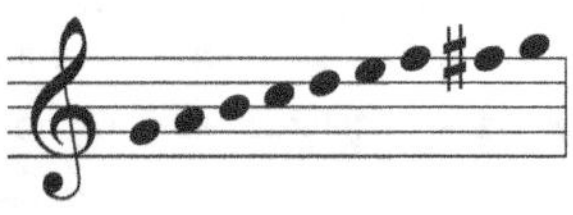

EX. 9.62
G dominant bebop scale and A harmonic minor scale

SPEED DRILL! See how fast you can play each example while keeping it accurate!

Dm7   G7   C Maj7   F Maj7
Bm7(b5)   E 7(b9)   A m7   A 7(b9)

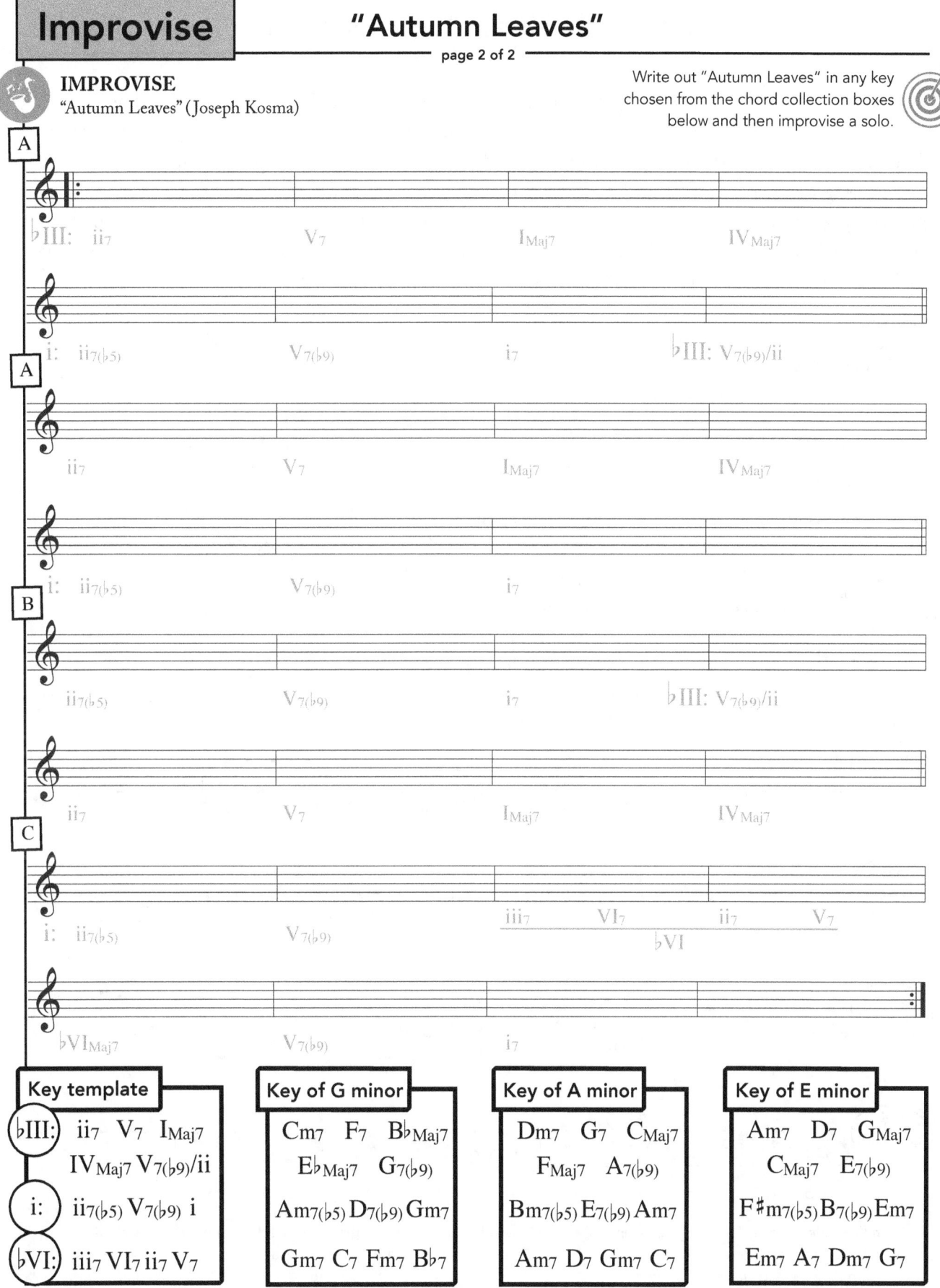

Improvise

"Autumn Leaves"
page 2 of 2

IMPROVISE
"Autumn Leaves" (Joseph Kosma)

Write out "Autumn Leaves" in any key chosen from the chord collection boxes below and then improvise a solo.

Chromatic Linear Improvisation
page 1 of 3

Chromatic linear improvisation keeps the focus on the melodic line rather than on the outline of each harmony in a chord progression. While chromatic linear improvisation can involve many approaches, "Grapes on a Vine" is one concept that helps introduce chromatics while keeping a line deeply melodic and relating to a parent key. Visualize a central melodic structure as a grapevine, with all other notes as grapes hanging from that central vine. In the illustration below, this structure (the "vine") is a C6 chord (pronounced "C major six"). All other notes (the "grapes") keep related to the C6, which remains the melodic focus even when the underlying harmony moves away from tonic C major.

EX. 9.63
"Grapes on a Vine"
based on a C6 chord

C6 chord (the "vine")

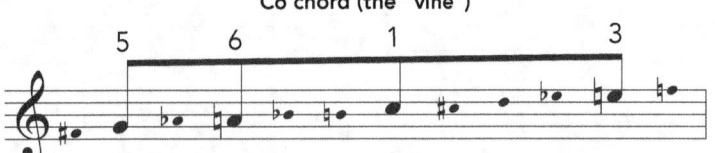

chromatic alterations and passing tones (the "grapes")

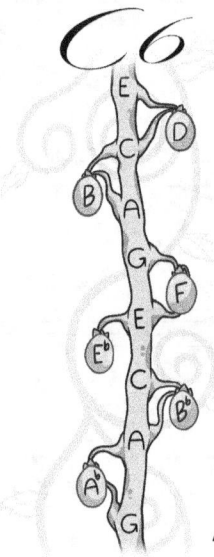

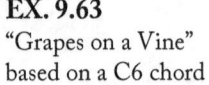

The C6 "vine" chord arpeggio above is presented in second inversion, starting from the 5th yet vines can involve any position, from root through 3rd inversion. Each position offers subtle melodic possibilities and differences.

"Grapes on a Vine"

Root position

1 3 5 6

EX. 9.64
C6 "vine" melody
(root position)

1st inversion

3 5 6 1

EX. 9.65
C6 "vine" melody
(1st inversion)

2nd inversion

5 6 1 3

EX. 9.66
C6 "vine" melody
(2nd inversion)

3rd inversion

6 1 3 5

EX. 9.67
C6 "vine" melody
(3rd inversion)

Write in the scale degrees for the "grapes" in the melodies above. Notice which "grapes" are diatonic and which are chromatic.

Keep in mind that **the improviser decides what to use as a "vine."** Parent chord vines are common because the key naturally suggests that all chromatics should return home to their parent key.

Chromatic Linear Improvisation
page 2 of 3

A "vine" across the chord progression

Melody matters! A melodic line based on a strong "vine" can sound good over multiple chords within the key. The melody below is based on a C6 "vine" and certainly sounds good when played over a C major tonic I chord yet the same melody also works over the ii chord and V chord even though it does not outline many of the chord tones in those harmonies.

EX. 9.68
C6 "vine" melody
(2nd inversion)

Case study
Don Byas
"I got rhythm"

Tenor saxophonist Don Byas' opening solo line on "I got rhythm" uses chromatics that relate to a central "vine" (a C6 chord), attributing logic and continuity to his melody. Instead of implying every underlying chord, the chromatics favor ornamentation of the tonic C major harmony.

EX. 9.69
Don Byas tenor sax solo
"I got rhythm"

EX. 9.70
Don Byas phrase analysis,
relating only to major C6

A "vine" can be any set of notes. While parent chords and scale fragments are common vines, the "vine" also could be a simple chord triad or even a combination of intervals.

Interval as motif

The interval as motif is another creative tool for chromatic linear improvisation. Pianist Bill Evans combines wider 4th, 5th, and 6th intervals with rising chromatic targets that stray from the chord progression, quite often landing on "wrong notes" that still sound right, in part because of the momentum and feeling of inevitability created by this melodic ascent.

EX. 9.71
Bill Evans piano solo
"Someday my prince
will come"

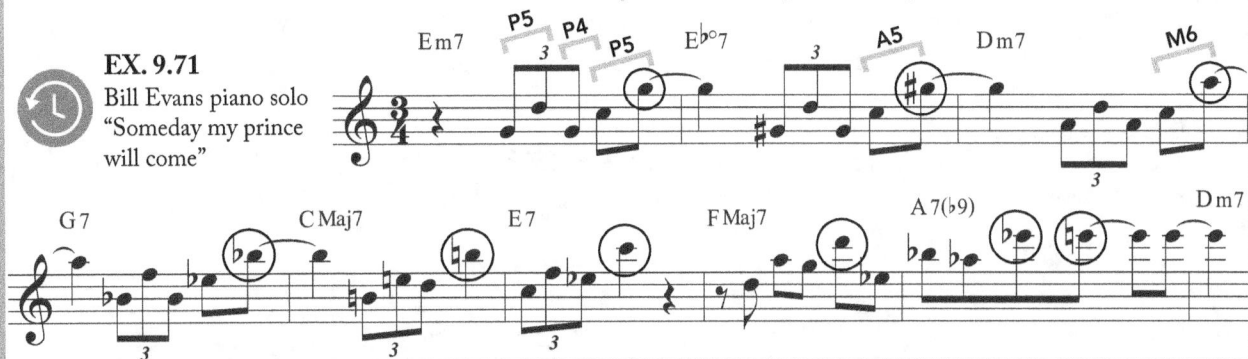

Chromatic Linear Improvisation
page 3 of 3

The chord progression below is common in many jazz standards, including "I can't give you anything but love" and "All of Me." Follow each step and begin developing an approach to moving from chord arpeggiation to creative chromatic linear improvisation, keeping the focus on a single key center.

Step 1 Know your chords (root position chord arpeggios).

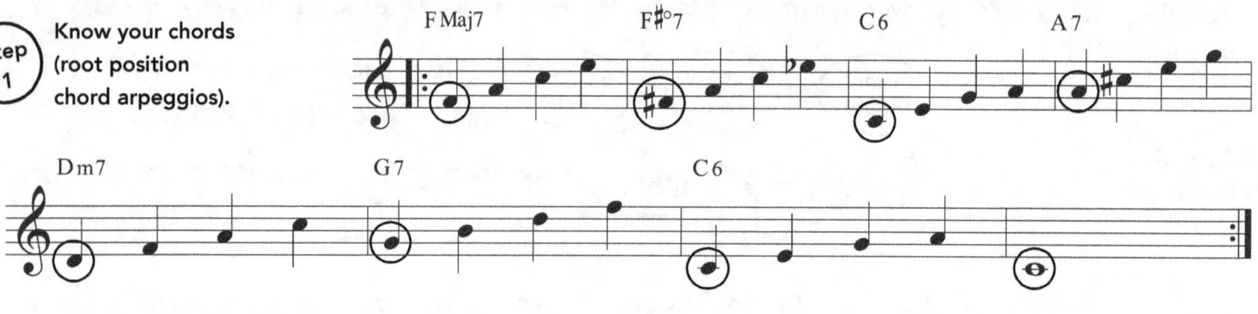

Step 2 Keep a focus on the parent key tonic (using chord inversions).

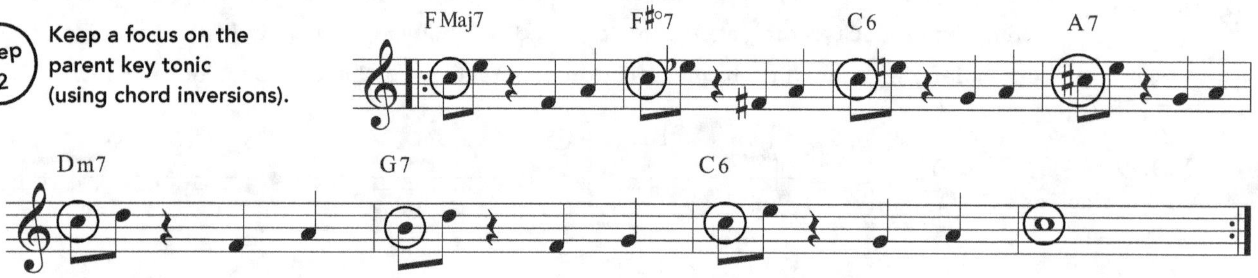

Step 3 Choose a "vine" (this example: C6 chord).

Step 4 Practice a solo that focuses on the chosen "vine."

Step 5 Over the 8-bar progression below, improvise using your "vine" and adding "grapes."

Case study
Valaida Snow
"I can't give you anything but love"

Trumpeter Valaida Snow navigates a classic chord progression that deviates regularly from its C major key center. Yet her melody remains firmly anchored in C major, its chromatics supportive of her diatonic major line. Notice within the first three chords the melody focuses on C tonic. When the line ascends, the melody still commits to the C major scale (in bar 4, B natural over the A7; in bar 5, a focus on C on the Dm7 chord). Even the melody's only chromatic target, the E-flat in bar 2, passes quickly, moving from D in bar 1 to E in bar 3.

EX. 9.72
Valaida Snow trumpet solo "I can't give you anything but love"

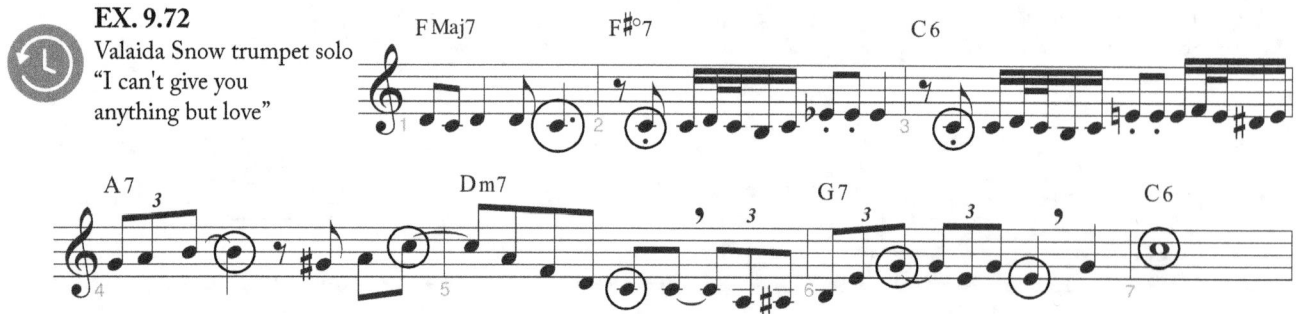

Smackdown! Linear vs. Vertical Improvisation

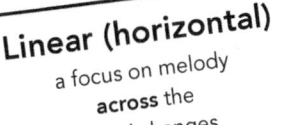

Linear (horizontal)
a focus on melody
across the
chord changes

Vertical
a focus on connecting
chord **arpeggios** within
the chord progression

Linear (or **horizontal**) **improvisation** keeps a focus on melody as it moves across the chord changes. **Vertical improvisation** keeps a focus on chord connection via arpeggios and is often more angular-sounding. Both approaches use scales and arpeggios (there are no exclusive rights to melodic devices!).

EX. 9.73
Linear melodic example

EX. 9.74
Vertical melodic example

EX. 9.75
Lester "Pres" Young
tenor sax solo
"Shoe Shine Boy"

Trace the circled chord tones of the I chord in Lester Young's "Shoe Shine Boy." Rather than outline the individual chords, Lester keeps a **linear/horizontal approach** and focuses throughout on melodic pitches belonging to the I chord.

EX. 9.76
Coleman "Hawk" Hawkins
tenor sax solo
"Body and Soul"

Coleman Hawkins changes to a new arpeggio on nearly every chord in "Body and Soul," yet he never simply runs through chord tones. Notice surprising chromatics that color underlying harmonies, providing intrigue and dissonance within Hawk's **vertical approach**.

Lester Young's "Shoe Shine Boy" and Coleman Hawkins' "Body and Soul" are seminal performances in jazz history that have inspired and influenced nearly all jazz musicians.

Chromatic Examples
page 1 of 2

The following solo examples include minimal chromatic usage. Each offers a model for using mostly diatonic pitches while also highlighting how even a single chromatic pitch can help color the melodic line. Notice Sonny Stitt's use of the flat-9, Kenny Burrell, Vi Redd, and George Coleman's use of a single chromatic, and Dexter Gordon's more extensive use of chromatic lower neighbors.

 As you listen to these masters, close your eyes to focus on learning the solo lines by ear.

Write out the scale degrees for each example then label the chromatics mentioned in the opening paragraph before learning these lines in multiple keys.

 EX. 9.77
Sonny Stitt tenor sax solo
"Avalon"

EX. 9.78
 Kenny Burrell guitar solo
"On the Sunny Side
of the Street"

 EX. 9.79
Vi Redd alto sax solo
"All the Things You Are"

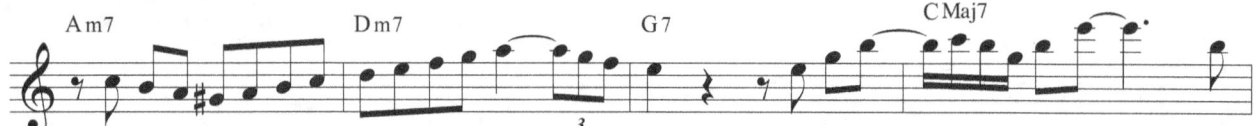

 EX. 9.80
George Coleman
tenor sax solo
"Autumn Leaves"

 EX. 9.81
Dexter Gordon tenor sax solo
"It's you or no one"

Dexter Gordon offers a quintessential example of **chromatic linear improvisation**. Rather than clearly outlining each harmony, his line sticks to a parent C major scale and includes chromatic lower neighbors throughout.

Chromatic Examples

— page 2 of 2 —

The following solo excerpts include more chromatics, typically chromatic neighbors or passing tones. Stan Getz crafts a pattern that targets chord tones 1 and 5 across multiple octaves while Sonny Stitt and Clifford Brown navigate chromatic lines that seem to glide over and across the chord changes yet Clora Bryant begins her melody by targeting chord tones and ends it by borrowing minor key chromatics.

EX. 9.82
Stan Getz
tenor sax solo
"Billie's Bounce"

EX. 9.83
Sonny Stitt
tenor sax solo
"Avalon"

Notice how Sonny Stitt **prolongs the guide tone line** (see circled notes) with an extended chromatic approach to each target note.

EX. 9.84
Clifford Brown trumpet solo
"Cherokee"

EX. 9.85
Clora Bryant
trumpet solo
"Makin' Whoopee"

Notice how Clora Bryant at first prioritizes the parent C major scale while using ornamental chromatics sparsely. In bars 1 to 4, Bryant's ascending targets (circled) move stepwise from $\hat{5}$ to $\hat{8}$. But particularly in bars 6 to 8, notice the shift from major, as every chromatic note is borrowed from the C natural minor scale.

Write out the scale degrees for all examples on this page. Relate each note to the underlying chord, not to the parent key.

Extended chromatics

EX. 9.86
John Coltrane
tenor sax solo
"Crescent"

An improviser may superimpose a melody that strays drastically from the underlying chord progression, incorporating chromatic notes that imply distant and chromatic harmonies. John Coltrane's chromatics below bring a deep dissonance to his melodic line. They move far away from the underlying minor ii-V-i progression, finally offering a complete resolution on his last three notes, which form a tonic i triad arpeggio.

Song Study   "Take the 'A' Train"

"Take the 'A' Train," composed by Billy Strayhorn and popularized by the Duke Ellington Orchestra, features one of the great melodies in jazz composition, supported by an inventive and celebrated chord progression. This song study focuses exclusively on this progression, beginning with the A-section of the song's 32-bar AABA form.

EX. 9.87
"Take the 'A' Train" A-section
(bars 1-8, 9-16, 25-32)

Learn the melody to "Take the 'A' Train" entirely by ear. Then write in the A-section and B-section (key of C) on the blank staves provided.

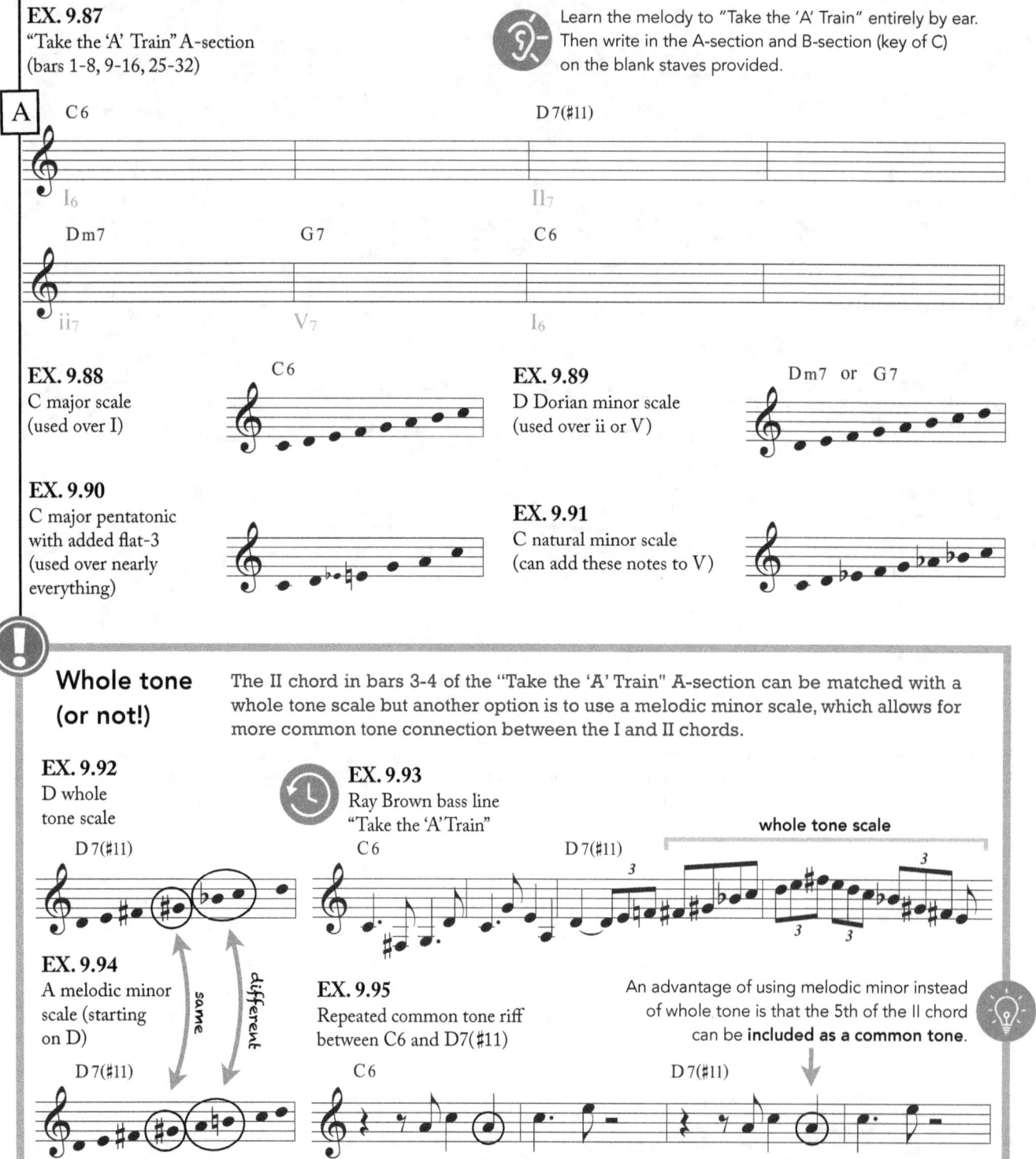

EX. 9.88
C major scale
(used over I)

EX. 9.89
D Dorian minor scale
(used over ii or V)

EX. 9.90
C major pentatonic
with added flat-3
(used over nearly
everything)

EX. 9.91
C natural minor scale
(can add these notes to V)

Whole tone (or not!)

The II chord in bars 3-4 of the "Take the 'A' Train" A-section can be matched with a whole tone scale but another option is to use a melodic minor scale, which allows for more common tone connection between the I and II chords.

EX. 9.92
D whole
tone scale

EX. 9.93
Ray Brown bass line
"Take the 'A' Train"

EX. 9.94
A melodic minor
scale (starting
on D)

EX. 9.95
Repeated common tone riff
between C6 and D7(♯11)

An advantage of using melodic minor instead of whole tone is that the 5th of the II chord can be **included as a common tone**.

Song Study

"Take the 'A' Train"
── page 2 of 2 ──

Bridge (B-section)

The bridge, or B-section, of "Take the 'A' Train" tonicizes briefly on the IV chord. In the key of C major, is a move to F major. The key contrast provides a welcome change of scenery before transitioning back to C major, ushering in the final A-section.

EX. 9.96
"Take the 'A' Train" B-section
(bars 17-24), preceded by bar 16

Learn the B-section by internalizing the chord progression here since the B-section melody of "Take the 'A' Train" **uses mostly chord tones.**

EX. 9.97
C Mixolydian scale
(used over V/IV, bar 16)

EX. 9.98
F major scale
(used over IV)

EX. 9.99
FMaj7 arpeggio
(used over IV)

Notice which chords contain **common tones.** Focusing on common tones will help provide melodic unity.

EX. 9.100
D Mixolydian scale
(used over II)

EX. 9.101
D9 arpeggio
(used over II)

EX. 9.102
Dm9 arpeggio
(used over ii or V)

EX. 9.103
G altered scale
(used over V7 or V7alt)

EX. 9.104
Fm9 arpeggio (includes notes used over V7 or V7alt)

Compose a simple melody over the bridge of "Take the 'A' Train," including carefully chosen common tones.

Transpose the newly composed melody to a new key of your choice.

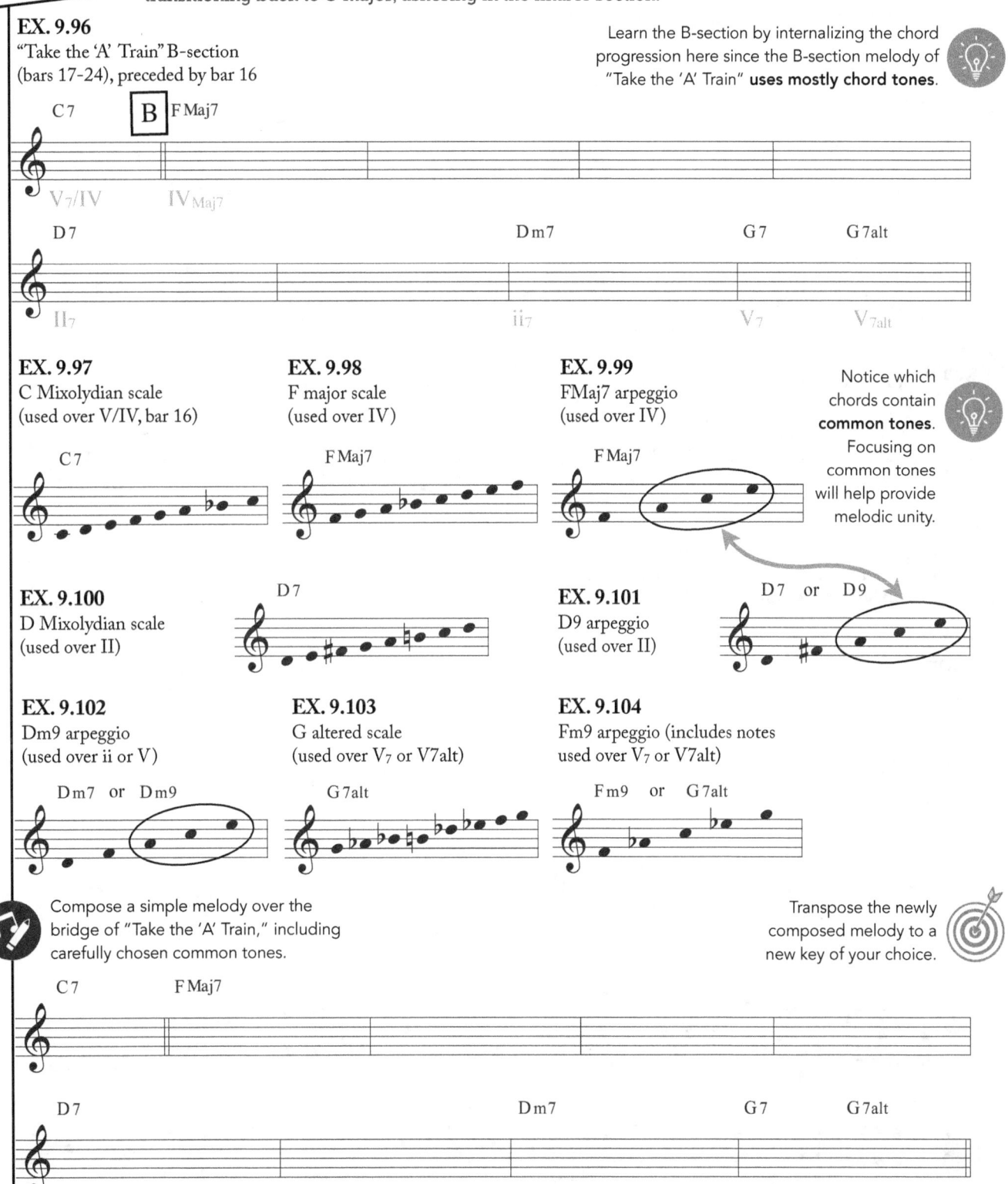

Masterclass

Super Scales
page 1 of 2

Super scales are formed by connecting various scales to create a perpetual motion exercise that can help establish fluency in scale application across any chord progression. The central premise is that a super scale moves stepwise at all times while altering scale notes to match each chord, sacrificing target note placements in favor of developing an eighth-note rhythmic continuity across the progression.

① Chords — Choose a chord progression. In this example, the chords come from the first eight bars of "Take the 'A' Train."

② Scales — Decide which scales to use. In this example, scales are largely diatonic.

This super scale will include the D whole tone scale over D7(#11).

③ Range limit — Choose a lower and upper limit. In this example, the wide range fits most instruments.

④ Super scale — Choose any starting note within the limit and begin the super scale.

WARNING! Use super scales at your own risk. They are **meant for practice** and may need to be edited for performance to include clearer target notes throughout, not to mention introducing more rhythmic variety, breaking up the eighth-note line.

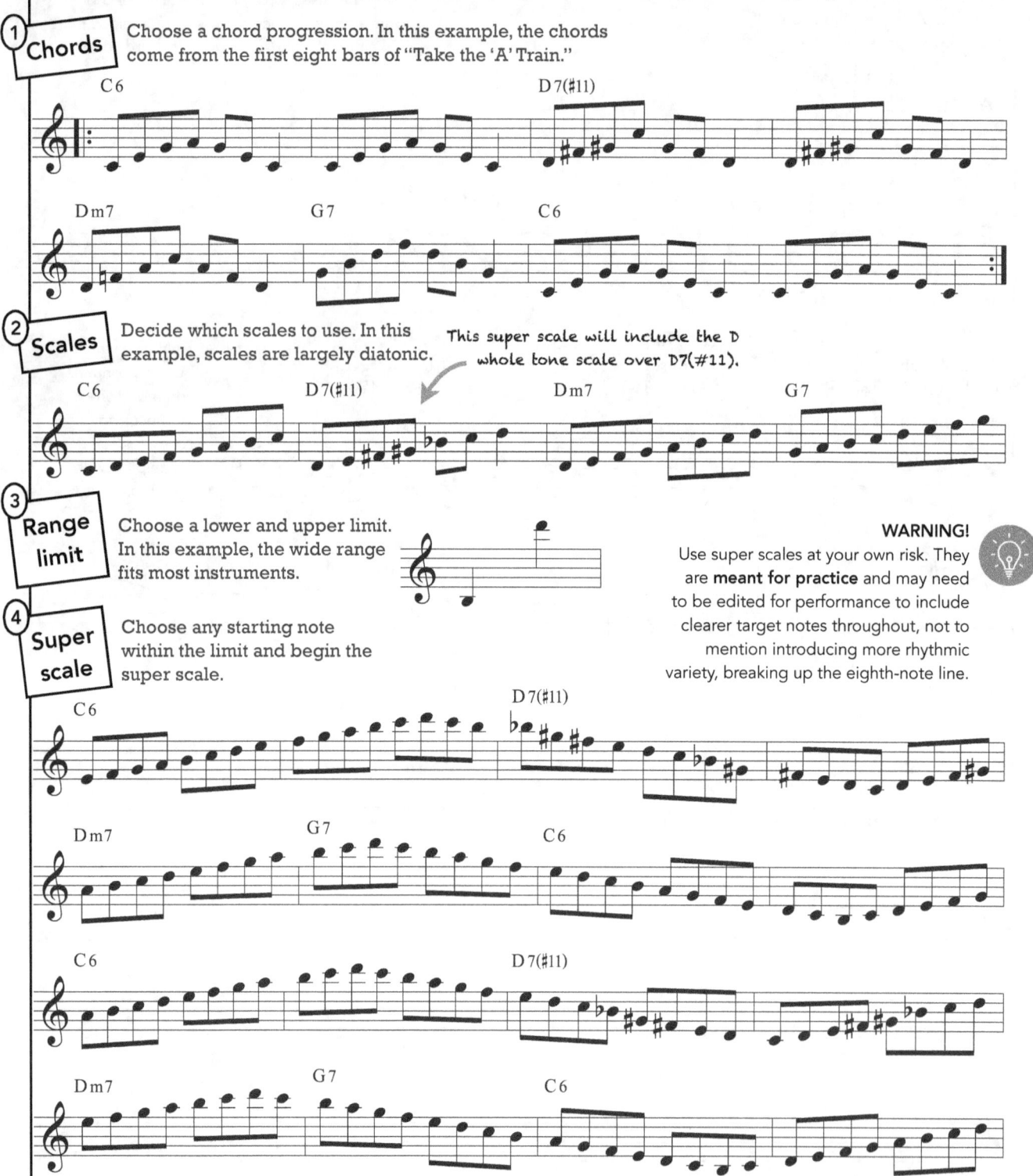

Masterclass

Super Scales
page 2 of 2

Super scales can be quite effective in developing familiarity with various scale options over chord progressions. Use the following alternative scales to create super scales over bars 1-8 of "'A' Train."

EX. 9.105
Alternate chords/scales over the first eight bars of "Take the 'A' Train"

Notice the change to the A melodic minor scale over D7(#11)...

...and the G altered scale over G7.

EX. 9.106
Alternate super scale over the first eight bars of "Take the 'A' Train"

EX. 9.107
Establish new upper and lower limits

EX. 9.108
Apply a scale pattern using the new limits

Keep in mind that a super scale can start on any note. The central aims are **perpetual motion**, fluency, and flow across multiple harmonies. The example below applies a **scale pattern** (diatonic thirds, first up then down) to the super scale.

IMPROVISE
Try various lower and upper limits while practicing super scales.

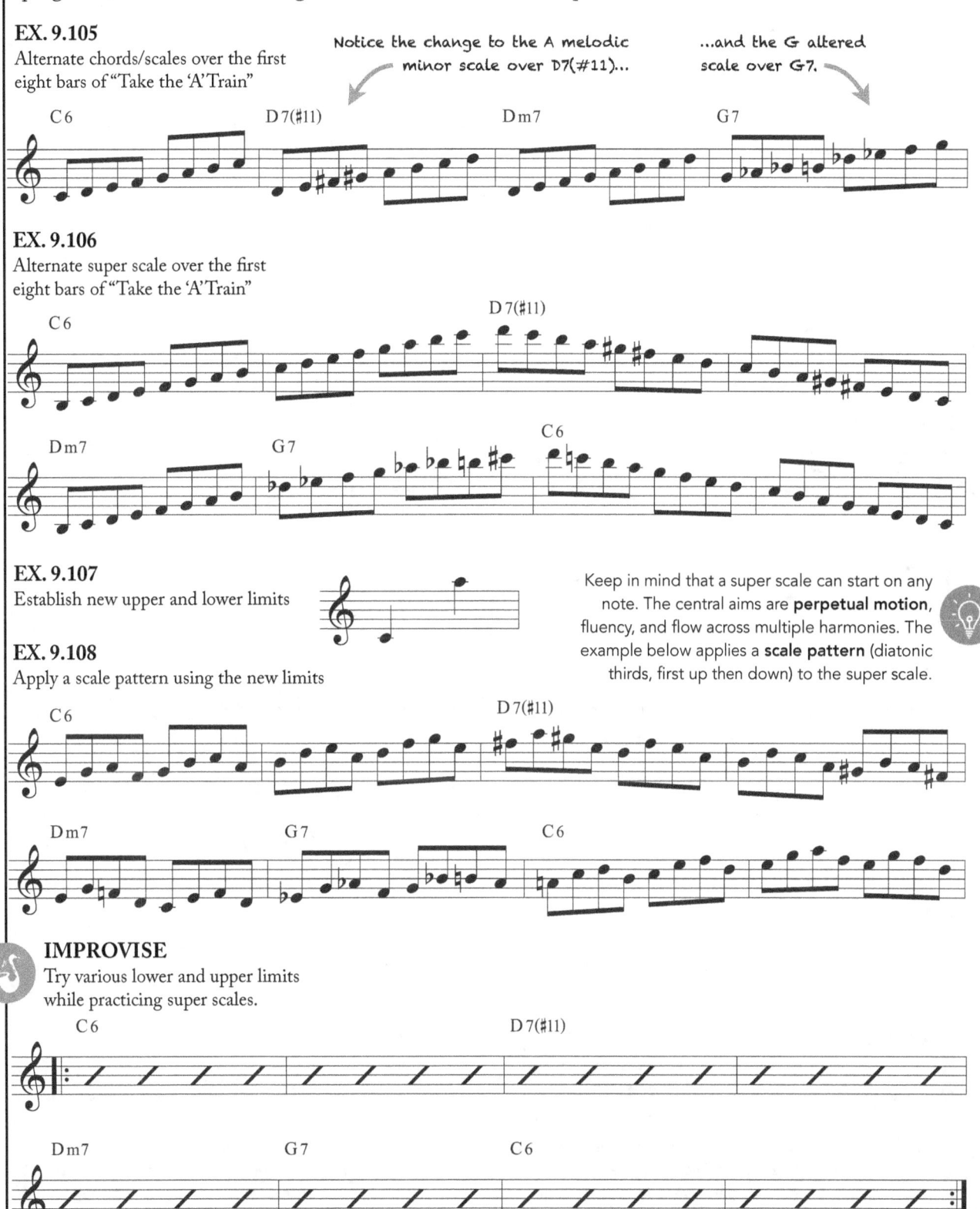

Solo Spotlight

Ray Nance, trumpet "Take the 'A' Train"

Ray Nance's iconic solo on "Take the 'A' Train" serves as a standard for thematic and melodic improvisation. Notice how Nance centers his solo on the tonic of the key while basing each phrase on small rhythmic statements. He also introduces chromatics only sparsely, never feeling compelled to include every chord tone.

EX. 9.109
Ray Nance trumpet solo
"Take the 'A' Train"

Notice when Nance moves away from his tonic center. Then consider **when and exactly how he returns back to tonic.**

Ray Nance's solo, from the most famous of many recorded versions by the Duke Ellington Orchestra, was so popular that Nance, and the trumpeters that followed, continued to record and perform variations of this exact solo.

Circle or mark any moments in Ray Nance's solo that are particularly intriguing or unusual. Then explain or consider why he might have chosen those particular notes.

Improvise

"Take the 'A' Train"

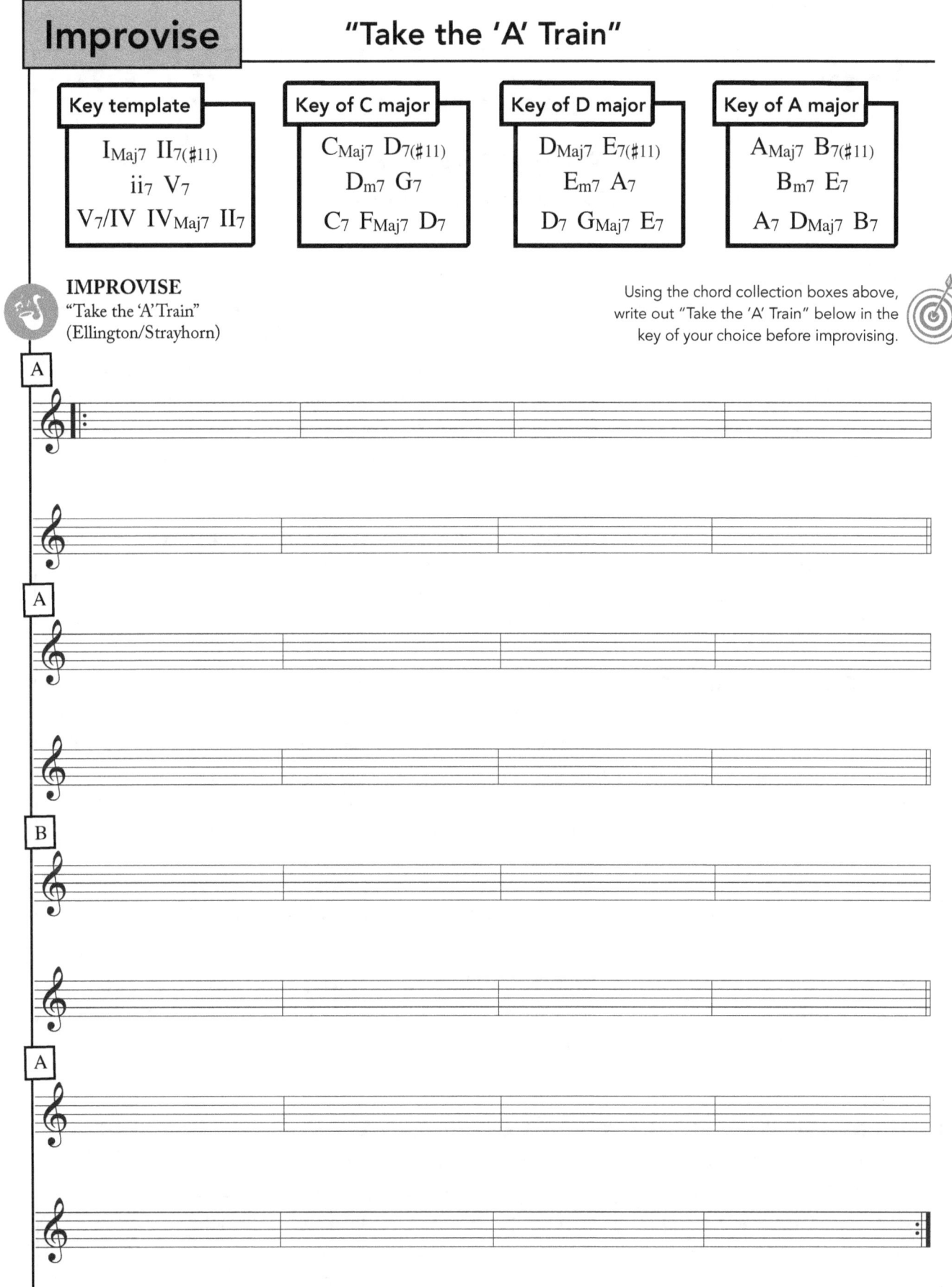

Key template

I_{Maj7} $II_{7(\sharp 11)}$
ii_7 V_7
V_7/IV IV_{Maj7} II_7

Key of C major

C_{Maj7} $D_{7(\sharp 11)}$
D_{m7} G_7
C_7 F_{Maj7} D_7

Key of D major

D_{Maj7} $E_{7(\sharp 11)}$
E_{m7} A_7
D_7 G_{Maj7} E_7

Key of A major

A_{Maj7} $B_{7(\sharp 11)}$
B_{m7} E_7
A_7 D_{Maj7} B_7

IMPROVISE
"Take the 'A' Train"
(Ellington/Strayhorn)

Using the chord collection boxes above, write out "Take the 'A' Train" below in the key of your choice before improvising.

A

A

B

A

Zen Jazz Master says:

Individuality
(No one plays like you!)

And now for a bit of Zen...

Developing fluency in a jazz language might take years of practice and experience but the most important part of your personal sound — your own personality — is already completely present! No one will ever sound just like you, no matter how hard they try. Conversely, if you strive to sound like someone else, you will only ever sound like you are imitating that player. This might at first sound like bad news, particularly if you really want to sound just like, say, Sonny Rollins or Michael Brecker, but it is actually very good news. The greatest jazz players in history all had one trait in common. They each had a personal sound. Most of these titans can be identified when you hear just a few notes of their playing.

The greatest improvisers never deny their own personalities in their playing. When Charlie Parker stormed onto the jazz scene, he spawned countless clones — saxophone players who denied their own personalities in an attempt to sound exactly like Parker. They are not remembered. So when you stand up and take a solo, always keep your own personality in the mix. No one will ever sound like you.

On the other hand...

You won't get too far on personality alone so make sure you take care of business and strive to really learn jazz language which supports your emerging personality. **Take the time and effort to learn from Parker and other masters.** Emulate their playing. The effort is worth it! The greats all learned from emulating, or mimicking, the masters who came before them. John Coltrane, in his early years, emulated the playing of Coleman Hawkins. Charlie Parker was influenced by Benny Carter and others. Both Coltrane and Parker moved beyond emulation and became innovators, both shaping and influencing the future of jazz.

Emulation: "Standing on the shoulders of giants"

Nearly all jazz players develop through emulating, or mimicking, jazz players they admire yet few players in history have become innovators. Don't be discouraged because you don't sound exactly like Parker or Coltrane (or Chris Potter or Joe Lovano). **Keep taking those giant steps to learn from the players you and your teachers enjoy.** Developing your own sound and style requires patience and gaining fluency with jazz vocabulary usually takes many years!

Innovation: "The shape of jazz to come"

Innovation is a tough concept. Most innovators don't set out to be innovative at all. They simply work hard at what they do and remain true to their own spirit. **Ultimately, history decides.** You may dream of being an innovator and you just might be someday. My advice to you as a student of jazz is to work hard now at emulating players you like. Don't worry at all about whether you are innovative or not.

Chapter 9 Achievements

Congratulations!

You are one step closer to jazz nirvana.

Here is a partial list of what you've achieved:

- Understanding how chromatic enclosures add color to your melody

- Using bebop and diminished scales to add chromaticism to your improvisations

- Extending chromatic concepts with tritone substitutions and hexatonic scales

- Improvising using chromatic linear improvisation

- Gaining a deeper understanding of the improvisations of jazz masters

SUBSTITUTIONS

DOUBLE-TIME TEMPOS

What's next?

Where do we go from here?

Conclusion

Three units and nine chapters later, this is an opportune moment for reflection and congratulations. It is no easy feat to navigate so many musical topics, applying it all in an effort to develop your own artistic voice. You committed yourself to growing as an improviser, becoming a more complete and thoughtful musician. There are countless ways to absorb all the material presented here. How did you delve in? Ironically, for all the pages and examples devoted to covering linear improvisation, reading from cover to cover is only one approach. Did you spend extra time in certain chapters, did you engage and apply yourself in every challenge and ear training example? Did you only read through the material without your instrument? Did you make the effort to listen to the actual recordings of the historical examples throughout? You might have used the book simply as a reference point, delving into a selected topic. Which topics are still shrouded in mystery and how will you continue to learn and grow?

One option is to start at the beginning again, trying novel approaches to your second (or third) read. The more active and curious you are, the better. This might manifest in the way you practice material at various speeds, changing tempo, lingering longer in an effort to master a given exercise or transcribed melodic line. This could mean moving deliberately from the key of C, the focal point for every chapter, and beginning a transposition journey through other key centers. Perhaps you take an active interest in select solos, moving beyond the presented excerpt of, say, Joe Henderson's "Song for My Father" solo and transcribing the full performance (and then learning it in all 12 keys!). Speaking of "Song for My Father," remember the chord collection boxes in that lesson? Try using chord collection boxes on "Bye Bye Blackbird" and other compositions. Although only two pages are devoted to super scales, this tool can be used over every composition introduced in the book, from 12-bar blues to "Oh, lady be good!" Speaking of "Oh, lady be good!", you might take the entire "Oh, lady be good!" lesson and work through it again, adapting it to a different jazz standard in its entirety. Only one page is spent introducing the difference between Lester Young and Coleman Hawkins yet their approaches need more than a survey. It is up to you to stay curious and keep exploring.

You have worked through so much material and developed many of your own insights in the process, all through careful and thorough practice, ear training, composing, and improvising. These topics included scale fragments as melodic building blocks, enclosures, target notes, rhythmic and octave displacements, functional harmony and the move from tonic to dominant, cadential moments of tension and release, architecture on a broad and small scale, independence of melodic line, motivic development, modal mixture and bebop structures built on chord extensions, diminished chords, and chromaticism, and so much more. What remains fascinating is how all these concepts are really ever-present in music and remain so inspired and fresh when put to use. When Sonny Stitt's "Avalon" solo had the spotlight in the book's introduction, it was shrouded in mystery. In closing, here is one more SOLO SPOTLIGHT, this time a full analysis of several lines from "Avalon" — the veil now lifted just enough that its anatomy finally starts making sense and artistic intent is revealed in all its beauty.

Solo Spotlight

Sonny Stitt, tenor sax "Avalon"

Saxophonist Sonny Stitt was a masterful improviser, able to weave intricate detail into each of his lines, all the while infusing them with propulsive and syncopated rhythm and style. The twelve measures presented below include myriad melodic devices, some quite simple and others filled with layers of complexity, all of which contribute to a memorable, creative, and artistic story.

Sonny Stitt tenor sax solo
"Avalon" (key of C major)

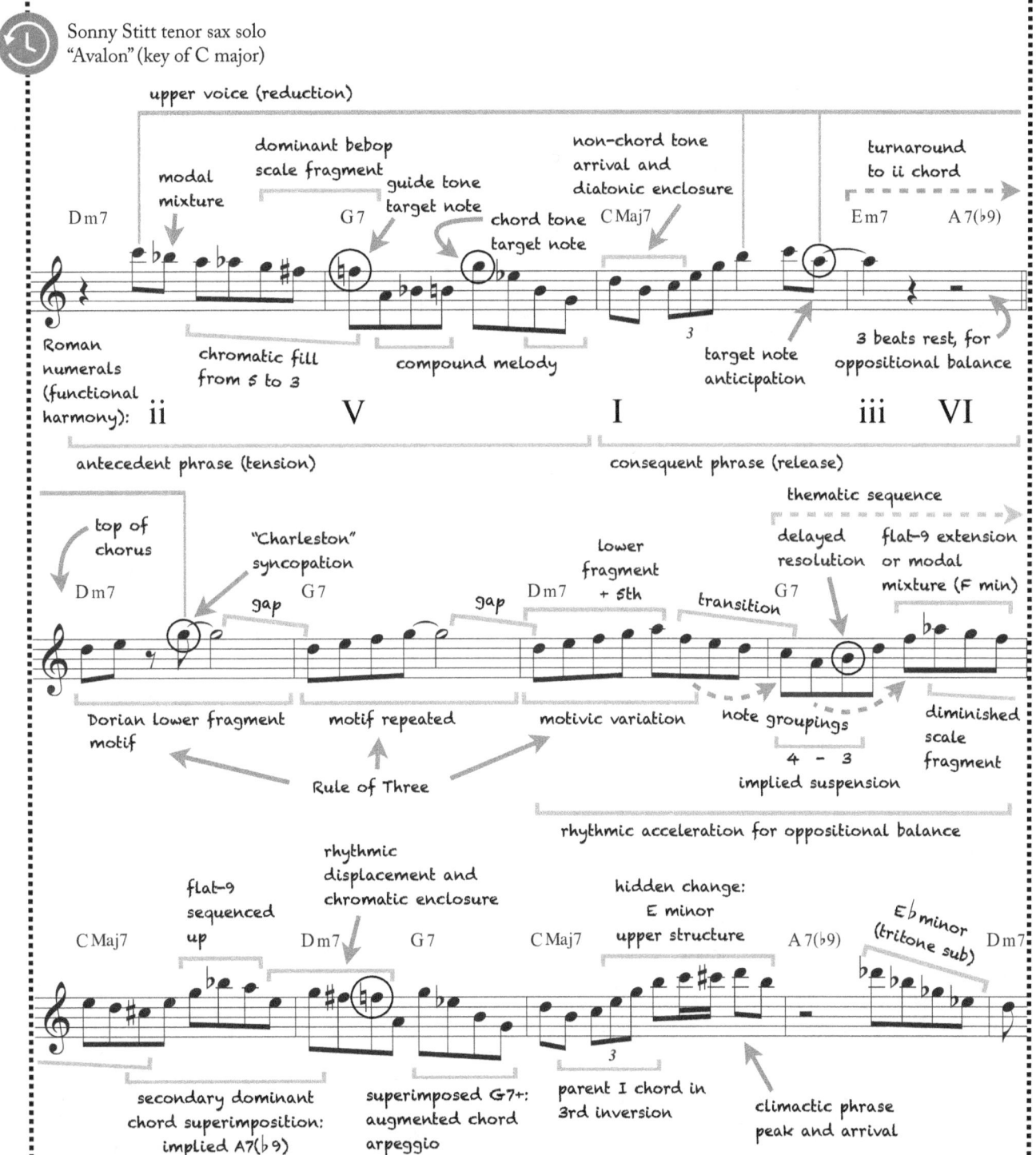

Notes

1. Coltrane, John. "An Interview with John Coltrane." Interview by Frank Kofsky. Recorded November 1966. Broadcast: KPFK Radio, January 1, 1973. Retrieved from https://www.pacificaradioarchives.org/recording/bc1266.

2. Armstrong, Louis. Brothers, Thomas. *Louis Armstrong, in his own words.* Oxford: Oxford University Press, 2001.

3. Isaac Stern quotation referenced by Yo-Yo Ma in an interview for *NPR Weekend Edition*, September 30, 2008.

4. Cohen II, Aaron. "Kenny Barron: Perfect Grace." *DownBeat Magazine*, Vol. 82, No. 4, April 2015, p. 25. Retrieved from https://issuu.com/smo34/docs/db__04.2015_.

5. Schenker, Heinrich. *Free Composition, Volumes 1-3.* Hillsdale: Pendragon Press London, 2001, 1935.

6. Russell, George. *George Russell's Lydian Chromatic Concept of Tonal Organization, Volume One: The art and science of tonal gravity.* Brookline: Concept Publishing Co., 2008, 1953.

7. Guthrie, Kenneth Sylvan. Fideler, David R. *The Pythagorean Sourcebook and Library: An Anthology of Ancient Writings which Relate to Pythagoras and Pythagorean Philosophy.* Newburyport: Red Wheel/Weiser, 1987.

8. Desmond, Paul. Parker, Charlie. "Interview with Charlie Parker and Paul Desmond." Interview by John McClellan (aka John T. Fitch). Recorded 1954. Broadcast: WHDH Radio, January 1954. Retrieved from https://www.youtube.com/watch?v=UvsqYo9r_dE.

9. Gillespie, Dizzy. Fraser, Al. *To be or not to bop: Memoirs of Dizzy Gillespie.* New York: Da Capo Press, 1979.

Bibliography

Arlen, Harold. Rose, Billy. Harburg, E. Y. "Yip." "It's only a paper moon." New York: Warner Bros., Inc. & Chappell Music, 1933 (Renewed).

Arlen, Harold. "Over the Rainbow" Nashville: EMI Feist Catalog, Inc. All rights administered by EMI Feist Catalog, Inc. (Publishing) and Alfred Music (Print), 1939.

Armstrong, Lil Hardin. "Struttin' with Some Barbecue." Public Domain, 1927.

Bach, J. S. *Violin Partita No. 2 in D minor*. Public Domain, 1723.

Barbarin, Paul. "Bourbon Street Parade." EMI United Partnership, Ltd., 1949.

Beethoven, Ludwig van. *Symphony No. 5*. Public Domain, 1808.

Beethoven, Ludwig van. "Für Elise." Public Domain, 1810.

Berlin, Irving. "Always." Public Domain, 1925.

Berlin, Irving. "Cheek to Cheek." New York: Irving Berlin Music Co. and Concord Music, 1935.

Bernie, Ben. Pinkard, Maceo. Casey, Kenneth. "Sweet Georgia Brown." Public Domain, 1925.

Carmichael, Hoagy. "Stardust." Public Domain, 1927.

Chambers, Paul. Davis, Miles. "So What." New York: Downtown Music Publishing, 1959.

Christy, Edwin Pearce. "Goodnight, ladies." Public Domain, 1847.

Cohn/Miller/Styne/Krueger. "Sunday."

Coltrane, John. "A Love Supreme." Woodland Hills: Jowcol Music, 1964.

Coltrane, John, "Giant Steps." Woodland Hills: Jowcol Music, 1974.

Davis, Miles. Kelly, Wynton. "Freddie Freeloader." New York: Downtown Music Publishing, 1959.

Davis, Miles. "Tune Up." New York: Prestige Music, 1963.

Donaldson, Walter. Kahn, Gus. "Love me or leave me." Public Domain, 1928.

Dorham, Kenny. "Blue Bossa." Beverly Hills: Orpheum Music, 1961.

Dvořák, Antonin. *Symphony No. 9 ("New World")*. Public Domain, 1893.

Ellington, Edward Kennedy "Duke". "C Jam Blues." New York: Sony/ATV and Famous Music Corporation in the U.S.A. Rights for the world outside the U.S.A. Controlled by EMI Robbins Catalog, Inc. (Publishing) and Warner Bros. Publications U.S. Inc. (Print), 1942 (Renewed 1969).

Ellington, Edward Kennedy "Duke." "Limbo Jazz." New York: Duke Ellington Music, 1962.

Ellington, Edward Kennedy "Duke." "Satin Doll." Santa Monica: Tempo Music & Duke Ellington Music, 1953 (Renewed 1958).

Ellington, Edward Kennedy "Duke." Strayhorn, Billy. "Take the 'A' Train." New York: Music Sales Corporation and Tempo Music Inc., 1941 (Renewed 1968).

Gershwin, George & Ira. "Oh, lady be good!" Public Domain, 1924.

Gershwin, George & Ira. Hayward, DuBose & Dorothy. "Summertime." New York: Downtown Music Publishing, George Gershwin Music, Ira Gershwin Music, and DuBose and Dorthy Hayward Memorial Fund. All rights administered by WB Music Corp., 1935 (Renewed 1962).

Handel, George Frideric. "Joy to the World/Antioch." Public Domain, 1719.

Handy, W. C. "St. Louis Blues." Public Domain, 1914.

Henderson, Ray. Dixon, Mort. "Bye Bye Blackbird." Public Domain, 1926.

Hill, Mildred & Patty. "Happy Birthday to You." Public Domain, 1893.

Hirsch, Walter. Rose, Fred. "'Deed I do." Public Domain, 1926.

Jackson, Milt. "Bag's Groove." Teaneck: Reecie Music, 1956.

Johnson, James P. Mack, Cecil. "The Charleston." Public Domain, 1923.

Jolson, Al. DeSylva, Buddy. Rose, Vincent. "Avalon." Public Domain, 1920.

Key, Francis Scott. Smith, John Stafford. "The Star-Spangled Banner." Public Domain, 1814.

Kosma, Josef. "Autumn Leaves." Paris: Enoch & Cie. Sole selling agent for U.S.A. (including its territories and possessions) & Dominion of Canada: Morley Music Co., by agreement with Enoch & Cie. Sub-publisher in British Commonwealth is Peter Maurice Co., Ltd., London, 1947, 1950, 1987 (Renewed 1975, 1978).

Lewis, Morgan. Hamilton, Nancy. "How High the Moon." New York: Chappell & Co., 1940.

Mills, Irving. "St. James Infirmary." Public Domain, 1929.

Mozart, Wolfgang Amadeus. "Minuet in C, K. 6." Public Domain, 1762.

Noble, Ray. "Cherokee." London: The Peter Maurice Music Co., Ltd. Copyright renewed and assigned to Shapiro, Bernstein & Co., Inc., New York for U.S.A. and Canada, 1938.

Parker, Charlie. "Perhaps." New York: Atlantic Music Corp., 1948 (Renewed 1978).

Pettiford, Oscar. "Blues in the Closet." Beverly Hills: Orpheus Music, Inc., 1954.

Puente, Tito. "Oye cómo va." Los Angeles: Planetary Music Publishing Co., 1971.

Rodgers, Richard. Hart, Lorenz. "Blue Moon." Public Domain, 1924.

Rodgers, Richard. Hart, Lorenz. "My heart stood still." Public Domain, 1927

Rollins, Sonny. "Sonnymoon for Two." New York: Son Rol Music Company, Inc., 1958.

Rollins, Sonny. "St. Thomas." New York: Prestige Music Co., 1963.

Romberg, Sigmund. Hammerstein II, Oscar. "Softly, as in a Morning Sunrise." Public Domain, 1928.

Shay, Larry. Fisher, Mark. Goodwin, Joe. "When You're Smiling." Public Domain, 1928.

Silver, Horace. "Song for My Father." Malibu: Ecaroh Music, 1964.

Van Heusen, Jimmy. Burke, Johnny. "But Beautiful." New York: Burke & Van Heusen, now Bourne Co. and Dorsey Bros Music. Rights for Germany, Austria, Switzerland & CSSR, assigned to Melodie der Welt, J. Michel GmbH & Co, KG, Musikverlag. Rights for Japan assigned to Chappell/Interson K. K., used by permission of JASRAC License #8670719, 1947.

Warren, Harry. Mercer, Johnny. "Jeepers Creepers." WB Music Corp., 1938 (Renewed).

Weill, Kurt. Brecht, Bertolt. *The Threepenny Opera (Die Dreigrschenoper)*. New York: Tams-Witmark Music Library, 1954. "Moritat (Mack the Knife)."

Youmans, Vincent. Caesar, Irving. "I want to be happy." Public Domain, 1926.

Youmans, Vincent. "Tea for Two." Public Domain, 1924.

Young, Lester. "Lester Leaps In." New York: WB Music Corp., 1940 (Renewed).

Young, Victor. "When I Fall in Love." New York: Chappell & Co., Inc. and Intersong-USA, Inc., 1952.

Zawinul, Joe. "Mercy, Mercy, Mercy." Edgewater: Zawinul Music, A Division of Gopam Enterprises, Inc., 1966.

Discography

Adderley, Julian "Cannonball." alto sax solo "Minority." *Cannonball Adderley Quintet — Portrait of Cannonball.* Riverside, 1958.

Armstrong, Louis. trumpet solo "Mack the Knife." *Louis Armstrong and His All Stars — Columbia and RCA Victor live recordings of Louis Armstrong and the all stars.* Mosaic, 2014 [1954].

Armstrong, Louis. trumpet solo "St. Louis Blues." *Louis Armstrong — The Essential Louis Armstrong.* Columbia/Legacy, 2004, 1979.

Armstrong, Louis. trumpet solo "When the Saints Go Marching in." *Louis Armstrong — The Gospel Train is leaving 1930-1945.* Iris Musique, 2002 [1950].

Baker, Chet. trumpet solo "Autumn Leaves." *Chet Baker — She Was Too Good to Me.* Legacy/Columbia, 1974.

Baker, Chet. trumpet solo "Summertime." *Jazz in Paris — Chet Baker Quartet Plays Standards.* Universal, 2002 [1955].

Barron, Kenny. piano solo "Softly, as in a Morning Sunrise." *Kenny Barron Trio — Green Chimneys.* Criss Cross, 1994 [1983].

Blakey, Art. drum solo "A Night in Tunisia." *Art Blakey — Theory of Art.* RCA Victor/Bluebird, 1997 [1957].

Brookmeyer, Bob. trombone solo "My Funny Valentine." *Jim Hall & Bob Brookmeyer — Live at the North Sea Jazz Festival.* Challenge, 1979.

Brown, Clifford. trumpet solo "Cherokee." *Clifford Brown & Max Roach Quintet — Study in Brown.* Verve, 1955.

Brown, Ray. bass line "Take the 'A' Train." *The Ray Brown Trio — Soular Energy.* Concord, 2006 [1984].

Bryant, Clora. trumpet solo "Makin' Whoopee." *Clora Bryant — …Gal With a Horn.* City Hall, 2008 [1957].

Burrell, Kenny. guitar solo "C Jam Blues." *Johnny Hodges & Earl "Fatha" Hines — Stride Right.* Verve, 2005 [1966].

Burrell, Kenny. guitar solo "On the Sunny Side of the Street." *Jimmy Smith — Back at the Chicken Shack.* Blue Note, 1963.

Byas, Don. tenor sax solo "I got rhythm." iTunes app, *Don Byas — At Nalen Live In the Swedish Harlem.* 2013.

Coleman, George. tenor sax solo "Autumn Leaves." *Miles Davis — In Europe (Live).* Columbia, 1964.

Coleman, George. tenor sax solo "There is no greater love." *Miles Davis — "Four" & More (Recorded Live in Concert).* Columbia, 1966.

Coltrane, John. tenor sax solo "All the Things You Are." *Johnny Griffin — A Blowing Session.* Blue Note, 1957.

Coltrane, John. tenor sax solo "Crescent." *John Coltrane Quartet — Crescent.* Universal, 2020 [1964].

Coltrane, John. tenor sax solo "Giant Steps." *John Coltrane — Giant Steps.* Atlantic, 1960.

Coltrane, John. tenor sax solo "Pursuance (A Love Supreme)." *John Coltrane — A Love Supreme.* Impulse!, 1965.

Curtis, King. soprano sax solo "Soul Serenade." *King Curtis — Best of King Curtis.* Blue Note, Capitol, 1996 [1965].

Davis, Miles. trumpet solo "Autumn Leaves." *Cannonball Adderley — Somethin' Else*, Blue Note 2021 [1958].

Davis, Miles. trumpet "Bye Bye Blackbird." *Miles Davis — 'Round About Midnight*. Columbia, 1957.

Davis, Miles. trumpet solo "So What." *Miles Davis — Kind of Blue*. Columbia, 1959.

Desmond, Paul. alto sax solo "Pennies from Heaven." *The Dave Brubeck Quartet — At Carnegie Hall (Live)*. Legacy/Sony, 2001 [1963].

Evans, Bill. piano solo "Someday My Prince Will Come." *Bill Evans Trio — Portrait in Jazz*. Riverside, 1960.

Fitzgerald, Ella. vocal solo "Mack the Knife." *Ella Fitzgerald — Live in Berlin*. Verve, 1960.

Flanagan, Tommy. piano solo "Moritat (Mack the Knife)." *Sonny Rollins — Saxophone Colossus*. Prestige, 1956.

Getz, Stan. tenor sax solo "Billie's Bounce." *Stan Getz & J.J. Johnson — Stan Getz And J.J. Johnson At The Opera House*. Verve, 1957.

Gillespie, John Birks "Dizzy." trumpet solo "All the Things You Are." *Dizzy Gillespie Sextet — Gettin' Dizzy: The High-flying Dizzy Gillespie*. Savoy, 2020 [1945-51].

Gordon, Dexter. tenor sax solo "Blow, Mr. Dexter." *Dexter Gordon — Dexter Rides Again*. Savoy, 2010 [1945-47].

Gordon, Dexter. tenor sax solo "It's You or No One." *Dexter Gordon — Doin' Allright*. Blue Note, 1961.

Gordon, Dexter. tenor sax solo "Shiny Stockings." *Dexter Gordon — Gettin' Around*. Blue Note, 1965.

Griffin, Johnny. tenor sax solo "Autumn Leaves." *Johnny Griffin — The Best of Johnny Griffin*. Galaxy/Fantasy, 1978.

Griffin, Johnny. tenor sax solo "The Way You Look Tonight." *Johnny Griffin — A Blowing Session*. Blue Note, 1957.

Hawkins, Coleman. tenor sax solo "Body and Soul." *Coleman Hawkins — Body & Soul*. Bluebird, 1988 [1939].

Henderson, Joe. tenor sax solo "Recorda-me." *Joe Henderson — Page One*. Blue Note, 1963.

Henderson, Joe. tenor sax solo "Song for My Father." *The Horace Silver Quintet — Song for My Father*. Blue Note, 1964.

Higginbotham, J.C. trombone solo "When the Saints Go Marching in." *Louis Armstrong — The Gospel Train is leaving 1930-1945*. Iris Musique, 2002 [1950].

Hodges, Johnny. alto sax "Limbo Jazz." *Duke Ellington — Duke Ellington Meets Coleman Hawkins*. Impulse!, 1962.

Jacquet, Illinois. tenor sax solo "Flying Home." *Lionel Hampton and His Orchestra — Flying Home*. Decca, 1942.

Johnson, J. J. trombone solo "Just Friends." *J. J. Johnson — Standards - Live at the Village Vanguard*. Universal, 2004 [1988].

Konitz, Lee. alto sax "Bye Bye Blackbird." *Lee Konitz — Dearly Beloved*. SteepleChase, 1997.

Lee, Peggy. vocals "Bye Bye Blackbird." *Peggy Lee — World Broadcast Recordings 1955*. Audiophile, 2017 [1955].

Liston, Melba. trombone solo "In Memory of." *Randy Weston & Melba Liston — Volcano Blues*. Universal 2009 [1993].

McPartland, Marian. piano solo "Jeepers Creepers." *Marian McPartland — Just Friends*. Concord, 1998.

Mobley, Hank. tenor sax solo "Home Cookin'." *Horace Silver — The Best of Horace Silver, Vol. 1*. Blue Note, 1988 [1957].

Nance, Ray. cornet solo "Limbo Jazz." *Duke Ellington — Duke Ellington Meets Coleman Hawkins*. Impulse!, 1962.

Nance, Ray. trumpet solo "Take the 'A' Train." *Duke Ellington and his Famous Orchestra — Take the "A" Train / The Sidewalks of New York*, Victor, 1941, 1943.

Parker, Charlie. alto sax solo "Anthropology." *"Bird" Charlie Parker — 1949 Concert & All Stars 1950-1951*. Forlane, 1991 [1951].

Parker, Charlie. alto sax solo "Lay your habits down." *Charlie Parker — Young Bird, Vol. 3: 1945*. Masters of Jazz, 1996 [1945].

Parker, Charlie. alto sax solo "Oh, lady be good!" *Charlie Parker — Live At The Philharmonic* 1946. Verve/Clef Records, 1992.

Parker, Charlie. alto sax solo "Oh, lady be good!" *Jay McShann Orchestra featuring Charlie Parker — Early Bird*. Spotlite Records, 2000.

Redd, Vi. alto saxophone solo "All the Things You Are." *Vi Redd — Bird Call*. Toshiba/EMI, 2013 [1962].

Remler, Emily. guitar solo "Softly, as in a Morning Sunrise." *Emily Remler — East to Wes*. Concord, 1988.

Rollins, Sonny. tenor sax solo "Moritat (Mack the Knife)." *Sonny Rollins — Saxophone Collosus*. Prestige, 1956.

Rollins, Sonny. tenor sax solo "Sonnymoon for Two." *Sonny Rollins — A Night at the Village Vanguard*. Blue Note, 1957.

Silver, Horace. piano solo "Song for My Father." *The Horace Silver Quintet — Song for My Father*. Blue Note, 1964.

Snow, Valaida. trumpet solo "I can't give you anything but love." *Valaida Snow — Queen of Trumpet and Song*, DRG, 1999 [1935-40]

Stitt, Sonny. tenor sax solo "Avalon." *Sonny Stitt Quartet — Stitt's Bits: The Bebop Recordings, 1949-1952*. Prestige, 2006 [1950].

Tipton, Billy. piano solo "Perdido." *Billy Tipton — Jazz 1955*. Calle Mayor, 2017 [1957].

Turrentine, Stanley. tenor sax solo "Impressions." *Stanley Turrentine — Sugar*. CTI, 1991 [1970].

Webster, Ben. tenor sax solo "Honeysuckle Rose." *Ben Webster — Ben Webster 1944-1946*. Classics, 1999 [1944].

Williams, Mary Lou. piano solo "St. Louis Blues." *Mary Lou Williams — A Grand Night for Swinging*. High Note, 2008 [1976].

Young, Lester. tenor sax solo "Blue Lester." *Lester Young — Blue Lester*. Savoy, 2010 [1956].

Young, Lester. tenor sax solo "Oh, lady be good!" *Count Basie, Harry James — Basie Rhythm*. Hep Records, 1991.

Young, Lester. tenor sax solo "Shoe Shine Boy." *Count Basie — Count Basie and the Kansas City 7*. Universal, 2020 [1936].

Young, Lester. tenor sax solo "When You're Smiling." iTunes app, *Teddy Wilson — When You're Smiling*, 1999 [1938].

Index of Historical Examples

Compositions (alphabetized by title)

Performances

(transcribed from the recordings by Javier Arau unless otherwise noted)

General Index

About the Author

Javier Arau, born in 1975, is an American saxophonist, composer, theorist and entrepreneur. The founder of New York Jazz Academy®, a prominent New York City-based music school now serving students in over 70 countries, his work as an educator and theorist has impacted musicians of all levels. A two-time quarterfinalist for Grammy® Educator of the Year and touted as "pioneering" by *DownBeat* magazine, Arau has been featured in *The New York Times*, as a cover artist for *Saxophone Journal*, and as an expert guest on PRI's *Science Friday*. A prolific composer, he scores the music for a nationally televised PBS series, leads the Javier Arau Jazz Orchestra, and has received awards from ASCAP, BMI, and *DownBeat*. Arau's jazz theory work has been cited in Cambridge University Press and discussed in *Music Theory Spectrum* (Oxford University Press), where he was described as a "rogue music theorist." He is an artist-endorser of Virtuoso Saxophones and has performed as a saxophonist at venues around the world, including the Montreux and Monterey Jazz Festivals, Carnegie Hall, and Lincoln Center.

Arau studied at New England Conservatory with composer Bob Brookmeyer, theorist George Russell, and saxophonist Jerry Bergonzi and was mentored as a young musician by jazz masters Joe Henderson, Dizzy Gillespie, and Dave Brubeck, who personally subsidized Arau's college music education. Arau's TED Talk, *Playing the Changes: What jazz teaches you about success*, offers inspiring insights and surprising solutions to forging a career in the arts, even when the odds are stacked against you. For more about Javier and his work, visit javierarau.com.

www.ingramcontent.com/pod-product-compliance
Lightning Source LLC
Chambersburg PA
CBHW080804120626

46556CB00009B/3213